THE INSANITY EDITION

Book 5
Tongue Twisting Series

Shaun Simpson

ATT PUBLISHING HOUSE

ISBN-13: 9798337765297

Cover design by: Nina Druzhkova
Library of Congress Control Number: 2018675309
Printed in the United State of America

CONTENTS

OTHER BOOKS BY THE SAME AUTHOR

Website\Patreon\Podcast\Instagram\Youtube\Tictok

The How to Series

How To Get Your Dream Job: When English isn't Your First Language

How to Talk to Anyone in English: Mastering Communication in the World Language

Talk Like a Boss: Phrasal Verbs for Business Success

The tongue-twisting series

Tongue Twisters for Perfect Pronunciation (Book 1)

Short, Sweet and Snappy Tongue Twisters (Book 2)

Lengthening the Challenge Tongue Twisters (Book 3)

Marathon for the Mouth Tongue Twisters (Book 4)

INTRODUCTION

The original volume provided tongue twisters for individual letters, letter combinations, and sound patterns, transforming a seemingly chaotic realm into a structured and engaging exploration of both funny and difficult linguistic challenges.

Each is divided into four levels of difficulty and lengths...

Short:

Short, Sweet and Snappy - This Book Two contains around 1000 brief, snappy "**short**" tongue twisters. Perfect for beginners or quick practice sessions, these concise challenges will get your tongue warmed up, in no time.

Long:

Lengthening the Challenge - As you have probably guessed, this Book Three contains around 700 twisters that ups the ante with "**long**" tongue twisters. These require more focus and stamina, pushing your linguistic skills to new heights.

Longer:

Marathon for the Mouth - Yeah, that's right. Book Four takes you on an extended verbal journey with even "**longer**" tongue twisters. With more than 500, these intricate phrases will test your concentration and articulation to the limit.

Insane:

The Insanity Edition - The final book in the series Book Five lives up to its name with **"insane"**ly long tongue twisters. These epic verbal challenges are not for the faint of heart and will push even the most skilled speakers to their limits.

Key Features:

Diverse Themes: Explore a variety of topics, including animals, food, people, and more.

Clear Pronunciation: Each tongue twister is carefully designed to highlight specific sounds and pronunciation challenges.

Educational Value: Improve your articulation, fluency, and vocabulary while having fun.

Who is this series for?

Language Learners: Practice pronunciation and improve fluency.

Speech Therapists: Use as a tool for articulation exercises.

Wordplay Enthusiasts: Enjoy a fun and challenging way to spend time. Families: Have fun together and improve your communication skills.

Now, we invite you to embark on a deeper linguistic adventure. These four new volumes present a vast collection of original tongue twisters, each carefully crafted to challenge and entertain. Expanding on the successful format of the first book, we have maintained the beloved difficulty levels of short, long, longer, and insane, ensuring there's a perfect fit for every tongue twister enthusiast.

Whether you're a casual wordplay aficionado seeking a lighthearted challenge or a seasoned linguistic athlete craving a rigorous workout, these books offer an immersive experience. Prepare to be captivated as you navigate the intricate twists and turns of these verbal labyrinths, sharpening your wit and verbal agility along the way.

PRONUNCIATION SYMBOLS LIST

The International Phonetic Alphabet (IPA) is quite comprehensive, with symbols for a vast array of sounds used in human languages. Here's an expansion of the previous list, aiming to cover the most common sounds with explanations:

Vowels:

- **/a/** - Open back unrounded vowel, like the "ah" in "father"
- **/æ/** - Near-open front unrounded vowel, short "a" sound, as in "cat"
- **/e/** - Close front unrounded vowel, long "e" sound, as in "beat"
- **/ɛ/** - Open-mid front unrounded vowel, short "e" sound, as in "bed"
- **/i/** - Close front rounded vowel, long "ee" sound, as in "see"
- **/ɪ/** - Near-close near-front unrounded vowel, short "i" sound, as in "sit"
- **/o/** - Close back rounded vowel, long "oh" sound, as in "boat"
- **/ɔ/** - Open-mid back rounded vowel, short "o" sound, as in "bought"
- **/u/** - Close back rounded vowel, long "oo" sound, as in "boot"
- **/ʊ/** - Near-close near-back rounded vowel, short "u" sound, as in "put"

- **/ʌ/** - Open central unrounded vowel, short "u" sound, but centralised, like the "u" in "but"
- **/ə/** - Mid central vowel, the schwa sound, like the "a" in "about"
- **/ɜː/** - Open-mid central rounded vowel, like the "er" sound in "nurse" (American English)

Consonants:

- **/p/** - Unvoiced bilabial plosive, like the "p" in "pin"
- **/b/** - Voiced bilabial plosive, like the "b" in "bin"
- **/t/** - Unvoiced alveolar plosive, like the "t" in "top"
- **/d/** - Voiced alveolar plosive, like the "d" in "dog"
- **/k/** - Unvoiced velar plosive, like the "k" in "kite"
- **/g/** - Voiced velar plosive, like the "g" in "go"
- **/f/** - Labiodental fricative, voiceless, like the "f" in "fish"
- **/v/** - Labiodental fricative, voiced, like the "v" in "van"
- **/θ/** - Dental fricative, voiceless, like the "th" in "thin"
- **/ð/** - Dental fricative, voiced, like the "th" in "this"
- **/s/** - Alveolar fricative, voiceless, like the "s" in "sip"
- **/z/** - Alveolar fricative, voiced, like the "z" in "zebra"
- **/ʃ/** - Postalveolar fricative, voiceless, like the "sh" in "ship"
- **/ʒ/** - Postalveolar fricative, voiced, like the "s" in "vision"
- **/m/** - Bilabial nasal, like the "m" in "man"
- **/n/** - Alveolar nasal, like the "n" in "nap"
- **/ŋ/** - Velar nasal, like the "ng" in "sing"
- **/l/** - Alveolar lateral approximant, like the "l" in "lip"
- **/r/** - Alveolar approximant, voiced, like the "r" in "rip" (American English)
- **/h/** - Glottal fricative, voiceless, like the "h" in "hat"
- **/j/** - Palatal approximant, like the "y" in "yes"
- **/w/** - Labial-velar approximant, like the "w" in "wet"

Suprasegmentals:

- /ˈ/ - Stress, placed before the stressed syllable (e.g., /ˈwater/)

- /ˌ/ - Secondary stress, placed before a syllable with less stress than the primary stress (e.g., /ˌencyclopedia/)
- /_/ - Syllable break (e.g., /teɪk/ /ˈaʊt/)

Other symbols:

- /ʔ/ - Glottal stop, a brief closure of the glottis (e.g., in some pronunciations of "button")
- / læng/ - Length

The IPA goes beyond representing individual sounds and also includes symbols for phenomena like tone and intonation. Here's an exploration of those aspects:

Tones and Intonation:

- Tone markers: These symbols indicate the pitch contour of a syllable, which can be crucial for meaning in tonal languages like Mandarin Chinese. Examples include:
  - /˥/ (high-tone)
  - /˧/ (mid-tone)
  - /˨/ (low-tone)
- Pitch contours: In non-tonal languages like English, intonation patterns are used to convey meaning and emphasis. IPA doesn't have specific symbols for these contours, but uses arrows to indicate relative pitch movement:
  - /↗/ (rising pitch)
  - /↘/ (falling pitch)
  - /¯/ (level pitch)

Other Symbols:

- /ǀ/ - Dental click, a sound produced by making a sucking motion with the tongue against the teeth (used in some African languages)
- /ǃ/ - Postalveolar click, a similar click produced against the alveolar ridge

- **/ɓ/** - Implosive bilabial stop, a sound produced by stopping airflow inwards

Additionally:

- **Diacritics:** These are small marks added to letters to indicate specific sounds. For example, /ɫ/ represents a velarised "l" sound, common in British English.
- **Ligatures:** These combine two or more symbols into one, like /ɛ/ (epsilon) for the short "e" sound.

IPA is a complex system, and perfect mastery may not be necessary for most purposes. However, this list provides a deeper understanding of the symbols used to represent the vast array of sounds used in human languages.

CHAPTER 1: INSANE A-CENTRIC TONGUE TWISTERS

Welcome to the **Absurd A's chapter** of Tongue Twisters: The Insanity Edtion, the fifth book in our *tongue-twisting series.* Here, we plunge into a perilous playground of linguistic lunacy, where the letter A reigns supreme in its most outrageous form.

Beyond the challenges of our previous books, these tongue twisters are insane iterations of intricate articulation, designed to drive even the most seasoned speaker to distraction. Each twister is an absurd amalgamation of audacious alliteration and astonishing auditory assault, pushing the boundaries of believability.

As you embark on this bewildering expedition, be prepared to battle baffling brain-busters and bewildering bewilderment. These ludicrous linguistic labyrinths will not only test your vocal resilience but also challenge your capacity for composure.

So, summon your sanity, steady your spirit, and step into this surreal soundscape. Remember, this is a test of tolerance as much as talent. Endure, and you will emerge a linguistic legend.

1. An ambitious aardvark architect, Arnold, avidly awaited an ample allotment of acorns to arrange an artistic

archway above an anthill. Along ambled an anxious Aunt Agatha, aching awfully after attempting an audacious afternoon aerial acrobatics act at an antique amusement park. Aghast, Agatha accidentally activated a faulty antique airbrush, aiming a vibrant array of avocado and aubergine hues across Arnold's aspiring artistry. Angrily, Arnold argued, "An archway adorned abundantly with acorns accents anthill aesthetics admirably, and absolutely avoids any abhorrent avocado and aubergine hues!" Aghast again, Agatha apologised abundantly, assuring the architect ample assistance acquiring acorns after all.

Arnold, appeased, accepted Agatha's apology. Agatha, always adventurous, announced, "Actually, Arnold, an abandoned antique airplane awaits assembly above an abandoned airstrip. Assembled aptly, it absolutely assures a spectacular aerial adventure!" Arnold astonished, abandoned anthill aesthetics altogether, accepting Agatha's adventurous alternative. Ascending aptly, Arnold and Agatha soared above the astonished ants, amidst a vibrant array of autumnal aromas.

2. An aardvark, ambitiously aiming at an apple as an ant angrily attacked another ant arrogantly perched atop an acorn, accidentally activated an alarm with its awkward attempt. Attracted by the awful racket, a swarm of angry ants abandoned their anthill, aggressively advancing towards the aardvark. Aghast, the aardvark abandoned its apple aspiration and ambled away amidst the ant assault.

As the aardvark awkwardly attempted to appease the ants with apologetic ahhhs, a wise old ant, adorned with an antique amulet, approached. Asking about the aardvark's actions, the ant archivist attentively awaited an answer.

Articulating its apple appetite amidst the ant attack, the aardvark awaited a solution. Astonishingly, the ant archivist advised the aardvark about abundant apricots awaiting across the abandoned anthill.

Accepting the advice with a grateful acknowledgement, the aardvark ambled across, appeasing its appetite and avoiding any ant arguments. However, as the aardvark ambled away, it accidentally attracted a gaggle of geese with its awkward gait. The geese, aggrieved by the aardvark's approach, angrily advanced, attempting to attack. The archivist ant, alerted by the escalating avian animosity, announced another assembly. Aiming to address aardvark-ant alliances and appetites, as well as appease the aggrieved geese, the archivist ant hoped to achieve an amicable accord across all parties.

3. At an auction, an aunt, affectionately addressed as "Aunt Agnes," outbid another aunt, known as "Aunt Agatha," for an antique amethyst ashtray. Agatha, absolutely aghast, accused Agnes of audacious avarice. An argument arose, attracting astonished attention from auction attendees. Amidst the altercation, an auctioneer, aiming for appeasement, announced another antique - an attractive art deco armchair adorned with amusing animal carvings.

   Aunt Agnes, abruptly abandoning her amethyst ashtray aspirations, angled aggressively towards the armchair. Aunt Agatha, equally ardent about acquiring the armchair with its amusing animal adornments, advanced alongside Agnes. Auction paddles poised, the aunts battled back and forth, bidding against each other with alarming alacrity. Auctioneer announcements accelerated as the aunts aggressively alternated raising their paddles.

As anticipated, the armchair achieved an astronomical asking price. Aunt Agnes, afflicted with auction anxiety and a sudden aversion to amusing animal adornments, abruptly abandoned her attempt. Aunt Agatha, although admittedly anxious, ultimately acquired the armchair. Approaching the auctioneer, Agatha, attempting aristocratic airs, announced, "Absolutely adore this armchair! Absolutely a steal, considering its amusing animal accoutrements!"

Auctioneer, accustomed to such antics, averted his eyes and announced another auction item – a collection of amusing animal artefacts, including an antique armadillo ashtray (somewhat similar to the one Agnes coveted), a pair of artfully crafted aardvark bookends, and a collection of alluring amethyst ashtrays (much to Agatha's amusement). Agatha, abruptly abandoning her aristocratic airs, ambled away, anxiously awaiting the animal artefacts with a newfound appreciation for amusing animal accoutrements.

4. An avid author, Amelia Aster, anxiously awaited an award announcement at a posh awards ceremony. As authors assembled, Amelia adjusted her attire, attempting to appear aloof. Around her, artists argued about abstract art, their animated voices adding to the already amped atmosphere. Amelia, afflicted by anxiety, absentmindedly ate an apricot Danish, accidentally acquiring a sticky apricot stain on her elegant emerald evening gown.

Aghast, Amelia attempted to appease a passing waiter with an awkward apology. Assured the stain was easily addressed with a special cleaning solution, Amelia anxiously awaited her turn. As anticipated awards approached, Amelia's anxiety amplified, transforming her practised air of aloofness into twitchy anticipation. Finally, the announcer, adorned in flamboyant attire, announced the "Author of the Year." Amelia's heart hammered in her chest as another author, Arthur Adams, arrogantly adjusted his spectacles, assuming victory with a practised smirk.

Astonishingly, the announcer declared Amelia Aster as the "Author of the Year!" Amidst a thunderous applause that seemed to shake the very foundations of the venue, Amelia, absolutely astonished, awkwardly approached the stage. Her steps felt like a dream, a surreal moment after months of relentless revisions and nervous anticipation. Accepting the award, a magnificent silver sculpture in the shape of a quill, Amelia addressed the audience. She spoke articulately, her voice trembling slightly at first, then gaining strength as she expressed her appreciation for the honour. Awarding Amelia a beautiful amethyst amulet, the announcer announced a celebratory after-party. Amelia, absolutely elated, abandoned the remnants of her anxiety and ambled towards the party, eager to celebrate her achievement with fellow authors, artists, and anyone else who cared to share in her moment of triumph.

5. An angry ape, Albert, flung a rotten apricot across the aviary. Alarmed, parrots squawked a cacophony, abandoning their preening and squabbling for prime perches. A mischievous monkey named Mike, notorious for pilfering treats from unsuspecting visitors, saw his opportunity. Swinging down from a vine with acrobatic agility, he snatched the apricot mid-air before any ants could claim it.

Albert, startled by the sudden silence and the disappearance of his projectile, let out a roar that echoed through the zoo. He thumped his chest and stomped his feet, accidentally dislodging a rusty latch on the aviary door. With a groan of ancient hinges, the door swung open, sending a kaleidoscope of colourful feathers skyward in a flurry of panicked squawks.

Attendants, alerted by the commotion, sprinted towards the aviary. One, Amelia, a quick-thinking young woman, grabbed a bag of apples – Albert's favourite afternoon snack. Another, Arthur, a seasoned veteran with a calm demeanour, grabbed a net and a whistle.

Spotting the open door and the scattered parrots, they knew immediate action was necessary. Amelia tossed a juicy apple towards Albert's enclosure. With a surprised grunt, Albert abandoned his agitated pacing and snatched the apple mid-air. The sweetness instantly calmed his ruffled feathers (figuratively, of course).

Arthur, meanwhile, expertly scaled the aviary wall with the agility of a spider monkey. He whistled a soothing tune, a familiar melody the parrots had come to associate with feeding time. Slowly, order was restored. The cacophony faded into a symphony of chirps and squawks, punctuated by the rhythmic munching of Albert contentedly devouring his apple.

Mike, however, perched precariously on a branch with the stolen apricot, wasn't quite finished with his mischief. As Arthur coaxed the last reluctant parrot back to its perch, Mike, emboldened by his daring feat, took a bite of the rotten fruit. His eyes widened in disgust. He spat it out, sending a shower of mushy apricots onto a particularly grumpy macaw below. The macaw, already ruffled by the earlier chaos, shrieked in outrage and launched itself at Mike, feathers ruffled and beak snapping.

With a yelp, Mike abandoned his perch, swinging wildly

through the aviary, the outraged macaw hot on his heels. Arthur, ever the professional, sighed and retrieved his net. With a practised flick of the wrist, he captured the squawking macaw in mid-flight, earning a grateful squawk from Mike who clung to the nearest branch, panting from his escapade.

As order was finally restored for good, Amelia and Arthur exchanged weary smiles. Another afternoon at the zoo, another unexpected adventure.

6. An awkward aardvark, Arnold, accidentally adopts an abandoned ant named Archie. Arnold, accustomed to ample anteaters, was astonished at the tiny ant clinging to his ankle. Archie, afraid and alone, clung desperately. Arnold, aiming to appease, attempted ant-appropriate actions – offering an acorn and awkwardly attempting to anthill-hop. Archie, alarmed, clung tighter, accidentally activating Arnold's allergy spray.

A plume of aerosolised antihistamines assaulted the area. Arnold, afflicted with a sneezing fit, accidentally abandoned Archie amidst a patch of dandelions. Archie, adrift in a sea of yellow, anxiously awaited Arnold's return. Appearing a moment later, Arnold, eyes watering, apologised profusely.

Suddenly, a booming voice echoed across the meadow. Agnes, a particularly assertive ant queen, approached, antennae bristling. "An aardvark adopting an ant? Absurd!" she declared. Archie, afraid of angering the queen, attempted to explain, but his tiny voice went unheard. Arnold, awkward as ever, attempted an apology, accidentally knocking over an anthill with his massive form.

Agnes, apoplectic, screeched at Arnold, a wave of angry

ants threatening to engulf him. Just then, a wise old ant, Arthur, intervened. "Antagonizing Arnold achieves absolutely nothing," Arthur croaked. "Perhaps a different approach?"

Agnes, appeased by Arthur's authority, considered her options. Arnold, anxious to help, suggested aiding in the reconstruction of the anthill. Agnes, astonished by the unexpected offer, agreed.

For the rest of the afternoon, Arnold, under Arthur's patient instruction, diligently assisted the ants. He carefully carried twigs and leaves, accidentally assembling a rather artistic ant sculpture in the process. Archie, emboldened by the teamwork, proudly led a contingent of ants to collect pebbles for the base. Finally, as the sun began to set, a magnificent new anthill stood proudly in the meadow.

Agnes, her anger replaced with appreciation, approached Arnold. "An admirable attempt, Arnold," she declared, "and Archie seems quite attached." Seeing Archie happily scurrying around Arnold's feet, Agnes offered a surprising solution. "Perhaps an aardvark and ant alliance isn't as absurd as it seems." Arnold, relieved and ecstatic, grinned. From that day on, Arnold became the honorary protector of the anthill, and Archie, his brave little companion, became a bridge between their two very different worlds.

7. An anxious artist, Agatha, arranged all available apples alphabetically across a massive antique artist's table. Aiming for an aesthetically alluring alliteration, Agatha meticulously categorised the apples: Ambrosias nestled beside Ashmeades, Baldwins bordering Braeburns, Cortlands clinging to Crispins.

Suddenly, a mischievous squirrel named Stanley spied the appetising arrangement. Scampering down a nearby oak branch, Stanley snatched a Scarlet Pippin, sending a cascade of Calvilles tumbling to the floor. Agatha, aghast, abandoned her alphabetical ambitions and angrily chased Stanley around the studio.

Alert to the commotion, Agatha's adorable Abyssinian cat, Alistair, awoke from his afternoon nap. Alistair, an avid apple admirer, also noticed the scattered fruit. Ambling towards the scene, he absentmindedly batted a Blenheim Orange with his paw, sending it rolling towards a rolled-up canvas.

The canvas, precariously balanced against an easel, began to wobble. Agatha, momentarily distracted by Stanley's daring acrobatics on a high shelf, didn't notice the impending disaster. With a crash, the canvas toppled over, splattering a vibrant abstract artwork across the pristine apples.

Agatha froze. Her carefully crafted alphabetical arrangement was a disaster area. Stanley, momentarily stunned by the chaos, paused mid-leap, a plump Granny Smith clutched in his tiny paws. Even Alistair, usually nonchalant, seemed to understand the gravity of the situation.

Agatha, taking a deep breath, assessed the situation. Acceptance washed over her. Art, after all, is often about embracing the unexpected. With a determined glint in her eye, she grabbed a brush and began transforming the splattered apples and spilt paint into a new, abstract masterpiece. She titled it "An Afternoon of Apples and Artistic Antics."

8. An anxious artist, Amelia, meticulously arranged apples alphabetically. A rogue Granny Smith tumbled from the table, attracting Amelia's perpetually curious cat, Alistair. Alistair, an apple aficionado, batted the apple with a playful paw, sending it on a rolling adventure under a rickety easel. The easel, precariously balanced with a blank canvas, teetered precariously. Panic turned Amelia's face ashen, but a strange calm washed over her as the canvas crashed down. Instead of a ruined artwork, spilt paint formed a graceful arc, mirroring the apple's unexpected path.

   Abandoning alphabetical anxiety, Amelia saw a new opportunity. Grabbing a brush, she transformed the chaos into a vibrant masterpiece. The spilt Granny Smith, now surrounded by swirls of amethyst, apricot, and avocado green, became the centrepiece. Amelia titled the work "Art and Apples: An Accidental Adventure." News of the accidental masterpiece spread like wildfire through the art world. Critics lauded Amelia's ability to capture the essence of serendipity. Galleries clamoured to exhibit "Art and Apples," and Amelia's anxiousness about artistic arrangements transformed into a newfound appreciation for the beauty of the unexpected.

   However, the story wasn't quite over. Alistair, sensing the commotion around his playful swipe, strolled nonchalantly into the art gallery during the opening night. Patrons, amidst admiring the painting, gasped as Alistair, ever the apple enthusiast, fixated on the central Granny Smith. With a mischievous glint in his eye, he leapt onto a nearby podium in a single, agile bound and, in a flash, snatched the "accidental" centrepiece from the canvas. Laughter erupted as Amelia, regaining her composure with surprising agility, chased after her mischievous muse. The art world, captivated by this new twist, declared it a performance piece, further solidifying Amelia's reputation as an artist who embraced the unexpected, both on and off the canvas.

News of Alistair's daring act spread like wildfire, turning him into an overnight internet sensation. Memes featuring the cat and the "stolen" apple flooded social media. Art critics debated the artistic merit of the "performance," with some praising its spontaneity and others scoffing at its lack of intention. Regardless of their opinions, everyone agreed that Amelia and Alistair had created a unique artistic experience that transcended the boundaries of a traditional painting.

Capitalising on this newfound fame, Amelia created a series of artworks featuring Alistair interacting with various fruits and vegetables. Galleries clamoured to exhibit these playful pieces, and Amelia found herself at the forefront of a new artistic movement – "Feline Food Frolics." Alistair, meanwhile, revelled in his newfound celebrity status, basking in the adoration of his fans and the abundance of catnip-filled gifts that arrived at Amelia's studio.

Their story became a testament to the power of embracing the unexpected, both in art and in life. Amelia learned to loosen her grip on control and embrace the beauty of serendipity. Alistair, ever the mischievous muse, continued to inspire her with his playful antics, reminding everyone that sometimes the greatest art comes from the most unlikely of sources.

9. An excited artist, Amelia, anxiously awaited another award announcement, absolutely ecstatic about her nomination. Aglow with anticipation, she absentmindedly arranged apricots according to artistic appeal, accidentally attracting a swarm of ants. Alarmed, Amelia abandoned her artistic ambitions and attempted ant appeasement.

Suddenly, the announcer's voice boomed, "And the winner is..." Amelia's heart hammered against her ribs as the name unfolded, agonisingly slow. "Beatrice Blake!" Amelia, although disappointed, applauded with a semblance of sportsmanship. Beatrice, beaming broadly, bounded towards the stage, breathless with bubbly acceptance.

As Beatrice basked in the afterglow of her award, a mischievous monkey named Milo, notorious for pilfering prizes, swung down from the rafters. With acrobatic agility, he snatched the coveted award, a stunning amethyst sculpture, before anyone could react.

Amidst the astonished audience, Amelia, ever the artist, saw an opportunity. Amused by the audacity of the act, she grabbed her sketchbook and began capturing the scene in rapid strokes. Absolutely captivated by the chaos, the audience fell silent, their attention transfixed on Amelia's artistic interpretation.

Meanwhile, security scurried after Milo, who, perched precariously on a chandelier, admired his prize. Alarmed by the approaching guards, he accidentally dropped the sculpture. It plummeted towards the ground, its fate seemingly sealed. However, with a stroke of luck, it landed perfectly in a large, antique aquarium filled with shimmering goldfish.

The unexpected turn of events left everyone speechless. The once intimidating award, submerged in the tranquil water, cast an otherworldly glow on the goldfish, transforming them into a mesmerising spectacle. As gasps of astonishment rippled through the crowd, Amelia completed her sketch, a masterpiece capturing the absurdity and unexpected beauty of the event.

The art critics, initially disappointed by the lack of a traditional winner, were captivated by Amelia's work. They declared it a groundbreaking performance piece, a commentary on the arbitrary nature of awards and the power of artistic interpretation. The award ceremony, intended to celebrate artistic achievement, had inadvertently become the stage for a far more profound artistic expression.

Amelia, once anxious for awards recognition, found herself celebrated for her ability to capture the unexpected. As for Milo, the mischievous monkey, he remained a fugitive, his act of thievery inadvertently sparking a new artistic movement – "Art in Absurdity." The story served as a reminder that sometimes, the most profound artistic experiences emerge from the most chaotic circumstances.

10. A brave astronaut, Amelia, aimed at an asteroid named Argus, accidentally activating an alarm awfully loud. Alarms blared, astronauts scrambled, anxiety ascending aboard the spaceship. Amelia, amidst the auditory assault, attempted analysis. A malfunction, absolutely certain!

Remembering her rigorous training, Amelia deactivated the alarm after a series of anxious button pushes. Announcing the all-clear, Amelia assessed the situation. Apparently, a rogue micrometeoroid had struck a stray antenna, accidentally activating the alarm.

Although relieved, a new concern arose. The impact had damaged a vital antenna, hindering communication with

Earth. Alone and adrift, Amelia activated her auxiliary antenna, a less powerful option. A faint, crackling signal emerged. After a tense ten minutes, Amelia established a weak connection with Mission Control.

Astronaut Arthur, ever the assured voice from Earth, calmly advised Amelia. They could guide her manually using a series of pre-programmed manoeuvres. Anxiety abated, Amelia agreed. For the next several hours, Amelia meticulously followed Arthur's instructions, a solitary pilot navigating by a threadbare connection.

Finally, with a collective sigh of relief on both Earth and in the spaceship, Amelia successfully manoeuvred around Argus. A wave of accomplishment washed over her. The incident, though alarming, had transformed into an unexpected adventure, a testament to Amelia's bravery, skill, and the unwavering support of Mission Control.

News of Amelia's harrowing yet successful mission spread like wildfire. Hailed as a hero for her cool head under pressure, Amelia became an inspiration to aspiring astronauts everywhere. She returned to Earth a celebrity, forever changed by her accidental adventure. The experience solidified her belief that the greatest journeys are often those that take unexpected turns.

Back on Earth, Amelia embarked on a whirlwind tour, sharing her story with captivated audiences. She spoke of the initial alarm, the tense silence during the weak connection, and the exhilarating moment of successfully navigating past Argus. She emphasised the importance of remaining calm under pressure, the value of rigorous training, and the unwavering support that astronauts receive from their teams on Earth.

Inspired by Amelia's experience, a young girl named Alice approached her after a particularly inspiring talk. Alice, wide-eyed and brimming with questions, confessed her dream of becoming an astronaut. Amelia, touched by Alice's enthusiasm, spent an hour mentoring the young girl, sharing stories, answering questions, and encouraging her to pursue her dreams.

This encounter sparked a new passion within Amelia. Beyond her piloting skills, she realised the power of inspiration. She decided to dedicate a portion of her time to visiting schools, sharing her story, and igniting a love for science and space exploration in young minds.

Years later, Amelia received a letter from Alice. Alice, now a young woman, had graduated top of her class in astrophysics and was about to embark on her own astronaut training program. Tears welled up in Amelia's eyes as she read the letter, a testament to the lasting impact of her unexpected adventure. The experience not only solidified Amelia's own place among the stars, but it also helped launch the dreams of a future generation of space explorers.

CHAPTER 2: INSANE B-CENTRIC TONGUE TWISTERS

This chapter is brimming with baffling brain teasers built around the **bellicose letter B**. Expect to battle your way through a bonanza of bewildering, bombastically brilliant wordplay. These buccaneeringly boisterous brainteasers will boldly challenge your ability to bridle your breath and balance your bilabial articulations. Are you brave enough to brave these bombastic barriers?

1. Busy beach bums, Barry, Brenda, and Beatrice, built beautiful sandcastles. Brenda, a brilliant architect, bragged about her intricate bridge, while Beatrice boasted of her breathtaking bastions. Barry, ever the beachcomber, busily beautified his with bits of broken seashells. But blissful building became bedlam as boisterous breakers began battering the shore. Bodies bounced, buckets bobbed, and beautiful sandcastles became blurry blobs.

   Beatrice, ever the optimist, began building anew. "Bigger, better, beach buddies!" she bellowed, her voice barely audible over the booming waves. Barry, brushing sand from his beard, brought bright blue bits of glass for windows. Brenda inspired braided bits of beach grass for bridges. Together, their laughter battled the roar of the waves, their resilience a beacon against the battering.

By the time the breakers calmed, their creation stood strong - a magnificent monument to misfortune made beautiful. Beachgoers, initially bemused by the bedlam, now bragged about the "Breakers-Beaten Beauty." Barry, Brenda, and Beatrice basking in their unexpected triumph, learned a valuable lesson: sometimes, the most beautiful things are built from the biggest blows.

News of the "Breakers-Beaten Beauty" spread like wildfire on the boardwalk. Tourists flocked to witness the beachside masterpiece, snapping pictures and marvelling at its improbable existence. Local businesses, seizing the opportunity, began selling miniature replicas, beach towels emblazoned with the "Breakers-Beaten Beauty" design, and even ice cream flavours inspired by the trio's creation: "Brenda's Bridgeberry Blast," "Beatrice's Bastion Berry," and "Barry's Bits of Blueberry."

The beach transformed into a buzzing bazaar, with Barry, Brenda, and Beatrice finding themselves accidental entrepreneurs. They used their newfound income to purchase sturdy tarps and shovels, building a weatherproof booth to sell their beach-themed creations. Brenda, a natural salesperson, charmed customers with her architectural anecdotes, while Beatrice, ever the artist, offered personalised sandcastle-building workshops. Barry, meanwhile, became the resident beachcomber extraordinaire, his keen eye unearthing an endless supply of unique shells and sea glass.

Life on the beach took on a whole new rhythm. The trio balanced their newfound business with their love for the sand and surf, their days filled with laughter, creativity, and the constant murmur of the ocean. The "Breakers-Beaten Beauty" remained a constant reminder:

challenges, like the boisterous breakers, could batter and break, but with resilience, collaboration, and a dash of creativity, something beautiful could always emerge from the wreckage. Their story became a beacon of hope for beach bums and dreamers alike, a testament to the transformative power of facing down life's biggest blows and building something incredible in their wake.

2. Big Bill bought a book about baboons battling for bananas. Bored by bedtime, Bill began embellishing the story. Bananas became bejewelled berries, baboons transformed into boisterous ballerinas, and battles morphed into breathtaking ballet competitions. His wide-eyed daughter, Beatrice, begged Bill to "bring them back!"

Suddenly, an idea bloomed! Bill grabbed his battered box of paints and began illustrating. Beatrice bounced with excitement, "Brilliant! Brilliant!" Bill, inspired, painted berried branches, baboons in ballet tutus, and a backdrop of a bamboo forest.

The next day, Bill brought his creation to school. "Beatrice's Bejeweled Baboon Ballet," he announced, launching into the story with newfound enthusiasm. The class, captivated, cheered and clapped. Beatrice, beaming with pride, whispered, "Thank you, Bill. You made my bedtime story beautiful!"

From then on, bedtime stories became a collaborative adventure. Bill, fueled by Beatrice's boundless imagination, crafted fantastical tales that stretched far beyond the pages of any store-bought book. Beatrice, his biggest fan, provided the artistic inspiration. Bill's stories transformed from simple narratives into interactive experiences. Beatrice would sketch fantastical creatures

Bill would weave into the stories, their bedtime routine evolving into a vibrant tapestry of words and pictures.

News of their bedtime ritual spread through the school, eventually reaching the ears of the librarian, Ms. Bookworm. Intrigued, she invited Bill and Beatrice to share their collaborative creation during story time. Nervous at first, Beatrice surprised everyone, including herself, by confidently narrating the story alongside her father. The library buzzed with excitement as the children ooh-ed and ahh-ed at Beatrice's colourful illustrations.

Their success at the library sparked a spark within Beatrice. She began drawing not just for bedtime stories, but for other children as well. Bill, a carpenter by trade, saw his daughter's blossoming talent and built her a beautiful wooden art stand. Soon, Beatrice's "Bejeweled Baboon Ballet" stand became a familiar sight at local fairs and markets.

Years later, Beatrice, now a renowned children's book illustrator, stood proudly beside her father at the launch of her first published book: "Beatrice's Bejeweled Baboon Ballet." The story, a testament to the power of imagination and the beauty born from boredom, a book, and a little bit of "bringing them back," had come full circle. It was a reminder that sometimes, the most magical stories aren't found on shelves, but created in the space between a father and daughter, a bedtime story, and a box of paints.

3. Blue butterflies bobbed between buzzing bumblebees on blooming bougainvillaea, their brilliant wings blending beautifully. Bernard, a bespectacled botanist, beamed, his notebook brimming with botanical brilliance. But beauty

bloomed briefly. Brown beetles, brown and bothersome, began devouring the bougainvillaea buds, their buzzing a constant annoyance. Bernard bristled, his brow furrowed. Battling the beetles became his botanical bane.

Suddenly, Beatrice, Bernard's bubbly daughter, bounced beside him. "Build birdhouses, Papa!" she chirped, her eyes bright with an unexpected solution. Bernard scoffed, "Birds bring bigger bothers! They'll gobble up all the berries the butterflies love!" Beatrice, undeterred, skipped off, returning with a brightly painted birdhouse, its colours blending with the bougainvillaea. The next day, a bluebird bobbed by, inspecting the birdhouse with a cocked head. Bernard watched, bewildered. Soon, a flurry of bluebird activity buzzed around the birdhouse as they happily built a nest.

Bernard's brow unfurrowed. The bluebirds, with their brilliant blue feathers, became more than just avian observers. They battled the beetles with a vengeance, beauty blooming anew in the bougainvillaea. Bernard, humbled, realised Beatrice's brilliance. "Birds begone beetles," he began to write in his notebook, a newfound respect blooming for both butterflies and his daughter. The bougainvillaea bloomed again, a vibrant testament to the power of observation, unexpected solutions, and a little girl's bright idea.

But the story didn't end there. As news of the bluebird's beetle-battling prowess spread, other birds joined the fight. Cardinals, known for their bold red plumage, arrived with a melodious chirp. Finches, their tiny bodies harbouring a fierce determination, joined the fray. The bougainvillaea, once under siege by brown beetles, became a bustling avian city. Tourists, drawn by the vibrant spectacle, began flocking to Bernard's garden. Bernard, initially hesitant, found himself transformed.

He started offering guided tours, sharing his botanical knowledge and the unexpected story of the birdhouses. Beatrice, ever the bubbly enthusiast, became his co-host, her laughter ringing out amongst the vibrant blooms and buzzing wings.

The once quiet corner became a haven for nature lovers, a testament to the interconnectedness of the natural world. Bernard, the botanist who battled beetles, became Bernard, the "Birdhouse Botanist," a reminder that sometimes the most unexpected solutions bloom from the boundless imagination of a child.

4. Beneath the boughs of a weeping willow, Baron Barnaby bellowed braggadocious boasts about his bewildering banjo beats, bemusing bemused butterflies basking on blooming bluebells. Bobbing beluga whales, baffled by his blustery pronouncements, breached the brackish bay, their baritone barks bouncing off bamboo bridges. But bold Beatrice, Barnaby's bookish beagle, bristled. "Balderdash!" she barked, "Barnaby's braggadocio belies his bungling ballads!" Bewildered, the Baron bungled a chord, his banjo blaring a bumbling cacophony that bounced between the bridges. Before the blustery bard could blurt another boast, Beatrice barked, "Better banish braggadocio, bring back beautiful beluga ballads!" Beatrice's booming barks bolstered the belugas, who bellowed beautiful melodies, blending with the babbling brook and buzzing bumblebees. Bewildered and bested, Barnaby bowed his blustery head, begging the belugas for a ballad. Blissfully basking in the bay, the belugas boomed a harmonious tune, a melody that brought butterflies back to the blooming bluebells and banished braggadocio from beneath the weeping willow. And so,

amidst the babbling brook and buzzing bees, Beatrice's bravery brought beauty back to the bay, proving that even blustery barons can be bested by ballads and brave beagles.

Baron Barnaby, bedecked in a blindingly bright blazer that seemed woven from a thousand blindingly bright butterflies, boasted about his bewildering banjo beats. Balancing precariously on a rickety bamboo bridge that swayed precariously with each boisterous strum, he blared baffling ballads, bombarding beluga whales basking beneath. Bewildered by the bizarre bravado, the belugas breached in a bewildered ballet, bubbles bursting by the bamboo bridge like miniature, bioluminescent bombs.

Barbara, a bespectacled biologist busy studying beluga behaviour, bristled with annoyance. Brandishing a butterfly net (borrowed for a butterfly census gone bust, a story for another bewildered day), she barged through a bewildered crowd of bemused bystanders. "Baron!" she bellowed, her voice barely audible above the banjo's blaring. "Belugas are best benefitted by a bit of blissful silence! Besides," she continued, brandishing a tattered book overflowing with scribbled notes and bewildering diagrams, "banjo beats demonstrably breach breeding behavior, based on my latest research!"

Baron Barnaby, momentarily bewildered by Barbara's bold outburst, blinked behind his bedazzled spectacles that shimmered with an unsettling rainbow effect. Briefly, he considered belligerent banter, a battle of bewildering barbs, but the sight of Barbara brandishing the butterfly net (adorned with a particularly magnificent butterfly she'd dubbed "Beatrice") convinced him otherwise. Beatrice, for her part, seemed utterly unfazed by the entire bewildering scene, her wings fluttering placidly in the gentle breeze.

Bowing with a flamboyant flourish that nearly sent him toppling off the rickety bridge altogether, he bid a blustering "bravo" to the bewildered belugas and beat a hasty retreat, his banjo bouncing wildly on his back like a belligerent backpack. Barbara, basking in the brief burst of bravado that had replaced her usual quiet demeanour, beamed at the bewildered bystanders. Buoyed by their bewildered but appreciative applause, she returned to her beluga observations, a triumphant glint in her bespectacled eyes.

The bamboo bridge, once a stage for bewildering banjo beats, now stood silent, a testament to Barbara's bravery and the belugas' blissful peace. A lone butterfly, a majestic blue morpho with wings that shimmered like stained glass, landed delicately on the bridge's weathered railing. Whether it was Beatrice, escaping the confines of the net, or simply a curious observer, no one knew. But for a brief, bewildering moment, it seemed to bask in the newfound tranquillity, its wings catching the last rays of the setting sun.

5. Baron Barnaby, his blindingly bright blazer a beacon of bewilderment, boasted about his baffling banjo beats, baffling beluga whales below the bamboo bridges. Barbara, a bespectacled biologist bristling with barely contained disapproval, brandished a butterfly net. "Blissful silence benefits belugas best!" she declared, her voice echoing across the glassy water. Baron, bewildered by her outburst, bowed flamboyantly, his plumed hat nearly tumbling off his head. "But surely, my dear," he stammered, "a spot of whimsical banjo wouldn't bring them to blows?"

Barbara, unimpressed by his theatrics, narrowed her eyes. "Their delicate hearing is attuned to the whispers of the deep, not the barbaric twang of your instrument," she retorted. "Besides," she continued, her voice softening slightly, "have you considered the effect on the ecosystem? The bamboo bridges, while undeniably picturesque, disrupt the natural flow of the river, and your boisterous music..." she trailed off, shaking her head. "It simply wouldn't do."

Baron, for all his bluster, was a surprisingly reasonable man beneath the flamboyant exterior. He contemplated her words, his brow furrowed. The belugas, surfacing for air, let out mournful calls that echoed in the sudden quiet. A pang of sympathy struck him. Perhaps, he mused, a different approach was needed. With a sheepish grin, he tipped his hat to Barbara. "Mea culpa, dear lady. It seems my appreciation for the finer things was misplaced. Perhaps a different tune is in order?"

Intrigued, Barbara lowered her butterfly net. "A more meditative melody, perhaps?" she suggested, a hint of a smile playing on her lips.

Baron chuckled, a deep, rumbling sound. "Indeed. Something to soothe the soul, not shatter it." He strummed a tentative chord on his banjo, a softer, gentler sound this time. The belugas, instead of recoiling, seemed to perk up, their calls turning into a soft, melodious chorus. A butterfly, its wings shimmering an iridescent blue, landed on the edge of Barbara's net, captivated by the unexpected harmony. The bamboo bridges, once a stage for bewildering banjo, now stood as silent sentinels to a newfound respect for the delicate balance of the ecosystem.

6. Beatrice, a bespectacled botanist, bent by the babbling brook, blushed as her baby bounced beside her, babbling away. Butterflies bobbed between blooming bluebells, beckoning the baby with their brilliant wings. Beatrice, briefly bewildered, realised the baby's babbling wasn't random. It mimicked the brook's gurgling rhythm, punctuated by bursts of bird calls. A symphony of buzzing bees joined the chorus, their bodies bobbing in the fragrant breeze.

Suddenly, a brown bear lumbered by, berries bulging in its belly. Beatrice braced herself, heart pounding a frantic rhythm against her ribs. But the bear, seemingly unbothered by the babbling baby, simply dipped its head into the brook and ambled on. Beatrice, breathing a sigh of relief that escaped in a shaky burst, realised the baby's babbling had become a bridge.

Bridge between brook and bird, bridge between human and bear, bridge between the baby and the beautiful chaos of the bramble-filled bank. The babble wasn't just sounds; it was a conversation, a language as old as the babbling brook itself. Beatrice, a woman who understood the whispers of wildflowers and the secrets hidden in the soil, began to understand the language of her child too.

Back at their cabin, nestled amongst the birch trees, Beatrice bounced the baby, humming a tune that echoed the brook's melody. The baby cooed, a blissful connection blooming between them. Beatrice, a brilliant botanist, discovered a new kind of brilliance in that moment – the boundless beauty hidden in a baby's babble, a bridge built on pure, unadulterated babbling. It wasn't just communication; it was a symphony of emotions, a boundless curiosity reaching out to the world, a bridge that transcended words and built connections on a deeper level.

As the sun dipped below the horizon, casting long shadows across the forest floor, Beatrice cradled her baby close, the babbling brook a gentle lullaby. The world was a symphony of sights and sounds, a beautiful, bewildering ballet of life. And in that moment, with the bridge of babbling connecting them, Beatrice knew she would spend the rest of her life learning to understand the language of her child, a language as captivating and ever-changing as the babbling brook itself.

7. Betty bought a box of bright, beautiful buttons for her best-bedazzled blouse. But, bewildered, Betty discovered a brown bat sleeping soundly amidst the bobbles. Betty shrieked, causing the bat to blunder blindly around the box. Bravely, Betty grabbed a butterfly net from the basement, hoping to gently capture the bat and release it outside.

The bat, however, took this as a bizarre ballet invitation. It swooped and soared around the net, Betty bobbing and weaving like a ballerina in a boxing match. Finally, with a burst of breath, Betty managed to scoop the bat into the net. Betty, breathless but brave, carried the bat outside and carefully released it into the twilight.

The bat, blinking in the sudden darkness, launched into the night sky with a grateful squeak. Betty, basking in the post-bat-battle breeze, noticed something peculiar. The bat, in its frantic fluttering, had accidentally brushed against the box of buttons, leaving behind a trail of shimmering, bat-wing dust. Betty peered closer, her eyes widening. The formerly bright buttons now shimmered with an otherworldly, bioluminescent glow!

Betty, ever the resourceful businesswoman, took advantage of this bizarre turn of events. She transformed her bedazzled blouse into a beacon of bioluminescent beauty, a sensation that swept the fashion world. "Betty's Bat-Kissed Buttons" became a fashion craze, with celebrities clamouring to wear the otherworldly glowing garments. Betty, once a simple seamstress, became a renowned designer.

But the story didn't end there. News of the bioluminescent buttons reached a team of biochemists at a nearby university. Intrigued by the bat's unique dust, they contacted Betty. Together, they embarked on a groundbreaking collaboration. Betty, with her keen eye for design, helped translate the bioluminescent properties into practical applications. The scientists, in turn, unlocked the secrets of the bat's dust, creating a sustainable, eco-friendly source of light.

Their work revolutionised the fashion industry. Clothes adorned with Betty's buttons no longer needed batteries or electricity to glow. The bioluminescent glow even possessed a calming effect, lowering stress levels in wearers. Betty's fashion line expanded beyond clothing, incorporating bioluminescent materials into home décor, creating a new wave of "bat-inspired" interior design.

The story of Betty's bat encounter became a heartwarming tale of ingenuity and the power of unexpected collaborations. It served as a reminder that even the most fearful experiences can hold unforeseen opportunities. Betty, the once-ordinary seamstress, became a beacon of innovation, forever grateful to the bewildered bat that blundered into her box of buttons.

8. Ben bounced the basketball badly, battling between frustration and a burning desire to improve. Brick after brick, the ball refused to cooperate, bouncing off the rim with a disheartening clang. Feeling defeated, Ben slumped onto a nearby bench, burying his face in his hands. The rhythmic thump of a worn-out leather ball echoed on the empty court, mocking his ineptitude.

Suddenly, a gentle voice broke through his dejection. "Basketball is about balance, young man." Ben looked up to see a weathered but wise-looking coach named Bob leaning against a nearby light pole. His kind eyes held a glint of experience that promised understanding. Intrigued, Ben listened as Bob began to explain the fundamentals of the game: balance, body positioning, and a calm focus. It wasn't just about brute strength or athletic prowess, Bob explained, but a delicate dance between mind and muscle.

Bob spent the next hour patiently guiding Ben through drills. He started with basic footwork, teaching him how to pivot and plant his feet for optimal shot preparation. With each repetition, Ben felt a sense of control he hadn't experienced before. Bob then moved on to ball handling, demonstrating the art of dribbling with both hands, keeping the ball low, and changing direction with a flick of the wrist. Ben practised diligently, the frustration slowly melting away as his movements became more fluid.

Finally, they reached the holy grail – shooting. Bob emphasised the importance of a consistent form, a balanced follow-through, and visualising the ball arcing through the net. Ben started close, focusing on perfecting his mechanics. As his confidence grew, Bob gradually nudged him back, extending the distance between him and the basket. By sunset, Ben's frustration had melted away, replaced by a newfound confidence. He dribbled with newfound control, his shots finding the net with a satisfying swish. The rhythmic thump of the ball against the court now echoed a melody of progress, a testament to his dedication and Bob's tutelage.

As Ben thanked Bob for his time, the coach smiled. "Basketball isn't just about talent," he said, "It's about bouncing back from bad bounces." Ben grinned, understanding the deeper meaning of Bob's words. He knew that his journey to becoming a better basketball player was just beginning, but he was no longer afraid of bobbling the ball.

News of Ben's transformation spread through the schoolyard. Kids who once scoffed at his clumsy attempts now watched with newfound respect. He wasn't a star player yet, but his dedication and coachable spirit were undeniable. Ben, emboldened by his progress, joined the school team. While he still had moments of frustration, he approached them with a newfound resilience, remembering Bob's words and the countless hours spent honing his skills on the empty court.

The journey wasn't always easy. There were losses, missed shots, and moments of self-doubt. But with each setback, Ben remembered the quiet wisdom of Coach Bob and the satisfying swish of a perfectly executed shot. He learned to celebrate his victories, big and small, and most importantly, to learn from his mistakes. Basketball became more than just a game; it became a metaphor for life, a testament to the power of perseverance and the transformative power of a mentor's guidance. Years later, Ben, now a skilled and respected player, found himself coaching a young boy struggling with his own shortcomings on the court. As he began explaining the fundamentals of the game, a sense of pride washed over him. He wasn't just passing on his knowledge, he was paying tribute to Coach Bob, the man who had ignited a passion within him and taught him the valuable lesson of bouncing back from bad bounces.

9. Blustery Barbara burnt blueberry muffins, blaming a broken burner. Before bickering with the repairman could escalate, Brenda, her bubbly friend and a baker extraordinaire, intervened. "Hold on, Barb," she chirped, her eyes sparkling with an idea. Brenda, ever the optimist, saw potential in the mishap. With a flourish, she scraped the burnt bits into a pan, adding a splash of balsamic vinegar, a squeeze of brown sugar, and a hint of smoky chipotle pepper. Soon, the kitchen was filled with the tantalising aroma of a bold blueberry barbecue sauce, a delicious twist on tradition.

The transformation was immediate. Barbara, initially sceptical, watched in awe as Brenda transformed a culinary disaster into a potential goldmine. The kitchen, once filled with the acrid scent of burnt muffins and Barbara's brewing frustration bloomed with creativity. Bob, Barbara's husband, who had been watching the scene unfold with a mixture of amusement and apprehension, was captivated. "Brenda," he boomed, his voice filled with newfound respect, "you've got magic in your hands. Why don't you take over that empty bakery space down the street? It's been gathering dust for months."

Brenda, her eyes widening with surprise, glanced at Barbara. Barbara, humbled by Brenda's ingenuity and Bob's unexpected proposal, knew she had misjudged the situation. With a sheepish grin, she reached out and squeezed Brenda's hand. "Partner?" she asked, a newfound respect colouring her voice.

And so, "Burnt to Brilliant Bites" was born. Their little bakery, built on the foundation of a burnt muffin and a sprinkle of serendipity, thrived. Brenda's culinary creations, fueled by her ability to transform even the most unexpected ingredients into delicious delights, attracted customers from miles around. Barbara, with her sharp business acumen and newfound appreciation for Brenda's talent, managed the financial side of things. Bob, meanwhile, became their biggest cheerleader, often regaling customers with the tale of the burnt blueberry muffins that launched a culinary revolution.

Their story became a beacon of hope for struggling home cooks and aspiring entrepreneurs everywhere. It was a testament to the power of unexpected opportunities, the transformative magic of embracing bold ideas, and the importance of seeing the potential for brilliance even in the face of burnt breakfast pastries.

10. Busy bakers, Beatrice and Ben, bustled around their bakery, balancing brightly-burning birthday candles on a mountain of birthday biscuits. But calamity struck! Clumsy Ben, while attempting an acrobatic flour sack manoeuvre (a questionable birthday tradition), bumped the table, sending a biscuit bouncing on a ballistic trajectory. Beatrice, ever the resourceful baker with reflexes honed by years of catching rogue sprinkles and runaway rolling pins, grabbed a butterfly net with the grace of a seasoned lepidopterist. In a blur of flour and focus, she expertly captured the biscuit mid-air before it splattered on the pristine frosting. Laughter filled the bakery as they righted the wobbly candles and dusted the flour off Ben's bewildered face.

Suddenly, the bakery door burst open, revealing a frantic bride, her veil askew and mascara threatening to join the fray. "Buttercream catastrophe!" she cried, her voice trembling. Tears welled up in her eyes as she explained how her three-tier wedding cake, a masterpiece of delicate sugar flowers and cascading fondant, had inexplicably collapsed moments before the ceremony. Beatrice, ever the picture of calm amidst the sugary storm, sprang into action. Ben, fueled by newfound biscuit-catching confidence and a healthy dose of adrenaline, scurried to gather supplies.

Working with the efficiency of a well-oiled baking machine, Beatrice and Ben began their culinary rescue mission. The birthday biscuits, initially destined for a joyous celebration, were repurposed. Using rolling pins with newfound reverence, they transformed the biscuits into a whimsical assortment of shapes – hearts, stars, and butterflies. These were meticulously layered, creating a base for a truly unique wedding cake. Vibrantly coloured berries and fluttering edible butterflies, crafted from the leftover biscuit dough with a dash of ingenuity, adorned the creation.

The bride, initially distraught, was overwhelmed with gratitude as Beatrice unveiled their "Biscuit to Bliss" masterpiece. Tears, this time of joy, streamed down her face. News of their heroic rescue mission spread like wildfire through the town. Beatrice and Ben, once known for their delectable birthday treats, became the city's go-to bakers for last-minute emergencies. Their story, a testament to quick thinking, teamwork, and the ability to transform misfortune into a thing of beauty, became a beacon for creative problem-solving and the unexpected magic that could arise from a simple biscuit mishap.

Furthermore, their ingenuity sparked a new trend in

wedding cakes. Soon, "deconstructed" cakes, featuring playful shapes and unexpected elements, became all the rage. Beatrice and Ben, at the forefront of this culinary revolution, found themselves not just saving weddings, but also redefining them, one delicious bite at a time.

11. Bashful Bess, a bookish barn owl, befriended Bartholomew, a brave black bull. Bess, with her oversized eyes perpetually glued to the pages of her salvaged novels, was an anomaly in the bustling barnyard. Bartholomew, on the other hand, was a gentle giant, his imposing size belying a surprisingly calm demeanour.

Their unlikely friendship blossomed over moonlit nights. Bess, perched atop Bartholomew's broad back, would narrate fantastical tales from the worn paperbacks she collected. The sight of the hulking bull with a delicate owl perched on his back, her voice weaving tales of brave knights and mythical creatures, became a barnyard marvel.

One particularly stormy night, a sudden power outage plunged the farm into an inky blackness. Panic rippled through the animals, their usual routines disrupted by the unfamiliar darkness. Bess, however, thrived in the gloom. Her exceptional night vision, a source of self-consciousness in the brightly lit days, became a beacon of hope.

With Bartholomew by her side, a silent and sturdy companion, Bess took flight. Her silent calls, a rhythmic "hoo-hoo," guided the confused animals back to their shelters. Farmers, stumbling blindly in the darkness, found their way thanks to the soft glow emanating from Bess' reflective eyes.

By morning, the storm had passed, leaving behind a

sense of gratitude and a newfound appreciation for the unlikely hero. News of the "Barnyard Batman," a moniker bestowed by a particularly imaginative farmhand, spread like wildfire. Bess, once a shy observer, found herself thrust into the spotlight. Bartholomew, ever the loyal friend, stood protectively by her side as she was showered with grateful chirps, moos, and the occasional grateful lick from a particularly enthusiastic cow.

Their story, however, became more than just a heartwarming local legend. A visiting wildlife photographer, captivated by the sight of Bess and Bartholomew, captured their image. The photograph, titled "An Unlikely Alliance," went viral. It sparked conversations about the beauty of unexpected friendships and the importance of embracing differences. Bess, who once found solace in the fictional worlds of her books, became a symbol of courage and the power of stepping out of your comfort zone.

Inspired by Bess' bravery, a group of introverted children started a nature club at the local library. They learned about owls, bats, and other nocturnal creatures, overcoming their initial fear of the dark. Bartholomew, in turn, became a local celebrity. Farmers from neighbouring communities invited him to their fields, not for his brawn, but for his calming presence. He became a symbol of gentle strength, a reminder that true power lies not just in physical might but also in kindness and quiet confidence.

Years later, Bess' stories continued to inspire. A young artist, captivated by the legend of the Barnyard Batman, created a series of murals depicting Bess and Bartholomew's adventures. These murals adorned the walls of schools and libraries, a constant reminder that even the most unlikely of friendships can change the world, one brave step, one whispered story, and one act of kindness at a time.

12. Balancing brilliantly, Bobby biked boldly down a bustling boulevard. Buildings blurred as he bobbed between buses and bewildered pedestrians. But Bobby wasn't just riding – he was racing. A bet with his best friend, Billy, had him vying to be the first to reach the bakery at the boulevard's end, known for its legendary blueberry babka.

Suddenly, a brown bag bounced off a bumpy brick, scattering colourful buttons across the path. Brakes biting, Bobby skidded to a halt, narrowly missing a bewildered Beagle. Looking around, he saw a flustered baker, her button box open, spilling its contents.

Without a beat, Bobby dismounted and began scooping buttons. Balancing precariously on one leg, he sorted and returned them with a bright smile. The baker, Brenda, beamed. "Bless you, young man! You've saved the day," she exclaimed, before disappearing into the bakery.

Bobby, momentarily forgetting the race, waited. Brenda returned with a warm, gooey babka. "Consider this a reward for your bravery and kindness," she said. Bobby, touched, thanked her and set off again, the babka tucked securely in his backpack.

Reaching the finish line, panting but victorious, Bobby found Billy waiting, a slightly stale bagel in hand. "Guess who got the real prize?" Bobby winked, pulling out the babka. Billy's eyes widened.

The race may have been won with balance and speed, but Bobby learned a bigger lesson – sometimes, the greatest rewards come from unexpected detours and acts of kindness. That day, the bustling boulevard became a reminder that a little bit of bravery, sprinkled with a dash of helpfulness, can create the sweetest victories.

CHAPTER 3: INSANE C-CENTRIC TONGUE TWISTERS

Brace yourself for a challenging collection of **C-centric tongue twisters**. These complex creations will test your speech skills to the limit. Are you ready to conquer these colossal challenges?

1. A crystal chandelier, crafted centuries ago, captivated by the captivating carnival carousel below. Its cascading prisms caught the coloured lights, transforming them into a dazzling display that rivalled the carousel's painted horses. Clara, a curious child, noticed the chandelier's forgotten magic. She tugged on a dangling chain, causing the crystals to chime softly, a counterpoint to the carnival's lively music.

   The carnies, initially dismissive, were captivated by the unexpected melody. Soon, Clara and the carnies were collaborating. Clara, perched on a carousel horse, tinkered with the chain, creating a rhythmic melody that perfectly complemented the calliope's tune. The carousel, once a silent spectacle, transformed into a captivating musical ride.

News of the "Crystal Carousel" spread like wildfire. Tourists flocked to experience the unique combination of light, sound, and movement. The once-forgotten chandelier became the star of the show, its forgotten beauty rediscovered by a curious child. Clara, an unlikely conductor, revelled in the unexpected joy of her creation.

The carnies, inspired by Clara's ingenuity, started incorporating found objects into their acts. A discarded hubcap became a rhythmic drum, a rusty swing set morphed into a trapeze act. The carnival, once a collection of tired routines, became a vibrant showcase of reinvention. The story of the Crystal Carousel became a testament to the power of collaboration and the unexpected magic that can be found in forgotten corners.

2. Candied carrots, cleverly concealed amongst colourful confetti, caused chaos at the costume contest. Confused contestants crunched on carrots, convinced they were costume components. Cleopatra, clad in customary Egyptian garb, choked on a candied carrot, causing confusion. Caesar, a toga-clad competitor, mistook a carrot for a jewelled sceptre, waving it triumphantly.

Chaos cascaded. A caped crusader, convinced carrots were Kryptonite for his cardboard kryptonite container, chucked them across the stage. A cloud-costumed contestant, sprinkled orange with the confetti, resembled a tangerine nightmare.

Amidst the mayhem, a young girl in a caterpillar costume, chomping on a carrot with glee, had an epiphany. "Carrots could be caterpillar candy!" she declared. Inspired, she hopped onto the stage, weaving a colourful tale of a caterpillar conquering a carrot patch. The crowd, initially confused, erupted in delighted cheers.

The judges, captivated by the unexpected turn, declared the contest a tie between Cleopatra (who recovered gracefully) and the caterpillar. The confetti-coated cloud contestant, now a crowd favourite, won the "Most Creative Costume" award.

The candied carrots, catalysts for confusion, became a symbol of creative chaos. The contest, forever etched in memory as the "Carrot Catastrophe," became a testament to finding humour and inspiration in the unexpected. From that day on, candied carrots were a quirky tradition at the contest, a reminder that even the most carefully planned events could be sweetened by a sprinkle of surprise.

3. Chubby cherubs, Charlotte and Charles, chortled contentedly. Cheeks crammed with chocolate chip cookies, crumbs cascaded onto the crimson carpets of the castle conservatory. Cecily, the stern-faced caretaker, cleared her throat, causing a collective clench in the cherubic cheeks.

Sensing trouble, Charles, the more cunning of the two, coughed dramatically, spewing a shower of chocolate crumbs onto Cecily's pristine white apron. "Oh dear!" he exclaimed, eyes wide with mock innocence. Charlotte, ever the accomplice, chimed in, "Perhaps a cup of chamomile could calm your clearly chagrined state, Cecily?"

Cecily, a woman easily flustered, sputtered incoherently. Taking advantage of her momentary disarray, Charles launched a charm offensive. "We could even share some of these celestial cookies, Cecily. They're crafted with care, from the choicest cocoa and clouds themselves!"

Hesitantly, Cecily accepted a cookie, her stern demeanour softening as the rich chocolate melted on her tongue.

By the time the last crumb was devoured, a ceasefire had been declared. Cecily, with a sugar-induced smile, agreed to overlook the carpet calamity. From then on, a curious custom emerged. Every Wednesday, the cherubs and Cecily would gather in the conservatory, sharing cookies and stories under the watchful gaze of the castle gargoyles. It became a testament to the power of a little creativity and a shared love for chocolate chip cookies in conquering even the most formidable frowns.

4. A clever calico cat named Clementine caught a clumsy cricket causing calamity in the kitchen. Christopher, the cook, chased Clementine with a whisk, convinced cricket chirps contaminated his carefully crafted creations. Clementine, cornered, launched the cricket into a cauldron of bubbling chocolate chip cookie dough.

   Christopher, expecting the worst, braced himself. But as he lifted the lid, a delightful surprise awaited. The cricket's chirp, combined with the chocolate's warmth, had created a symphony of unexpected flavours. The cookies were a hit! Christopher, ever the curious cook, christened them "Chirpy Chip Cookies."

   News of the cricket cookies caused a confectionary craze. Bakeries across town began experimenting with insect-inspired ingredients, each creation more curious than the last. Clementine, the unlikely muse, became a local celebrity, her catnip-filled collar a badge of honour. Christopher, once a stickler for tradition, embraced the unexpected, his kitchen a playground of chirpy crickets and culinary capers.

   The story, however, didn't end there. Professor Charles

Cadence, a renowned entomologist, became fascinated by the "Chirpy Chip Cookies." He theorised that specific insect chirps, combined with certain frequencies, could unlock unique flavour profiles. Partnering with Christopher, they embarked on a series of experiments, their kitchen transformed into a laboratory of bubbling concoctions and chirping crickets.

Their research unearthed a whole new world of culinary possibilities. Honeybee hum cookies buzzed with citrusy sweetness, while firefly flicker fudge glowed with a hint of cinnamon. The food world was captivated. Restaurants offered "Entomophagic Evenings," featuring insect-inspired dishes that tantalised taste buds and challenged perceptions.

Clementine, meanwhile, became the mascot of the movement. Her image, a mischievous grin framed by a catnip collar, adorned packaging and promotional materials. Christopher, the once-traditional chef, became a celebrity himself, his name synonymous with culinary innovation.

Their story transcended cookies. It became a testament to the delicious potential of chance encounters, the power of collaboration between seemingly disparate fields, and the importance of embracing the unexpected. It reminded everyone that a little chaos in the kitchen, a clever cat with a penchant for crickets, and a curious entomologist with a passion for flavour could lead to something truly extraordinary – a revolution in taste, fueled by a single chirpy cricket.

5. Captain Calamity, clad in a crimson cape crusted with candy corn, cackled gleefully as he commandeered his colossal contraption. This wasn't your average carnival ride, oh no! This behemoth boasted a whirlwind of

whirling wonders: a carousel crazed with candy-cane steeds, a catapult flinging fuzzy frogs far and wide, and a candy cannon spewing sprinkles of swirling sherbet. The result? A chaotic concoction of creatures caught in a cacophony of calamity!

Curious capybaras clung to candy canes, their cries swallowed by the carousel's calliope clang. Cackling cockatoos careened through the candy cannon, their feathers dusted with sherbet snow. Clumsy camels collided with colourful carts, sending cotton candy clouds billowing into the air. Cats, cast from the catapult, clung comically to carrousel creatures, their claws tangled in candy corn manes.

Amidst the mayhem, the courageous crew scrambled to contain the catastrophe. Clara, the quick-witted captain, steered the contraption with steely resolve, her voice booming above the bedlam. Carlos, the nimble acrobat, leapt between leaping llamas, untangling their teetering towers of taffy. Crystal, the cunning chemist, concocted a calming concoction of candied chamomile tea, soothing the ruffled feathers of flustered flamingoes.

But Captain Calamity wasn't finished yet! With a mischievous glint in his eye, he cranked the contraption into overdrive. The carousel spun faster, the catapult flung further, and the candy cannon erupted in a rainbow of sugary shrapnel. Could the courageous crew quell the calamity before it consumed them all? Or would Captain Calamity's chaotic creation spell their sugary doom?

Only time, and your tongue-twisting prowess, will tell! So pucker up, practise your pronunciations, and prepare to embark on this whirlwind adventure with Captain Calamity and his candy-coated crew!

6. A curious cerulean cat named Cleo clung cautiously to a creaky clothesline. A clumsy crow, mistaking a flapping sheet for a potential meal, swooped down, sending Cleo tumbling into a bed of colourful calla lilies. Beatrice, the botanist below, gasped in horror at the sight of her prized flowers in disarray. But as Cleo emerged, dusted with pollen and sporting a disgruntled expression, Beatrice noticed something unexpected. The lilies, normally a pristine white, now sported streaks of vibrant cerulean and charcoal grey, mirroring the cat's fur and the crow's feathers.

   Intrigued, Beatrice saw an opportunity. Carefully collecting pollen from both the cat and the crow, she embarked on a daring experiment – cross-pollinating the lilies. Weeks later, her efforts bore fruit (or rather, flowers). The once-uniform lilies bloomed in a stunning array of colours – cerulean blues, charcoal greys, and even a smattering of inky black. News of Beatrice's "Cleo's Canvas" calla lilies spread like wildfire. Gardeners from across the region flocked to see the breathtaking blooms, a testament to the unexpected beauty that can arise from a messy tumble and a touch of creative inspiration.

   Cleo, the reluctant muse, became a local celebrity, her mischievous spirit forever immortalised in the vibrant hues of the calla lilies. Beatrice, in turn, learned that even the most meticulously planned gardens could yield surprising beauty with a little help from chance and a curious cat.

   But the story didn't end there. Inspired by Beatrice's success, a young boy named Christopher, captivated by the crow's role in the pollen transfer, started sketching intricate crow sculptures. Soon, his creations, crafted from recycled materials, adorned the gardens alongside the calla lilies. These sculptures, depicting crows perched on lily pads or mid-flight, became a captivating addition to the landscape. Tourists marvelled at the harmonious blend of nature and art, a testament to the interconnectedness of creativity and the ripple effect a single event can have.

Beatrice, Christopher, and Cleo, an unlikely trio, became symbols of embracing the unexpected. Their story resonated with artists and scientists alike, reminding everyone that inspiration can come from the most curious creatures, the clumsiest tumbles, and the most unexpected collaborations.

7. Clara carefully chopped colourful carrots, concentrating on creating crunchy coleslaw. A curious crow, captivated by the rhythmic chopping, cawed loudly and swooped down. Clara, startled, dropped her knife, sending carrots cascading across the counter like a confetti explosion. The mischievous crow, convinced she'd unearthed a hidden treasure, grabbed a carrot chunk and flew off in triumph.

Clara, initially frustrated, noticed something peculiar. The scattered carrots, haphazardly arranged on the counter, resembled a vibrant mosaic. Inspired, she abandoned the traditional coleslaw and began chopping other vegetables – cucumbers with a cool green, red bell peppers with a fiery hue, purple cabbage adding a touch of whimsy. She arranged them carefully, mirroring the pattern created by the crow's chaotic act. The result? A stunning "Crow's Creation Salad," a kaleidoscope of colours and textures.

Clara entered the salad in a local competition, its unorthodox beauty captivating the judges. "Crow's Creation" won first prize, with its story becoming a sensation. Restaurants clamoured to feature Clara's "accidentally artistic" salads. Clara, once a meticulous cook, embraced the unexpected. She started incorporating "controlled chaos" into her dishes, collaborating with the crow (who, surprisingly, seemed to enjoy the attention) by leaving enticing carrot pieces strategically placed.

The once-ordinary kitchen became a stage for creative culinary chaos. News crews filmed Clara and her feathered partner, documenting their collaborative cooking process. Clara, initially hesitant about the spotlight, found herself enjoying the shared creative energy. The crow, christened "Cornelia" by the internet, became a viral sensation, her playful antics adding a dash of humour to Clara's artistic presentations.

Their fame wasn't limited to the internet. Local art schools began offering "Crow and Cook" workshops, where students explored the intersection of creativity and chance. Aspiring chefs flocked to Clara's cooking classes, eager to learn her techniques of incorporating "controlled chaos" into their dishes.

The story of Clara and Cornelia transcended the culinary world. It became a symbol of the unexpected beauty that can arise from mistakes and collaboration. From a dropped knife and a startled crow, Clara and Cornelia reminded everyone that inspiration can come from the most unlikely places, and that even the most meticulously planned creations can benefit from a touch of feathered chaos.

8. Curious children, clad in colourful costumes that clashed in a delightful cacophony, clamoured for cotton candy clouds spun by clumsy clowns cavorting in the centre ring. Chaos reigned as candy floss rained down, sticking to sequined shirts and sparkling tutus like a whimsical snowstorm. But calamity became creativity when clever Clara, crowned Queen Cupcake for the day, noticed the mess.

With a mischievous grin that could outshine the mirrored balls above the big top, Clara corralled the cotton candy chaos. She fashioned leftover candy floss into colourful crowns for the children, transforming the sticky situation into a delightful surprise. The crowns, adorned with spun sugar jewels and fluffy pink peaks, were an instant hit. Soon, every child sported a confectionary crown, a symbol of their reign over the sugary mayhem.

The clowns, inspired by Clara's ingenuity, incorporated the candy into their act, their initial clumsiness morphing into comical dexterity. They juggled sticky strands with the grace of seasoned acrobats, weaving the cotton candy into their routines like a magician pulling scarves from a hat. Laughter erupted as clowns sported cotton candy beards that defied gravity and juggled pink puffs that resembled oversized lollipops. The "Candy Catastrophe" became a carnival highlight, a testament to turning chaos into creative capers.

News of Clara's cotton candy crown and the carnival's clever calamity spread through the land like wildfire on a windy day. Children across the kingdom started hosting "Cotton Candy Chaos" parties, revelling in the playful mess. Bakeries began crafting confections specifically designed for creative calamity, with flavours like bubblegum blue and sunshine orange replacing the traditional pink and purple. Clowns honed their skills in candy-coated comedy, their routines evolving into dazzling displays of sugary slapstick. The once-dreaded "Cotton Candy Catastrophe" became a symbol of embracing the unexpected, reminding everyone that a little mess can lead to a lot of magic.

But the story didn't end there. Inspired by Clara's resourcefulness, a young inventor named Carl began experimenting with ways to capture the fleeting beauty of the cotton candy clouds. He tinkered and toiled in his workshop, emerging weeks later with a contraption that resembled a giant lollipop with a spinning funnel. When spun, the contraption transformed sugar into shimmering, edible sculptures – delicate spun sugar dragons soaring through the air, sparkling castles fit for a candy kingdom, and swirling lollipops that resembled miniature galaxies.

Carl's invention revolutionised the carnival, adding a layer of artistic wonder to the cotton candy chaos. Soon, carnies across the land were incorporating his "Sugar Sculpting Spinners" into their acts, creating fantastical landscapes and edible masterpieces that delighted audiences of all ages. Clara, Carl, and the cotton candy clowns became symbols of collaboration and unexpected inspiration, their story a testament to the transformative power of a little chaos and a lot of creativity.

9. Carefree cyclists, Charlie and Chloe, cruised comfortably along cobblestone streets. Cars congested the crossings, causing confusion. Charlie, ever cautious, called a halt. But Chloe, a champion of creativity, noticed colourful construction cones blocking a narrow alleyway. With a mischievous grin, she led Charlie down the cobbled path.

The alley, crammed with colourful crates, transformed into a cyclist's paradise. Weaving through the vibrant maze, Charlie and Chloe emerged onto a hidden riverside path, a peaceful oasis amidst the city chaos. They christened it "The Cobbled Caper," a secret route known only to adventurous cyclists.

News of the hidden path spread virally through cycling forums and social media. Soon, colourful clusters of cyclists navigated the cluttered alleyway, a testament to the joy of discovery hidden within the city's chaos. Shopkeepers along the route, initially surprised by the influx of customers, quickly adapted. "Caper Coffee" and "Cobbled Cake" became bestsellers, with vibrant murals depicting Charlie and Chloe adorning the cafes.

The city council, initially hesitant about the sudden popularity of an unmarked path, saw the positive impact. They commissioned a study, which revealed a significant decrease in traffic congestion on the main roads and a rise in cycling tourism. Inspired, the council installed cycling lanes along the river path, transforming it into a scenic artery for both commuters and leisure riders.

Charlie and Chloe, the carefree cyclists who dared to explore, became accidental urban architects. Their story resonated with city dwellers, reminding everyone to look beyond the obvious. It sparked a movement encouraging creative solutions for urban planning, with citizens organising "Caper Walks" to discover hidden gems in their own neighbourhoods. The cobblestone streets, once a symbol of congestion, became a testament to the transformative power of curiosity and a little bit of colourful chaos.

Years later, Charlie and Chloe, now established urban

planners themselves, received an award for their contribution to the city's infrastructure. As they stood on stage, surrounded by a sea of colourful cycling jerseys, they couldn't help but smile. The "Cobbled Caper" had become a symbol of possibility, reminding them that even the smallest act of exploration can lead to unexpected beauty and lasting change.

10. Clever Chloe cleverly concealed a crumpled chip underneath a cute, colourful coat. Lunchtime loomed, and Chloe craved a crunchy companion to her cafeteria concoction. But alas, a rogue "No Chip" policy cast a shadow over the school cafeteria. Instituted to promote healthy eating, the policy backfired, turning forbidden chips into contraband coveted by all.

Undeterred, Chloe channelled her inner MacGyver. With the grace of a magician, she produced the crumpled chip, transforming it into a magnificent "Chip Crown." Using a napkin as a makeshift base and securing the chip with a strategically placed rubber band, she created a crunchy couture masterpiece.

Her classmates, captivated by her creativity and a touch envious of her crunchy crown, erupted in cheers. News of Chloe's "Chip Caper" spread like wildfire, reaching the ears of Principal Campbell, a man known for his love of crossword puzzles and a healthy dose of scepticism. Intrigued by the commotion, Principal Campbell met Chloe, a meeting that sparked a cafeteria revolution.

Chloe, nervous but determined, explained her craving for a little crunch and the absurdity of a chip ban. Principal Campbell, surprised by the eloquence of the normally quiet Chloe, listened intently. He saw a spark of ingenuity in her eyes and a reflection of his own youthful mischief in her crumpled chip crown.

Together, they hatched a plan. Chloe's "Chip Caper" became a catalyst for change. Principal Campbell, a reformed sceptic, announced the creation of a "Creative Crunch Corner." This corner, overseen by Chloe and a rotating committee of students, offered a selection of healthy snacks like carrots and celery sticks. But the real magic happened in the condiment section. A sprinkle of everything bagel seasoning here, a drizzle of hot sauce there, students could customise their healthy snacks with a sprinkle of surprise.

Chloe's crumpled chip became a symbol of student voice and a testament to the power of a little creativity and a whole lot of crunch. From that day on, lunchtime was no longer just about sustenance; it became a celebration of student ingenuity. The cafeteria echoed with the sounds of chopping vegetables, the clatter of condiment containers, and the satisfied munching of students enjoying their customised creations. It was a delicious reminder that rules can sometimes be deliciously crunched, and even the smallest act of defiance can spark positive change.

CHAPTER 4: INSANE D-CENTRIC TONGUE TWISTERS

This section is a veritable vault of verbal challenges designed to test the limits of your diction. From the deceptively simple to the downright diabolical, these tongue twisters will demand your undivided attention. Whether you're a seasoned word warrior or a novice adventurer, you'll find yourself dodging, dipping, and diving to conquer these convoluted concoctions. So, sharpen your skills, steady your nerves, and step into a world where the **letter D** reigns supreme.

1. Devoted doodler Drew dreamt diligently, depicting dragons dancing disco in a dazzling display. Daylight dispelled the dream, but Drew didn't dismiss it. Determined to capture his vision, Drew dug out dusty drawing pads and dusted off his dormant talent. Dragons, once confined to the dream world, danced across his pages. Their scales shimmered with disco glitter, their fiery breath transformed into bursts of neon light. Drew, initially doubtful, discovered his doodles delighted his co-workers. Soon, discarded cardboard boxes became dragon disco floors, detailed with markers and shimmering tape. His cubicle, once dull, became a dazzling disco den, attracting lunchtime crowds eager to witness the dancing dragons.

News of Drew's "Dream Disco Dragons" spread through the office. The CEO, a man known for his no-nonsense demeanour, was intrigued. He visited Drew's cubicle, a flicker of amusement dancing in his eyes. Impressed by Drew's creativity and the unexpected boost in employee morale, the CEO decided to embrace the disco fever. He declared a "Dress-Up Disco Day," a day to celebrate whimsy and the power of dreams. The office, once a sea of drab suits, transformed into a kaleidoscope of colours. Dragons adorned ties, disco balls twirled from the ceiling, and laughter replaced the usual hum of productivity.

Drew, the devoted doodler, became a champion of dreaming big. His story resonated with employees of all levels, a reminder that even the most whimsical ideas can spark joy and transformation. His cubicle remained a vibrant disco den, a constant nudge to daydream and dare to bring those dreams to life. It was a dazzling display – a testament to the power of a devoted doodler, a disco-dancing dragon dream, and the unexpected joy that can bloom in the most ordinary office cubicles.

2. Dazzling diamonds danced across Diana's dress, designed specifically for dazzling disco domination. Disappointment dimmed her smile – the disco was decidedly dull. The pulsating music felt pedestrian, the dance floor devoid of daring dips. Diana, ever the determined disco diva, decided to defy the dreary scene.

With a dramatic flourish, she spun, the diamonds catching the meagre spotlight and exploding into a kaleidoscope of colour. The once-dull dance floor transformed into a disco dream. People stopped, mesmerised by the spectacle of light and movement. A lone man, emboldened by Diana's dazzling display, shuffled onto the floor, resurrecting a forgotten move with surprising grace. A shy couple, inspired by the unexpected energy, followed suit, their tentative steps blossoming into a hesitant twirl. The DJ, inspired by the burgeoning dance floor, cranked up the tempo, the bass thrumming through the room like a revitalising beat.

The disco, once a dud, became a destination. News of "Diamond Diana" and her disco revival spread through the city. Discos, struggling to compete with the latest trends, saw a resurgence. Dingy dance floors were polished, forgotten disco balls dusted off, and DJs unearthed classic vinyl. Diana, the reluctant revolutionary, became a disco ambassador. Her dazzling dress, a symbol of taking a chance and defying expectations, hung proudly in a museum exhibit celebrating the disco era. It served as a reminder that even the dullest disco can be transformed by a single dazzling diamond and a touch of determined spirit. But more importantly, it became a testament to the power of one person's audacity to ignite a collective spark, reminding everyone that the magic of disco wasn't just in the lights and the music, but in the uninhibited joy of movement, the shared experience of letting loose and losing yourself in the rhythm. Diana's story transcended the disco scene, becoming a beacon of hope for struggling businesses and communities everywhere. It whispered a simple truth: sometimes, all it takes to revitalise a dying trend or a forgotten passion is a single person willing to take a chance, to step out onto the dance floor and shine their light, no matter how dim the spotlight may seem.

3. Dapper Duke Desmond, renowned for his dashing dance moves, decided to defy dancing doctor Dorothy's dire diagnosis. Dorothy declared Desmond's dancing days done, deeming his dazzling disco detrimental to his

delicate digitals. Dreading despair, Desmond devised a daring plan. Dawn found him disguised as a delivery driver, dropping dazzling disco doughnuts at Dr. Dorothy's door. Delighted by the delicious distraction, Dorothy devoured the delectable discs, leaving Desmond free to dash to the disco. Determined to disprove Dorothy's dismal declaration, Desmond donned dazzling disco duds, dazzling the dance floor with dizzying dexterity. Disco diva Donna, impressed by Desmond's defiance, declared him the undisputed disco dominator. Dr. Dorothy, drawn by the din of dazzling disco beats, discovered Desmond dancing divinely. Delighted by his determination, Dorothy admitted defeat, declaring Desmond's dancing dreams decidedly dazzling, not detrimental. Dancing the night away, Desmond and Donna dethroned the disco duo, their dazzling display demonstrating that dreams, like doughnuts, should always be devoured, doctor's doubts or not.

4. A dapper dachshund named Douglas, sporting a diamond-patterned collar, dug diligently down a dusty, dark ditch, determined to dislodge a particularly delightful dirt dweller. Down, down he dove, his dachshund legs churning dust devils in his wake. Disappearing completely, Douglas left only a dishevelled disturbance in the ditch's edge.

Distraught, his owner, Diana, dropped her delicate gardening gloves. Dread descended upon her. Douglas, with his digging desires dooming him to disappearances, had vanished. Diana darted desperately around the delightful garden, desperately calling his dachshund name. Distress dripped from her voice.

Suddenly, a muffled "Woof!" erupted from the depths

of the ditch. Relief descended upon Diana. But then, another distinct sound emerged – a rhythmic din. Diana, discarding decorum, dove down into the ditch, her eyes widening in astonishment. There, amidst the displaced dirt, gleamed a dazzling display of diamond earrings. Douglas, ever the determined digger, had unearthed a delightfully decadent diamond-encrusted jewellery box, doubtless deposited decades prior.

Diana carefully retrieved the sparkling jewels, a priceless diamond dynasty heirloom she hadn't even known existed. News of Douglas's delightful discovery disseminated through the delightful village, and the once-ordinary dachshund became a local legend. Diana, deeply grateful, used the recovered diamonds to establish a new dog park, designated delightfully for diligent digging dogs. Douglas, the dapper dachshund, sporting a new diamond-encrusted collar, became an ambassador for delightful digging, forever remembered as the day a dusty ditch yielded dazzling diamonds.

5. Diligent dancers, Donna, Drew, and Beatrice, dipped dramatically during a dazzling disco demonstration. Disco balls dangled, dazzling the dance floor with a kaleidoscope of colours. Determined to impress the judges, Donna executed a daring double pirouette, but disaster struck! Her disco ball-inspired sequined shoe snagged on a loose floorboard, sending her tumbling towards a display of delicate disco ducks decorating the stage.

Donna braced for impact, but strong arms encircled her midsection. Drew, with his signature dazzling smile, had instinctively caught her just in time. Beatrice, ever the quick thinker, didn't miss a beat. With a flourish, she incorporated Donna's stumble into their routine, transforming it into a playful display of synchronised spins and dips. The crowd erupted in delighted cheers, their initial gasp of surprise morphing into roaring approval.

Donna, flustered but grateful, winked at Drew. Beatrice beamed her creativity on full display. The judges, initially taken aback by the unexpected turn of events, were captivated by the dancers' ability to adapt and transform a near-disaster into a showstopping moment.

News of the "Disco Duck Dodge" spread like wildfire. Donna, Drew, and Beatrice, once diligent dancers, became renowned for their improvisational brilliance. Disco halls across the country clamoured to book them, eager to witness their electrifying performances. Their story became a testament to the power of presence and quick thinking on the dance floor. Even the most dazzling routines could benefit from a dash of duck-dodging dexterity, proving that sometimes the most memorable moments emerge from the unexpected.

6. Delighted Daisy discovered dozens of delightful Dalmatian puppies digging diligently in the dirt. Disarray reigned as the spotted pups unearthed daisies, their black spots blending with the white petals in a whirlwind of playful chaos. Daisy, a dog devotee with a heart as big as her smile, knew she had to divert their attention before her prized flowers became completely buried. With a mischievous glint in her eye, Daisy darted to the shed and emerged triumphantly with a dusty dog biscuit bag, its enticing aroma a guaranteed pup-pleaser.

Laughter erupted as Daisy led the pack of playful pups on a merry chase around the garden, their wagging tails a blur of black and white. The joyful yelps and excited barks echoed through the air, a symphony of pure, unadulterated canine enthusiasm. But amidst the joyous chaos, a seed of inspiration was planted in Daisy's mind. Why not channel this boundless digging energy into something productive?

The very next day, Daisy, armed with a shovel and a determined glint in her eye, transformed a neglected corner of the daycare into a "Digging Discovery Zone." A sandbox overflowing with colourful balls, plastic bones, and hidden treats became the centrepiece, surrounded by a low fence crafted from recycled wood. The once-disorderly digging was now transformed into a dedicated space for exploration and reward.

Whining ceased to be a background noise, replaced by the happy sounds of paws enthusiastically scratching at the dirt. The "Dalmatian Digging Diva," as Daisy was now affectionately known, had become a champion for canine enrichment. Her ingenuity not only saved her flowers but also provided a much-needed outlet for the pups' natural digging instincts. News of Daisy's innovative approach spread through the dog-loving community, inspiring other daycare centres to incorporate similar "dig pits" into their playgrounds. Daisy, the flower-loving dog devotee, had inadvertently become a pioneer in the world of canine happiness, all thanks to a delightful discovery of digging Dalmatians and a well-timed bag of dog biscuits.

7. Disgruntled diners drummed their fingers, a symphony of discontent echoing through the dimly lit restaurant. Their double-decker cheeseburgers, recently devoured with gusto, seemed to have left a void of sugary yearning. Doris, the delightful dessert chef with a twinkle in her eye, knew this symphony all too well. But instead of churning out predictable plates of pie and pudding, Doris

decided to conduct a culinary concerto of a different kind.

With a flourish, she disappeared into the kitchen, a secret smile playing on her lips. Doris wasn't just a dessert chef; she was an architect of edible adventures, a sculptor of sugary satisfaction. This time, inspired by the diners' double-decker dilemma, she envisioned a playful deconstruction – a whimsical rebellion against the tyranny of traditional desserts.

Gone were the predictable plates piled high with predictable pastries. Instead, Doris created a masterpiece of playful proportions: a deconstructed burger sundae. Pillowy cheesecake clouds, once the foundation of a classic New York-style, became the fluffy "buns" of this daring dessert. Juicy burger toppings metamorphosed into a vibrant berry compote, their tangy sweetness a delightful counterpoint to the creamy cheesecake. And a drizzle of barbecue sauce, a mischievous reminder of the recently departed burgers, transformed into a sinfully delicious chocolate sauce.

When Doris presented her "Deconstructed Delight," a hush fell over the previously disgruntled diners. The sight of their familiar cheeseburger whimsically reimagined on a dessert plate sparked curiosity and laughter. The first tentative spoonfuls yielded gasps of surprised delight. The creamy cheesecake, the vibrant berries, and the rich chocolate sauce danced on their taste buds, a symphony of flavours far exceeding the sum of their parts. The disgruntled drumming transformed into delighted discourse, a chorus of praise for Doris's daring culinary composition.

News of Doris's "Deconstructed Delights" spread like wildfire through the foodie community. Food critics, with their jaded palates and penchant for pronouncements, flocked to the restaurant. But even they were left speechless, their expectations shattered in the most delightful way. They lauded Doris for her ability to dismantle tradition and deliver delicious disruption. Doris, once a well-respected but predictable dessert chef, became a culinary daredevil, her playful plates a testament to the power of embracing the unexpected, even on the dessert menu.

Her restaurant, once known for classic fare and predictable portions, became a destination for culinary curiosity. Patrons ventured in not just for a meal, but for an experience – a delightful gamble on what playful deconstruction Doris might conjure next. It was a reminder that sometimes the most delightful dishes, the ones that leave a lasting impression and inspire a dance on the taste buds, emerge from deconstructing the familiar, from taking a whimsical leap of faith into the unknown realm of culinary possibilities. And at the helm of this delicious revolution stood Doris, the dessert chef who dared to dream beyond the double-decker cheeseburger, forever changing the way diners viewed the art of dessert.

8. Duncan diligently dusted dusty drawers, discovering dozens of delightful dime-sized diamonds. Disbelief danced in his eyes. Duncan, a dedicated but down-on-his-luck dishwasher, dreamt of a different life. These diamonds, a forgotten family fortune, could be his ticket out. Yet, a dilemma developed. Selling them discreetly seemed dishonest, a betrayal of his past.

Suddenly, inspiration dawned. Duncan, with his dexterous dishwashing digits, possessed a hidden talent – delicate jewellery design. Diamonds in hand, he embarked on a daring decision. He enrolled in a night class, his days spent scrubbing plates, his nights spent meticulously crafting exquisite jewellery. Duncan's designs, infused with a dishwasher's unique perspective, captured light in unexpected ways, each piece a testament to his past and his newfound passion.

Months later, at a prestigious jewellery fair, Duncan unveiled his collection – "Diamonds from the Dishwasher." The glittering display, a stark contrast to his usual dishcloth uniform, captivated the audience. Judges, initially sceptical, were blown away by the raw talent and unexpected beauty. Duncan, the dishwasher-turned-designer, won the grand prize.

News of his overnight success spread like wildfire. People marvelled at the man who transformed dusty diamonds into dazzling dreams. Duncan, once diligently dusting, now diligently designed. He opened his own studio, his past a badge of honour, a reminder that sometimes the most unexpected places hold the key to a dazzling future. His story resonated with dreamers everywhere, a testament to the power of hidden talents and the unexpected discoveries that can lie dormant in the dustiest of drawers.

9. Dexter, the determined delivery driver, dodged dozens of darn ducks dabbling in the delivery depot, delaying his deliveries dreadfully. Disgruntled drivers drummed their fingers, their daily deliveries dangling in the dubious depths of Dexter's dented delivery van. But Dexter wasn't fazed. He understood the ducks' dilemma – a flooded nest hidden beneath a stack of dented disco balls destined for the Dollar Disco down the road.

Dexter devised a daring diversion. With a delightful disregard for his already delayed deliveries, he dashed to the nearby dollar store, returning with a dazzling display of colourful duck decoys. He strategically placed them around the flooded nest, creating a decoy duck haven. The real ducks, mesmerised by their mirrored reflections, waddled away from the disco balls, quacking with delight.

The flooded nest, now accessible, was carefully relocated to higher ground by Dexter, a makeshift raft constructed from leftover delivery boxes keeping the precious eggs dry. News of Dexter's ducky diversion and delivery day debacle reached the local news.

Instead of reprimands, Dexter received a hero's welcome. The Dollar Disco owner, touched by Dexter's compassion, offered him a lifetime discount on disco balls. The delighted ducks became the disco's unofficial mascots, their quacking a quirky soundtrack to Saturday night fever. Dexter, the once-delayed delivery driver, became a local legend – the "Duck Deliverer." His story, a testament to the transformative power of a little detour and a whole lot of duck decoys, became a beacon of kindness in the fast-paced world of deliveries. From that day on, Dexter carried a bag of duck decoys in his van, always prepared to divert a delivery disaster into a heartwarming detour.

CHAPTER 5: INSANE E-CENTRIC TONGUE TWISTERS

This collection presents a sophisticated series of tongue twisters centred around the **letter E**. Designed to enhance articulation and precision, these exercises offer a rigorous test of verbal dexterity. Prepare to encounter intricate phrases that demand exceptional enunciation and cognitive engagement.

1. Eleven elves, Elara, Elara's energetic elder Evelyn, and their eager apprentices, meticulously embroidered exquisite evening gowns. Eagerness sometimes eclipsed expertise, and Elara discovered a misplaced emerald earring embedded in a shimmering sapphire gown. Elara's heart sank. Disgruntled designers demanded delicate dismantling, delaying the delivery.

   Evelyn, ever the optimist, saw an opportunity. "Embrace the emerald!" she declared. With nimble fingers, she transformed the misplaced gem into a dazzling centrepiece. The sapphire fabric shimmered anew, the emerald adding an unexpected elegance. The designers, initially disappointed, were enthralled. News of Elara's "Emerald Encore" gown spread like wildfire. Every elf, from Elara to the youngest apprentice, became inundated with requests.

Their workshop, once echoing with the rhythm of embroidery needles, now hummed with excitement. Evenings became a flurry of creativity, with emeralds adorning gowns in unexpected ways. Elara learned a valuable lesson: sometimes, even errors could be embroidered into something extraordinary. The "Elven Emerald Emporium" became renowned, a testament to the power of embracing the unexpected and the artistry that thrives even amidst misplaced gems.

2. Elroy, the eccentric elephant, with ears flopping like emerald flags, dreamt of vast empires adorned with exquisite elegance. He envisioned every inch, from towering trees sculpted into emerald arches to meadows embroidered with fragrant flowers. His passion, however, was not for grand palaces, but for the delicate artistry of embroidery.

Elroy would spend hours meticulously stitching using his trunk as a needle and vines as thread. He'd weave intricate patterns on enormous envelopes, transforming them from mundane mail carriers into breathtaking works of art. Flowers bloomed in vibrant hues, landscapes unfolded in miniature, and whimsical creatures frolicked across the surface.

The recipients, upon receiving these extraordinary envelopes, were utterly astonished. Mailboxes overflowed with gasps and delighted squeals as people marvelled at the exquisite craftsmanship. Elroy's fame grew, whispers of the "Embroidering Elephant" spreading far and wide.

Important dignitaries, socialites, and even royalty sought

out Elroy's talents. He stitched invitations to grand balls, announcements of royal births, and even delicate love letters, each one imbued with his unique style and whimsical charm.

One day, the Queen herself requested Elroy's expertise. She needed a magnificent tapestry to adorn the grand hall of her palace, a testament to the kingdom's grandeur. Elroy, ever the enthusiast, devoted himself to the project. For months, his trunk danced across a canvas the size of a tennis court, weaving stories of the kingdom's history, its noble heroes, and its bountiful landscapes.

When the tapestry was unveiled, the entire court gasped. It was a masterpiece, a breathtaking fusion of art and storytelling. Elroy, the once-eccentric elephant with a passion for embroidery, had become a national treasure, his legacy forever stitched into the very fabric of the kingdom.

3. Exuberant Emily's elbow jabs punctuated her jokes, leaving envious elephants eyeing their empty enclosure. The zoo, while meticulously maintained, lacked the spark of unexpected fun. Emily, a volunteer with a boundless supply of enthusiasm and a penchant for mischief, sensed the elephants' disgruntlement.

   Determined to inject some joy into their day, Emily hatched a plan. With the help of her friends and a generous donation of cardboard boxes from a local recycling centre, she embarked on an ambitious project - "The Cardboard Castle Caper." Armed with colourful markers, rolls of recycled paper, and a mischievous glint in her eye, Emily transformed the central exhibit into a sprawling cardboard kingdom. Towers soared, bridges connected, and dangling disco balls, salvaged from a forgotten attic, shimmered overhead.

The elephants, initially hesitant, were soon captivated. Trunks twirled, ears flapped, and playful trumpeting echoed through the enclosure as they explored their new domain. Emily, ever the entertainer, used her trusty elbows to propel giant cardboard balls across the makeshift moat, sending the elephants on a lumbering charge filled with mock roars. The zookeepers, initially concerned about the chaos, were surprised to witness the elephants' renewed energy and playful spirit.

News of Emily's "Cardboard Castle Caper" spread like wildfire. Parents flocked to the zoo, eager to see the elephants cavorting in their cardboard kingdom. The zoo, once a place of quiet observation, transformed into a vibrant hub of laughter and interaction. Emily's elbows, once a source of friendly jabs, became a symbol of creativity and the unexpected joy that can bloom from a little bit of mischief and a whole lot of cardboard. The elephants once resigned to their routine, became unexpected stars, their playful antics a reminder that sometimes the greatest enrichment comes from the simplest of interventions. The zoo, inspired by Emily's ingenuity, incorporated "Creative Creature Capers" into their weekly schedule, ensuring that both animals and visitors continued to experience the thrill of the unexpected.

4. Elroy, the eccentric elephant, envisioned emerald empires while meticulously embroidering exquisite designs on enormous envelopes. Dismissed by the other elephants for his delicate desires, Elroy dreamt of dazzling dignitaries with his dazzling designs. Days turned into weeks, envelopes piled high, each a testament to Elroy's

dedication. Dejected by a lack of recognition, Elroy slumped beside his embroidery basket, a single tear splashing onto a vibrant emerald thread.

Suddenly, a distinguished dodo dabbling in diplomacy stumbled upon Elroy's enclave. Duncan, the dodo, was instantly captivated by the intricate embroidery. "Exquisite!" he exclaimed, his voice echoing through the dusty enclosure. Elroy, astonished, explained his aspirations of adorning envelopes for dignitaries. Duncan, delighted, offered a solution.

Utilising his diplomatic connections, Duncan arranged for Elroy's envelopes to be delivered to embassies around the world. Ambassadors, accustomed to sterile stationery, were enthralled by Elroy's artistry. Elroy's emerald envelopes became coveted collectors' items, his name whispered with reverence in diplomatic circles.

News of Elroy's success trumpeted through the elephant community. The once-mocking herd now marvelled at his talent. Elroy, ever the eccentric elephant, emerged from his enclave a star, a symbol of following your dreams, no matter how different they may seem. From that day on, Elroy's embroidery sessions were no longer solitary endeavours but joyous gatherings, filled with the rhythmic thump of trunks and the delighted trumpeting of a herd finally inspired by their once-ridiculed friend. Elroy's emerald empires, born from dedication and a touch of derision, became a testament to the transformative power of pursuing your passions, even if you're an elephant with a penchant for embroidery.

5. Eleven energetic elves, Elaine, Elara, Eleanor, Elora,

Elphaba, Elsie, Elwin, Emery, Esther, and Eunice, eagerly embroidered exquisite evening gowns in Elara's enchanting workshop. Every evening, Elara extolled the importance of elegant execution. Each elf possessed a unique style, their emerald eyes gleaming with focus as needles danced across silks and satins, weaving ethereal dreams into wearable art.

Elara, esteemed for her meticulous precision, experienced exceptional emotional distress upon discovering a misplaced emerald embedded in a sapphire dress destined for the Duchess of Diamondshire. Dreadful visions of the Duchess' disdain danced in Elara's head. Yet, amidst the escalating emergency, Evelyn, ever the enthusiastic encourager and renowned for her elegant embellishments, espied an exciting opportunity.

"Embrace the unexpected, Elara!" Evelyn exclaimed, her ever-present effervescent smile widening. "This emerald could evolve into a dazzling centrepiece!" With energetic efficiency, Evelyn orchestrated the error's elegant eradication. Ever so meticulously, she extracted the misplaced emerald, encircling it with a delicate swirl of sapphire threads, exquisitely evoking a blooming flower. The end result was an exceptionally elegant effect, the emerald's vibrant green a captivating counterpoint to the cool elegance of the sapphire dress.

Elara, initially hesitant, eventually embraced Evelyn's enthusiastic encouragement. Together, they enthusiastically presented the "Emerald Encore" gown to the Duchess. The Duchess, a woman esteemed for her exquisite taste, was rendered speechless. The unexpected emerald, a symbol of both a near-disaster and the elves' extraordinary expertise, effectively elevated the essence of the dress. News of the "Emerald Encore" evening gown effervesced like effervescent bubbles through the fashion world. Esteemed fashion editors extolled the elves' exceptional ability to not only create exquisite gowns but to also enthusiastically embrace the unexpected, transforming a potential flaw into a focal point of fascination.

Elara's enchanting workshop swiftly evolved into an esteemed establishment, a pilgrimage site for fashionistas and socialites alike. Each elf, emboldened by Evelyn's enthusiastic encouragement, embarked on a creative exploration, subtly incorporating unexpected elements into their designs. A tiny misplaced pearl could become a delicate dewdrop adorning a rosebud bodice, while a wayward thread transformed into a whimsical vine gracefully cascading down a flowing skirt. Elara's enclave transcended mere dressmaking; it became a testament to the artistry that thrives even amidst misplaced gems, a reminder that sometimes the most extraordinary creations arise from embracing the unexpected. The elves, once renowned for their meticulous precision, became celebrated for their enchanting ability to weave both flawlessness and surprise into their breathtaking gowns.

CHAPTER 6: INSANE F-CENTRIC TONGUE TWISTERS

This collection of **F-filled tongue twisters** is designed to challenge even the most fluent of speakers. From the frivolous to the ferocious, these phrases will put your pronunciation to the ultimate test. Whether you're a seasoned twister or a fresh-faced fanatic, prepare to be fascinated and frustrated in equal measure. So, fasten your seatbelt and embark on this fun yet ferocious journey through the letter F.

1. Beneath the fully flourishing boughs of a thousand-year-old firn, flooded in the ethereal glow of fluorescent fungi, Fiona, a firefly fuelled by an insatiable curiosity and a fearless spirit, flitted freely. Unlike her friends, forfilled with the fenced safety of the undergrowth, Fiona fixated on fun.

   Finally a fullmoom filled the funnels, forcing the family to flee their fortified family home. filled with fear fiona's family frantically forgaged for food. Fretful of a foodless night. But Fiona, thrilled by forced fleeing floated with festivity. Freed from the family fears an their fruitful nightmares faulter, freed from a fragmented picture of the world.

2. A frantic fan, Frances, frantically fanned a flustered friend, Felix, facing a flagpole. Fearful of Felix's faintiquette, Frances devised a daring distraction. Dipping a dusty denim handkerchief in a delightful dew-covered daisy, she doused Felix's forehead, drawing a gasp and a giggle.

Suddenly, a mischievous idea danced in Frances' eyes. With a playful wink, she grabbed a discarded red balloon and began a dazzling display of balloon artistry. Dogs delighted, ducks dived, and the crowd, momentarily diverted, roared with laughter. Felix, revitalised by the joyful din, refocused on the flagpole. His routine, imbued with newfound energy and playful flourishes, became a crowd favourite, a delightful defiance of decorum.

Days later, news announced Felix as the "Dazzling Flagpole Champion." Frances, the frantic fan, became an unexpected hero. Her story, a testament to the power of friendship and delightful distractions, resonated with fans everywhere. Flagpole competitions transformed – a splash of colour, a dash of silliness, all encouraged. Frances, a testament to the transformative power of a single, daring moment, became a symbol of unwavering support and the joy found in defying expectation.

3. Flustered Fred fumbled with flimsy folding furniture, facing faulty floodlights. Dinner guests dwindled, deterred by the disastrous décor. The air crackled with awkward tension, a stark contrast to the joyous evening Fred had envisioned. Determined to salvage the soiree, Fred delved into the dusty recesses of his garage, a treasure trove of forgotten dreams and abandoned hobbies. There, nestled amidst forgotten tools and faded sports equipment, lay a box of disco balls – relics of a bygone era. A mischievous glint sparked in Fred's eye.

With a flurry of activity, Fred hung the disco balls from the failing floodlights. A dazzling display of refracted light danced across the patio, transforming the flimsy furniture into shimmering silhouettes. The once-dismal scene became a kaleidoscope of colour and movement. Fred, fueled by desperation and a dash of disco inspiration, whipped up a dip of dazzling colours with discarded vegetables languishing in the crisper drawer. The result? A vibrant "Disco Delight Dip," a testament to resourcefulness and a sprinkle of serendipity.

The guests, initially hesitant, ventured out, drawn by the mesmerising disco glow. Laughter erupted as they bumped into the mirrored furniture, their reflections adding to the delightful disarray. The tension evaporated, replaced by a sense of playful camaraderie. Fred's frantic fumble had become a fortuitous foundation for fun. News of the "Dazzling Disco Dinner Disaster" spread like wildfire through the neighbourhood. Friends clamoured for invitations, eager to experience the unexpected. Fred, the flustered host, became an accidental party extraordinaire, his story a testament to the transformative power of a little disco magic and a whole lot of delightful disaster.

Evenings spent with Fred became synonymous with surprise, reminding everyone that sometimes the most dazzling moments emerge from the most disastrous beginnings. Invitations to Fred's gatherings were coveted, not for the promise of a perfectly curated event, but for the guarantee of unexpected delights. From disco ball disasters to vegetable-based masterpieces, Fred's soirees became a celebration of imperfection, a reminder that laughter and joy can be found even in the most chaotic of settings. Fred's initial fluster transformed him into a local legend, a beacon of positivity and a testament to the simple truth: a dash of disco spirit and a willingness to embrace the unexpected can turn a disastrous dinner party into an unforgettable evening.

4. Farmer Fred, with fastidious focus, filled fifty feedbags full of fluffy, freshly-fallen feathers, specifically selected for fifty fluffy female finches. Finding fulfilment in feeding his feathered friends, Fred fostered a flourishing flock in his fertile fields. His feathered friends, fed with fervour and finesse, flourished fantastically, forming a fascinating flock that filled the fields with fanciful flight.

   Fred's farm, a haven for happy hens, became a favoured feeding ground for these feathered friends, fostering a friendly and familial atmosphere amongst the flock. The farm's fertile fields, filled with fragrant flora, provided a feast for the eyes as well as a food source. Fred's fowl, free to forage and frolic, found fascination in the farm's familiar features.

   As the first faint flickers of dawn filled the farm, the flock would flutter forth, filling the fields with frantic flapping. Fred, fortified with fresh fruit and fulfilling fantasies of fowl-friendly fields, would follow, focused on fulfilling the flock's feeding frenzy. The farm, a fortress for feathered freedom, flourished under Fred's fervent care.

CHAPTER 7: INSANE G-CENTRIC TONGUE TWISTERS

Get ready to be gob-smacked by these **G-loaded challenges!** We've gathered a galaxy of gnarly tongue twisters to test your verbal might. Can you handle the gauntlet?

1. Deep within the heart of Mount Glimmering, nestled amongst meadows dotted with luminous wildflowers, lay the Glittering Glade. Here, beneath a canopy of shimmering crystals, resided Gnome Gladys, a creature renowned for her boundless enthusiasm and unwavering passion for gemstones. Unlike her kin, content with tending their gnomish gardens, Gladys possessed an insatiable curiosity and a keen eye for a sparkling treasure. Every sunrise found her armed with her trusty pickaxe, a smile plastered on her face, ready to embark on her daily quest. The rhythmic clanging of her pickaxe against the rocky earth echoed through the glade, a melody as cheerful as Gladys herself. Each unearthed gem, a ruby the colour of a dragon's fire, a sapphire as blue as a kingfisher's wing, or an emerald that rivalled the verdant heart of the forest, filled her with an unmatched glee. Her pockets were a treasure trove in themselves, a testament to her dedication and her ability to spot a glistening gem from a mile away.

However, Gladys's sunny disposition was a stark contrast to the residents of Gloom Grotto, a network of caverns that burrowed deep beneath the Glittering Glade. Here resided a band of goblins, a perpetually grumpy bunch whose only passion was the accumulation of wealth. Unlike Gladys, who saw beauty in the intrinsic value of each gemstone, the goblins viewed them as mere tools for acquiring gold. Their days were spent hunched over dusty ledgers, their guttural grumbles echoing through the caverns as they tallied their dwindling gem stock and cursed the ever-cheerful gnome who seemed to unearth every valuable stone before they could get their greedy hands on it.

One particularly crisp autumn morning, Gladys, guided by a mischievous glint in her eye and a map drawn on the back of a discarded napkin, stumbled upon a hidden crevice veiled by a curtain of emerald vines. Curiosity, a constant companion on her adventures, propelled her forward. Squeezing through the narrow opening, she found herself in a cavern unlike any she had ever seen. The air shimmered with an otherworldly glow emanating from a colossal mountain of glistening gemstones. Rubies the size of apples, sapphires brighter than a summer sky, and emeralds that pulsed with an inner light - it was a treasure trove beyond her wildest dreams! Gladys gasped, her eyes wide with wonder. But just as she reached out to touch a particularly dazzling ruby, a guttural growl echoed through the cavern. Gladys whirled around to find.

Gladys whirled around to find a gaggle of grotesque gargoyle-esque goblins, their grotesque green mugs contorted in grotesque grimaces. Their beady eyes, usually glued to grimy gold-tallying ledgers, were now fixated on the glistening, glimmering, gigantic gem-mountain. Grog, the goblin leader, his girth groaning against a greasy green jerkin, gleefully grabbed a gigantic gleaming great axe, his gnarled green grasping appendages flexing greedily.

"Well, well, well," Grog gargled, his voice dripping with a grotesquery that could curdle gallons of goat's milk. "Lookie here, lads, the glitter-grubbing gnome has gambled her way into our glistening, glimmering grotto and stumbled upon our secret stash!"

A guttural, gravel-throated chorus of grumbles gurgled grotesquely from the goblin horde. They shuffled closer, their grasping, green-gloved claws scraping against the glistening, gem-encrusted cavern floor, their stench of stale sweat and mildew growing gamier by the grotesque groan. Gladys, however, remained gleefully grinning. Her boundless enthusiasm, a force as potent as a shimmering sapphire, refused to be dampened by the goblins' grotesque grumpiness.

"Greetings, grumpy goblins!" Gladys gurgled, her voice echoing through the glistening, gem-studded cavern. "What a gloriously gigantic collection of glimmering gems! There seems to be enough for everyone, wouldn't you grotesque goons agree?"

Grog snorted, a sound like a gargantuan, congested gargoyle attempting to wheeze out a Gregorian chant. "Enough for everyone? Don't be daft, gnome! These gems are rightfully ours, a glittering goldmine guaranteed to grant a goblin a good, gluttonous grub-filled lifetime!"

Gladys, ever the diplomat, refused to be discouraged. A gloriously mischievous glint glinted in her glistening green eyes, a twinkle that could rival the brilliance of a gigantic gemstone. With a flourish, she gleefully grabbed a gigantic, glimmering pouch woven from glistening gossamer spider silk, overflowing with a kaleidoscope of glistening, gemstone-shaped pebbles.

"Perhaps," Gladys gargled, her voice dripping with gleeful glee, "we can strike a grotesque, glittering bargain? These are but ordinary, grey-glistening pebbles, perfect for practising your gemstone-grading gibberish! In exchange, you grotesque goblins could graciously guide me through your glistening, glimmering gem grotto, showcasing the most spectacular specimens in your collection, the ones that truly make your glum green gobs glitter with glee!"

The goblins, momentarily bewildered by Gladys's gloriously grandiose proposition, grounded to a halt. Grog grotesquely scratched his grotesquely green head with a gnarled green claw, his beady eyes flickering between the gigantic pouch of pebbles and the glistening, glimmering mountain of gemstones. The idea of grotesquely gullible-grubbing the cheerful gnome with glittering gravel was strangely appealing. A guttural, gargantuan guffaw escaped his throat, a sound as unsettling as a gaggle of geese gargling in a graveyard.

"Very well, gnome," Grog gargled, a glimmer of glee glistening in his eyes. "But if these turn out to be nothing more than glistening gravel, you'll be gnome stew for our next goblin grub-fest!"

Gladys, with a gloriously grandiose grin that could outshine a gigantic, glorious golden goblet, readily agreed. Thus began a grotesquely glittering game of trickery that echoed through the glistening, gem-studded caverns of Gloom Grotto. Gladys, armed with her gigantic pouch of glistening pebbles and her boundless enthusiasm, would gleefully gamble fabricated gemstone-grading gibberish for glimpses of the goblins' grotesquely glittering, glimmering prized collection.

Each encounter was a chaotic, grotesque ballet of glum grumbles, gleeful giggles, and the shimmering, glistening dance of real and imagined gemstones.

The once-greedy goblins, their avarice momentarily tempered by Gladys's grotesquely infectious cheer, found themselves strangely entertained. Even Grog, his perpetual frown etched a little less grotesquely into his grotesque face, couldn't help but grotesquely guffaw at Gladys's gloriously grandiose tales of mythical gemstones that glowed in the glistening glow-worm light and gargled gnomish lullabies.

As the days grotesquely gargled into weeks, an unlikely bond began to grotesquely glimmer between the cheerful gnome and the glum goblins. They grotesquely learned to appreciate each other's quirks - the gnomes, the goblins' grotesquely meticulous record-keeping (even if it was for stolen treasure), and the goblins, Gladys's grotesquely infectious joy and her uncanny ability to grotesquely find beauty in the most unexpected places, even a perfectly round, glistening pebble.

CHAPTER 8: INSANE H-CENTRIC TONGUE TWISTERS

Ready for some seriously tricky tongue twisters? This book is packed with **H-heavy phrases** that'll put your speaking skills to the test. We're talking crazy hard, brain-bending stuff here. Think you can handle it? Let's see if you can spit out these H-bombs!

1. Hubert, a history buff with an insatiable thirst for knowledge and a penchant for physically demanding hikes, embarked on a historical trek that promised adventure around every hidden bend. His journey: to conquer the highest hill overlooking Hidden Hollow, a historical hamlet shrouded in whispered tales of headless horsemen who galloped through the mist on moonlit nights. Hubert, fueled by his passion for the past, hoped to happen upon hidden historical happenings – perhaps an unearthed artefact, a forgotten inscription, or some other clue that would unlock the secrets of Hidden Hollow. However, Hubert's ambitious trek was far from a historical holiday. His path was hampered by hurdles that tested his endurance and historical knowledge. He had to decipher cryptic historical riddles to unlock gates, hurdle hefty hay bales stacked precariously by unseen hands,

hop over hidden holes that could send him tumbling into forgotten cellars, and even help hysterical horses tangled in thorny hedges (apparently, even headless horsemen weren't immune to getting lost!). Would Hubert's hectic hike hold historical hidden treasures or just heaps of hardship? Only time, and his unwavering historical hunger, would tell!

2. Hilarious Hector, a hapless handler with a penchant for the peculiar, had hired a hefty hippopotamus hoping to heighten the hilarity of his holiday happenings. The hippopotamus, however, was a hefty, hulking behemoth with a hidden habit of haphazardly hurling heavy haystacks, hindering Hector's hopes of hosting a harmonious holiday. Hector, having hired a helpful helper to handle the hippopotamus's hefty habits, had hoped to harness the hippopotamus's hidden helpfulness. However, the hippopotamus's habitual, harmful habits had hindered Hector's happiness, leaving him helplessly hopeless.

Hector, however, held onto a glimmer of hope. Perhaps he could harness the hippopotamus's hefty heft for a different purpose. With heroic hope, Hector hatched a plan. He would harness the hippopotamus's strength to haul heavy holiday decorations, transforming the hapless hippopotamus into a helpful holiday helper.

The plan was hatched, and Hector, with heart pounding with hope, approached the hefty hippopotamus. Surprisingly, the hippopotamus, despite its habitual haphazardness, seemed to understand Hector's hopeful intentions. With a hearty huff, the hippopotamus hefted the heavy holiday decorations, hoisting them higher and higher. Hector, heartened by the hippopotamus's helpfulness, had finally found a harmonious harmony between man and beast. The holiday, once hindered by the hippopotamus's habits, was now heightened by the hippopotamus's helpfulness.

3. Hazy Hal, a hapless herdsman, had hired a horrifically huge, hairy hound to help him herd his hundred hardy, horned Highland heifers. The hound, a horrendous, howling hound, had a habit of haphazardly herding the heifers, hindering Hal's hopes of having a harmonious herd.

The hound's howling had heightened the heifers' hysteria, causing them to haphazardly hoof it homeward. Hal, having hired the hound to help, had hoped to have a happier herd. However, the hound's horrendous herding had hindered Hal's happiness, leaving him helplessly hopeless.

Hal, however, held onto a glimmer of hope. He had heard of a helpful herbalist who had helped other hapless herdsmen with similar hound-related horrors. With heart pounding with hope, Hal hurried to the herbalist's home.

The herbalist, hearing Hal's heartbreaking tale, handed Hal a handful of healing herbs. The herbalist hinted that the herbs, when handled correctly, had the hidden power to help calm even the horniest heifers. Hal, hopeful the herbs would help, hurried home, heart heavy with hope and heavy with herbs.

4. Hideous Hubert, a hapless human, habitually hid from hazardous happenings. His current hiding place, a hefty hedge, was a hurried choice, born of a horrifying hunch about hungry hedgehogs. Hubert had heard harrowing tales of hedgehogs, their insatiable hunger and uncanny ability to unearth hidden humans. His heart hammered with horror as he huddled behind the hedge, hoping his hiding place held.

The hedge, however, was hardly a haven. Hedgehogs were known to be highly intelligent, their honed hunting skills honed for hours. Hubert held his breath, hoping his hidden heart wouldn't betray him with a heavy heartbeat. A horrifying thought hit him: perhaps he should have heeded his heart's warning and chosen a higher hiding place. But it was too late for hindsight.

He heard the hedgehogs' hurried huffs, heralding their hungry hunt. Their hollow hollers echoed through the hushed haven, heightening Hubert's horror. He huddled closer, his heart heavy with fear. He had heard of hedgehogs having a heightened sense of smell, and he feared his fear was fueling a foul odour that might attract the hungry horde.

5. Hasty Harriet, her heart heavy with hopeful anticipation, hurriedly heated heavenly hot chocolate, harbouring hidden hopes of Hannah's hidden hoard of heavenly, healthful hazelnut halvah. Her heightened heart hammered with hopeful hunger as she hunted for hidden treats, her hands hovering over hidden havens, her heart heavy with the haunting hope of finding her hidden treasure. Her hurried heart heightened her hopes, hands growing hotter with each hidden haven, her heart heavy with the haunting hope of discovering her delectable desire. Her heightened hopes of harvesting hidden happiness were hindered by Hannah's hidden habits, her heart heavy with the haunting possibility of her hidden hoard being hidden away, her hopes of happiness hanging by a thread.

6. Hairy Harry's huge, hungry hound, howling with horrific hunger, hunted harrowing Halloween horrors, haunting haunted houses, hoping to horrify hapless humans hiding hurriedly. Harry, however, had heard harrowing tales of horrifying haunts, hindering his hound's hunting habits. His heart pounded with a haunting hunger, his hound howling with heightened hope, as they hunted through the hallowed halls of the haunted house. His heart hammered harder, his hound's howls heightened, as they hunted deeper into the darkened depths of the dreadful dwelling, their hopes of horrifying humans heightened with each harrowing hallway. Their heightened hopes of horrifying humans were hindered by the house's haunting history, their hearts heavy with the haunting possibility of horrifying happenings, their hopes of horrifying humans hanging by a thread.

7. Humble Harriet's handy, homemade helicopter hovered higher, humming a harmonious hymn, helping harassed hikers hurry homeward, hoping to hinder horrible headaches haunting hapless humans, having hurried homeward. Having helped the hapless hikers, Harriet hurried homeward, harbouring a hopeful heart, her helicopter hovering higher, her hopes of happiness heightened as she hurried homeward. Her helicopter hummed happily, her heart hopeful, her mind humming with happiness. Having helped the hapless hikers, Harriet harboured a hopeful heart, her helicopter hovering higher, her hopes of happiness heightened as she hurried homeward, her heart heavy with the haunting hope of hindering Hannah's hidden hoard of hazelnut halvah. Her heightened hopes of hindering Hannah's hidden hoard were hindered by Hannah's hidden habits, her

heart heavy with the haunting possibility of her hidden hoard being hidden away, her hopes of harvesting hidden happiness hanging by a thread.

8. Hubert held high the heavy, hairy hippopotamus hide, a heart-pounding hope flickering within him. The humid highland heat hung heavy in the hazy atmosphere, a hostile environment that heightened his heightened anxiety. Horrifying tales of hyena hordes had haunted his dreams, their howls echoing in his head like a haunting harbinger of doom. These hungry, hateful creatures were known for their relentless pursuit, their hidden hunger a harrowing threat to his hopeful heart. His hand hovered over the hilt of his hidden hunting hatchet, a heavy heart filled with hope as fragile as frost. This was his hideaway, his last hope, a hidden haven that must hold against the hyena's hungry horde. A hushed hope hummed in his heart, a hesitant hope hinged on his hidden haven holding firm. His heart raced as he heard a haunting howl, a hideous herald of the hyena's impending hunt. He gripped the hilt of his hatchet tighter, his hope hardening into a hardened resolve. He would not be a helpless hostage to these hungry horrors. He would hold his ground, his heart heavy but his hope unwavering, until the sun sank below the horizon and the hyenas' hunt was hopefully halted.

9. Happy Henry hiccuped horrendously, his head hurting horribly. A hapless victim of this hateful hiccup, he held his head high, a hopeful heart heavy with despair. Honey, herbs, and holding his breath had proven hopeless remedies. He yearned for a healing hand, a helpful hint to hinder his horrid hiccups. His heart hammered with every hiccup, a haunting rhythm that echoed his helplessness. He hoped for a heroic healer, a hallowed helper to halt this harrowing ordeal. His hopeful heart yearned for a halt to this harrowing ordeal. A hapless, humiliated Henry hoped his hopeful heart would hold on. He had heard of hypnotists, healers with hidden talents, who could halt hiccups with a hypnotic hand. Henry hoped such a healer existed, a hallowed helper who could hinder his horrific hiccups. He was a hapless hostage to this hateful hiccup, and his hope for a healing hand held him together.

10. Henry hunted for a house hidden high on a hilly heath, his heart heavy with a hope for home. He envisioned a hearty hearth, casting a hopeful hue on the wintry night. A humble home, a haven from the howling winds, was his heart's desire. He dreamed of hot cocoa, a heartwarming drink to help him heal from the day's hunt. A hopeful heart yearned for a house, a humble home to call his own. He hoped to find a house with a hospitable host, a haven hidden from the harsh, howling world. A hopeful heart held high the hope of a hidden home, a hearth to heal his weary soul. He hunted tirelessly, his heart heavy with hope, determined to find a home hidden high on the hill, a haven from the howling world outside. He imagined a home filled with warmth, a hearty hearth casting a hopeful glow, a place where he could finally heal and rest.

CHAPTER 9: INSANE I-CENTRIC TONGUE TWISTERS

Brace yourself for an icy inferno of **Intricate I-twisters**. These icy challenges are designed to ignite your intellect and inspire incredible intonation. From ignoble alliterations to impossible imagery, each icy utterance will invigorate and inspire. Remember, impeccable intonation is the ideal, not inept imitation. Ready to investigate this intriguing icy itinerary?

1. A collective of improvisational actors, illustrious for their irrepressible energy that could illuminate even the most impenetrable blackout, initiated a spontaneous spectacle. These weren't your stereotypical thespians reciting insipid scripted lines in an intimidating theatre. No, this troupe thrived on instigating chaos and igniting interactive involvement with the audience. With no insipid script or predetermined plot, they ingeniously improvised, relying on the unpredictable inclinations of the crowd and their own wildly imaginative ideas. The inevitable outcome? Infectious insanity, indisputably guaranteed to induce inevitable laughter that would leave your sides in insufferable pain!

   The actors, invigorated by the electric energy emanating

from the audience, instantaneously improvised hilarious stories on the fly. A singular suggestion, like "imaginary invisible iguana," could instantaneously morph into a side-splitting scene. Improbable props, like an inflated, inexpensive beach ball or a stapler inexplicably missing a staple, became integral aspects of the performance. And the characters? Well, let's just say they were a motley crew of improbable individuals, ranging from an incessantly inquisitive talking teapot with an undeniable Napoleon complex to a mime afflicted with an uncontrollable case of the hiccups. The actors' infectious enthusiasm was undeniably contagious, igniting uncontrollable laughter and chaotic delight within the audience. Who knew what these improvisational imps would ingeniously conjure up next? Perhaps a singing sock puppet opera or a tap-dancing dinosaur? The possibilities were truly infinite, and the only limitations were their (and the audience's) imaginations. So, fasten your seatbelts and prepare yourselves for a wild ride – because with these improvisational masters, anything is imaginable!

2. Iridescent Isabelle's intricately interwoven illustrations ignited an intense, insatiable, and irrepressible interest in indelible ink. Her images, imbued with an iridescent, incomparable, and illuminating glow, introduced a novel, neoteric, and noteworthy aesthetic paradigm to the art world. Isabelle's innovative, ingenious, and incomparable use of ink inspired imitation and experimentation, as artists sought to capture the same luminous, lovely, and lasting quality in their own work.

Her illustrations were more than mere pictures; they were invitations to immerse oneself in the infinite, intriguing, and inspiring potential of ink as a medium. Isabelle's work elicited a deep, devoted, and durable appreciation for the artistry and versatility of this humble, helpful, and historically significant material. Her influence extended beyond the visual, inspiring intellectual inquiry into the interplay of light and colour, the psychology of perception, and the very nature of creativity itself.

Isabelle's impact on the art world was immeasurable. She transformed ink from a simple tool into a complex and evocative medium, elevating it to a status previously reserved for more traditional materials. Her legacy is a testament to the power of imagination and the enduring allure of the unexpected.

3. Intelligent Ian's impressive igloo inspired immediate imitation. Its imposing, icy edifice irresistibly invited individuals to immerse themselves in the intriguing intricacies of ice architecture. This innovative igloo ignited a fervent fascination, fostering an influx of imaginative ideas. From intricate ice sculptures to ingenious igloo enhancements, the possibilities seemed infinite. Ian's architectural archetype had inadvertently initiated an icy insurrection, inspiring innumerable individuals to investigate the incredible, inexplicable properties of this often overlooked, ordinary object.

   The once quiet, quaint, and commonplace realm of ice construction was suddenly saturated with activity. Architects, engineers, and enthusiastic amateurs were intoxicated by the challenge of crafting captivating, colossal, and complex structures from this ephemeral, elusive element. Ian's igloo had become a catalyst for countless experiments, pushing the boundaries of the imaginable and implausible. As winter intensified, interest in ice architecture increased exponentially, inspiring the inauguration of the annual "Igloo Invitational," a spectacular showcase of ice-based ingenuity. The event illuminated the immense potential of ice as a building material, attracting international attention and igniting a global interest in this innovative, intriguing art form.

Ian's legacy extended far beyond the confines of his initial inspiration. His igloo had sparked a broader, burning inquiry into sustainability and resourcefulness. As the world grappled with the growing, global crisis of climate change, the idea of constructing with ice offered a tantalising, theoretical solution. Ian's igloo had not only inspired a new generation of imaginative, intrepid architects but had also ignited a worldwide movement towards innovative, intelligent, and inspiring building practices.

4. Icy iguanas, in their infinite, idiosyncratic inquisitiveness, insisted on indulging in icy indigo ice cream instantly. Their insatiable, impulsive cravings for icy treats ignited an intense interest in indigo ingredients. Intrigued by the ice cream's unusual hue, these intelligent invertebrates initiated an investigation into the ice cream's intriguing ingredients.

In their icy, isolated island habitat, these intelligent reptiles imagined innovative ice cream inventions. Inspired by the initial indulgence, they initiated an ice cream industry, introducing intriguing, icy flavours to the island. Their initial indigo ice cream became an iconic indulgence, inspiring imitators to innovate with other unexpected ingredients.

From iridescent, insect-infused ice cream to exotic, evergreen-enhanced flavours, the iguanas' icy inventions intrigued island inhabitants and intrigued international ice cream aficionados. Their ingenious ice creamery became an iconic island institution, attracting inquisitive tourists eager to experience the extraordinary.

Ultimately, these idiosyncratic iguanas, in their infinite wisdom, inspired imitation, igniting an international ice cream innovation revolution. Their icy ingenuity influenced ice cream artisans worldwide, encouraging experimentation with unconventional, unexpected ingredients. From the icy peaks of the Andes to the infinite expanse of the Antarctic, ice cream connoisseurs craved creative, captivating concoctions inspired by the iguanas' initial icy indulgence.

CHAPTER 10: INSANE J-CENTRIC TONGUE TWISTERS

Prepare for a wild ride through the jungle of the **letter J**. These aren't your average tongue twisters; they're colossal challenges designed to test your verbal might. Get ready to twist, turn, and tangle with the letter J as we explore intricate phrases and perplexing puzzles. Can you conquer these colossal conundrums? Let's find out!

1. Jimmy, Jojo, and Janine, a jubilant juggling juggernaut, were the undeniable jewels of the annual Jitterbug Jamboree. Their joint act was a jaw-dropping display of dexterity and joyful jubilation that jolted the jaded and jiggled the jittery in the audience. Jimmy, the seasoned maestro of the juggling mayhem, masterfully manipulated a multitude of multicoloured juggling clubs. Their flamboyant forms, a kaleidoscope of joyous hues, blurred in a mesmerising dance that defied description. Jojo, the youngest and most effervescent jester, spun a dazzling display of jubilant jester-adorned plates. The plates, each featuring a different jovial jester with a wide, infectious grin, whirled with astonishing speed, their laughter echoing through the jubilant throng like joyous, jingling bells. Janine, the graceful jester of the trio,

twirled an array of jewel-encrusted hoops adorned with an orchestra of jangling bells and jubilant jingles. Each intricate twirl of the hoops sent a cascade of shimmering jewels and jubilant sounds cascading outwards further captivating the enthralled crowd. The audience, a jubilant jumble of jitterbugging jam-seekers, roared with unrestrained delight as the juggling juggernauts flawlessly navigated their routines. The infectious energy of their joyful performance jolted even the most jaded audience member to their feet, leaving them in a state of joyous jubilation long after the final juggling club had been caught. The Jimmy, Jojo, and Janine juggling juggernaut had truly secured their place as the jewels of the Jitterbug Jamboree, leaving a lasting impression of joyful brilliance in their wake.

2. Jazzy jaguar jauntily jammed a jangled jubilee, juggling juicy jalapenos for jovial jungle creatures. Jealous jackals joined joyfully, their jaws jutting jubilantly as they joined jubilant jays in jaunty jigs. Juvenile jaguars joined joyfully, their joyful yelps joining jaunty jackdaws in jubilant jive. Jovial jumbos joined joyfully, their joyous jumps joining jaunty jackrabbits in jubilant jive. Joyous jellyfish joined jubilantly, their jiggling jellies joining jaunty jaguars in jaunty jigs. Juvenile jaguars, with jaw-dropping agility, joined jubilant jays in joyous jive. Jovial jumbos, juxtaposed with jaunty jackals, joined jubilant jive. Joyous jellyfish, jiggling jauntily, joined jubilant jays in joyous jigs. Juvenile jaguars, juxtaposed with jolly jumbos, joined jaunty jive. Joyful jellyfish, juxtaposed with jaunty jackals, joined jubilant jive.

3. A jolly juggler juggled juicy jiggly jelly jars, jangling a joyful tune. Juvenile jackdaws joined joyfully, their joyful yelps joining jaunty jaguars in jubilant jigs. Jubilant jays joined joyfully, their joyful calls joining jovial jackals in jaunty jive. Jovial jumbos joined joyfully, their joyous jumps joining jaunty jackrabbits in jubilant jive. Joyous jellyfish joined jubilantly, their jiggling jellies joining jaunty jaguars in jaunty jigs. Jittery jackals, joining joyfully, juxtaposed their jerky jabs with jubilant jigs. Jubilant jays, joining joyfully, joined jaunty jaguars in joyous jive. Jovial jumbos, juxtaposed with jaunty jackals, joined jubilant jive. Joyous jellyfish, juxtaposed with jaunty jackdaws, joined jubilant jive. Jovial jumbos, juxtaposed with juvenile jaguars, joined jubilant jive.

4. Jolly juggling Jeff, jaunty and jubilant, juggled joyful jewel-toned juggling jewels, juggling jets of joyous laughter. Jumping jackals, jovial and joyous, joined joyfully, their jaws jutting jubilantly as they joined jubilant jays in jaunty jigs. Juvenile jaguars, juxtaposed with jolly juggling Jeff, joined joyfully, their joyful yelps joining jaunty jackdaws and jittery jackrabbits in jubilant jive. Jovial jumbos, juxtaposed with jumping jackals, joined joyfully, their joyous jumps joining jaunty jackdaws and jittery jackrabbits in jubilant jive. Joyous jellyfish, jiggling and jittery, joined jubilantly, their jiggling jellies joining jaunty jaguars and jovial jumbos in jaunty jigs.

Jubilant jays, joining joyfully, joined jaunty jaguars in joyous jive, their joyous calls juxtaposed with the jaguars' joyful yelps. Jovial jumbos, juxtaposed with jaunty jackals, joined jubilant jive, their joyous jumps juxtaposed with the jackals' jittery jaws. Joyous jellyfish, juxtaposed with jaunty jackdaws, joined jubilant jive, their jiggling jellies juxtaposed with the jackdaws' joyful calls. Jovial jumbos, juxtaposed with juvenile jaguars, joined jubilant jive, their joyous jumps juxtaposed with the jaguars' joyful yelps.

5. Jumping Jane juggled juicy jellybeans, jeering at jittery Jimmy who jammed his thumb. Jealous jackals joined joyfully, their jaws jutting jubilantly as they joined jubilant jays in jaunty jigs. Juvenile jaguars joined joyfully, their joyful yelps joining jaunty jackdaws in jubilant jive. Jovial jumbos joined joyfully, their joyous jumps joining jaunty jackrabbits in jubilant jive. Joyous jellyfish joined jubilantly, their jiggling jellies joining jaunty jaguars in jaunty jigs. Jittery Jim joined joyfully, his jerky jabs joining jubilant jellyfish in jaunty jigs. Jubilant jays, joining joyfully, joined jaunty jaguars in joyous jive. Jovial jumbos, juxtaposed with jaunty jackals, joined jubilant jive. Joyous jellyfish, juxtaposed with jaunty jackdaws, joined jubilant jive. Jovial jumbos, juxtaposed with juvenile jaguars, joined jubilant jive. Jittery Jim, juxtaposed with jovial jumbos, joined jubilant jive.

6. Jealous jackals, jaunty and jittery, joined joyfully, their jaws jutting jubilantly as they joined jubilant jays in jaunty jigs. Juvenile jaguars, jovial and joyous, joined joyfully, their joyful yelps joining jaunty jackdaws and jittery jackrabbits in jubilant jive. Jovial jumbos, juxtaposed with jaunty jackals, joined joyfully, their joyous jumps joining jaunty jackdaws and jittery jackrabbits in jubilant jive. Joyous jellyfish, jiggling and jittery, joined jubilantly, their jiggling jellies joining jaunty jaguars and jovial jumbos in jaunty jigs.

Juvenile jaguars, juxtaposed with jovial jumbos, joined jaunty jive, their joyful yelps juxtaposed with the jumbos' joyous jumps. Joyful jellyfish, juxtaposed with jaunty jackals, joined jubilant jive, their jiggling jellies juxtaposed with the jackals' jittery jaws. Jittery Jim, juxtaposed with joyous jellyfish, joined jubilant jive, his jittery jumps juxtaposed with the jellyfish's jiggling jellies. Jubilant jays, juxtaposed with juvenile jaguars, joined jubilant jive, their joyous calls juxtaposed with the jaguars' joyful yelps. Jovial jumbos, juxtaposed with jittery jackals, joined jubilant jive, their joyous jumps juxtaposed with the jackals' jittery jaws. Joyous jellyfish, juxtaposed with jubilant jays, joined jubilant jive, their jiggling jellies juxtaposed with the jays' joyous calls.

CHAPTER 11: INSANE K-CENTRIC TONGUE TWISTERS

Prepare for a linguistic labyrinth filled with formidable K-focused fun. **Kolossal K's** offers a kaleidoscope of complex challenges designed to kindle your cognitive capabilities and cultivate keen articulation. These knotty tongue twisters will keep your mind nimble, your mouth moving, and your spirits high. From kooky alliterations to killer wordplay, each concoction is crafted to challenge and entertain. Are you ready to embark on this captivating quest for verbal mastery? Let's kick off this kooky linguistic adventure together!

1. King Kenneth, a king known for his keen cultivation of knightly knowledge, decreed a kingdom-wide competition to cull the cream of his courageous cavalry. The coveted crown awaited the knight conquering countless contenders, culminating in a clash between two combatants crowned kings of knife-fighting. Sir Kevin, a knight commended for his meticulous manoeuvres and killer counters, met his match in Sir Kristopher, whose krakens of strength and killer kicks kept crowds captivated. Knives kissed with a chilling clang, carving chaotic constellations in the air as the knights commenced their combat. King Kenneth, keenly focused,

kept his eyes glued to the whirlwind of gleaming steel. Would Sir Kevin's killer knowledge and knightly finesse prevail, or would Sir Kristopher's knock-out kracht (power) overpower his opponent? The kingdom's collective breath hitched as the knights parried and thrust, a kaleidoscope of kinetic energy keeping the crowd on the knife-edge of their seats

Suddenly, with a knightly kowtow (deep bow), Sir Kevin feigned a retreat, luring Sir Kristopher into a ferocious forward charge. In a flash, Sir Kevin executed a cunning kick, knocking the pommel of Sir Kristopher's knife askew. The crowd gasped as Sir Kristopher's weapon clattered to the ground, leaving him momentarily vulnerable. But underestimate Sir Kristopher at your own peril! With a ferocious knee strike aimed at Sir Kevin's midsection, the crowd erupted in a cacophony of cheers and jeers. Sir Kevin, with a knightly nimbleness honed over years of relentless training, barely managed to deflect the blow with his elbow, the impact sending tremors through his arm. The knights, now locked in a fierce grapple, wrestled for dominance, their grunts echoing through the arena. King Kenneth rose from his throne, his kingly composure momentarily shaken by the intensity of the duel. Would either knight gain the upper hand, or would this epic encounter culminate in a double disqualification, a knightly faux pas unheard of in the kingdom's history?

2. Klutzy, kindhearted, and keenly capable Karl's kooky, kaleidoscopic kitchen kindled knowingly keeping kooky, key-lime, kale-based kebabs, keeping keen, knowledgeable, and kind koalas keenly cultivating their keen knack for knocking kettles with kinetic, captivating force. Karl's culinary creations, however, kindled controversy among the koala community. Some koalas, known for their kind and calm nature, keenly criticised Karl's kooky concoctions, claiming the key to koala contentment was not kale-based kebabs, but rather, calming eucalyptus leaves.

Despite the koala community's critique, Karl, known for his kind and carefree nature, continued to kindle his kitchen kingdom, keeping his kooky culinary creations at the forefront of his kooky kitchen kingdom. Undeterred, Karl embarked on a quest to quell the koala community's qualms. He knew that to keep the koalas content, he needed to concoct culinary creations that captured the essence of the eucalyptus, while still embodying his kooky kitchen style.

Karl spent countless hours in his kitchen, experimenting with exotic spices and unique ingredients. He kneaded, chopped, and stirred, his kitchen becoming a kaleidoscope of colours and aromas. Finally, after countless kitchen calamities and culinary conundrums, Karl created a masterpiece: eucalyptus-infused kebabs, coated in a key-lime glaze, and served with a side of kale and kiwi chutney.

The koalas were sceptical at first, their keen noses accustomed to the calming scent of eucalyptus. However, one bite of Karl's creation and their scepticism was silenced. The kebabs were a harmonious blend of familiar and extraordinary, a testament to Karl's culinary creativity. From that day forward, Karl's kitchen became a haven for happy koalas, and his kooky, kaleidoscopic culinary creations became the talk of the eucalyptus-loving community.

3. Kermit's kinetic, kiwi-shaped kite, knowingly kept aloft by keen, knowing kids, was a captivating centrepiece to their kaleidoscopic day. As the kite danced and dipped, its cerulean hues contrasting vividly with the verdant sky, the children were inspired to create their own vibrant world. They kicked with calculated precision, transforming the once uniform kale patch into a kaleidoscope of green, punctuated by the occasional crimson kick. Their hands, once idle, became instruments of creation as they kneaded clay with keen focus, moulding it into intricate, knobby sculptures. And with nimble fingers, they knitted, their needles clicking rhythmically as they brought to life knee-high knickers in a kaleidoscope of colours.

The kite, a kinetic masterpiece, served as a catalyst for their creativity. Its constant motion mirrored the children's own dynamic energy, encouraging them to explore the limitless possibilities of their imaginations. As they worked, they felt a growing kinship with the kite, a sense of shared adventure and exploration. It was as if the kite was a kindred spirit, soaring through the sky while they soared through the realms of their own minds.

The children's creations, born from the inspiration of the kite, were as diverse as the colours of the rainbow. Some sculpted intricate, knobby creatures, while others crafted kaleidoscopic landscapes. The knitters produced a vibrant array of knee-high knickers, each pair a unique testament to their creativity. As the day wore on, the children's creations transformed their surroundings into a kaleidoscope of colour and texture, a testament to the power of imagination and the inspiration that can be found in the simplest of things.

The day ended as it began, with the kite soaring high above, a symbol of the boundless potential that resides within each of us. As the sun began its descent, casting long shadows across the land, the children looked up at the kite with a sense of wonder and fulfilment. They had spent the day exploring the depths of their creativity, and in doing so, had discovered a new appreciation for the beauty and magic of the world around them.

4. Keen karaoke king Karl, consumed by an insatiable craving for chaos, cruelly kicked the karaoke kiosk with considerable force, creating a colossal commotion that captivated the curious crowd. Kindhearted Karen, a knowledgeable karate expert known for her courageous composure, calmly confronted Karl, conveying her concern for the compromised kiosk in a clear and concise manner. Karl, cognizant of Karen's karate capabilities and the potential consequences of continued chaos, complied cautiously.

   Karen, keen to keep the peace and promote positive pursuits, proposed Karl channel his creative energy into composing captivating karaoke compositions. Intrigued by the idea, Karl committed to crafting calming and captivating karaoke content, hoping to curtail his chaotic tendencies and cultivate a calmer demeanour. With Karen's encouragement, Karl began composing compelling choruses and catchy melodies, discovering a newfound passion for performance. As Karl's confidence grew, so too did his reputation as a karaoke connoisseur, and his once chaotic energy transformed into charismatic charm.

5. Keen knitter Kathy, known for her quick-witted knitting, kept kittens kicking with knitted kickballs, creating chaotic commotion and concern among cautious caregivers. Concerned about the kittens' chaotic conduct

and potential for injury, Kathy crafted calming catnip cushions and captivating cricket-shaped toys to redirect their rambunctious energy. The kittens, captivated by the colourful creations, ceased their chaotic kicking, allowing Kathy to continue knitting quietly.

Kathy, knowing the importance of kitten care and cognitive stimulation, continued crafting countless colourful creations, ensuring the kittens' contentment and comfort while cultivating a calm and controlled environment. As Kathy's knitting skills flourished, so too did her reputation as a knitting virtuoso. Kitten caregivers, impressed by Kathy's creativity and compassion, began commissioning custom-knit creations, transforming Kathy's hobby into a thriving business. With each new project, Kathy's knitting became more intricate and imaginative, and her kittens, now grown into graceful cats, continued to inspire her creativity.

6. Keen cook Kelly, consumed by a capricious craving for chaos, carelessly kicked the kooky kettle, causing kitchen chaos that culminated in a culinary catastrophe. Clever cook Connie, known for her culinary calmness and composure, confronted Kelly calmly, convincing her to control her chaotic conduct through controlled breathing exercises and cognitive coping mechanisms. Kelly, recognising the repercussions of her reckless actions and the potential for real-world harm, cooperated, cleaning up the kitchen and calming down considerably.

   Kelly, keen to keep the kitchen calm and conducive to culinary creations, committed to crafting delectable dishes rather than causing kitchen catastrophes, cultivating a calmer and more controlled approach to cooking. With Connie's guidance, Kelly began exploring the intricacies of flavour combinations and the artistry of food presentation. As her culinary skills improved, Kelly discovered a passion for creating dishes that not only satisfied hunger but also delighted the senses. Kelly's kitchen, once a chaotic battlefield, transformed into a culinary sanctuary, where the aroma of delicious food filled the air and the sounds of sizzling ingredients filled the silence.

7. Kickboxing kangaroos, careless in their conduct and devoid of concern, kicked kumquats with reckless abandon, knocking koalas kooky with karate kicks, creating chaos in the kangaroo kingdom. Kindhearted kookaburras, concerned for the koalas' well-being and the kangaroo kingdom's reputation, cautioned the kangaroos about the consequences of their careless conduct, emphasising the importance of considering the impact of their actions on others. Kangaroos, considering the kookaburras' concerns and fearing potential repercussions, ceased their chaotic kicking, keeping the koalas calm and the kumquat crop intact.

   The kangaroos, keen to keep the peace and preserve the peaceful environment, committed to cultivating calmer kangaroo conduct and considering the consequences of their actions before engaging in chaotic behaviour. With the guidance of the wise kookaburras, the kangaroos began to develop a deeper appreciation for the delicate balance of their ecosystem. They learned to respect the rights of other creatures and to find joy in cooperative activities. As the kangaroos matured, they became leaders within their community, promoting harmony and understanding among all creatures great and small.

CHAPTER 12: INSANE L-CENTRIC TONGUE TWISTERS

Launch into **Legendary L's!** These longer, tougher tongue twisters will elevate your language skills. Get ready for lyrical challenges that will test your tongue and mind. Let's conquer these L-laden labyrinths together!

1. Lethargic Lola, luxuriating in languid leisure, lovingly lingered over a large, lemon-infused lemonade. Its luscious, lavender hue lured Lucy from her languid lounging, leading to laughter-filled libations and lively lunchtime conversations. Lola, lifted from her lethargy by Lucy's lively spirit, launched into a lengthy discourse on local lore, leaving Lucy laughing and longing for more leisurely afternoons. As the sun began its descent, casting long, languid shadows, the ladies lingered, lost in lighthearted laughter, their lovely companionship a luminous beacon in the lengthening day.

   Lola's laughter, like a gentle lullaby, lulled Lucy into a state of languid relaxation. As the last rays of sunlight disappeared, leaving the land cloaked in twilight, Lola's luminous eyes seemed to linger on the horizon, lost in contemplation. Lucy, leaning against the cool, comforting cushions of their lounge, felt a sense of tranquillity wash over her, like the gentle lapping of lake water.

2. Lively Lucy, leaping lithely into the lake, left little lily pads limp and lifeless. Laughing loudly, Lucy looked longingly at the lovely, lush landscape, luxuriating in the leisurely life. Later, Lucy, laden with laughter, lounged lazily on the lake's edge, listening to the lyrical lapping of the water. Lost in reverie, Lucy imagined leaping like a lithe leopard, living life to the fullest, leaving no lingering regrets.

   Lucy's laughter was like a light, lifting the spirits of all who heard it. As the sun began its descent, casting long, languid shadows, Lucy lingered by the lake, lost in thought. The last rays of daylight danced on the water, creating a luminous display that left Lucy mesmerised. She imagined leaping into the lake one last time, feeling the cool water envelop her like a liquid embrace. With a sigh of contentment, Lucy reluctantly left the lake, her heart filled with a lingering sense of peace.

3. Lively lions, lolled lazily in the long, lush lawns, leaving lunch leftovers scattered. Little lizards, lurking in leafy leaves, lingered longingly, hoping for leftover morsels. Lucky for the lizards, a lengthy lunch break allowed for leisurely feasting. As the sun began to sink, casting long, languid shadows, the lions lifted their large heads, looking towards the distant horizon, their lion-like roars lost in the lengthening twilight.

   The lions, their lion hearts content after a leisurely lunch, lay languidly in the long grass. The last rays of sunlight painted their golden manes with luminous hues, creating a majestic spectacle. As darkness enveloped the land, the lions let out low, rumbling growls, a lullaby to the night.

The little lizards, their bellies full and their spirits lifted, scurried back to their leafy lairs, leaving the lions to their nocturnal slumber.

4. Lively laundry lady Lucy, lugging large loads of laundry, left little lint lingering on the lovely linens. Laughing loudly at the ludicrous laundry load, Lucy launched into a lively, lyrical song, lifting her spirits as she laboured. Lost in a world of laundry, Lucy located lovely lace and luxurious linens, leaving her laundry list of chores temporarily forgotten. With laundry lines laden with linens, Lucy looked like a laundry queen, her laughter like a light breeze, lifting the spirits of all who lingered nearby.

Lucy's laughter, like a light, filled the laundry room with a lively atmosphere. As the last item of laundry was hung, Lucy felt a sense of accomplishment. The lovely, fresh linens filled the air with a delicate fragrance, creating a luxurious ambience. Looking at her handiwork, Lucy felt a surge of pride. She had transformed a mundane chore into a labour of love. With a satisfied sigh, Lucy left the laundry room, her heart light and her spirit lifted.

5. Lily, the littlest librarian's loyal llama companion, lumbered alongside, laden with leather-bound ledgers and lyric-laden literature. Lily, known for her lightning-fast leaps, longed to locate legendary lost libraries alongside Lulu. Legends whispered of labyrinths lurking beneath limestone landscapes, littered with luminous lore.

Leaving the library's lofty lamplight, Lulu and Lily launched themselves into the lavender twilight. Lush landscapes loomed large, lit by a luminous lacework of stars. Lulu, ever the leader, led the way, her lilac llama fur luminescing faintly in the moonlight. Lily, lithe and loyal, followed closely, her large, luminous eyes scanning the landscape for lurking lanky lynxes.

Legends spoke of lyrical libraries laced with lost languages, lurking beneath limestone landscapes. Lulu, longing to learn these languages, longed for a legendary linguist to lead the way. Luckily, lurking in a luminous lavender luminescence, Lulu spotted a lone, lanky leprechaun lounging languidly on a lichen-covered log.

Lulu, ever the lively llama, let out a loud, lilting "Lilt!" The leprechaun, startled from his slumber, sat bolt upright, his emerald eyes gleaming with surprise. "Lost, lass?" he boomed in a lilting brogue.

"Not lost, kind leprechaun," chirped Lulu, "but on a quest for lyrical libraries!"

The leprechaun's face broke into a wide grin. "Lyrical libraries? Lovely ladies! I might just know the lore you seek. But first, answer this riddle – what has no voice, yet speaks volumes?"

Lulu pondered for a moment, then a smile spread across her face. "A book!" she exclaimed.

The leprechaun cackled with delight. "Correct, clever critter! Follow me, then, and I'll lead you to a legendary library unlike any you've ever seen!"

And so, led by the leprechaun's luminous lantern, Lulu and Lily embarked on the next leg of their llama-venture, a labyrinthine journey towards a library lost to the ages, its lyrical secrets waiting to be unveiled...

CHAPTER 13: INSANE M-CENTRIC TONGUE TWISTERS

Welcome to **Mammoth M's**! Bigger, bolder tongue twisters await. These monstrous mouthfuls will test your verbal might. From mesmerising alliterations to mind-bending mayhem, prepare for a magnificent linguistic workout. Let's master these mammoth M's together!

1. Dr. Millie Moore, a renowned museum conservator lauded for her meticulous methodologies, meticulously mends mammoth molars and mesmerised museum professionals with her masterful mending. Many marvel at Dr. Moore's meticulous microscale manipulations, marvelling at how massive molars are meticulously miniaturised for maximised museum display. Museum murmurs mentioned mammoth molars, the most magnificent marvels meticulously mastered by Dr. Moore. Dr. Moore, ever modest, merely murmured, "Museum conservation practices make mammoth molar mending a model of modern scientific methods."

   Morning routines within the esteemed museum commenced with meticulous molar mending for Dr. Moore. Moonbeams filtering through the expansive museum windows cast an ethereal glow on her workspace as she meticulously matched mammoth molar fragments under a high-powered microscope. Micrometres, meticulously calibrated, mattered most in this meticulous mending mission. Each molar, once a magnificent marvel in the maw of a mighty mammoth, now a fragmented fossil, found its missing pieces thanks to Dr. Moore's masterful manipulations.

Museum professionals, mesmerised by Dr. Moore's meticulous manipulations, would gather around her workbench, their murmurs mixing with the rhythmic tapping of her miniature hammer. Dr. Moore, ever mindful of the delicate procedure, would momentarily pause, her high-powered magnification momentarily lowered. With a professional demeanour, she'd murmur, "While mammoth molars may seem mundane, meticulous conservation practices practised within museums transform them into marvels, models of modern scientific methods."

2. Meticulous Marcus, a masterful mechanic with a meticulous mind, meticulously measured myriad minuscule mechanisms. His masterful manipulation of minuscule metal marvels moulded magnificent machines, mesmerising onlookers with their mesmerising movements. Marcus' mental models, meticulously mapped and mastered, made magnificent machines masterpieces of motion. This methodical marvel meticulously moulded marvellous mechanisms, showcasing his masterful mechanical might. More than merely meticulous, Marcus' mechanical marvels mesmerised multitudes, making him a monumental master of machinery. Moreover, Marcus' meticulous methods and masterful manipulations made his machines more than mere mechanisms; they were mesmerising manifestations of mechanical mastery, marvels that moved minds as much as they moved metal.

3. Mysterious Madame Mim, a mesmerising magician, manifested marvellous, mind-boggling marvels through her miraculous magic mirror. Madame Mim's mystical mind, a marvellous mosaic of magical might, produced monumental marvels that mesmerised mortals and mystified magicians alike. Her magical manipulations, masterful and mysterious, transformed mundane moments into magnificent memories. Madame Mim's magical mastery made mundane matters magical, mesmerising minds with marvellous manifestations. Moreover, Madame Mim's magical milieu was a mysterious maze of marvels, making her a monumental mistress of magic. More than a mere magician, Madame Mim was a masterful manipulator of the mystical, creating mesmerising moments that lingered long after the magic faded.

4. Mumbling museum member Marvin, a methodical mastermind, meticulously memorised monumental mammoth molar measurements. Marvin's mental manoeuvres, marvellous manifestations of meticulous memory, made mammoth molar metrics memorable to all who met him. His monumental mental might made mundane museum matters mesmerisingly memorable. Marvin's methodical mind, a marvellous museum marvel, mastered mammoth molar measurements with meticulous might. More importantly, Marvin's monumental memory made him a magnificent museum mainstay, mesmerising multitudes with his mammoth molar mastery. Moreover, Marvin's methodical musing on mammoth molars made him more than a mere museum

member; he became a mesmerising maestro of mammoth molar minutiae, a monumental marvel of memory.

5. Majestic Mara, a magnificent mask-maker, crafted captivating, colourful creations. Her masterful manipulation of materials made mesmerising masks, each a masterpiece of meticulous design. Mara's marvellous masquerade masks made men murmur in amazement, their minds mesmerised by her magnificent motifs and meticulous mastery. Mara's magical masks, marvellous manifestations of her masterful mind, made memorable moments for all who marvelled at her magnificent creations. Moreover, Mara's marvellous mask-making made her a monumental muse for many, inspiring myriad admirers to marvel at her magnificent masterpieces. More than a mere mask-maker, Mara was a masterful magician of materials, creating mesmerising masks that mirrored the magic of masquerade.

6. Magnificent, meticulous mushroom munchers, mindful of their munching, munched mightily on marvellous, moist mushrooms. These merry makers of memorable moments mastered the magic of mushroom munching. More than mere mortals, they were mythical in their munching, their mouths filled with mouthwatering morsels.

   Each mushroom, meticulously measured and munched, was a masterpiece of flavour. These marvellous munchers, with meticulous manners, made the most of their mushroom moments. Their munching missions were monumental, making them the most memorable mushroom munchers in mushroom mythology. Moreover, their munching methodology was masterful, maximising the mushroom's marvellous taste.

Beyond mere sustenance, these mushrooms were more than morsels; they were mystical, magical manifestations of nature's magnificence. Munching these mushrooms was a meditative moment, a mindful meander through the marvellous world of mushrooms.

7. Mighty, masterful musicians, marching with meticulous might, made magnificent music. These melodic marvels mesmerised multitudes with their masterful manipulation of musical instruments. More than mere melody makers, they were magicians of music.

   Their marching was majestic, their music mesmerising. With each movement, they made magic, moving minds and mountains momentarily. These musical maestros, with meticulous musicality, made their mark on the world. Their music was more than marvellous; it was monumental, a masterpiece of melody that mattered. Moreover, their musical momentum was unmatched, making them the most memorable marching musicians in musical history.

   Beyond mere entertainment, their music was a meaningful meditation, a masterful manipulation of mood. With every note, they navigated the nuances of emotion, creating a musical masterpiece that moved mountains and mended minds.

   Would you like me to try a different approach, perhaps focusing on internal rhyme or alliteration?

CHAPTER 14: INSANE N-CENTRIC TONGUE TWISTERS

This section presents a series of advanced tongue twisters centred on the **letter N.** Designed to challenge and refine articulation, these exercises demand precision, clarity, and fluency. Participants will encounter intricate phrases that necessitate careful enunciation and nasal resonance.

1. Navigator Nellie, nestled near the needle of her compass, navigated never-ending nebulae, a nightly odyssey through the cosmos' darkest corners. Nebulae, shimmering with an ethereal glow, cast an ever-shifting nautical tapestry across the bridge of Nellie's nimble spaceship. Never nervous in the face of the unknown, Nellie narrated nautical nonsense to keep her nimble narwhal crew entertained. Nestled amongst the navigational instruments, these narwhals, known for their narcoleptic tendencies, needed constant nudges to stay awake. Nellie's narratives, nonsensical as they were, never failed to rouse the narwhals from their slumber.

   Night after night, Nellie navigated, her nimble fingers dancing across the holographic star charts. Nebulae, named with nonsensical nicknames ("Nebulous Nancy," "Nebulous Ned"), became familiar companions on their cosmic quest. New navigational nuances necessitated Nellie's nightly narrations. Nebulae, once navigated by instinct, now required precise calculations to avoid nasty near-collisions with nebulous nasties – rogue asteroids and nebulous nebulas prone to unpredictable fluctuations.

Nellie's narrations, nonsensical at first glance, became infused with subtle navigational knowledge. Narwhals, no longer simply entertained, began to nibble on the nuggets of wisdom Nellie sprinkled throughout her stories. Soon, the narwhals were not just nimble swimmers, but nascent navigators themselves, nudging Nellie towards new nebulae and navigating near misses with newfound navigational prowess.

Nightmares of never-ending nebulae never haunted Nellie. Navigator Nellie, with her crew of nimble, now nearly nocturnal narwhals, navigated the never-ending nebulae, her nonsensical narrations evolving into a symphony of spacefaring knowledge.

2. Navigating nigh-infinite, nebulous, nocturnal nebulae, Nellie, a nautical navigator, nobly navigated nuanced, nautical nonsense, nurturing nimble narwhals' nascent navigational needs. Her neural networks, normally navigating normative narratives, now negotiating novel, nebulous nomenclature, necessitated neurological nuance. Normally navigating navigable nautical waters, Nellie now navigated nebulous, nocturnal, nautical nothingness, necessitating newfound navigational norms. Necessitated by newfound, nebulous, nautical necessities, Nellie's neural networks, now navigating novel, nautical narratives, necessitated neurological normalisation. Notwithstanding the nuanced nature of navigating nautical nothingness, Nellie's navigational

nous necessitated nimble, neurological navigation, neutralising navigational nightmares.

To navigate such nebulous, nocturnal nautical nonsense, Nellie needed not merely navigational nous, but neurological nimbleness. Navigating these nigh-infinite, nebulous nebulae necessitated a nuanced, nimble mind, neutralising the neurological nightmares inherent in navigating such nautical nothingness. Nellie's navigational narratives, normally normative, now needed to navigate novel, nebulous nautical nuances, necessitating neural network normalisation.

3. Nervous Nellie, normally nurturing, now neglecting normalcy, nervously narrated nonsensical, nauseating news nonstop, neglecting neutral neutrality. Notably neurotic, Nellie's neurological network, normally navigating normative news, now navigating nonsensical, nauseating nonsense, nearly neglected neurological normality. Necessitating neurological normalisation, Nellie needed to neutralise the nonsensical news, normalising neural networks, navigating normalcy anew. Notwithstanding the newfound normality, Nellie's neurotic nature necessitated continual cognitive correction, combating continual cognitive chaos caused by continual consumption of convoluted content. Notably, Nellie's neural network needed nurturing, not neglecting normative news, necessitating neurological normalisation, neutralising nonsensical news, and normalising neural network navigation.

To neutralise the neurological nightmares induced by nonstop, nonsensical news, Nellie needed to navigate a neural pathway to normalcy. Normalising neural networks was necessary to nullify the negative neurological effects of the nonsensical news. Nellie's neurotic nature, however, necessitated navigating this neural network normalisation with nuance, not neglecting the need for neutralising the negative neurological noise.

4. Nimble, naturalistic Nancy, navigating nature's nooks and navigating narrow, neglected niches, noticed nesting nighthawks, normally nocturnal, now nesting nearer. Nancy, notably naturalistic, normally nurturing nature's nuances, now navigating nature's novelties, noting notable, natural phenomena. Needlessly navigating nigh-time nature, Nancy noticed nocturnal nuances, needing new naturalistic narratives. Nonetheless, Nancy, navigating nature's nuances, noticed notable, naturalistic necessities, necessitating nuanced narratives, narrating nature's nuances naturally. Notably, Nancy's naturalistic nature necessitated navigating nature's nuances with nuance, noting noteworthy nuances, neglecting needless narratives, and nurturing nature's naturalness.

   Nancy's naturalistic nature necessitated navigating nature's nuances with nuance. Navigating these narrow, neglected niches, noting the nocturnal nuances of nesting nighthawks, required a naturalistic nimbleness. Normally navigating normative natural narratives, Nancy now needed to navigate novel, naturalistic narratives, noting nature's noteworthy nuances. Neglecting needless narratives, Nancy needed to nurture naturalistic narratives, navigating nature's nuances with naturalistic nuance.

5. Neat, nimble Nick, normally nurturing noodles, now neglecting nutritional needs, negligently nested noodles, neglecting necessary nutrients, in narrow, nauseating

nests. Nick, normally noted for nutritional nuance, now neglecting nutritional norms, notably neglecting noodle normality, nesting noodles negligently. Necessitating nutritional normalisation, Nick needed to neutralise noodle neglect, nurturing noodles normally, navigating noodle normality anew. Notwithstanding the newfound normality, Nick's noodle-nesting notoriety necessitated nutritional nuance, necessitating novel noodle norms, neutralising noodle neglect, and normalising noodle nutrition. Notably, Nick's noodle-navigating nous necessitated nutritional nuance, neutralising noodle neglect, and normalising noodle normality, navigating noodle nirvana.

Nick's noodle-nesting notoriety necessitated nutritional normalisation. Navigating the nuances of noodle nutrition, Nick needed to neutralise the neglect of noodle normality. Normally, nurturing noodles with nutritional nuance was Nick's norm, but now, negligent noodle nesting needed neutralising. Navigating this noodle nightmare necessitated nimble neurological navigation, normalising noodle nutrition, and nurturing noodle normality.

CHAPTER 15: INSANE O-CENTRIC TONGUE TWISTERS

This exercise presents a rigorous linguistic challenge: constructing complex sentences with a preponderance of words beginning with the **letter O.** Participants will be required to demonstrate exceptional verbal dexterity and creativity.

The **O-Challenge** is designed to enhance articulation, fluency, and cognitive flexibility.

1. Optimistic opera-loving Omar, obsessed with obscure orchestral oddities, often overbooked odd oboe offerings, orchestrating oboe extravaganzas that outlandishly outshone other instruments. Orchestra owls, perched patiently in the rafters, observed with owlish curiosity, occasionally ogling Omar's outlandish oboe overtures. Seasoned symphony subscribers, accustomed to soaring strings and sonorous symphonies, sat stoically, occasionally stifling stifled sighs. One stoic subscriber, a stout soprano named Sonia, scribbled scathingly in her souvenir program, "Omar ought only orchestrate oboe operas occasionally!"

   Unfazed by such scribblings, Omar, oblivious to the orchestra's off-key oboe odyssey, ordered oddest oboe oddities for upcoming orchestral offerings. One outrageous overture, ominously titled "Ode to Overcooked Omelettes," featured an obsessive oboe solo that droned on for over eight agonising octaves. Orchestra owls, overwhelmed by the onslaught of oboe, oozed out of the opera obscurely, leaving only Omar oblivious to the oboe overload. Backstage, befuddled bassoonists bemoaned the bizarre blowhard brilliance bestowed upon the oboe, muttering amongst themselves about "obnoxious oboe overplays."

Undeterred by the disgruntled dissenters, Omar, optimistic as ever, ordered a custom-built contra-oboe, an outlandish orchestral oddity specifically designed to overpower the entire orchestra. Opening night arrived, and the audience, a curious collection of oboe enthusiasts and disgruntled subscribers, awaited with apprehension. Omar, oblivious to the audience's anxiety, approached the podium, a triumphant twinkle in his eye. As he raised his baton, a lone, disgruntled voice bellowed from the balcony, "Omar, enough oboes already!"

The audience erupted in agreement, their pent-up frustration overflowing into a cacophony of boos and hisses. Omar, for the first time, seemed to notice the orchestra's off-kilter expressions and the audience's obvious agitation. Perhaps, he pondered, a touch of orchestral balance wouldn't be the worst thing. With a sheepish grin, he lowered his baton and announced, "Alright, alright, I get it! Tonight, let's orchestrate a symphony of instruments, not just an oboe opera!" Relief washed over the orchestra and the audience alike, a collective sigh escaping their lips as normal orchestral normalcy returned.

2. Opinionated Olga's obnoxious octopus, once only

occupying Ollie's obsolete, oval-shaped offshore office, had outgrown its original oceanic office, obliging Olga to offer other outlandish octopus accommodations. Owing to the octopus's outrageous appetite for oysters and other oceanic organisms, Olga's original oceanic office options often proved overly onerous. Only occasionally could Olga overlook the octopus's obvious overindulgence, offering opportunities for other occupants to occupy Olga's original oceanic office.

Olga's obstinate outlook on octopus ownership often obligated Olga to offer other outlandish options. One option involved obtaining a larger offshore office, outfitted with optimal octopus accommodations. Other options included outsourcing octopus ownership or organising an oceanic octopus orphanage. Ultimately, Olga opted for obtaining a larger offshore office, outfitted with opulent octopus accommodations, overlooking the octopus's occasional outrageous outbursts.

3. Optimistic opera lover Omar, overtly obsessed with obscure oboe oddities, often overloaded orchestras with outrageous, overly opulent oboe extravaganzas. Orchestral owls observed with owlish, occasionally offended outlooks, while seasoned subscribers sat stoically, silently stifling sighs. Unaware of the overwhelmingly obvious annoyance, Omar continued his obsessive, often offensive oboe orchestrations, ordering a custom-built, contra-oboe contraption to overpower the orchestra's overall output. Opening night offered an opportunity for Omar's orchestral overindulgence and a lone voice from the balcony, obviously outraged, obliterated Omar's obliviousness. "Omar, only obstinate oboe offenders offer such offensive orchestrations!" the outraged observer offered. The audience, obviously overwhelmed by the oboe onslaught, erupted in overwhelming agreement. Omar, observing the overall

opposition, obviously overwhelmed, offered a sheepish, "Okay, only occasional oboe offerings." Relief, openly offered, overwhelmed the orchestra as ordinary, orchestral operations once again occurred.

CHAPTER 16: INSANE P-CENTRIC TONGUE TWISTERS

This exercise is designed to enhance precision and clarity in speech. Participants will encounter a progression of progressively challenging sentences featuring the **letter P.** By mastering these patterns, individuals can improve their overall pronunciation and fluency.

1. Professor Penelope Periwinkle, perched atop her plush purple pouffe, perfected peculiar potions peculiar Professor Peabody, a paragon of pedantic profundity, possessed an unparalleled passion for the perplexing. His purview, primarily palindromes, presented peculiar problems that provoked prodigious ponderance. With meticulous methodology, Professor Peabody pursued perfection in palindromic patterns, producing perplexing puzzles that perplexed even the most perspicacious pupils.

2. Prolific in his production of palindromic prose, Professor Peabody penned poetry, prose, and plays that possessed peculiar properties. His ponderous ponderings produced paradoxical phrases and perplexing patterns, perpetually pushing the boundaries of palindromic possibilities.

3. Despite public praise for his prodigious pursuits, Professor Peabody remained perpetually preoccupied with the pursuit of perfection. His peculiar penchant for palindromes persisted, prompting persistent pondering and producing prodigious quantities of palindromic perplexities. Ultimately, Professor Peabody's pursuit of palindromic parity proved to be a perpetual pursuit, a pleasurable pastime that provided purpose and fulfilment.n her perpetually pink laboratory. Sunbeams, slanting through stained-glass windows emblazoned with playful pigs, cast a kaleidoscope of colours across bubbling beakers and overflowing vials. Penelope, perpetually perky in her polka-dotted lab coat, hummed a jaunty pirate shanty while meticulously measuring powdered peacock feathers and pulverised porcupine quills.

   Her most peculiar project involved a potent potion designed to propel pumpkins. Not just any pumpkins, mind you, but prize-winning pumpkins, plump and perfectly round, pilfered (with permission, of course) from the annual Pumpkin Palooza down the lane. Penelope envisioned these pumpkins, propelled by her potent purple potion, participating in a spectacular pig-piloted pumpkin race across the sprawling patch.

   Now, Penelope wasn't one to shy away from a challenge. Finding pig pilots, however, proved a peculiar predicament. After meticulously posting flyers plastered with pictures of plump pumpkins and purple potions, Penelope finally attracted a gaggle of giggling girls, all sporting fetching fuchsia jumpsuits and an undeniable affinity for all things pink.

   The night of the Pumpkin Palooza arrived, a vibrant tapestry of twinkling fairy lights and excited onlookers.

Penelope, her purple potion bubbling ominously in a cauldron the size of a bathtub, carefully calibrated each dose. The giggling girls, now christened the "Pink Pig Posse," scurried around, outfitting their porcine partners in custom-made purple pyjamas (courtesy of Penelope's ever-overflowing sewing basket).

With a theatrical flourish, Penelope declared the "Pigkin Pumpkin Prix" officially underway. A chorus of "oinks" erupted as the pigs, surprisingly adept pilots, steered their potion-powered pumpkins across the dewy grass. The race was a riot of rolling rinds, squealing snouts, and splattered pumpkin guts, much to the amusement of the cheering crowd.

In the end, a piglet named Penelope Jr. (owned by a petite girl named Penelope Jr. Jr.) emerged victorious, her pumpkin leaving a trail of glistening purple goo in its wake. Professor Penelope, ever the gracious champion, awarded the winners a lifetime supply of her prized pastries (potent potions were strictly for research purposes, of course). As the festivities came to a close, Penelope, surrounded by giggling girls, grateful pigs, and a single, slightly singed pumpkin, knew this peculiar potion had unearthed a most peculiar kind of magic – the magic of community, camaraderie, and a good old-fashioned pig-piloted pumpkin race.

4. Proceeding with his perplexing pursuit, Professor Peabody painstakingly plotted potential palindromic phrases. Placing particular emphasis on precise phrasing, the professor produced progressively perplexing patterns. Patiently persevering, Professor Peabody perfected his peculiar process, producing palindromic phrases possessing unparalleled precision. Pursuing further profundity, the professor pondered potential pitfalls, prudently preventing premature proclamation of perfection. Ultimately, Professor Peabody produced palindromes of prodigious proportions, proving his prowess in puzzling pursuits.

Proceeding beyond previous ponders, Professor Peabody precipitated a plethora of palindromic possibilities. Pondering profounder patterns, the professor produced palindromic phrases possessing unparalleled potency. Patiently persisting, the professor perfected his perplexing process, producing palindromes progressively more perplexing. Pursuing perfection with unwavering passion, Professor Peabody produced palindromic puzzles perplexing even the most perceptive pundits. Ultimately, Professor Peabody's prodigious performance produced palindromic phrases proving his preeminence in the pursuit of puzzling perfection.

CHAPTER 17: INSANE Q-CENTRIC TONGUE TWISTERS

Ready to quench your **Q Quest** for quick-wittedness? Dive into a deluge of difficult, delightful dilemmas. These quirky, convoluted conundrums will unquestionably challenge your quickest queries. Prepare to puzzle over perplexing phrases as you pursue perfection. Let the quixotic challenge commence!

1. Quintessential quilter, Dr. Quintilia Quinn, a whirlwind of creative energy, conjured quilts with captivating celerity, consistently conquering complex chromatic compositions that left seasoned spectators speechless. Connoisseurs coveted her creations, queuing curiously at quarterly quilting congresses just to contemplate her audacious colour choices. Where others saw clashing hues, Dr. Quinn envisioned captivating constellations – a cerulean sky sprinkled with lemon-yellow stars, a fiery sunset bleeding into a tranquil lavender twilight.

   Dr. Quinn, ever-quotable, peppered her lectures with captivating quotes from quilting icons, calmly quelling critics with her quilt-making virtuosity. "A quilt is not just a utilitarian object," she'd declare, her voice echoing through the hushed halls, "it's a canvas, a chronicle, a conversation stitched in thread." One could almost hear the collective gasp of awe from the audience as Dr. Quinn unveiled her latest masterpiece – a quilt depicting a fantastical underwater metropolis inhabited by quilted creatures in shades of cerulean, coral, and aquamarine.

Countless accolades adorned Dr. Quinn's trophy shelf – "Queen of Quilting Color," "Curator of Chromatic Compositions," "Quilting Virtuoso." Yet, none of these could quench Dr. Quinn's insatiable pursuit of perpetual quilting perfection. Each new quilt, a testament to her boundless creativity, pushed the boundaries of the craft, leaving the quilting world breathlessly awaiting her next masterpiece. In her mind's eye, Dr. Quinn envisioned a future where quilts transcended mere bedcovers, evolving into breathtaking tapestries that adorned museums, captivating the hearts and minds of all who beheld them. And with each meticulously placed stitch, Dr. Quintilia Quinn, the quintessential quilter, was one step closer to realising this audacious dream.

2. Quintessential Quanah, quickly quitting questionable questioning, quietly questioned the quaintly quiet quill, quickly quoting questionable quotations quietly questioning questionable quail quandaries. Quite curiously, Quanah quickly quantified the questionable quail's quirky qualities, quietly questioning the questionable quacking quotient, quickly querying questionable quotations questioning questionable quail quandaries. Quite quickly, Quanah questioned questionable qualities of questionable quail quarters, quietly questioning questionable quotients and questionable quail quantities. Quite quickly, Quanah questioned the questionable quail's quietude, quite quickly querying questionable quail quotations, quite curiously questioning the questionable quail's quaint qualities. Quite quickly, Quanah questioned the questionable quail's questionable quest, quite quickly quitting questionable questioning, quietly questioning the questionable quail's questionable quietude.

Quantifying quaintly questionable quail quandaries quickly became Quanah's quintessential quest. Quicker questions quelled questionable qualms, quickly quenching quietude's questionable qualities. Quite curiously, Quanah questioned the questionable quail's quirky quotient, quickly qualifying questionable quail quandaries as quite questionable. Quantifying questionable quail qualities quickly quelled questionable qualms, quietly questioning the questionable quail's questionable quest for quietude. Quite quickly, Quanah questioned the questionable quail's quaint quietude, quickly quitting questionable questioning, quite curiously questioning the questionable quail's questionable quandaries.

3. Quirky Queenie, quietly questioning questionable quilting quandaries, quickly quantified the quaint, quilted quarters, qualifying quite quickly as a quite qualified quilt queen. Questioning questionable quilting quotients, Queenie quietly questioned the quaint quality of the queen's quilted quarters, quickly quenching questionable queries concerning quilt quantities. Quite curiously, Queenie questioned the questionable quotient of the queen's quilted quarters, quickly quantifying the quaint, quilted quarters' questionable quality. Quickly quitting questionable questioning, Queenie quietly questioned the quaint, quilted quarters, qualifying quite quickly as a quite qualified quilt queen, unquestionably quenching questionable queries concerning quilt quantities.

Quite curiously, Queenie questioned the questionable

quotient of the queen's quilted quarters, quickly quantifying the quaint, quilted quarters' questionable quality. Quietly questioning the quaint, quilted quarters, Queenie quickly questioned the questionable quilting quotient, qualifying quite quickly as a quite qualified quilt queen. Questioning questionable quilting quandaries, Queenie quietly questioned the quaint, quilted quarters, quickly quenching questionable queries concerning quilt quantities. Quite curiously, Queenie questioned the questionable quotient of the queen's quilted quarters, quickly quantifying the quaint, quilted quarters' questionable quality.

4. Quick quail quickly queued for quirky quartz, quietly quarrelling with quirky ducks, quickly questioning questionable quacking qualities. Quite curiously, quarrelling quickly quelled the quail's quietude, quickly quenching the quail's questionable quest for quirky quartz. Quixotic quail, quickly quitting the queue, quietly questioned the questionable quality of the quirky quartz, quite curiously questioning the questionable quacking of the quarrelling ducks.

Quite quickly, the quail questioned the questionable quacking of the quarrelling ducks, quietly quitting the queue for quirky quartz. Questionable quacking quickly quelled the quail's quietude, quite curiously culminating in a quite complex quandary concerning the quail's questionable quest for quirky quartz. Quickly quitting the queue, the quail quietly questioned the questionable quality of the quirky quartz, quite curiously questioning the questionable quacking of the quarrelling ducks.

CHAPTER 18: INSANE R-CENTRIC TONGUE TWISTERS

Get ready to rumble with the **letter R**! This chapter is packed with rapid-fire tongue twisters designed to test your recitation skills. From rolling R's to resonant rhymes, these riddles and repetitions will challenge even the most articulate speaker. Are you ready to rise to the challenge?

1. Rugged rancher Rex rode rapidly round rugged Rocky Ridge Ranch, the rising sun glinting off the rusty spurs of his scuffed boots. His loyal red rottweiler, Rusty, bounded beside him, tongue lolling out in a red blur as they chased the receding mist clinging to the canyons. Rex, a renowned wrangler with a reputation as rough as the ranch itself, was on a mission to round up a rowdy bunch of range ropers known for their reckless wrangling techniques.

   These ropers, notorious for their rambunctious personalities, roamed the ranchlands with a reckless disregard for the well-being of the ranch's prized rodeo rams. Rex, a stickler for responsibility and respect for the animals, wouldn't tolerate their rowdy ways. The rams, magnificent creatures renowned for their impressive horns and fiery tempers, were easily riled by the ropers' rough techniques. Rex, with a deep respect for the animals entrusted to his care, knew their well-being was paramount.

As Rex and Rusty crested a rocky ridge, a plume of dust rose in the distance, followed by the unmistakable sounds of bawling rams and raucous laughter. Rex, tightening his grip on his reins, urged his horse, Ringo, into a gallop. Reaching the source of the commotion, Rex found the ropers exactly as he'd expected - wrangling rams with a reckless disregard for proper technique. Their laughter echoed across the ranchland as they chased the bellowing beasts through the tall ryegrass.

Rex, his voice booming with authority, halted their rambunctious behaviour. "Hold on there, rowdies!" he bellowed. The ropers, startled by Rex's sudden appearance, reined in their horses, their faces flushed with defiance. Rex, ever the pragmatist, knew a harsh scolding wouldn't solve the problem. He reminded them of the ranch's regulations, emphasising the importance of respectful handling of the rams to avoid injuring the valuable animals or hindering their training.

The ropers, initially resistant, grudgingly acknowledged Rex's point. Their leader, a lanky fellow named Rory, mumbled an apology through gritted teeth. Seeing a flicker of understanding in their eyes, Rex offered them a compromise. "Alright, ropers," he said, a hint of a smirk playing on his lips. "Since you seem keen on roping rambunctious critters, how about we put those skills to good use?" He pointed towards a nearby field where a large group of rabbits, notorious ranch pests, grazed nonchalantly. The ropers' faces lit up with a mixture of amusement and relief.

With renewed purpose, the ropers rode out, their earlier recklessness replaced by a focus on their task. Soon, the ranch echoed with the sounds of laughter once more, but this time it was infused with a sense of camaraderie and accomplishment. Rex, watching them round up the rabbits with newfound respect for the ranch's rules, felt a wave of satisfaction wash over him. The tranquillity of Rocky Ridge Ranch had been restored, not through harsh reprimands, but by channelling the ropers' rowdy energy into a productive task. As the sun began its descent, casting an orange glow across the vast expanse of the ranch, Rex knew that tomorrow might bring new challenges, but for now, Rocky Ridge Ranch basked in the rare moment of peace, thanks to Rex's sharp wit and unwavering commitment to his role as a rancher.

2. Rowdy Rory rarely rearranged ripe, red raspberries, rather rapidly running 'round rusty railings. Reckless Rowdy relentlessly raced rival riders, recklessly risking ruinous results. Reluctant Rowdy reluctantly repaired rusty railings, realising risks remained, resolutely resolving to reinforce them. Relentlessly, Rowdy ripe, reducing risks, and reclaiming his/her reputation as a rusty rider. Relishing the renewed reputation, Rowdy revelled in rapid rides, recognising the risks remained, reminding himself/herself of the rugged reality of racing.

   Regrettably, Rowdy's reign as a resolute rider remained restricted, reminders of recent races replaying relentlessly. Rethinking the risks, Rowdy recognised the need for rigorous training, realising the reality of racing required relentless refinement. Resolutely, Rowdy resumed rigorous routines, recognising the rewards would be reaped, resulting in renewed readiness.

3. Restless Renee repeatedly rehearsed riveting, rhythmic rhymes, rarely resting, rendering raucous results. Reckless Restless relentlessly raced rival riders, recklessly risking ruinous results. Reluctant Restless reluctantly

repaired rusty railings, realising risks remained, resolutely resolving to reinforce them. Relentlessly, Restless riveting, reducing risks, and reclaiming his/her reputation as a raucous rider. Relishing the renewed reputation, Restless revelled in rapid rides, recognising the risks remained, reminding himself/herself of the rugged reality of racing.

Regrettably, Renee's rhythmic rhymes remained rudimentary, rendering results relatively restrained. Recognising the need for refinement, Renee resolved to relentlessly research renowned rhymesters, recognising the reality of refining rhymes required relentless repetition. Resolutely, Renee resumed rehearsing, realising the rewards would be reaped, resulting in renewed reputation as a riveting rhymester.

4. Roaring race cars roared around racetracks, Ricky the racer revving relentlessly for victory. Reluctant rivals recognised Ricky's relentless rhythm, realising the race required remarkable resilience. Ridiculous rumours regarding Ricky's racing prowess rapidly spread, resulting in renewed respect for the relentless racer. Rather than resting on his reputation, Ricky remained resolutely focused, refining his racing technique. Recognising the rivalry's relentless nature, Ricky resolved to remain resilient, refusing to relinquish his determination. Relentless practice and rigorous routines became Ricky's regimen, reinforcing his resolve to reach the racing pinnacle.

   Ultimately, Ricky's relentless pursuit of perfection propelled him past his rivals, resulting in a resounding victory. The roaring crowd's rapturous response resonated with Ricky, reinforcing his reign as the racetrack's unrivalled champion. However, Ricky realised that racing remained a realm of relentless rivalry, requiring rigorous re-evaluation after each race. Recognising the need for continued refinement, Ricky resolved to remain relentlessly focused, reducing risks while retaining his reputation as a resolute racer.

Reluctantly, Ricky recognised the reality of racing, where rivals relentlessly seek to replace reigning champions. Rather than resting on past victories, Ricky realised the need to remain resilient, refusing to relinquish his focus on the road ahead. Rigorous routines and relentless practice remained essential elements of Ricky's regimen, ensuring his readiness for the relentless challenges that racing would undoubtedly present.

CHAPTER 19: INSANE S-CENTRIC TONGUE TWISTERS

Prepare to embark on a sensational journey through a sonic labyrinth of serpentine syllables. Here, we've meticulously crafted a collection of sophisticated sentence structures, each a singular showcase of the seductive **Sound of S**. These sublimely slippery statements will surely stimulate your speech and stretch your skillset. So sharpen your speech organs and step into this stimulating sphere of sibilant sorcery. Can you conquer these convoluted concoctions of consonants and vowels?

1. Señorita Sofia, a sculptor of sensational sandcastles, surveyed the sun-drenched shore with squinting, sea-salt-crusted eyes. Sunrise shimmered on the sapphire surface of the sea, promising another day of crafting fantastical creations from sand. Today, inspiration struck in the form of a sleek, silver sea serpent Sofia had spotted gliding through the waves at dawn.

   With a sand pail in hand and a seashell shovel clutched between her sun-kissed toes, Sofia set to work. Her nimble fingers sculpted a magnificent sandcastle, its turrets reaching for the sky like the spires of a forgotten underwater kingdom. Shimmering moats, meticulously carved with seashells, encircled the castle, and a grand, spiralling seashell staircase led to the highest tower.

But a sandcastle, no matter how grand, was incomplete without inhabitants. So, Sofia, with a mischievous glint in her eyes, began sculpting a magnificent sea serpent alongside her castle. Its sinuous form stretched out along the shoreline, its scales meticulously crafted from crushed seashells that shimmered in the sunlight like scattered jewels.

As the day wore on and the sun climbed higher, Sofia's creation began to attract attention. Seashells, bleached white by the sun and polished smooth by the waves, became curious onlookers, clustering around the base of the sandcastle. Seagulls, their calls echoing across the beach, swooped down for a closer look, their white wings flashing against the azure sky.

But the most magnificent visitor arrived just as the sun dipped towards the horizon, casting the beach in a warm, golden glow. A real sea serpent, its scales gleaming silver in the fading light, emerged from the waves. It circled Sofia's sandcastle, its inquisitive black eyes seeming to take in every detail.

Sofia, her heart pounding with a mixture of excitement and trepidation, held her breath. Then, to her utter astonishment, the sea serpent nudged its sleek head against the base of the sandcastle, its movement surprisingly gentle. It let out a low hiss, almost a purr, before gracefully turning and gliding back into the sea.

As the last rays of sunlight dipped below the horizon, painting the sky in hues of orange and pink, Sofia stood on the shore, a wide smile on her face. Her sensational sandcastle, once a solitary creation, now stood as a testament to the magic that could be found at the intersection of imagination and the wonder of the sea. The memory of the real sea serpent, its scales shimmering like scattered jewels, would forever be etched in her mind, a reminder that sometimes, the most fantastical creations have a way of summoning their real-life counterparts.

2. Sly Sammy the snake charmer, seeking sizzling serpents at sunrise, stumbled upon a stunning sight – seven sunbathing sun snakes sprawled on a sandstone slab. Startled, Sammy shuffled sideways, scrutinising the scaly scene. "Seven sun snakes!" Sammy stammered, squinting sceptically. "Surely, such a sight shouldn't simply slip by a seasoned snake charmer such as myself!

   Slowly, Sammy sauntered closer, his silver snake-charming staff shimmering in the sunlight. The snakes, startled by the shuffling and shimmering, slithered sluggishly, seeking shelter beneath smooth, sun-warmed stones. Sammy sighed softly, his sly smile fading slightly. "Sun snakes shy away from such shenanigans," Sammy sang, hoping his soothing voice would coax the serpents back out.

   Suddenly, a slithering sound snaked across the sandstone slab. A shimmering silver snake, its scales gleaming like polished steel, emerged from behind a stone. Sammy's eyes widened. This wasn't your average sun snake! This magnificent creature, a rare silver sun serpent, was a sight worth seeing for any seasoned snake charmer.

   Sammy, his voice regaining its sly charm, began to sway gently, singing a soothing song specifically designed to entice silver sun serpents. The serpent, seemingly mesmerised by Sammy's song and shimmering staff, slowly emerged from its hiding place. Its mesmerising silver scales shimmered in the sunlight as it swayed hypnotically to Sammy's song.

Sammy, thrilled by his success, carefully scooped up the silver serpent, his sly smile returning in full force. "Seven sun snakes," he chuckled, "and one spectacular silver sun serpent! Surely, this is a story worthy of sharing with seasoned snake charmers from sea to shining sea!"

CHAPTER 20: INSANE T-CENTRIC TONGUE TWISTERS

This volume presents a sophisticated collection of tongue twisters centred on the **letter T.** Designed to challenge and refine verbal articulation, these exercises offer a rigorous test of linguistic skill. Prepare to encounter intricate phrases that demand precision, clarity, and fluency.

1. Tremendous tightrope walker Tony, a titan of tenacity, tiptoed triumphantly across a taut tightrope, transforming the tranquil terrain into a thrilling theatre of the extraordinary. His tiny toes, trembling yet tenacious, traversed the treacherous tightrope, turning terror into triumph. The taut wire, a tangible test of Tony's talent, transformed the timid spectators into trembling tributes to his tenacity.

   Tony's towering talent, a testament to tireless training, transformed the tranquil town into a tumultuous spectacle. The tiny tottering tightrope walker, a tantalising target for the terrified, transformed their terror into rapturous applause. The town's tranquillity, temporarily transformed by Tony's thrilling feat, returned to its former state, yet the memory of the tremendous tightrope walker lingered, a tantalising tale told time and again.

Tony, the tightrope titan, transformed himself from a timid toddler to a towering talent, his triumph a testament to the transformative power of tenacity. The tightrope, once a terrifying obstacle, became a triumphant trajectory, propelling Tony to unprecedented heights. The town's transformation, though temporary, left a timeless imprint, a testament to the transformative power of one man's tenacity.

2. Tricky Trevor, a tactical titan, tactically transported twenty-two terrific, teetering towers to Timbuktu, transforming the tranquil town into a towering tapestry. These titanic structures, though teetering on the precipice of peril, transformed the timid townsfolk into triumphant tourists. The town, once tranquil and tame, transformed into a turbulent theatre of towering triumphs. Trevor's tactical talents, tested by the treacherous task, transformed the timid technician into a triumphant tower-builder. The towering, teetering titans, a testament to Trevor's tenacity, transformed Timbuktu into a tourist trap.

The town's tranquil tempo transformed into a tempestuous tumult as tourists thronged to witness the towering spectacle. Trevor, the town's unlikely hero, transformed from a timid technician to a towering talent. The town's treasury, once depleted, transformed into a treasure trove thanks to the tourist traffic. The towering titans, though temporary, transformed the town's trajectory, turning it from a tranquil backwater to a thriving tourist destination. Trevor's triumph, a testament to tenacity and talent, transformed Timbuktu from a forgotten frontier to a favoured focal point.

3. Timid turtle trainer Tom, a testament to tireless patience, toiled tirelessly at his tranquil tank, dedicated to the delicate art of terrapin twirling. His tiny trainees, a trembling throng of translucent turtles, huddled together, their tiny translucent tails twitching in a symphony of timidity. Tom, a tower of tranquillity in a tank full of trepidation, understood their terror. Twirling translucent tassels was a tall order for tiny terrapins accustomed to the tranquillity of the tank's murky bottom.

But Tom, a titan of turtle taming, wouldn't be deterred. Armed with a toolbox of turtle-tempting techniques, he tirelessly toiled to transform these timid tremblers into twirling titans. Tempting tuna treats, Tom's trump card, tempted even the most timid terrapin from their trembling huddle. With a twinkle in his eye, Tom would tap a translucent tassel gently against the water's surface, the ripples mimicking the movement he desired. Slowly, ever so slowly, a tiny turtle would emerge, its translucent tail twitching a hesitant inquiry.

This was Tom's moment. With a calm, coaxing voice, he'd guide the terrapin's tiny beak towards the tassel. The first tentative touch, a testament to Tom's tireless training, would be met with a triumphant tuna treat. Soon, the tank echoed with the click-clack of tiny beaks against translucent tassels, a symphony of terrapin triumph.

Tourists, initially intrigued by the tranquil tank, were soon thronging around, their eyes wide with wonder. Tom, a titan of turtle trivia, revelled in regaling them with turtle-tastic tales. He'd recount the tale of Timothy, a particularly timid terrapin who, through tireless training, became the tank's top twirler, his translucent tassel a blur of triumphant motion. He'd share the struggles of Tammy, a terrapin with a penchant for pirouettes, and the eventual triumph of her unorthodox twirling style.

Tom's tales, tinged with the tranquillity of the tank and the triumphant tinkling of translucent tassels, captivated the tourists. They'd bombard him with turtle-training tips, most of them outlandish and ultimately unhelpful. But Tom, ever the tranquil trainer, took it all in stride. He knew, in the quiet moments between tourists, that the real magic wasn't in the tips or the tales, but in the trust that blossomed between him and his timid terrapins. As the sun dipped below the horizon, casting long shadows across the tranquil tank, Tom couldn't help but feel a surge of pride. These trembling terrapins, once terrified of translucent tassels, were now twirling titans, a testament to his tireless patience and the transformative power of tiny turtle triumphs.

4. Tom's trumpet, a tonal talisman, transformed the timid into titans of the tango, their tiny triumphs testifying to the trumpeter's talent. The tigers' taut tongues, tasting the thrill of the tempestuous tango, transformed their timid thoughts into triumphant triumphs. Their tireless twirls and turns, tinged with tantalising tenacity, turned the tranquil terrain into a theatre of thrilling triumph.

Tom's trumpet tune, a tapestry of tonal textures, tantalised the tigers' tender tympani. Their tiny tails, twitching in tandem with the trumpeter's tempo, transformed the tranquil terrain into a tempestuous tumult. The tigers' timid trepidation transformed into a torrent of triumphant tenacity, their tiny bodies twisting and turning with tantalising tenacity.

The trumpeter's triumphant tune, a testament to his

tonal talent, transformed the theater into a temple of triumph. The tigers, once timid, now titans, their tails tapping in time to the trumpeter's tantalising tune, transformed the tranquil terrain into a tempestuous, thrilling spectacle.

5. Tenacious Theo's twenty-two taut, tidy tents totally transformed Timbuktu's tranquil terrain, turning the torrid, tiresome trek through the treacherous, tangled thicket into a tranquil, tempting, temporary tourist trap. The tents, towering tall and taut, transformed the barren, bleak badlands into a bustling, beautiful, blossoming bazaar. These temporary testaments to Theo's tenacity, though, were tragically terminated by a tempestuous thunderstorm that tore through the tranquil terrain, transforming the towering tents into tattered, twisted tributes to the treacherous, turbulent weather.

   The tempestuous tumult, terrifying to timid travellers, transformed the tranquil terrain into a treacherous trap. The towering trees, their branches tangled and torn, transformed the once-tranquil thicket into a terrifying labyrinth. The travellers, trapped and terrified, sought temporary shelter in the tattered remnants of Theo's tents, their trembling bodies taut with terror.

   The tempestuous turmoil, though, was temporary. The terrifying thunder and torrential rain, though terrifying, transformed the terrain, turning the barren badlands into a verdant, vibrant valley. The travellers, their terror transformed into tranquillity, emerged from their tattered tents to witness the transformation. Theo, tenacious as ever, though his tents were torn, transformed the tragedy into triumph, turning the tattered remains into a temporary tourist attraction.

CHAPTER 21: INSANE U-CENTRIC TONGUE TWISTERS

Uncover ultimate **U-twister challenges**. These intricate phrases will test your speech skills to the utmost. Prepare for unusual, unyielding tongue twisters designed to uplift your verbal ability. Ready to unravel these unique utterances? Let's begin!

1. Unveiling underground utopias, these unassuming unicorns united unlikely understudies, urging unprecedented urban upgrades. Unquestionably, these unusual events unveiled the university's untapped potential, ultimately ushering in a unique era of unparalleled achievement.

   Underneath the university, unexpected underground utilities united unique urban undercurrents, ultimately unlocking unprecedented urban opportunities. Unbelievably, these underground utopias unveiled unknown underground utilities, ushering in unprecedented urban uplifts. Unquestionably, these underground undertakings united urban upstarts, ultimately unlocking unprecedented urban advancements.

   Under the watchful eyes of these unyielding unicorns,

underground urban uprisings unfolded, ultimately ushering in unprecedented urban transformations. Unprecedented urban undertakings united urban visionaries, ultimately unlocking unimaginable urban advancements. Underneath the city's surface, unexpected urban undercurrents united unlikely urban upstarts, ultimately ushering in unprecedented urban triumphs.

2. Her heart, a hidden harbour of hopes, held higher aspirations than the mundane monotony of household hauling. Beneath the facade of habitual helpfulness, a hidden hunger for heroic endeavours yearned for expression. Her housemate, however, hindered her heroic pursuits with habitual hindrance, his heart heavy with hopeless hesitation.

Holly, however, harboured a hidden heroism, her heart hardened against hindrance. Her hopeful heart held higher hopes, her head held high, her hands hauling heavy hatboxes with habitual haste. Her hidden hunger for higher horizons, however, haunted her heart, a persistent whisper of what could be beyond the confines of her current circumstances.

Her housemate's habitual hindrance had hitherto hampered her heroic endeavours, but Holly, her heart hardened against such hindrance, held her head high. Her hopeful heart harboured a heroic resolve, a hidden strength that would not be hindered by her housemate's hesitation.

Her hands, hardened by household chores, held a hidden potential for higher accomplishments. Her heart, a hidden harbour of hope, held higher aspirations. Her hidden heroism, however, had yet to be fully realised, hindered as it was by her housemate's habitual hindrance.

Holly, however, was a woman of hidden depths. Her heart, a hidden harbour of hope, held higher aspirations than the mundane monotony of her current life. Her hands, hardened by household chores, held a hidden potential for greatness. Her housemate's habitual hindrance, however, had hitherto hampered her heroic pursuits.

Yet, Holly, her heart hardened against hindrance, held her head high. Her hopeful heart held higher hopes, her hands held heavy hatboxes with habitual haste, but her heart held higher aspirations. Her hidden heroism, however, had yet to be fully revealed.

3. Her helpful hands, hardened by helpful habits, hauled heavy hatboxes with habitual haste. Her hopeful heart, however, held higher hopes than mere household hauling. Hidden beneath her habitual helpfulness, a hidden hunger for higher horizons yearned.

Her housemate, however, hung his head in helpless horror, his heart heavy with hopeless hindrance. His habitual hindrance hampered Holly's hopeful endeavours, hindering her heroic household haul. However, Holly, her heart hardened against hindrance, held her head high, her hopes higher, and hauled the heavy hatboxes with heroic haste.

Her hidden heroism, however, heralded a hidden hunger for higher achievements. Beyond the household haul, a hidden hope for higher horizons held her heart. Her housemate, however, hindered her heroic hopes with habitual hindrance, halting her hopeful journey. However, Holly, her heart hardened against hindrance, held her head high, her hopes higher, and hauled the heavy hatboxes with heroic haste.

Her hidden heart held higher hopes than mere household hauling. Hidden beneath her habitual helpfulness, a hidden hunger for higher horizons yearned. Her housemate, however, hindered her heroic hopes with habitual hindrance, halting her hopeful journey. However, Holly, her heart hardened against hindrance, held her head high, her hopes higher, and hauled the heavy hatboxes with heroic haste.

4. Unhappy unicorns, united in their unyielding opposition to unusual uniforms, unequivocally urged a unanimous return to their usual, unadorned attire. This unexpected unity, a unique phenomenon in the usually uncooperative unicorn community, unveiled an unprecedented understanding and appreciation for their original, unassuming appearance.

Ultimately, these united unicorns ushered in a unique era of unicorn unanimity, characterised by unparalleled unity and unprecedented uniformity in their unadorned attire. Their unexpected and unwavering solidarity served as an unforgettable example of united opposition to unwanted external impositions, inspiring other unyielding individuals to stand united for their unalienable rights.

Moreover, this unexpected upheaval underscored the unicorns' underlying unity, a unifying force that transcended their usual individuality. Their united front against the imposition of unusual uniforms unveiled a deeper, underlying understanding of their shared identity. This newfound unity, once unearthed, became an unshakeable foundation for future endeavours, ensuring the unicorns' continued cohesion in the face of unforeseen challenges.

In the grand tapestry of unicorn history, this episode of united defiance against unwanted attire will undoubtedly be remembered as a turning point, a testament to the unicorns' unyielding spirit and unwavering unity. Their unexpected and unwavering stand against uniformity serves as an enduring emblem of their innate individuality and their unyielding determination to preserve their unique identity.

5. Dr. Ursula Unruh, a seasoned utility engineer, meticulously untangled a network of unruly underground lines during a routine infrastructure inspection. Her routine unearthing, however, took an unexpected turn when she unearthed a cluster of unidentified metallic objects. Unfazed by the anomaly, Dr. Unruh utilised her specialised equipment – universal wrenches, uniform pliers, and an ultrasonic utility locator – to carefully extract the objects. Upon closer examination, she muttered under her breath, "Unidentified Aerial Vehicles...subterranean? Unbelievable."

Intrigued by the discovery's potential historical or technological significance, Dr. Unruh uploaded high-resolution video footage to a secure online forum frequented by reputable aerospace archaeologists and engineers. The forum erupted in a flurry of professional discourse, with participants unanimously highlighting the objects' resemblance to early prototypes of unidentified aerial vehicles. News outlets, ever eager for a captivating story, quickly picked up the thread, thrusting Dr. Unruh into the unfamiliar spotlight.

Unprepared for the media frenzy, Dr. Unruh issued a public statement urging the public to utilise a critical lens. While acknowledging the objects' unusual nature, she emphasised the possibility of these being long-forgotten subterranean utility prototypes, unidentified for decades due to a lack of proper documentation. Worried about the narrative straying too far from scientific reasoning, Dr. Unruh uncharacteristically emphasised, "This discovery, while unexpected, falls within the realm of historical utility infrastructure, not extraterrestrial phenomena."

The public, however, remained captivated by the narrative of unearthed UFOs. Social media continued to churn with speculation, with users uploading a cacophony of unrelated content – ukulele tutorials, unicycle tricks, and underwater unboxing videos – further obscuring the scientific significance of the find.

Undeterred by the online commotion, Dr. Unruh returned to her work, her focus unwavering. The discovery served as a quiet reminder of the universe's capacity to surprise, even within the seemingly mundane world of subterranean infrastructure. Dr. Unruh, ever the professional, remained committed to unearthing the truth, one meticulous excavation at a time.

CHAPTER 22: INSANE V-CENTRIC TONGUE TWISTERS

This volume presents an advanced collection of tongue twisters centred around the **letter V.** Designed to challenge and refine verbal articulation, these exercises offer a rigorous test of linguistic skill. Prepare to encounter intricate phrases that demand precision, clarity, and fluency.

1. Vacationing vintners, with a penchant for premium pours and verdant vistas, visited a verdant vineyard, a veritable viticultural Valhalla. Venturing very, very close to a very vocal vulture, perched precariously on a very vine-covered vine, they were vexed by the vulture's vociferous vocalisations. The vintners, vigilant and wary, visualised various venomous vipers venturing very visibly, their venomous visages vaguely visible in the vineyard's verdancy.

   With valour and verve, the vintners ventured further, vowing to verify the vineyard's vulnerability to such vile visitors. Vigilantly viewing the vineyard, they vowed to vanquish any venomous vermin vexing the vineyard, their vigilant vigilance a veritable vanguard against vineyard villains. Venturing deeper into the verdant expanse, they vowed to verify the vineyard's vitality and vowed vigorous vigilance to preserve its verdancy.

2. Vibrant violin vipers, their vivacious verses vibrating with venomous verve, vex villainous vultures with virtuosic violin vignettes. Vexed by these viperine virtuosos, villainous vultures, voracious and vengeful, vow vicious vindication. Venturing valiantly, vultures visualise victorious vanquishing of these venomous vipers, their virulent venom notwithstanding. Yet, these vibrant violin vipers, with unwavering valour, visualise victorious vignettes, their virtuosity vanquishing villainous vultures.

A veritable vortex of venomous vitriol ensues as vultures and vipers vie for victory. Vultures, their vulpine visage filled with venomous vengeance, visualise vipers vanquished. Conversely, vipers, their viperine venom vibrating with vitality, visualise vultures vanquished. This visceral verbal volley, a veritable vortex of venom and vitality, vibrates through the verdant valley, a veritable spectacle of serpentine skill versus vulture voracity.

Ultimately, the victor of this venomous vendetta remains veiled in obscurity, a victim of the vicissitudes of viperous virtuosity versus vulpine vengeance.

A verdant valley, once tranquil and serene, now vibrates with venomous vitriol. Verdant vegetation, once vibrant and vivacious, withers under the venomous atmosphere. The verdant valley, once a haven for varied wildlife, now vacillates between fear and fascination as the venomous vendetta unfolds. Villagers, vigilant and wary, venture forth cautiously, their verdant vitality vanquished by the venomous spectacle.

Yet, amidst the venomous vortex, a valiant vision

emerges. A visionary villager, with unwavering valour, ventures forth to vanquish the venomous vendetta. This visionary, visualising a verdant valley restored, vows to vanquish the venomous vipers and vultures. With verve and vigour, the visionary begins their quest, their vision of a verdant valley, vibrant with life, their ultimate victory.

3. Vivian, a vivacious veterinarian with a penchant for vibrant vests, vigorously vacuumed various venomous vipers very vexing to vicious vampire bats venturing into her vast violet-veined van. Vincent, Vivian's verbose ventriloquist of a brother, vehemently voiced his vehement vexation. Venomous vipers, Vincent vehemently insisted, were valuable valuables, not vile vermin victuals for vampire bats! Vivian, vindicated, vowed vengeance on Vincent's vindictive ventriloquist vendetta. Venturing valiantly into Vincent's velvet-lined ventriloquist vault, Vivian vigorously vacuumed voluminous velvet ventriloquist dummy heads, vowing to vanquish Vincent's vicious ventriloquist virtuoso vanity. Vincent, visibly vanquished, vowed virtuous veganism, vowing to value vegetables verily, verily!

   Meanwhile, Victor, Vivian's verbose violin virtuoso of a brother, vehemently voiced his *own* vehement vexation. Vegetables, Victor vehemently insisted, were valuable valuables, not vile vermin victuals for vampire bats! Vivian, visibly vexed, vowed vengeance on Victor's vindictive violin vendetta as well. Venturing valiantly into Victor's velvet-lined violin vault, Vivian vigorously vacuumed voluminous velvet violin cases, meticulously avoiding valuable varnish while vanquishing Victor's vicious violin virtuoso vanity. Victor, visibly vanquished, also vowed virtuous veganism, vowing to value vegetables verily, verily!

But the vampiric villainous vow-breaking wasn't over! Vivian, venturing out for a vigorous victory vegetable vendor visit, vehemently voiced her vehement vow to vanquish vicious vegetables Vincent and Victor vehemently insisted were vile. Vowing virtuous veganism was vastly different from vehemently vilifying vegetables Vivian valued! Vincent and Victor, visibly vilified, vowed vehemently to vindicate Vivian's valuable vegetables, venturing vigorously into various vegetable vendors, vowing vast quantities of vibrant verdant vegetables for Vivian's victory van. Vivian, visibly vindicated, vowed virtuous vegetarianism with Vincent and Victor, vowing vengeance only on vicious vampire bats venturing very near their vast violet-veined van.

4. Valiant Vincent, a vigilant vintner, embarked on a venturesome voyage through his verdant vineyard. Verdancy veiled the valley, a verdant vista that Vincent valued immensely. Vigorously verifying vine vigour, Vincent vowed to vanquish any vexatious vermin that ventured into his vineyard. Visualising a victorious vintage, Vincent ventured forth, wielding various vineyard tools with verve.

   Vincent's vineyard was a veritable haven for verdant vegetation, yet venomous vipers and voracious vermin ventured there, vexing the vintner. With vivid determination, Vincent vowed to vanquish these vile visitors. Venturing valiantly, he ventured deeper into the vineyard, vigilant for any signs of these vexatious creatures.

   Vincent's vineyard was his vocation, his verdant sanctuary. He valued the verdancy and vitality of his vines, and vowed to protect them with vigor. As the sun began its descent, casting violet hues over the vineyard, Vincent vowed to return the following day, vigilant in his pursuit of a vermin-free vineyard.

CHAPTER 23: INSANE W-CENTRIC TONGUE TWISTERS

Get ready for **Wild W-Word Wonders!** These wacky challenges will test your word wizardry. From winding wordplay to whimsical wonders, prepare to be wowed. Ready to wrestle with these wordy workouts? Let's whirl into it!

1. With winter's wrath waning, warmer weather was welcomed with wild, welcoming waves. Workers, weary of winter's woes, willingly washed away winter's whitewash, revealing wondrous window views.

   Wearing warm woollen wraps, women watched with wonder as winter's weary winds whispered weakly, while wise women wove whimsical wishes for wonderful weather. Within weeks, warm weather welcomed wildlife, with wildflowers waving wildly in welcoming winds.

   Wanting warmer weather without worry, workers worked with willing workers, weeding wildflower beds with worn-out tools. With weary wrists and wobbly legs, workers worked willingly, while watchful wardens wandered within, wondering when weary workers would withdraw.

Within weeks, wild weather warnings were whispered, with wicked winds whipping wildly, while weary workers wished wildly for wonderful weather. Wearing warm woollen wraps, workers waited within, watching weather warnings with worried whispers.

Worried workers wondered where to wait, while wise women whispered warnings of worse weather woes. With winter's wrath returning, workers wrapped windows with weatherproof wood, while wise women wished wildly for warmer weather wonders.

Wanting warmer weather without winter's woes, workers worked with willing workers, while wise women watched, wondering when winter would withdraw. Wearing warm woollen wraps, women waited within, while winter's wrath worsened, with wicked winds whipping wildly.

With winter's wrath worsening, workers worried wildly, while wise women whispered words of wisdom. Wondering where to wait without worry, workers wrapped windows with weatherproof wood, while wise women watched, wondering when winter would withdraw.

Wearing warm woollen wraps, women waited within, while winter's wrath worsened, with wicked winds whipping wildly. Within weeks, workers worried wildly, while wise women whispered words of wisdom, wondering where to wait.

2. With wistful wishes for wider walkways, the waiters worked with willing, wonderful women who wore whimsical wigs and waved welcoming white wands. Watermelon wedges were wrapped in wet, white

wipes, while watermelons were weighed with worn-out weights. Watching the waiters waddle wildly, worried workers wondered where the wider walkways were, while whimsical waiters whispered worriedly of wider world wonders.

Wanting wider, welcoming walkways without worry, workers wondered where wooden wedges would work well, while wise women whispered wittily of wonderful ways to widen the walkways without wasting water or weakening walls. With weary wrists and wobbly legs, waiters worked with willing women, weaving wonderful walkways with wooden wedges, while wise women watched, wondering when the walkways would be wide enough to walk without worry.

Weaving wider walkways with wooden wedges was wearying work, but the workers were willing. With wonderful whitewash, they whitened the wooden wedges, while wise women watched, wondering when the walkways would be wide enough for the waiters to walk without wobbling. Wearing wide, welcoming smiles, workers waved wooden wedges wildly, while wise women whispered words of wisdom, warning of wayward wanderers who might wander wrongly.

3. Enveloped in woolly winter wear, these wary wolves wandered through windswept woodlands, their wide eyes watchful for wildlife. With winter's white world a wondrous wilderness, they witnessed wildlife weathering the winter with wild wonder.

While wandering, the wolves were wary of winter's wrath, the wind whipping wildly, a worrisome weather woe. With winter's worst weather, wildlife were often weary, their wintery world a world of wonder and worry.

Watching the wildlife with wide-eyed wonder, the wolves wished for warmer weather, their woolly winter wear a weighty burden in the wind. With winter's waning warmth, the wolves wondered where wildlife would wander when winter's worst was weathered.

4. Wilfred, a world-renowned watchmaker, meticulously wields his well-worn welding torch while working with white gold. Whispering whimsical watch designs, Wilfred welds watch wheels with watchmaker's wax, ensuring watertight wristwatch wonders. Working with unwavering focus, Wilfred welds watch winder mechanisms with white-hot precision. Suddenly, a wayward wind whips wildly through Wilfred's workshop window, weakly wobbling his worktable.

   Worried, Wilfred whirls to ward off the wind, wobbling precariously with his welding torch. With a swift, well-practised wrist movement, Wilfred extinguishes the flame, narrowly avoiding watery disaster. Wiping sweat from his brow, Wilfred walks wearily to the window, witnessing the wind whip wildly at the weeping willows outside. "Whew," Wilfred whispers, "waterproofing those wristwatch winders was a wise decision."

   Wandering outside, Wilfred wrestles with a wayward wooden window shutter threatening to break free. Winnie, Wilfred's wise old watchdog, wags her wet tail, whining worriedly. Wilfred, with weathered hands, wrestles the wooden window shut, whistling a well-known watchmaker's tune to calm his nerves. With the wind waning, Wilfred wanders back to his workbench, wiping water from his spectacles. Whew, what a wild Wednesday! Now, back to those wonderful watch winder mechanisms...

Wilfred whistles while wiping, watching Winnie wander westward, sniffing wildly for wet weather worms. Whistling a working waltz, Wilfred wonders when work will wrap up – wristwatch wonders wait! Suddenly, a window-washing whiz named Wanda walks by, whistling a warbling waltz while wheeling a wobbly wagon full of water and window-washing tools. With a wink and a wave, Wanda winks, "Want your windows washed, Wilfred?" Wilfred, woefully wet, winces at the water-warped wood and wobbly window panes. "Wonderful, Wanda!" he wheezes, "Wash with a will, weather permitting!" Wanda, with a winning smile, whips out a worn whisk, whipping window-washing wonder-water wildly. Wilfred, watching Wanda work with watery wisdom, wonders, "Will Wanda's work withstand this wild wind?" Whew, what a whirlwind Wednesday!

CHAPTER 24: INSANE X-CENTRIC TONGUE TWISTERS

Welcome to **Xenial X's**, where X-treme tongue twisters await. Brace yourself for complex phrases that will challenge your speech. From Xerographic alliterations to xylophone-like wordplay, test your verbal skills. Ready to tackle these X-tra tricky tongue twisters? Let's begin!

1. Dr. Xylander, a xenolinguistics professor extraordinaire, expertly executed an exceptional xenon-illuminated xerographic presentation for a symposium of sceptical xenolinguists. Exuberantly elaborating on the intricacies of extraterrestrial communication, Dr. Xylander emphasised xenolinguistics' potential for extracting extraterrestrial knowledge previously deemed exceptionally elusive. Expertly executed examples, projected with xenon illumination, showcased the science's ability to decipher encoded extraterrestrial transmissions, exceeding expectations held by the sceptical xenolinguists. The previously perplexed professors, experiencing a paradigm shift, excitedly exchanged questions. "Explain exactly, Dr. Xylander," one exclaimed, "the extraordinary xenolinguistic techniques employed to achieve such an exceptional feat!"

Emboldened by their enthusiasm, Dr. Xylander embarked on an explanatory expedition. They elaborated on xenolinguistic analysis – the meticulous extraction of meaning from encoded transmissions, considering factors like extraterrestrial syntax and unique communication protocols. But Dr. Xylander didn't stop there. They delved into the fascinating history of xenolinguistics, tracing its humble beginnings from deciphering cryptic messages on ancient artefacts to the cutting-edge analysis of complex interstellar dialogues. The previously sceptical xenolinguists, utterly enthralled, peppered Dr. Xylander with further inquiries. Questions ranged from the theoretical – "How do we account for vast differences in extraterrestrial intelligence?" – to the practical – "Can xenolinguistics help us navigate potential interstellar conflict?"

Finally, Dr. Xylander covered ethical considerations in xenolinguistic communication, emphasising the importance of respectful first contact and responsible message dissemination. They highlighted the potential pitfalls of cultural misunderstandings and the need for carefully constructed communication protocols. Exhausted but exhilarated, the xenolinguists exchanged final remarks, one exclaiming, "Enough explanations! Dr. Xylander, your expertise is truly exceptional!"

Dr. Xylander, exceeding expectations once more, expertly selected a relevant research paper for immediate group discussion, reigniting the symposium's intellectual fervour. The unexpected shift from presentation to participatory analysis underscored Dr. Xylander's commitment to fostering collaboration, leaving the xenolinguists not only impressed but inspired. Perhaps, Dr. Xylander mused, xenolinguistics could indeed be the key to unlocking the secrets of the cosmos, one meticulously deciphered message at a time. But the journey had just begun. New research questions swirled in the minds of the newly converted xenolinguists, a testament to the infectious enthusiasm Dr. Xylander had ignited. As the symposium drew to a close, a collective determination hung in the air – a determination to push the boundaries of xenolinguistic understanding and forge a path towards meaningful communication with the unknown.

CHAPTER 25: INSANE Y-CENTRIC TONGUE TWISTERS

This chapter focuses on the **Yarns of letter Y**, exploring its complex role in English phonology. Through intricate exercises, readers will refine articulation and enhance phonological awareness.

1. Youthful Yara, a yodelling yogini, yearned for yonder yellow yachts. Yanked by youthful yearning, she yanked yellow yarns, yielding yeasty yams. Yearning for yonder, she yearned for youthful yet yearning adventures. Young yachtsmen, yearningly yearning, yearned for yonder yellow yonder. Yielding to youthful yearnings, Yara yodelled anew, yearning for yet another yellow yam, and perhaps a yielding, yellow yak. Yearning for yonder yellow yonder, yet yearning for yet another yellow yam, Yara yearned for something truly unique. Yearning for a yapping yellow yak, yielding yummy yoghurt, Yara yearned for a youthful yearning. Yet, yearning for more, Yara yearned for a year-long yacht voyage, yielding to youthful yearnings for yellow yaks and yummy yams. Yearning for the unexpected, she yearned for a yodelling yak, yielding yummy yoghurt, and a year-long yacht voyage.

2. Yancy's yappy Yorkie, yelping youthfully, yearned yearningly for yesterday's yams. Yearning for yonder yellow yachts, he yearned for youthful yet yearning adventures. Young yachtsmen, yearningly yearning, yearned for yonder yellow yonder. Yielding to youthful yearnings, Yancy's Yorkie yelped again, yearning for yet another yellow yam, perhaps a yielding, yellow yak, and a youthful, yellow yonder. Yearning for yonder yellow yonder, yet yearning for yet another yellow yam, Yancy yearned for something truly unique. Yearning for a yapping yellow yak, yielding yummy yoghurt, Yancy yearned for a youthful yearning. Yet, yearning for more, Yancy yearned for a year-long yacht voyage, yielding to youthful yearnings for yellow yaks and yummy yams. Yearning for the unexpected, he yearned for a yodelling yak, yielding yummy yoghurt, and a year-long yacht voyage.

3. Yeasty yoghurt, yielded yearly, yielded yummy yellow yams, yodelling youthfully yonder. Yearning for yonder yellow yachts, she yearned for youthful yet yearning adventures. Young yachtsmen, yearningly yearning, yearned for yonder yellow yonder. Yielding to youthful yearnings, yeasty yoghurt yielded yet another yummy yellow yam, and perhaps a yielding, yellow yak. Yearning for yonder yellow yonder, yet yearning for yet another yellow yam, yeasty yoghurt yearned for something truly unique. Yearning for a yapping yellow yak, yielding yummy yoghurt, yeasty yoghurt yearned for a youthful yearning. Yet, yearning for more, yeasty yoghurt yearned for a year-long yacht voyage, yielding to youthful yearnings for yellow yaks and yummy yams. Yearning for the unexpected, it yearned for a yodelling yak, yielding

yummy yoghurt, and a year-long yacht voyage.

4. Yawning yogis, yielding gracefully yet yawningly during yoga class, yearned for yummy yoghurt afterwards. Yearning for yonder yellow yachts, they yearned for youthful yet yearning adventures. Young yachtsmen, yearningly yearning, yearned for yonder yellow yonder. Yielding to youthful yearnings, yawning yogis yielded, yearning for yet another yellow yam, perhaps a yielding, yellow yak, and a youthful, yellow yonder. Yearning for yonder yellow yonder, yet yearning for yet another yellow yam, yawning yogis yearned for something truly unique. Yearning for a yapping yellow yak, yielding yummy yoghurt, yawning yogis yearned for a youthful yearning. Yet, yearning for more, yawning yogis yearned for a year-long yacht voyage, yielding to youthful yearnings for yellow yaks and yummy yams. Yearning for the unexpected, they yearned for a yodelling yak, yielding yummy yoghurt, and a year-long yacht voyage.

5. Young yacht broker Yannick meticulously yawned, yearning for yesterday's lucrative yacht sale. Yawning yet again, Yannick yearned for a yard sale, yearning to unearth yet another yellow yachting accessory. Yacht pennants, yellow life vests, a yearning for a yard-long yacht model - Yannick yearned for it all. Yet, yearning for yesterday's hefty commission, Yannick yanked open the classifieds, yellow highlighter poised. "Yacht club yard sale!" Yannick yelped, yellow highlighter circling the ad with fervour. "Yachts galore!"

Suddenly, Yvonne, Yannick's yellow Labrador, yowled, yearning for yesterday's juicy yellow jack tuna. Yannick, yielding to Yvonne's yowls, yanked a yellow chew toy from a nearby yacht magazine. Yvonne yelped with delight, her yellow eyes fixated on the toy. With a determined yell, Yannick yanked on his yellow yachting jacket and shoved Yvonne into his car - yard sale adventures awaited!

The yard sale overflowed with yellow yachting paraphernalia: yellow yacht flags, a yellow yacht captain's hat, a yearning for a yellow yacht christening model. Yannick yearned to buy it all, yet his yearning for yesterday's commission prevailed. Finally, his keen eye spotted it - a yellow yacht fender, the very one he'd been yearning to replace. Yannick yelped triumphantly, his yellow highlighter marking the purchase with glee. Yvonne, meanwhile, munched contentedly on her yellow chew toy.

As Yannick stowed his yellow fender, a yard sign caught his eye - "Yacht detailing services needed!" Yannick yelped once more. His yearning for yesterday's sale could wait. A new opportunity shimmered on the horizon, a chance to secure yet another hefty commission. With a sigh of satisfaction, Yannick tossed the sign into his car – fate had intervened, and Yannick was ready to seize it. Yvonne, sensing an adventure, barked eagerly, ready to explore yet another yacht while her master worked. As Yannick sped off, a determined glint in his yellow eyes, his phone buzzed – a potential client! "Yachts ahoy!" he muttered, a symphony of sales pitches already formulating in his mind.

CHAPTER 26: INSANE Z-CENTRIC TONGUE TWISTERS

This chapter is a whirlwind of **Z Zoomed-in challenges**. Expect complex linguistic puzzles designed to test your articulation and verbal agility.

1. Zealous zoologists, zapped with zealous zest, zombified zebras with zirconium-tipped zephyrs. Zigzagging through the zoo, these zany zoologists, zapped with a zesty zeal, zombified zebras, zapping zoo visitors with unwavering zest. Zombified zebras, zigzagging with zany zeal, zoomed through the zoo, zapping zoologists with zeroed-in zest. Zesty zephyrs, zooming with zealous zest, zapped zombified zebras, zigzagging with zany zeal. Zookeepers, zapped with a zesty zeal, zoomed into the zoo, zapping zombified zebras with zirconium-tipped zephyrs. Zany zoologists, zigzagging with zealous zest, zapped zombified zebras, zapping zookeepers with unwavering zest. Zealous zoologists, zapped with a zesty zeal, zoomed into the zoo, zapping zombified zebras with zirconium-tipped zephyrs, zigzagging through the zoo.

2. Zesty Zoe, zeroing in on zillions of zigzagging zephyrs, zoomed through the zoo with zealous zest.

Zany zoologists, zapped with a zesty zeal, zoomed to Zoe, zapping zephyrs with zirconium-tipped zephyrs. Zigzagging zephyrs, zapped with zealous zest, zoomed through the zoo, zapping zookeepers with unwavering zest. Zombified zebras, zigzagging with zany zeal, zoomed towards Zoe, zapping zoologists with zeroed-in zest. Zesty Zoe, zigzagging with zealous zest, zapped zombified zebras with zirconium-tipped zephyrs. Zookeepers, zapped with a zesty zeal, zoomed to Zoe, zapping zephyrs with unwavering zest. Zigzagging zephyrs, zapped with zealous zest, zoomed through the zoo, zapping zookeepers with zeroed-in zeal. Zany zoologists, zapping zebras with zirconium-tipped zephyrs, zoomed into Zoe, zigzagging through the zoo.

3. Zesty zebras zoomed to Zachary's zany pizza party, happily devouring zucchini-topped pizzas. Zillions of zoologists, zigzagging with zealous zest, zoomed to Zachary's zany party, zapping zebras with zirconium-tipped zephyrs. Zombified zebras, zigzagging with zany zeal, zoomed to Zachary's zany party, zapping zoologists with zeroed-in zest. Zesty zebras, zigzagging with zealous zest, zoomed through the zoo, zapping zombified zebras with zirconium-tipped zephyrs. Zookeepers, zapped with a zesty zeal, zoomed to Zachary's zany party, zapping zebras with unwavering zest. Zany zoologists, zigzagging with zealous zest, zoomed to Zachary's zany party, zapping zookeepers with zeroed-in zeal. Zesty zebras, zigzagging with zealous zest, zoomed through the zoo, zapping zombified zebras, zigzagging with zany zeal.

4. Zeno, a zealous zebra, zigzagged through Zimbabwe's zany, zoological zone. Zesty zephyrs, zooming with zany zeal, zigzagged through the zanzibar, zapping Zeno's zestful spirit. Yet, Zeno, with zealous zest and unwavering zeal, zoomed onward, navigating zany, zigzagging zones. Zillions of zebras, zigzagging with zany zeal, zoomed towards Zeno, zapping Zeno's zestful spirit. Zeno, zigzagging with zealous zest, zoomed through the zoo, zapping zany zebras with zesty zeal. A zany zoologist, zooming to Zeno's zenith, zapped zebras with zesty zeal, zapping Zeno with zany zest. Zeno, zigzagging with zealous zest, zoomed away, leaving zookeepers zapped and zany. Zigzagging through the zoo, Zeno encountered zealous zoologists, zapping zebras with zesty zeal. Zeno, zigzagging with zany zeal, zoomed past, leaving zookeepers zapped and zesty.

5. Zippy Zack, a zany zester of zucchinis, zinged zingy zest into zany zinc zones. Zillions of zombified zebras, zigzagging with zany zeal, zoomed towards Zack, zapping zucchinis with zesty zest. Zack, with zany, zealous zeal, zigzagged, zapping zebras with zucchini zest, zombifying zebras with zesty zaps. Zesty, zigzagging zephyrs, zooming through the zoo, zapped zombified zebras, zapping Zack with zany zeal. Zack, zigzagging with zesty zeal, zoomed away, leaving zookeepers zapped and zany. A zany zoologist, zooming to the scene, zapped Zack with zesty zeal, zapping zombified zebras with zany zest. Zack, zigzagging with zealous zest, zoomed through the zoo, zapping zany zookeepers with zucchini zest. Zigzagging through the zoo, Zack encountered zealous zoologists, zapping zombified zebras with zesty zeal. Zack, zigzagging with zany zeal, zoomed past, leaving zookeepers zapped and zesty.

6. Zephyrs zipped zestfully, zigzagging zealously through Zambia's zoological zones. Zany zebras, zapping with

zesty zeal, zoomed through the zoo, zigzagging with zany zest. Zillions of zookeepers, zigzagging with zealous zeal, zoomed to the zebras, zapping zephyrs with zesty zest. Zesty, zigzagging zephyrs, zooming through the zoo, zapped zombified zebras, zapping zookeepers with zany zeal. Zany zoologists, zooming to the scene, zapped zebras with zesty zeal, zapping zephyrs with zany zest. Zesty, zigzagging zebras, zooming through the zoo, zapped zookeepers with zucchini zest, zapping zoologists with zany zeal. Zigzagging through the zoo, zephyrs encountered zealous zoologists, zapping zombified zebras with zesty zeal. Zephyrs, zigzagging with zany zeal, zoomed past, leaving zookeepers zapped and zesty.

7. Izzy zipped up her fuzzy zebra jammies, humming a zany zucchini jingle. Suddenly, a bloodcurdling "Zzzooooommmm!" shattered the night's tranquillity. A dozen dizzy zombies, looking more tattered than a tattered tapestry, zipped by her window. Izzy froze, her zesty tune replaced by a strangled gasp. "Zoinks!" she squeaked, frantically zipping her jammies tighter. Her heart thumping a frantic jazz solo, Izzy peeked through the blinds. There, bathed in the dim moonlight, the zombified horde was gleefully zapping Zinnias in Mrs. Zest's prize-winning garden!

A fiery glint ignited in Izzy's eyes. Grabbing her trusty zucchini zapper (a birthday gift from her slightly eccentric Aunt Zelda, don't ask!), Izzy zipped out the door. Tonight, fuzzy jammies were out; zombie-zapping was on the agenda! With a determined zip and a zap, Izzy zapped the nearest zombie, transforming him from a zany flower-zapping fiend to a snoring, zombified lump. One down, eleven to go!

But the remaining zombies weren't fazed. With a chorus

of groans that could curdle milk, they turned towards Izzy, their vacant eyes gleaming with a hunger for zinnias (and possibly brains). Unfazed, Izzy weaved through the zygocactus hedge, her fuzzy zebra slippers a blur against the dewy grass. Zapping zombies with the precision of a seasoned zookeeper zapping zebras, Izzy cackled with manic glee. A zing here, a zap there, the once vibrant zinnias became collateral damage in Izzy's one-zebra-jammied crusade.

Meanwhile, the commotion had woken Mr. Zest, a portly fellow with a penchant for polka-dotted pyjamas. Peeking out his window, he witnessed the bizarre battle. "Zounds!" he exclaimed, rushing outside with his trusty bug zapper (mistakenly purchased during a particularly enthusiastic late-night shopping spree). Mistaking the zombies for particularly large, luminous mosquitoes, Mr. Zest zapped with abandon. The combined efforts of Izzy's zucchini zapper and Mr. Zest's bug zapper proved too much for the zombified flower fiends. One by one, they crumpled to the ground, moaning softly about the injustice of it all.

With the last zombie subdued, Izzy slumped to the ground, her fuzzy zebra jammies streaked with glowing green goo (a side effect of the zucchini zapper, not recommended by the manufacturer). Mr. Zest, still bewildered, approached her cautiously. "Zestfully done, young lady," he stammered, offering her a steaming mug of chamomile tea (much needed after that ordeal). Izzy, too exhausted to speak, simply grinned and took a sip, the calming chamomile a welcome contrast to the night's zany events. As dawn painted the sky a soft lavender, the zinnias may have been singed, but peace had returned to the neighbourhood, thanks to a brave girl in fuzzy zebra jammies and a well-meaning, polka-dotted pyjama-clad gentleman.

CHAPTER 27: INSANE WH-CENTRIC TONGUE TWISTERS

This chapter offers **wheeling wh** focused tongue twisters. Expect complex wordplay and articulatory demands. These exercises aim to enhance phonological skills and verbal dexterity.

1. Whence whippets whistle, wholesome wheat whirls wildly, whisking whey wherever whirlwinds whip with wanton wildness. Whimpering wharfs, weakened by the weather's wrath, withstand the relentless rhythm of the roaring waves. While weary wharf workers watch the water with wary eyes, wondering when wondrous whales will emerge, they wield their work with unwavering willpower. With wistful wishes for whale watching, they wait, their weary spirits warmed by the whimsy of the world around them.

   What wondrous wonders will unfold when the wind wanes and the waves weaken? Will wondrous whales emerge from the watery depths, their white forms a welcome wonder in the world? With unwavering hope, the wharf workers watch, their weary bodies warmed by the winter sun, waiting for the whimsical whims of the wind to whisper wondrous tidings of the water's wealth.

2. Whirlpool's whimsically wicked ways wreak havoc on hapless whales, hurling them helplessly into a hypnotic, hellish vortex. Whistling with worry, watchful whales struggle against the swirling, sucking surge, their weary bodies weakened by the water's wildness. With unwavering will, the whales wrestle with the whirlpool's wrath, their white bodies a stark contrast to the water's wild, watery world.

   When will the whirlpool's wicked ways weaken? Will the water's wildness wane, allowing the whales to wander away, weary but whole? With watchful wonder, the world waits for the whirlpool's wrath to subside, for the water's wildness to wane, and for the whales' well-being to be restored. Will the whimsical whims of the wind work wonders and weaken the whirlpool's grip? Only time will tell.

3. Wheezing Whittaker, a whimsical wanderer, wheels wondrous whelks with wild abandon, while whistling whimsical tunes that weave through the wind. With watchful wonder, Whittaker waits for the wondrous appearance of a white whale, its white body a beacon in the boundless blue. While waiting, Whittaker's world is filled with whimsical wonders, from wave-washed wonders to windswept wonders. With unwavering willpower, Whittaker will withstand the wait, his weary spirit warmed by the whimsy of the world.

   What wondrous wonders will Whittaker witness when the white whale appears? Will the whale's watery world be as wild and wondrous as Whittaker's wildest dreams? With watchful wonder, Whittaker waits, his weary heart filled with hope. Will the whale's presence bring with it a wave of wonder that will wash away Whittaker's weariness and fill his world with whimsical joy?

4. White whale Whistler, a wondrous creature of the deep, whipped by with a whirlwind of wake, leaving Wharf Worker Wanda with a world of wonder. With wide-eyed wonder, Wanda watches the whale's wake, weaving whimsical wishes into the wind. While waiting for Whistler's return, Wanda wonders where the whale will wander, what wondrous worlds it will witness, and what wild waters it will weather. With unwavering hope, Wanda watches the water, waiting for the whale's return, a white speck on the blue canvas of the sea.

   What wondrous wonders await Whistler in the watery world? Will the whale's journey be filled with whimsical wonders or wild and treacherous waters? With watchful wonder, Wanda waits for Whistler's return, her heart filled with hope and her mind with whimsical thoughts. Will the whale's wisdom and wonder inspire Wanda to embark on her own wondrous journey?

5. While waiting patiently for whales, whimsical whalers whisper wistful wishes, their hearts heavy with hope and anticipation. With watchful eyes, they scan the horizon, hoping to happen upon a hidden haven for whales. When the white whale finally emerges, the whalers' world is transformed, their weary waiting rewarded with wondrous wonder. With unwavering enthusiasm, they witness the whale's watery world, a world of wonder and wildness, where waves whisper secrets and the wind whispers wishes.

   What wondrous wonders will the whalers witness as they watch the whale? Will the whale's watery world reveal hidden treasures or mysterious marvels? With watchful wonder, the whalers will explore the whale's world, their hearts filled with hope and their minds with questions. Will the whale's wisdom inspire the whalers to protect and preserve the wonders of the watery world?

CHAPTER 28: INSANE AI-CENTRIC TONGUE TWISTERS

This section focuses on refining the **quaint 'ai'** diphthong through complex linguistic patterns. These exercises enhance articulatory precision, fluency, and overall vocal quality.

1. A quaint quail, quaintly qualified in quaint qualities, quailed at the quaintly quiet aquarium. Acquainted with aquatic anxieties, the avian adventurer aimed to alleviate avian apprehension. Armed with aerial agility, the agile avian ascertained an appropriate approach.

   Ascending above the aquatic abode, the audacious avian assessed the aquatic ambience. Aiming to avoid alarming aquatic inhabitants, the airborne adventurer adopted an amiable attitude. As the avian approached, aquatic attention amplified. Anxious aquatic animals, accustomed to aquatic tranquillity, anticipated an atypical aquatic encounter.

   Amidst the aquatic anticipation, the audacious avian executed an aerial acrobatic, aiming to amuse and assure the aquatic audience. Agilely altering altitude, the airborne adventurer averted aquatic alarm. Ultimately, the avian's aerial artistry achieved aquatic acclaim, and the quaint quail, once quivering with quaint qualms, quietly quivered with quaint contentment.

2. Maids braided their hair while debating the merits of baiting snails with stale grains on a rainy day in Spain. Meanwhile, a playful pair of twins, aiming to attain fame, trained to entertain, while abstaining from complaining about the rain, painstakingly practising their entertaining refrain. Their aspirations aligned with acquiring acclaim, aiming to ascend to the apex of entertainment, and avoiding any taints on their reputations. As the rain intensified, they remained contained within a quaint cabin, their minds ablaze with imaginative scenarios, awaiting the anticipated arrival of an agent, eager to aid their ascent to stardom.

   Intriguingly, an antiquated airship, adorned with avian-inspired attachments, appeared amidst the aerial acrobatics of acrobatic athletes, aiming to amaze the astonished audience. Its arrival amplified the anticipation, as it was anticipated to transport the talented twins to a distant city, where a grand audition awaited. Amidst the aerial excitement, a mischievous alligator, aware of the impending adventure, aimed to ambush the airship, awaiting its anticipated ascent. The twins, ever alert, aimed to avoid such an audacious assault, their adrenaline amplified by the approaching adventure.

3. Frail Gail's nails failed to snail-mail framed paintings of sails, derailing her trail of retail sales. Agitated and annoyed, she abandoned her antiquated approach. Acquiring an automated airplane, she aimed to airdrop artistic advertisements, anticipating an avalanche of attention. Agile and adventurous, she anticipated

ascending above all adversaries.

Alas, a sudden air current altered her aircraft's alignment. Avoiding an appalling accident, she adeptly adjusted the airplane's attitude. Although alarmed, she acted admirably, applying aerodynamic alterations to assure altitude.

Arriving at her appointed airspace, she activated the airborne apparatus, allowing artwork to ascend. As artistic aesthetics adorned the atmosphere, a sense of achievement arose. Anticipating acclaim, she awaited audience appreciation.

Ultimately, the aerial artistry achieved astonishing acclaim. Aficionados applauded the audacious approach, acknowledging the artist's acumen. Amidst the accolades, Gail's anxiety abated. At last, affirmation arrived, and artistic aspirations appeared attainable.

Yet, amidst the acclaim, a subtle suspicion arose. A rival artist, known for acrimonious actions, appeared agitated. Aware of the attention, Gail's alertness amplified. Anticipating potential antagonism, she adopted a vigilant attitude. After all, in the arena of art, attention often attracts animosity.

4. Ailing airline analyst Alistair Finch awaited an airlift, aiming for aisle D amidst anxious attendants. Alistair, a renowned authority on airline efficiency, adjusted his seatbelt with practised ease. "Air turbulence expected," the pilot announced in a calm, authoritative voice. Alistair, meticulously studying in-flight data on his tablet, barely registered the announcement. Suddenly, a high-pitched "Aieeee!" pierced the cabin. Several aisles away, a young passenger clutched a stuffed airplane, wailing about the approaching "airpocalypse."

Alistair, ever the professional, understood passenger anxieties weren't easily alleviated. Discreetly, he leaned across the aisle. "Air turbulence is a common occurrence during flight," he offered in a reassuring tone. "The aircraft is perfectly engineered to handle such situations." The child, momentarily silenced by Alistair's calm demeanour, peeked from behind her stuffed toy.

With a gentle smile, Alistair pointed to the window. "Look, observe the aircraft's ailerons adjusting. This aids in maintaining stability amidst air fluctuations." Intrigued, the child focused on the movement of the wing controls. As the airplane levelled off, a hush fell over the cabin. Alistair, discreetly returning to his data analysis, noticed the child quietly observing the wing movements.

Suddenly, a voice crackled through the intercom. "Attention passengers," the pilot announced. "Unforeseen air traffic necessitates a diversion to a nearby airfield. Please remain seated." Alistair winced internally. Diversions disrupted airline schedules, impacting efficiency. He glanced at the child, whose wide eyes mirrored his own concern.

Clearing his throat, Alistair tapped the child's shoulder. "While a diversion isn't ideal," he explained in a professional yet friendly tone, "it sometimes proves necessary for optimal air traffic management." He pointed to a map on his tablet. "See, this diversion allows for a smoother reintegration into the airspace, minimising delays for all passengers."

The child, captivated by the map and Alistair's explanation, nodded slowly. In that aisle seat, amidst a minor aviation hiccup, Alistair had not only soothed a young passenger's anxieties but also offered a glimpse into the complex world of airline efficiency.

CHAPTER 29: INSANE EI-CENTRIC TONGUE TWISTERS

This section presents a focused exploration of the **'ei' veils.** Readers will encounter progressively complex linguistic patterns designed to enhance phonological awareness and articulatory precision.

1. Deirdre's eccentric, elderly neighbour, with evident eagerness and enigmatic enthusiasm, seized upon the opportune moment to flaunt his fabricated expertise. Weighting in with an abundance of absurdly inaccurate assessments regarding the exact height of foreign ceilings, he executed this performance with a convincingly casual demeanour. His exaggerated emphasis on entirely extraneous and evidently erroneous elements elevated his erroneous estimations to an entirely erroneous expertise, evidently entertaining everyone within earshot except the increasingly exasperated Deirdre. His eccentric exhibition, executed with extraordinary energy, elevated the everyday encounter to an extraordinary event, etching itself into the collective memory as an enduring example of elderly eccentricity.

2. The freight of eighty-eight beige veils weighed heavily on the sleigh, its reins seized by a feisty reindeer feigning innocence. Enraged by the extra effort exerted, the exhausted equine erupted in exasperation, ejecting everything from the elegant equipment. The ensuing event ended in everyone's embarrassment, especially the elusive elf who engineered this elaborate escapade.

   Enveloped in escalating exasperation, the equine eventually expelled everything from the elegant equipment, including eight expensive, embroidered envelopes. Each envelope, embossed with exquisite emblems, encased eight emerald earrings, each earring estimated to be eighteen carats. The ensuing eruption of expletives echoed through the entire encampment, exposing the elf's elaborate deception.

   Eventually, the embarrassed elf emerged from their encampment, expressing elaborate excuses and offering extravagant reparations. Everyone, exhausted by the extraordinary events, eventually extended exoneration, expecting exemplary execution of the elf's promises.

   The entire escapade emphasised the importance of evaluating every element before embarking on endeavours, especially those involving eighty-eight exquisite items.

3. Deirdre's dauntless dog, despite debilitating discomfort, demonstrated dogged determination in defending its domain. Daily, during daylight hours, this diligent defender diligently detected disturbances, displaying an uncanny capability for capturing culprits. Equipped with extraordinary endurance and exceptional eyesight,

this eager explorer eagerly embarked on exploratory expeditions, examining external environments for potential perils. Every evening, exhausted from exhaustive exertions, this empathetic entity eagerly awaited evening's embrace, envisioning eventual eradication of enemies.

Enthralled by the enigma of endless exploration, this extraordinary animal exhibited exceptional eagerness, enduring every encounter with unwavering enthusiasm. Eventually, emerging evidence exposed elusive enemies, ensuring enduring equilibrium and eternal ease. The dog's devoted dedication deterred destructive delinquents, delivering domestic tranquillity.

Diligently discharging its duties, this devoted defender became a distinguished defender of the domicile, earning esteemed eminence among esteemed experts in canine capabilities.

4. Eight-year-old Leigh, perched precariously on a creaky, beige beach cruiser, excitedly eyed the eight tiny seine nets she'd carefully crafted from beige string. Her goal: to seize eight feisty little hermit crabs scuttling sideways across the beige, sun-bleached sand. Leigh, feigning disinterest, eased the seine nets ever closer, a mischievous glint in her eight-year-old eyes.

The hermit crabs, eight tiny tenants in their beige, borrowed shells, sensed the impending beige siege. With eight synchronised scurries, they executed an eight-legged escape plan, their eight beady eyes scanning for an eight-way egress. Leigh, ever eager, expertly anticipated their eight escape routes, strategically repositioning her beige seine nets. The eight tiny tenants, trapped in a beige ballet of evasion, scuttled side-to-side, their eight legs a blur.

Suddenly, eight beige seagulls swooped down, mistaking Leigh's beige seine nets for a smorgasbord of eight wriggling, beige worms. Leigh, ever elegant, shrieked in surprise, her eight fingers flailing as eight feathered fiends dive-bombed. The eight tiny tenants, seizing the eight-second window of opportunity, executed a final, eight-legged escape manoeuvre, disappearing into eight beige crevices beneath the beach.

Leigh, eight seagulls circling overhead, sighed in beige-tinged defeat. Eight empty seine nets lay crumpled on the beige sand, a testament to the eight quick hermit crabs and eight very confused seagulls. Exhausted, Leigh pushed off on her beige beach cruiser, her eight-year-old spirit unbroken, vowing to return for another eight-legged, beige beach escapade tomorrow.

CHAPTER 30: INSANE OI-CENTRIC TONGUE TWISTERS

This section presents advanced exercises focused on the **noisy 'oi'** diphthong. Readers will encounter increasingly complex linguistic patterns designed to enhance articulation and phonological awareness. These challenges aim to develop precision and fluency in producing the 'oi' sound within a variety of phonetic contexts.

1. Loathsome Lois, lacking foresight and filled with foolish frivolity, applied a spoiled, oily ointment, inadvertently causing noisy, annoying chaos as it soiled her favourite, oil-stained silk dress. The oily, obnoxious odour overwhelmed the once-pleasant perfume, transforming the room into a noxious, nauseating environment. The oily residue, spreading like wildfire, stained not only Lois's lovely attire but also the luxurious, leather armchair upon which she lounged. The once-joyful occasion was now a chaotic, cacophonous calamity, filled with wailing, whining, and whispered accusations. Lois, oblivious to the olfactory offence she had committed, continued to apply the offensive ointment, oblivious to the growing outrage of those unfortunate enough to be within olfactory range.

   The oily ordeal escalated as Lois, in a fit of oily-induced insanity, attempted to clean the oily mess with oily, ineffective cleaning products. The oily substances combined to create a slick, slippery surface, causing Lois to lose her footing and land with a loud, ungraceful thud. The ensuing chaos was indescribable, as furniture toppled, ornaments shattered, and angry voices filled the room. In the end, Lois was left alone, covered in oil, surrounded by the remnants of her ruined reputation and her beloved but now oil-soaked belongings.

2. The poignant, pulsating percussion of the boiling koi pond roiled Lois's previously poised demeanour, disrupting her delicate, dexterous task of joining the fragile foil to the intricate doily. The incessant, irritating intrusion was a constant, unwelcome companion, distracting her focus and frustrating her efforts. With each belligerent bubble, Lois's frustration grew, her patience dwindling to a perilous precipice.

Determined to complete her delicate task, she toiled on, her mind a tumultuous tempest of conflicting emotions. The once-peaceful pursuit had transformed into a battle against both the belligerent, boiling koi and her own burgeoning belligerence. The cacophony of the cascading chaos was a cruel contrast to the serene silence she had sought.

Her once-steady hands trembled, her vision blurred by a growing sense of despair. She longed to escape the cacophonous confines of the koi pond's vicinity, but a perverse sense of pride compelled her to persevere. The doily, a symbol of serenity and sophistication, seemed to mock her with its delicate defiance against the discordant din.

As the minutes ticked by, Lois found herself on the brink

of a breakdown. The boiling water, once a source of life, now seemed a malevolent force, intent on destroying her sanity. With a final, desperate effort, she forced herself to focus, her mind a fortress against the onslaught of noise. And then, as abruptly as it had begun, the chaos ceased. The koi pond had quieted, the water returning to a serene stillness.

Exhausted but triumphant, Lois completed her task, her hands trembling slightly as she admired her handiwork. The doily, now adorned with its foil embellishments, was a testament to her determination and resilience. As she looked at her creation, she felt a sense of peace wash over her, a calm that had been shattered by the cacophony but was now restored. The ordeal had been a crucible, testing her strength and revealing her inner fortitude.

3. A boisterous, boisterous boy named Roy enjoyed noisy exploits with his noisy toys. Roy's favourite? A box of ten noisy, coiling Slinkys! Roy, with a mischievous grin, would hoist himself into a rickety, old stool, his ten fingers poised to unleash the chaotic joy of the Slinkys.

   Down they'd go, ten shiny, metallic serpents, boinging, coiling, and clanging their way down the rickety steps. The noise! Oh, the glorious, glorious noise! A symphony of clanging, boinging, and coiling that echoed through the boisterous boy's boisterous house. Downstairs, Roy's poor, stoic grandmother, enjoying a moment of quiet with her cup of chamomile tea, would jolt upright, her face a mask of worried disapproval.

   "Roy!" she'd bellow, her voice a beacon of order amidst the metallic chaos. Roy, ever the charmer, would peek his head around the corner, a mischievous glint in his eyes, a single, shiny Slinky dangling from each finger like ten metallic question marks. "Just enjoying my toys, Grandma!" he'd declare, his voice dripping with mock innocence.

Undeterred, Roy's grandmother would embark on a mission – to foil the noisy Slinkys. Armed with a worn-out, but sturdy, cloth shopping bag, she'd ascend the rickety steps with surprising agility. With a practised swoop and a determined glint in her eye, she'd scoop up the remaining Slinkys, their metallic forms disappearing into the depths of the shopping bag.

Roy, momentarily defeated, would stare longingly at the now-empty bag, a silent promise of future Slinky-filled escapades forming in his mind. His grandmother, with a satisfied sigh, would settle back into her armchair, the quiet house a testament to her victory, at least until Roy unearthed another noisy delight for his next boisterous exploit.

CHAPTER 31: INSANE GR-CENTRIC TONGUE TWISTERS

Prepare to embark on a grueling linguistic gauntlet in **gritty gr's**. Here, you'll encounter a formidable forest of formidable phrases, each fraught with fricative fervour. These gnarled and grotesque grammatical constructs are designed to galvanise your vocal cords and gyrate your grey matter. Expect to grapple with guttural sounds and grapple with the complexities of the English language. This is not merely a matter of generating glib gibberish; rather, it's a rigorous regimen to refine your rhetorical repertoire and reinforce your resilience. So, gird your loins, gather your grit, and get ready to grapple with the greatest linguistic challenge yet.

1. Grizzled grizzlies, gargantuan and gruff, grumbled and groaned as they traversed the gnarled terrain. Their gargantuan appetites necessitated a gruelling quest for sustenance. Grasping at green grasses and grubbing in the gravelly ground, they exhibited a grim determination to satisfy their growling stomachs. Their guttural growls echoed through the gloomy glade, a grating and ghastly sound that galvanised the ground-dwelling creatures into a state of guarded vigilance.

   In stark contrast to the solitary, solitary grizzlies,

gregarious grackles gathered in great, noisy groups. Their grating, gravelly calls were a cacophony that grated on the nerves of even the most grounded and patient individual. These gregarious gatherings of grackles were a grievous grievance to the groundskeepers, whose green grounds were subjected to a relentless barrage of bird-brained behaviour.

With a gluttonous gusto, the grackles descended upon the grounds, their greedy grasps plucking at the precious grains. The groundskeepers, their patience gradually giving way to growing irritation, grew increasingly grumpy as they grappled with the grackles' gluttony. Their green grounds, once pristine and perfectly groomed, were gradually being transformed into a graceless, grain-deprived wasteland.

The battle between the beleaguered groundskeepers and the brazen birds became a daily drama, a grotesque spectacle of nature versus nurture. The groundskeepers, armed with only their grit and determination, fought valiantly to protect their green domain. The grackles, with their guile and numbers, seemed to grow bolder with each passing day.

2. A gargantuan gathering of disgruntled individuals congregated at the grotesque garage sale, their greedy grasps yearning for the glittering gewgaws on display. The garage, a grim and grimy graveyard of discarded goods, was a grotesque gallery of unwanted items. Greta, the grumpy guardian of the garage, glared at the growing throng, her grievances growing with each passing moment.

The grasping guests, a grotesque group of greedy individuals, grabbed at everything in sight, their grumbling growing louder with each passing minute. Greta, growing increasingly irritated, gritted her teeth and glared at the growing chaos. The garage was gradually transforming into a ghastly, gaping maw of consumerism.

As the sun began its gradual descent, the gathering grew more desperate. The greedy guests, their patience growing thin, began to grapple with each other over the remaining goods. Greta, growing weary of the whole affair, began to dream of a tranquil, green garden, far removed from the grotesque spectacle unfolding before her.

Finally, the garage was emptied, a ghastly graveyard of discarded cartons and crumpled bags. Greta, with a groan of relief, began the grim task of cleaning up the gruesome mess. As she gathered the garbage, she couldn't help but feel a growing sense of gratitude that the ordeal was over.

3. Grocer Greg's grin gleamed generously as he greeted graphic designer Gillian rummaging through the grocery aisles. Groaning softly, Gillian grumbled about a grotesque green and grey grotesque gargoyle gracing a new graveyard brochure with a gruelling deadline. "Grim, grotesque gargoyles?" Greg guffawed. "Graphic design can get gruesome at times, Gillian?" Gillian glared. "Precisely, Greg! Green grapes, Greek yoghurt, grapefruit, and granola bars, please, and quickly!"

Greg, grabbing a gigantic green grocery cart, guided Gillian through the labyrinthine aisles. Green garlands, grated ginger, grotesque green gourds, and grapes galore filled the cart. Greg, ever the enthusiastic salesman, even grabbed a grubby green grinding stone. "Green grinding stones for that extra gritty graphic texture, Gillian?"

Gillian grimaced. "Absolutely not, Greg! Get grilling supplies instead!"

Reaching the grilling section, Greg procured ground lamb, gruyère cheese, and gourmet sausages. Gillian gasped. "Ground beef, not gourmet, and green peppers, not greasy sausages!" Greg chuckled good-naturedly, replacing the sausages with green peppers. As Gillian meticulously selected groceries, Greg regaled her with tales of gregarious greengrocers from bygone eras, their gruff greetings, and their guaranteed green-thumbed gardening tips. Gillian, momentarily captivated by the grocer's gregarious grin and grandfatherly charm, almost forgot about her grotesque gargoyle deadline.

At checkout, the cashier, a gruff fellow named Gruff Grunt, greeted them with a grumpy grunt. "Green groceries galore," he grumbled as he scanned Gillian's haul with a practised eye. "Going green for graphic design?" Gillian sighed. "Just fulfilling a green graphic guru's grilling grocery list," she muttered. As they left, Greg, hefting the green grocery cart with a groan, declared, "Green groceries guarantee graphic greatness, Gillian! Now, how about grilling some grouper for good measure?" Gillian, defeated but with a hint of a smile playing on her lips, simply shook her head.

CHAPTER 32: INSANE QU-CENTRIC TONGUE TWISTERS

Embark on a curious expedition through a labyrinth of language in **quirky qu's.** This chapter is a quintessential quarry of convoluted constructions centred on the capricious character q. Prepare to question your quotidian quietude as you grapple with quirky quandaries and quixotic queries. Within these pages, you'll discover quaint curiosities and questionable quotations that will unquestionably quicken your cognitive capacities. So, quit questioning and quickly quench your curiosity with these convoluted concoctions.

1. Queen Quigley, quite a quirky queen, embarked on a questionable quest for quaint, quiet quarters. Her kingdom, once quiet and quaint, was now quite chaotic due to a quarrelling quorum of quarrelsome knights. She quickly quit the clamorous castle, seeking solace in secluded seclusion.

   Her quest led her to a questionable quarry, where she encountered a queer quarryman. Despite his questionable quarryman qualities, he proved quite helpful, quickly querying the queen about her quest. With a quick wit, Queen Quigley explained her quandary, and the quarryman, quite curiously, suggested a quiet cottage in the quaint countryside.

The cottage was a quiet haven, perfect for pondering her predicament. As she pondered, she realised the problem wasn't as insurmountable as she thought. With a quick change of plans, she devised a questionable, yet quite cunning, strategy. Returning to the castle, she quelled the quarrelling knights with a quick, quiet ultimatum: quit quarrelling or quit the castle.

The knights, quite taken aback by the queen's quiet but firm command, quickly quieted down. The castle was once again tranquil, and Queen Quigley returned to her cottage, content in the knowledge that her quest had been a qualified success.

2. Quentin, a quilting conservator of unparalleled renown, received a peculiar package – a dusty, intricately stitched quilt rumoured to possess a hidden history. Its arrival sent a thrill through the usually composed Quentin. The quilt, a kaleidoscope of curious squares crafted from an unknown fabric, emanated an undeniable mystique. With a practised eye, Quentin quickly discerned the fabric originated from Quebec, its intricate stitching hinting at a bygone era's exceptional craftsmanship.

Quentin meticulously documented the quilt's provenance, his curiosity piqued by the presence of peculiar quatrains – four-line poems – delicately stitched along the borders. These cryptic verses, he surmised, were more than mere decoration; they offered a tantalising glimpse into the life and customs of the quilt's maker. Intrigued, Quentin embarked on a quest to decipher their meaning, venturing beyond the confines of his workshop.

His journey led him to the quaint villages of Quebec,

where he consulted with cultural experts and weathered textile historians. Together, they poured over dusty archives and faded photographs, deciphering the archaic language of the quatrains. Slowly, like a tapestry coming to life, a captivating narrative began to unfold. The quatrains, once unravelled, revealed a story of resilience – a tale of a close-knit community celebrating a bountiful harvest despite a harsh winter. This discovery transformed the quilt from a mere textile into a window into a bygone era, imbuing it with immense value beyond its exquisite craftsmanship.

News of Quentin's success spread like wildfire through the quilting community. Museums clamoured for the opportunity to exhibit the quilt, but Quentin, ever the custodian of history, refused. Instead, he spearheaded a painstaking restoration project, ensuring the quilt's story – and the artistry of its anonymous maker – would be preserved for generations to come.

CHAPTER 33: INSANE VE-CENTRIC TONGUE TWISTERS

Embark on a verbal voyage through intricate tongue twisters centred on the **veiled ve sound**. These challenges demand vocal verve and mental vigour. Expect velveteen alliterations and veracious wordplay. Let's venture forth!

1. Veronica's monumental, meticulously curated archive, a veritable vault of vanished ages, miraculously withstood the vicious, violent invasion, preserving invaluable, irreplaceable vestigial artefacts from previously undocumented, primordial civilisations. Her vigilant valour and the vault's verdant, vibration-dampening fortifications were vital in safeguarding these vestiges of antiquity. These extraordinary relics, unearthed from the enigmatic epochs of yore, offer unprecedented insights into the enigmatic existence of our earliest ancestors, promising to revolutionise our understanding of human origins and evolution. Encased within the archive's verdant depths, these artefacts are a testament to the tenacity of human spirit, enduring against the ravages of time and the brutality of invasion. Their preservation is a pivotal victory for the pursuit of knowledge, ensuring that the echoes of the past will continue to reverberate through the corridors of time, inspiring

future generations of explorers and scholars.

2. Five bold, burrowing voles, venturing valiantly through the vibrant, vehicular vortex, evaded vicious, voracious wolves with verve while vigilantly delivering velvety, verdant leaves to voraciously starving calves. Their valiant voyage, a testament to their tenacity and tactical acumen, was a vital victory for vegetation and a crucial contribution to the survival of the succulent-seeking, starving young. This daring deed, demonstrating the diminutive creatures' determination and dexterity, has become a celebrated saga, inspiring countless tales of triumph against adversity and igniting a fervent fascination with the fauna of the field. Beyond their immediate impact, these intrepid rodents have become emblematic of the indomitable spirit found in even the smallest of beings, showcasing the power of perseverance in overcoming seemingly insurmountable obstacles. Their story serves as a vibrant reminder of the intricate interconnectedness of all life, demonstrating how the actions of a few can ripple through an ecosystem, fostering balance and ensuring the continuation of the delicate tapestry of nature.

3. Beloved, bold Oliver, a veritable virtuoso of the vast, volatile waters, bravely battled the vehement, vengeful waves, diving deep into the cavernous cove to retrieve seven scintillating, surviving starfish from the cove's massive, mysterious reserves. This audacious aquatic adventure was a testament to Oliver's unwavering will and unparalleled prowess. His perilous plunge into the perilous depths, where pressure and darkness converged, was a feat of extraordinary endurance. Emerging victorious, Oliver's valiant venture was a vital victory for marine conservation, ensuring the survival of these

stellar sea creatures. His heroic haul has since become the stuff of legend, inspiring countless courageous souls to explore the enigmatic ecosystems beneath the ocean's surface.

4. Every naive, unsuspecting native unquestioningly believed the clever, cunning raven's deceitful, deceptive narrative about the elusive, enigmatic vine's purportedly curative properties. The raven, a master of manipulation, wove a web of whispered wonder, cloaking the vine's venomous, virulent nature in a veil of verbal veracity. The raven's velvety vocalisations, a symphony of seductive sounds, lured the unsuspecting into the vine's verdant, treacherous trap. This verdant villain, a viperous vegetation, was a veritable vortex of venomous vitality, capable of vanquishing even the most vigorous of victims. The naive natives, their minds muddled by the raven's mesmerising mirage, ventured forth with unwavering faith, ultimately falling victim to the vine's insidious influence. This tragic tale serves as a poignant parable, cautioning against the perils of unchecked credulity and the importance of critical thinking.

5. Vivian, a visionary inventor with a mane of vibrant violet hair, ventured into her five-story laboratory. The air crackled with creative energy, buzzing with the whir of gears and the soft glow of strategically placed ultraviolet lamps. Five valves, vital for reviving her most marvellous, malfunctioning machines, lay scattered on her velvet workbench. Each machine, a marvel of Victorian engineering adorned with intricate brass gears and polished copper pipes, was shrouded in a layer of dust, remnants of years spent in slumber.

"Fear not, my mechanical marvels!" Vivian declared, her voice echoing through the cavernous space. A determined glint shone in her violet eyes as she surveyed the challenge before her. With a flourish, she swept a velvet glove across the workbench, the gesture a silent summons to her ever-reliable assistant, Kevin.

"Kevin," Vivian boomed, her voice cutting through the rhythmic hum of the laboratory, "delivering five velvet visors with utmost haste! We wouldn't want a rogue puff of valve vapour venturing into our vital visages, would we?"

Kevin, a young man with a mop of unruly brown hair and a thirst for knowledge that rivalled Vivian's own, nodded fervently. He scurried across the polished metal floor, his footsteps echoing in the vastness of the laboratory, and returned moments later with the requested visors.

Vivian, visor firmly secured, approached the first machine. Its intricate gears, once gleaming, were now coated in a film of grime. Undeterred, she set to work, her movements practised and precise. Valves were meticulously replaced, each one a perfect fit. Gears were painstakingly degreased and relubricated, their metallic surfaces regaining their former lustre. Levers, once frozen in time, were lovingly lifted and lowered, coaxing the machine back to life.

Following this pattern, Vivian tackled each machine in turn. The laboratory slowly filled with the symphony of reawakened invention: the rhythmic whir of gears, the satisfying hiss of steam, and the gentle clinking of metal against metal. Finally, with a triumphant heave, Vivian pulled the final lever on the last machine. The room pulsed with renewed energy as the machine roared to life, its mechanical heart beating once more.

Vivian, a wide grin splitting her face, raised her velvet-gloved fist in the air. "Another inventive endeavour achieved!" she declared, her voice filled with the satisfaction of a challenge overcome. The laboratory, once filled with dormant potential, now hummed with the vibrant energy of creation, a testament to Vivian's unwavering spirit and inventive genius.

CHAPTER 34: INSANE URE-CENTRIC TONGUE TWISTERS

This chapter presents a sophisticated exploration of phonological complexity centred on the **treasure ure sound**. Readers will encounter intricate linguistic structures designed to challenge articulation and fluency. These exercises are intended to refine enunciation and enhance verbal dexterity.

1. Pure, potent manure, meticulously manipulated and masterfully merged with mineral-rich marl, served as the cornerstone of an agricultural revolution, securing an unprecedentedly bountiful harvest and ensuring unbridled joy for the mature, methodical farmer. This unparalleled utilisation of often overlooked organic matter ushered in a new era of sustainable, self-sufficient agriculture, transforming barren, unproductive land into fertile, flourishing fields.

   The farmer's innovative approach, a testament to his unyielding pursuit of agricultural advancement, garnered widespread acclaim and inspired countless cultivators to embark on similar endeavours. As news of his extraordinary success spread far and wide, a global movement towards regenerative agriculture emerged, characterised by a profound respect for the earth's resources and a commitment to producing nutrient-dense food.

The once-humble farmer became a revered figure, his name synonymous with agricultural ingenuity. His legacy extended far beyond the boundaries of his farm, as his pioneering spirit ignited a passion for holistic land management and inspired the development of innovative farming practices. The world witnessed a resurgence of rural communities as young people, drawn to the promise of a sustainable livelihood, returned to the land.

The transformation was nothing short of miraculous. Degraded ecosystems began to rejuvenate, biodiversity flourished, and the overall health of the planet improved. The farmer's initial success story had blossomed into a global movement, demonstrating the power of one individual to catalyse positive change on a planetary scale. His journey serves as an enduring inspiration, reminding us that even the most humble of resources can be harnessed to create a more sustainable and prosperous future for generations to come.

2. Ten trembling tourists, their tenacity tested by a tempestuous Tuesday, tentatively tackled the treacherous "Twister and the Treasure" trial. This tumultuous ordeal, a torturous test of their tolerance for the unexpected, was a terrifying torment. The twisting, turning tunnel, a labyrinthine passage illuminated by flickering, fearsome flames, plunged them into a profound state of panic. Their hearts pounded in their chests like panicked percussionists, their palms perpetually perspiring.

As they progressed through the perilous passage, each twist and turn revealed tantalising glimpses of treasure, tantalising them with the prospect of prodigious profits.

Yet, the proximity of potential peril prevented them from progressing with purpose, their progress punctuated by paralysing pauses.

Would they emerge from this ordeal unscathed, their spirits unbroken and their pockets plump with precious plunder? Or would they succumb to the sinister secrets lurking within the labyrinth, their dreams of fortune dashed against the daunting dangers of the deep? The tension was palpable, the anticipation agonising.

3. During a routine inventory curation, curator extraordinaire Ms. Purifoy meticulously reviewed a new shipment of obscure artefacts. Ensuring the provenance of each procured treasure was paramount. One particular item, a weathered wooden chest secured with a rusty lock, piqued her curiosity. Rumours of its pure gold contents had preceded its arrival, but Ms. Purifoy, ever the astute professional, remained unsure. Undeterred by the allure of potential riches, she opted for a thorough examination.

With practised precision, Ms. Purifoy donned protective gloves and carefully examined the chest. The humid storage facility did little to obscure the faint musty odour emanating from the aged wood. As she pried open the lock, the rusty hinges groaned in protest, a sound that echoed through the cavernous room. Anticipation hung heavy in the air.

Ms. Purifoy braced herself, then lifted the lid. A gasp escaped her lips. The chest wasn't overflowing with gold as anticipated, but with hundreds of shimmering, iridescent seashells. Their pearly lustre, unlike anything she'd encountered before, captivated her. A momentary disappointment was quickly eclipsed by a surge of professional intrigue. These weren't ordinary shells; their intricate patterns and otherworldly glow suggested a potentially significant historical or cultural origin. Perhaps, she mused, these unexpected treasures held a story yet to be unravelled.

CHAPTER 35: INSANE IGH-CENTRIC TONGUE TWISTERS

The **high igh** combination presents a unique linguistic challenge, as its pronunciation can vary across different words. This section offers a series of tongue twisters designed to help you navigate the intricacies of this sound. Whether it's the long "i" sound as in "high," the diphthong in "sigh," or other variations, these exercises will enhance your ability to accurately produce the "igh" sound in various contexts. Get ready to tackle this linguistic puzzle!

1. Sighing with delight, a child clad in vibrant, thigh-high high-tops, their tiny toes tingling with excitement, tightly gripped the high handlebars of a shiny, silver bicycle, its sleek silhouette shimmering in the sunlight. With each mighty push of the pedals, a symphony of exhilaration echoed through the child's being, as the bicycle accelerated, its tyres humming a rhythmic tune against the tarmac. The wind, a playful accomplice, whipped through the child's hair, creating a whirlwind of joy as they soared past towering trees and vibrant flowerbeds. The world seemed to shrink as speed amplified the child's senses, transforming the ordinary into extraordinary. The once mundane journey became a high-flying adventure, the child's imagination taking

flight alongside the bicycle. With every passing moment, the child ascended to new heights, not just physically, but emotionally and spiritually, leaving behind the weight of the world and embracing the pure, unadulterated thrill of the ride.

2. Highlighting the most prominent and picturesque sights, a writer, their spirit ignited by a fervent passion for prose, delved deep into the labyrinthine depths of their imagination, conjuring captivating compositions about the extraordinary and eclectic array of exciting spectacles that adorned the world. From the vertiginous peaks of majestic mountains, their summits kissed by ethereal clouds, to the abysmal depths of mysterious oceans, teeming with otherworldly creatures, the writer's mind was a boundless canvas, teeming with vibrant hues, intricate details, and evocative imagery. With each deft stroke of the pen, a new world was brought to life, a realm where dreams took tangible form and reality blurred with fantasy. The writer's heart, a fervent furnace of creativity, was ignited anew with each revelation, each discovery, each extraordinary sight that ignited their imagination. The insatiable desire to share these vivid visions with the world propelled the writer forward, their fingers dancing across the page with a fervour that belied the quietude of their surroundings. In this solitary pursuit, the writer found solace, fulfilment, and a profound connection to the world around them, their words a bridge between the extraordinary and the ordinary, inviting readers to embark on unforgettable journeys of the mind.

3. Lieutenant Higgins, a rising star amidst the prestigious ranks of fighter pilots, embarked on a daring training mission amidst the ethereal expanse of the stratosphere.

High above the world, his cerulean eyes narrowed in concentration as he meticulously calibrated his targeting sights. A squadron of five rival MiG fighters, their pilots visibly fuming over Lieutenant Higgins's exceptional reputation, tightened their flight formations in a desperate attempt to outmanoeuvre him. These rivals, though boasting mightier jets bristling with high-tech weaponry, were no match for Lieutenant Higgins's piloting prowess. His nimble F-18 fighter danced through the sapphire canvas of the sky, an enigmatic enigma against the brilliant sunlight. His lightning-fast reflexes and intuitive understanding of his aircraft defied expectations, leaving his rivals trailing in his contrails like bewildered gnats.

Suddenly, Lieutenant Higgins spotted a critical sight – a malfunctioning weather satellite on a collision course with a vital civilian communications relay. The stakes had just skyrocketed. With a split-second decision, Lieutenant Higgins executed a series of daring manoeuvres, his fighter screaming in protest as he weaved through a treacherous asteroid field, a legacy of a bygone celestial collision. The rival pilots, caught off guard by this unexpected turn of events, could only watch in awe as Lieutenant Higgins, with nerves of steel and a sigh of exertion, nudged the malfunctioning satellite off course just moments before impact. Back at mission control, amidst a flurry of activity and flashing lights, the exercise director, his voice thick with emotion, declared Lieutenant Higgins not just the victor, but a true hero. His victory, a testament to the gruelling high-intensity training regimen he'd endured, echoed through the halls, inspiring a new generation of aspiring pilots. News of his triumph, along with his heroic act, spread like wildfire, igniting a passionate fire within countless young minds who dreamt of soaring through the endless blue, replicating Lieutenant Higgins's mastery of the skies and his unwavering commitment to protecting life, both military and civilian.

CHAPTER 36: INSANE TH-CENTRIC TONGUE TWISTERS FOR BOTH VOICED & UNVOICED

This chapter delves into the complexities of the **th sounds**, a frequent stumbling block for non-native English speakers. We'll navigate the nuances between the voiced and voiceless "th," often represented orthographically as "th" and "th." These sounds are produced by placing the tongue between the teeth, with subtle adjustments in airflow determining the voiced or voiceless quality. Through a series of carefully crafted exercises, you'll develop the precision and control necessary to confidently produce these challenging phonemes. Whether you're aiming to eliminate lisping tendencies or simply refine your pronunciation, this chapter offers a comprehensive approach to mastering the "th" sounds.

The Voiced "th" Sound:

1. With thunderous pronouncements, the youthful thespians rhythmically thrummed their theologies, thrillingly thrashing through their theatrical Thursday throngs. Their thespian thunder echoed throughout the theatre, their thoughtful thespian talents thriving under the theatrical spotlight. The enthralled audience, their emotions thoroughly thrashed, thirsted for more theatrical thrills.

Act three, the theatrical pièce de résistance unveiled a wealthy clotheshorse with otherworldly pronouncements. This flamboyant figure, draped in shimmering attire, therapeutically thwarted the thin Duke's dastardly plot to thieve the Queen's precious amethyst trinket. The thin Duke, thwarted in his thievery, threw a theatrical tantrum, his thin limbs thrashing about in a display of theatrical thunder.

The youthful thespians, their thespian talents on full display, thunderously triumphed! The throngs, thoroughly thrilled by the theatrical spectacle, thundered their applause, their voices echoing through the theatre like a chorus of thunder. Thus, the theatrical Thursday evening extravaganza concluded with a resounding success, a testament to the thespians' thrilling thespian talents.

2. With thunderous thumps, Theresa the thoughtful housewife rhythmically stirred the thick Thanksgiving broth, the therapeutic thiamine thoroughly thickening the theatrical concoction. The throaty thrum of the simmering broth echoed throughout the thankful throng's thankful Thursday gathering. Their thankful thoughts swirled with the steam, their thirsting throats yearning for Theresa's theatrical Thanksgiving treat.

The centrepiece, a triumphant turkey, was unveiled with theatrical flourish. This thankful Tom, thoroughly thawed and meticulously marinated, promised a taste of Thanksgiving thunder. Theresa, triumphant in her thoughtful preparation, theatrically carved the bird, the glistening gravy trickling down in a cascade of thankful thrumming.

The thankful throng, their thankful tummies

rumbling, eagerly devoured the theatrical Thanksgiving feast. Theresa, the thoughtful Thanksgiving therapist, tirelessly tended to their thankful needs, her thankful spirit thriving amidst the thankful thundering merriment. Thus, the Thanksgiving Thursday throng's thankful celebration concluded with a chorus of thankful thumps, a testament to Theresa's thoughtful Thanksgiving theatrics!

3. They scoff and sputter, these social butterflies fluttering from soirée to soirée, their whispers laced with envy and a touch of fascination. "The Rothschilds," they coo, their voices dripping with dramatic flair, "bathe in bathtubs overflowing with a thousand thimbles, wouldn't you rather bathe in blissful bubbles?" But can anyone truly say for certain? Perhaps it's a mere allegory, a jab at their supposed extravagant lifestyle. Maybe they bathe in bathtubs sculpted from the finest Italian marble, or perhaps they indulge in a simple shower, the kind enjoyed by the hoi polloi. The truth, like a luxurious bathrobe, may forever remain hidden, a whispered secret exchanged over clinking champagne flutes and caviar canapés. But one thing's undeniable: these rumours, these fantastical tales of thimble-filled tubs, only serve to solidify the aura of mystery that surrounds the ultra-wealthy.

Imagine, if you will, the scene: a grand manor house, its opulent rooms echoing with the distant strains of a string quartet. Inside a lavish bathroom, a bathtub crafted from a single block of jade gleams beneath crystal chandeliers. Does a Rothschild, adorned in a silk robe, recline amidst a thousand thimbles filled with exotic bath salts? Or is it all a grand illusion, a fabrication woven from whispers and speculation? The answer, like the steam rising from a luxurious bath, remains tantalisingly out of reach.

Perhaps the truth is far less exciting. Maybe the Rothschilds, like many of us, simply enjoy a relaxing soak in a hot tub, the gentle bubbles massaging away the day's stresses. Or maybe they prefer a bracing cold shower, a jolt of energy to kickstart their morning routine. The reality, stripped of its fantastical embellishments, might be far less glamorous. Yet, the allure of the unknown persists. After all, wouldn't a simple shower seem mundane compared to the legend of a thimble-filled bath? In the absence of concrete evidence, the rumours continue to swirl, a testament to our enduring fascination with the lives of the obscenely wealthy.

The Unvoiced "th" Sound:

4. The midday sun beat down on the meadow, turning the thistles a dusty silver. A thin thistle thrush, his throat brimming with a repertoire of morning melodies, perched precariously on a slender stalk. Below, a sprawling thicket of thistles bristled with unyielding spines, their sharp points glinting menacingly in the harsh light. The thrush, his brow furrowed in thought for a moment, puffed out his chest and began his song.

"Those thick-headed thistles," he chirped, his voice clear and strong, "think they'll enthral me with their prickly grandeur! But a thin thistle thrush, like myself, finds their roughness rather troublesome. Their attempts at intimidation are nothing more than a bothersome bother." He fluttered his wings, scattering thistle fluff like snowflakes in a summer breeze, and landed on a nearby sunflower. Its golden face, a beacon of warmth and cheer, stood in stark contrast to the thistles' steely demeanour. From his new perch, bathed in the sunflower's golden light, the thrush continued his song. It was a melody filled with the joy of freedom, the sweet defiance of a small creature against a prickly world, and a celebration of the beauty that could bloom even in the most unexpected of places.

The thistles, unfazed by the thrush's bravado, swayed gently in the breeze. Their sharp points continued to glint in the sun, a silent warning to any creature foolish enough to venture too close. Yet, amidst their prickly defences, a single, delicate wildflower bloomed. Its soft petals, a vibrant shade of purple, defied the harshness of its surroundings. It stood tall and proud, a testament to the tenacity of life and the unwavering beauty that could exist even in the most unpromising of places. The wildflower, the thrush, and the thistles - three elements of the meadow, each existing in a delicate balance, a silent story of resilience, defiance, and the quiet beauty that thrives in the wild embrace of nature.

Both Voiced and Unvoiced “th” Sound:

5. Timothy, a tireless tongue twister enthusiast, thumped his chest with theatrical flourish. "Thirty thumbnails!" he declared, his voice thick with excitement. "Thumped thrice upon this very table, a thrilling feat that few can fath!" With a determined glint in his eye, he grabbed a thimble and, with lightning speed, began tapping rhythmically on the tabletop. "One, two, three..." he counted, his brow furrowing in concentration. But as he neared the thirtieth thump, a throbbing sensation pulsed through his teeth. "Thirty!" he finished with a triumphant yell, only to wince and clutch his jaw. His teeth, unused to such a rapid and forceful tapping, throbbed in protest. Timothy, his enthusiasm slightly dampened, sheepishly rubbed his jaw. "Perhaps," he muttered, "thirty thrilling thumps in a row might be a bit too much for these teeth."

   He sighed, defeated, but the cogs in his ever-active tongue twister mind were already turning. "But there's always tomorrow," he thought, a mischievous glint flickering in his eye. "And forty forceful finger taps might just be the next ultimate tongue twister challenge!" However, a flicker of doubt crossed his mind. Forty-finger taps sounded impressive, but was it truly achievable? He envisioned his fingers flying across the table, a blur of motion punctuated by the rapid-fire clicks of his fingernails. The thought sent a shiver down his spine, a delightful combination of anticipation and trepidation. Yet, the challenge was too tempting to resist. Timothy, ever the enthusiast, resolved to embark on a rigorous training regimen. He'd start with a modest ten taps, gradually increasing the number each day. He'd strengthen his finger muscles, improve his dexterity, and prepare his teeth for the inevitable onslaught of clicks. The prospect of conquering the forty-tap feat fueled his determination. He could almost picture the awestruck faces of his friends as he flawlessly executed the tongue twister, his fingers drumming a rapid rhythm on the table. Yes, forty forceful finger taps was a worthy goal, a true testament to his tongue twister prowess. Timothy, a wide grin spreading across his face, grabbed a practice thimble and began his training montage. The rhythmic tapping echoed through the room, a testament to his unwavering dedication to the art of the tongue twister.

6. Thirty thankful thrushes, their throats throbbing with a melody of gratitude, decided to thank the thin Thatcher with a thousand thimbles. These weren't your ordinary thimbles, mind you, but miniature silver ones filled with plump, juicy berries, a delightful offering for the esteemed Thatcher. The thrushes, a feathery flurry of brown and grey, practised their chirps and trills, rehearsing their song of thanks.

But alas, on their way to Thatcher's doorstep, disaster

struck! A sprawling patch of thick thyme, its fragrance heavy in the air, tangled beneath their feet. With a flurry of flustered feathers and frantic flapping, the thrushes tripped and tumbled, their precious thimbles scattering like glittering hail. Disappointment settled over the feathered troupe. Their meticulously planned presentation was in tatters!

Thatcher, alerted by the commotion, peeked out her window. There, amidst the thyme-tangled chaos, she saw the bedraggled thrushes, their tiny chests puffed with a mixture of frustration and apology. Understanding dawned on her face. With a gentle chuckle, she stepped outside and began gathering the scattered thimbles. "No worries, little ones," she said, her voice warm. "The thought is truly what matters." The thrushes, relieved and grateful, chirped their thanks, a melody this time tinged with a touch of sheepishness.

That evening, Thatcher enjoyed a delightful cup of tea, sweetened with a few of the berries the thrushes had so thoughtfully (and clumsily) offered. The thimbles, gleaming on her windowsill, served as a reminder of the day the thirty thankful thrushes, with their good intentions and unfortunate thyme tangle, brought a touch of avian amusement to her doorstep.

7. With a theatrical thunder, Bartholomew, the bothersome brother, threw himself beneath the birch branches, thirsting for a therapeutic Thursday bath. Bertha, bewildered by his bizarre bathing behaviour, bristled, "But Bartholomew, wouldn't bathing by the thick, thorny thickets be both bothersome and brutal?"

Bartholomew, brimming with bravado, scoffed, "Brotherly brawn beats bothersome branches any day! Besides, these birch branches boast therapeutic benefits, supposedly banishing bothersome blemishes and bringing forth breathtaking beauty!"

Bertha, unconvinced, bit her tongue, then muttered under her breath, "Those branches boast bothersome barbs, more likely to bring bloody blemishes than breathtaking beauty!"

Undeterred, Bartholomew brandished a bristly brush, boasting, "Behold, Bertha! This bristly brush battles bothersome bugs before bath time!"

Bertha, bristling at his bravado, blurted, "But Bartholomew, beneath the thickets, those bothersome bugs become a bristling battalion, breathing threats and biting with bothersome brawn! Better bathe by the birch branches, belligerent brother!"

Bartholomew, bewildered by Bertha's brash outburst, mumbled, "Brotherly bonding bested by bothersome bathtime banter? Perhaps Bertha's right..."

With a theatrical sigh, Bartholomew abandoned his bizarre bathing plan, muttering, "Bothersome brother bows to Bertha's brilliance. Birch branches beckon for a less bothersome bath, beneath the benevolent blue sky!"

Thus, the battle of the bathtime location ended, with both Bartholomew's bothersome bravado and Bertha's brilliance bringing forth a breathtaking bath beneath the birch branches! Bathed and bewildered, Bartholomew thanked Bertha with a brotherly thump on the back.

8. A throng of thirty thrilled thrushes, their tiny throats throbbing with thanksgiving, gathered with thunderous theatrics to express their gratitude to the thin Thatcher, a kindhearted farmer renowned for his thyme-infused treats. These feathered thespians, their wings shimmering with an otherworldly iridescence, had meticulously practised a theatrical thanksgiving extravaganza unlike any other.

Their performance? A rhythmic symphony of thimble-tapping, each tiny footfall a testament to their thoughtful appreciation. The plan? To enthral Thatcher with the mesmerising display under the autumn sun. With tireless enthusiasm, they practised the rhythmic clinking of thimbles echoing through the trees.

The day arrived, and the thrushes, their theatrical zeal overflowing, fluttered towards Thatcher's farmhouse. Perched on the windowsill, their tiny throats throbbing with anticipation, they launched into their performance. Hopping from foot to foot, they clinked their silver thimbles in a dazzling display.

But alas, beneath the window lurked an unexpected villain – a thyme-dwelling troll with a thunderous temper! Disgruntled by the racket, the troll emerged from his leafy lair, his voice a guttural bellow that echoed through the crisp autumn air. In a fit of rage, the troll hurled handfuls of pungent thyme, throwing the thimble symphony into utter chaos. Thimbles scattered, feathers ruffled, the once-graceful thespians transformed into a flurry of feathered frenzy.

Startled by the commotion, Thatcher rushed to the window. Witnessing the bizarre scene – a flurry of flustered thrushes dodging airborne thyme, a grumpy troll with a leafy mane – he burst into laughter. To appease the thyme-throwing terror and his thankful avian visitors, Thatcher threw a generous helping of birdseed. The troll, momentarily mollified by the tasty offering, grumbled under his breath before retreating back to his leafy haven.

The thrushes, their hunger pangs temporarily soothed, chirped their thanks, albeit a little sheepishly. Though their theatrical extravaganza ended in a bizarre display of thyme-hurling fury, it remained a testament to their thoughtful intentions and Thatcher's kind heart. As the sun dipped below the horizon, casting long shadows across the thyme-scented fields, a sense of peace settled over the farmyard. The thrushes, their feathers ruffled but spirits high, fluttered away, already chirping about next year's even-more-theatrical Thanksgiving extravaganza.

9. Thirteen thick-thighed thistle gatherers, their thighs throbbing with the aftermath of a brutal uphill trek, huddled beneath the ominous thirteen-thundercloud congregation thundering ominously overhead. Visions of their exquisitely thickened broth, lovingly prepared for this annual gathering, danced tantalisingly in their thirsting throats. Alas, time, the relentless thief, had not been kind to the weathered thatched roofs above. Thinned by years of relentless weather, they provided little defence against the thrillingly thickened torrent about to unleash. With a thrillingly thick crack that echoed through the valley, a sizable section of thatch succumbed, raining a chillingly thin, rain-soaked thatch-thinning down upon the thirsty thistle gatherers and their prized broth.

Disgruntled but not defeated, the thirteen, their thick-thighed determination undimmed, huddled even closer, thick eyebrows furrowed in contemplation. They wouldn't let this thrillingly thickened tragedy thin their spirits or their legendary broth-brewing prowess. A solution, thicker and more robust than the downpour itself, would be found. Perhaps thicker, sturdier thatch could be scavenged from the abandoned barn on the hill, or maybe a generous villager with a thick, cast-iron cauldron could be persuaded to lend a hand. One way or another, their meticulously thickened broth would be salvaged, their thirsting throats soothed, and the symphony of flavours they envisioned would not be silenced by a mere downpour.

The storm raged on, thunder still thrillingly thundering, but beneath the thinning thatch, a thrillingly thick plan began to take shape. Voices, thick with determination, mingled with the drumming rain. One by one, the thirteen thick-thighed thistle gatherers, their thick-skinned resilience on full display, began to delegate tasks. Some, with a swiftness born of years of experience, set about gathering any salvageable broth, while others, their thick-fingered dexterity unmatched, devised a makeshift shelter using the remaining thatch and sturdy branches. Laughter, thick and hearty, eventually rose above the din of the storm, a testament to their unwavering spirit. This thrillingly thickened tragedy, they realised, wouldn't be the end of their annual gathering. It would simply be another thrilling chapter in the legend of the thirteen thick-thighed thistle gatherers, their thirst for adventure and their love for a perfectly thickened broth forever intertwined.

10. Authoritative Barth, a horse-obsessed historian with a penchant for headwear, held a highly-anticipated hullabaloo on a blustery Thursday. He'd invited thirty throngs of history buffs, each clad in hefty helmets, to his sprawling hilltop homestead. Barth, boasting a booming baritone, bellowed a hearty "Huzzah!" as his guests, brandishing hefty hunks of ham, hollered back with enthusiasm.

The highlight? A horse-drawn historical reenactment! Thirty hefty horses, harnessed to rickety replicas of Roman chariots, thundered across the hillside. Helmeted heads bounced, hearty laughter echoed, and hats of every hue flew off in the hullabaloo. Barth, his handlebar moustache bristling with excitement, hollered instructions through a hefty horn. Horses huffed, hooves hammered the hard-packed earth, and the chariots hurtled towards a hay bale finish line.

Triumphant knights, their helmets askew, hoisted heavy trophies made of hefty hocks (pig trotters), the highest honour in Barth's historical hodgepodge. As the hilarity subsided, a hush fell over the gathering. High above, hidden in the hazy heavens, a hot air balloon emblazoned with a historical hero hovered into view. A hidden hatch opened, and a hail of hard candies and history-themed hats rained down upon the happy historians.

Hearts full and hats askew, the throngs of history buffs happily hoofed it homeward, forever hoodwinked by Barth's horse-drawn historical hullabaloo!

11. The salty spray swirled skyward, whipped into a frenzy by a stiff southerly breeze. Atop the weathered lighthouse, perched precariously against a backdrop of churning grey clouds, stood the weathered weather vane. Crafted in the form of a proud pirate ship, its once-gleaming copper hull was now a tapestry of greens and blues, a testament to the relentless assault of the salty air. Yet, despite the ravages of time, the weather vane retained a surprising agility. With a sudden gust, it swivelled with a metallic screech, its weathered figure tracing a graceful arc against the stormy sky. Then, with a theatrical flourish that would put any thespian to shame, it dipped low, its weathered copper hull scraping the salty air. Below, a weathered fisherman named Bartholomew, bundled in a thick woollen sweater that strained against his burly frame, chuckled. "There you go again, matey," he muttered, his voice hoarse from the salty spray and years of bellowing commands at the unforgiving sea. "Always putting on a show, even when there's not a soul to see."

The weather vane, as if in response, dipped its weathered figure once more, then bobbed back up with a flourish, its weathered Jolly Roger flag snapping in the wind like a tattered black tongue. A constant companion to the lonely lighthouse keeper, who spent his days battling the elements and his nights navigating the treacherous shoals by the faint glow of the lighthouse lamp, the weather vane seemed to relish its role as both weatherman and entertainer. Its weathered form, a silent sentinel against the ever-changing moods of the sea, was a testament to the enduring power of the elements and the whimsy of the wind. Perhaps, in its silent dance with the sky, the weather vane found a solace that mirrored the solitude of the lighthouse keeper, both forever bound to their solitary posts, locked in an eternal embrace with the untamed ocean.

CHAPTER 37: INSANE H SOUND-CENTRIC TONGUE TWISTERS

This section is dedicated to refining the articulation of the **h sound**. Through targeted exercises, learners will develop the ability to produce a clear and consistent "h" phoneme. Consistent practice with these exercises will significantly enhance speech clarity and intelligibility.

1. Heaving Harry the hippo, happiest hat hoarder ever, hid hundreds of hand-painted headwear in his humongous hat hut. Hundreds of hilarious hats hung haphazardly, handcrafted with horsehair, hemp, and hibiscus hues. Happy hippos hoping for headwear hunted through Harry's hut, hollering for hidden headgear.

   Hurried Helen, a hat-hunting hippo, huffed and puffed, her hooves hammering the hut's hard-packed floor. "Has Harry hidden a hooded hat for hefty hippos?" Helen hollered hopefully. Harry, hidden amongst the hats, held his breath, hoping Helen wouldn't find his favorite hooded headwear.

   Helen, her hunt unsuccessful, huffed out of the hut in a huff. Harry, heaving a sigh of relief, hung his head, his hat-hiding heart hammering. News of Harry's hidden hat hoard reached hungry hat hunters. Hundreds of hippos descended upon Harry's hut, their hooves hammering a chaotic rhythm.

Harry, overwhelmed by the hungry hat horde, hesitantly flung open the hut's heavy hinges. Hundreds of happy hippos hooted with glee, happily hunting for hidden headwear. Harry, his heart heavy, watched as his hat hoard dwindled. But as the happy hippos hauled away their hand-painted hats, a heartwarming hush fell over the hut.

Harry, humbled by the hat hunters' happiness, decided hat-hoarding wasn't so heavenly after all. He hung his head, a hopeful plan hatching. The next day, Harry, hammer in hand, happily hung hundreds of hooks in his hut. He'd transform his hat hut into a hat-sharing haven, a place for happy hippos to hang out and hanker for headwear whenever they wished.

2. Hurried Harold, a house-hunter with high hopes, hired Heidi, a highly-hyped house-flipper, to handle his haunted house hassle. Heidi, humming happily, hammered holes haphazardly, hoping hidden horrors wouldn't hinder her house-flipping hustle. Harold, horrified by the hammering, held his head, his heart hammering a frantic rhythm.

Suddenly, a hysterical house-elf named Humphrey hopped out of a hidden hollow, holding a harmonica. Harold, heart hammering even harder, hollered, "Heidi, have you hired hysterical house-elves hiding harmonicas?" Heidi, her hammering halted, hung her head, her high hopes for a horror-free house-flip fading fast.

Humphrey, his harmonica held high, hummed a haunting house-elf tune. Harold, horrified, hightailed it out of the house, his hopes for a haunted-house-free home dashed. Heidi, her head hung low, hesitantly followed Harold, hoping he hadn't hired her for her lastfavouritelipping job.

News of Harold's horrifying house-elf harmonica hustle reached hungry house-hunters. Hundreds of hopeful homebuyers, headlamps held high, hunted for haunted houses hidden amongst the happy homes. Heidi, her house-flipping career hanging by a thread, hatched a hopeful plan.

She hired Humphrey, the harmonica-playing house-elf, to help. Together, they transformed Harold's horrifying house-elf haven into a haven for happy house-elves. They hung hammocks for house-elf relaxation, hid harmonicas for house-elf entertainment, and even built a hidden hollow for Humphrey to hum his haunting house-elf tunes.

The house-hunters, hearts pounding with excitement, hunted through the happy house-elf haven, hoping to find a harmonious home. Harold, hearing the news, hesitantly returned. He peeked inside to find Heidi and Humphrey, harmoniously humming a house-elf tune. Harold, his heart filled with hope, hesitantly stepped inside, ready to give his haunted house-elf haven a second chance.

3. Hoarding Henrietta, a hungry hamster with a hefty hidden hoard, hauled hundreds of Hershey's Kisses into her hideaway hollowed from a hollowed-out head of hollowed-out Swiss cheese. Happy hamster helpers hurried behind Henrietta, helping her haul her hefty hoard.

Suddenly, a hefty hound named Humphrey happened

upon Henrietta's hidden hideaway. Humphrey, sniffing hungrily, hoped to happen upon hidden hot dogs. Henrietta, horrified by the hefty hound, held her breath, hoping Humphrey wouldn't happen upon her hidden Hershey's hoard.

Humphrey, his hopeful hot dog hunt unsuccessful, huffed out of the hideaway in a huff. Henrietta, heaving a sigh of relief, hurried her hamster helpers back into the hideaway. News of Henrietta's hidden Hershey's hoard reached hungry hamster hoarder hordes. Hundreds of hungry hamsters hurried to Henrietta's hideaway, hoping to happen upon hidden Hershey's Kisses.

Henrietta, overwhelmed by the hungry hamster horde, hesitantly flung open the hideaway's hollowed-out head entrance. Hundreds of happy hamsters hooted with glee, happily hunting for hidden Hershey's Kisses. Henrietta, her heart heavy, watched as her hefty hoard dwindled. But as the happy hamsters happily hauled away their Hershey's Kisses, a heartwarming hush fell over the hideaway.

Henrietta, humbled by the hamster hoarders' happiness, decided Hershey's hoarding wasn't so heavenly after all. She hung her head, a hopeful plan hatching. The next day, Henrietta, hammer in hand, happily hung hundreds of hooks in her hideaway. She'd transform her hideaway into a Hershey's-sharing haven, a place for happy hamsters to hang out and hanker for Hershey's Kisses whenever they wished.

4. Hurried Henry, a hysterical hypnotist hyped for high hilarity, hurried Hilda the hippopotamus into his hidden hypno-hut. Holding hypnotising hands high, Henry hummed a hypnotising tune, hoping to hypnotise Hilda into hilarious hiccups. Hilda, hefty and hesitant, hoped

Henry's hypnotism wouldn't hurt.

Suddenly, Henry hissed, "Hilda the hippopotamus, hiccup hilariously hundreds of times!" Hilariously hypnotised, Hilda hiccuped! One hiccup. Two hiccups. Three...hundred hiccups later, Hilda halted, hyperventilating, her hefty belly heaving.

Henry, horrified by Hilda's hiccuping hysteria, hung his head, his hopes for hilarious hypnosis hanging by a thread. Hilda, hiccuping helplessly, hurried out of the hypno-hut, hoping a handful of hay would help.

News of Henry's horrific hippopotamus hiccuping hypnosis hit the headlines. Hundreds of hypno-hopefuls, holding hands and hoping for hilarity, huddled around Henry's hypno-hut. Henry, his hypnotism career hanging by a hair, hatched a hopeful plan.

He hung a huge horseshoe high on his hypno-hut, hoping for a happy hypno-healing henceforth. Henry then hesitantly hypnotised Hilda once more, this time focusing on happy horse races. Hilda, hypnotised anew, hopped out of the hut, hiccups replaced by a happy horse-racing hum.

The hypno-hopefuls, hearts thumping with hope, huddled closer, eager for their turn at hilarious hypnosis. Henry, his head held high, happily hypnotised henceforth, focusing on happy hobbies and hilarious habits. His hypno-hut, once a haven for horrific hiccups, became a happy haven for hilarious hypnosis.

5. Haphazard Humphrey, a heedless hedgehog with a head full of high hopes, hopped haphazardly through a hedge hoping for hidden honeysuckles. Hundreds of hungry hawks hovered hopefully high above the hedge, their hungry eyes hunting for hapless hedgehogs.

Suddenly, Humphrey, his head held high, hopped out of the hedge, heading straight for a hungry hawk hovering hopefully nearby. The hawk, heart hammering, halted its hovering, hoping for a helpless hedgehog lunch.

Humphrey, however, his head held even higher, puffed out his prickly pockets, hoping his prickly points would deter the hawk's hungry hovering. The hawk, hesitant due to Humphrey's prickly presentation, hooted hesitantly, its hungry hovering halted.

Humphrey, heaving a sigh of relief, hopped haphazardly back into the hedge, his head full of happy honeysuckle hunting. The hawk, hungry hopes dashed, hooted in frustration and hungrily hovered higher, hoping for a hapless hedgehog lunch later.

News of Humphrey's harrowing hawk encounter reached hundreds of hedgehogs. Huddling together in hidden hollowed-out hedgerows, the hedgehogs hatched a hopeful plan. They'd headhunt for helpful humans with high-powered hoses.

The next day, hundreds of hedgehogs hiding in the hedges hollered for the helpful humans with high-powered hoses. The humans, happy to help, hurried over, their hoses held high. The hungry hawks, hovering hopefully high above, were helpless against the humans' high-powered hoses.

The hawks, drenched and defeated, hooted in dismay and hungrily hovered away. The hedgehogs, hearts filled with happy hollers, hopped out of the hedges, their honeysuckle hunt a happy success. The hedges, once a haven for hapless hedgehogs, became a happy haven for hundreds of honeysuckle-hunting hedgehogs, forever safe from hungry hawks and high-powered hoses.

6. Huddled Harold, a hairy hedgehog happy in his holey haven, hummed a high-pitched, haunting hymn hidden amongst hundreds of holey hockey pucks. Harold's house, a haven for happy hedgehogs, held hidden hollowed-out logs and heaps of helpful household hints for hiding from hungry hawks.

Suddenly, a hungry hound named Humphrey happened upon Harold's hidden house. Humphrey, sniffing hungrily, hoped to happen upon hidden hot dogs. Harold, horrified by the hungry hound, held his breath, hoping Humphrey wouldn't happen upon his hidden haven.

Humphrey, his hopeful hot dog hunt unsuccessful, huffed out of the house in a huff. Harold, heaving a sigh of relief, hurried back into his hidden house. News of Harold's hidden haven reached hundreds of happy hedgehogs. Huddling together, the hedgehogs hatched a hopeful plan.

They'd headhunt for helpful humans with high-powered hoses. The next day, hundreds of hedgehogs hiding in the houses hollered for the helpful humans with high-powered hoses. The humans, happy to help, hurried over, their hoses held high.

A hungry hawk, hovering hopefully high above, hoped to happen upon a hapless hedgehog. But with the help of the humans' high-powered hoses, the hedgehogs were safe inside their houses. The hawk, drenched and defeated, hooted in dismay and hungrily hovered away.

The hedgehogs, hearts filled with happy hollers, hurried out of the houses, their high-spirited hide-and-seek a happy success. Harold's house, once a haven for just one happy hedgehog, became a happy haven for hundreds of hedgehogs, forever safe from hungry hawks and high-powered hoses.

7. Huffing Heather, a hiker known for her habanero obsession, hiked uphill, her heart hammering a hurried rhythm against her ribs. Holding a hefty handful of fiery-red habaneros, Heather hoped her hike would help her handle the heat. Hopping hordes of happy hummingbirds hovered hopefully around Heather, their tiny wings whirring.

   Suddenly, a heavy-handed hiker named Hank happened upon Heather's habaneros. Hank, hankering for a hot-pepper handout, held out his hand hopefully. Heather, horrified by Hank's habanero hunger, hesitated, her heart hammering even harder.

   "Have you handled habaneros before, Hank?" Heather hesitantly inquired, hoping to hinder Hank's habanero habit. Hank, head held high, scoffed, "Habitually handle heaps of habaneros, hardly a hindrance!"

   Heather, hesitant no more, held out a single, fiery-red habanero. "Here's one, Hank," she warned, "handle with care!" Hank, happily accepting the habanero, hungrily halved it and popped it in his mouth.

   His face flushed fiery red in a flash! Hank, hiccupping and hopping haphazardly, huffed and puffed, his heart hammering a frantic rhythm. Heather, her habanero handover a hesitant success, hurriedly hiked onwards, her heart gradually calming. News of Hank's habanero hiccups reached hundreds of hungry hikers. Holding hands and hoping for a hot-pepper handout, they hurried after Heather.

   Heather, however, her habanero hoard hidden safely in her backpack, held her ground. "Hot habaneros only for hardened hot-pepper handlers!" she declared, her voice firm. The hungry hikers, hesitant after witnessing Hank's habanero hiccups, happily opted for handfuls of healthy huckleberries Heather offered instead.

Heather, her hike a happy habanero-free success, reached the hilltop, her heart filled with the healthy rhythm of her hike. The view from the top, a haven of happy hikers and healthy huckleberry bushes, was a far better reward than any fiery habanero.

8. Heaving Hector, a hefty hedgehog with a head full of high hopes, hurriedly herded hundreds of hedgehogs behind humongous hats hidden amongst hay bales. Hungry hawks hovered hopefully high above, their hollow eyes hunting for hapless hedgehogs.

Hector, his heart hammering a frantic rhythm, hissed, "Hawks hover hungrily! Hedgehogs huddle here! Hatch a hurl-handfuls-of-hickory-nuts plan!" The hundreds of hedgehogs huddled closer, their tiny heads held high.

Suddenly, a single, silly-looking hawk swooped down, hovering hesitantly a hair's breadth from Hector's hat. Hector, horrified, held his breath, hoping the hawk wouldn't happen upon his hidden hedgehog haven.

The silly hawk, however, held a handful of hickory nuts in its talons. It hesitantly dropped the nuts near Hector's hat, hooted a high-pitched hello, and hovered back up to rejoin its hungry hawk companions.

Hector, heaving a sigh of relief, hesitantly peeked out from under his hat. The other hedgehogs, their heads held even higher, hooted with happy surprise. The silly hawk, they realised, wasn't hungry for hedgehogs, but for hickory nuts!

Hector, hatching a hopeful plan, held up a handful of

hickory nuts for the silly hawk to see. The silly hawk swooped down, happily snatched the nuts, and hooted a high-pitched "Thank you!" before hovering back up to its hungry hawk companions.

The other hawks, hungry for hickory nuts too, followed suit, swooping down, hovering hesitantly, and trading handfuls of hot dogs for handfuls of hickory nuts. The hedgehogs, hearts filled with happy hollers, hurled handfuls of hickory nuts with newfound enthusiasm.

News of the hedgehogs' hickory-nut-hurling hawk-distraction plan reached hundreds of happy hedgehogs. Huddling together in hidden hollowed-out hedgerows, the hedgehogs happily hoarded hickory nuts, forever prepared for hungry hawks with a hankering for high-protein snacks.

9. Henry the Hippopotamus, renowned for his hospitality, hosted a high-society soiree. He'd hired the hottest chefs, ordered heaps of hors d'oeuvres – hot habanero hummus, hickory-smoked hocks, and heaps of honey-glazed halibut. The high-hatted hippo guests hummed with anticipation.

But disaster struck! As Henry hovered over a heaping helping of hors d'oeuvres, a horrifying hiccup erupted from his hefty belly. He tried holding his breath, hoping for a hush, but another hiccup, louder and hoarser than before, echoed through the high-ceilinged hall.

The high-society guests, initially horrified by Henry's hiccupping, stared wide-eyed. Had he devoured a hidden habanero by mistake? Was this a highbrow hippo prank? The tension hung heavy in the air.

Henry, mortified, tried everything to quell the hiccups. He hastily chugged a hefty helping of hibiscus tea, held his breath till his head felt like a hot air balloon, and even attempted a headstand (a hilarious sight for a hefty hippo!). But the hiccups only intensified.

Each hiccup was a hurricane of sound, punctuated by horrified gasps from the guests. Helena, a high-strung hippo known for her herbal remedies, hurried forward. "Hold your breath, Henry," she hollered, "and hum a happy hippopotamus tune!"

With a desperate hope, Henry followed Helena's advice. He held his breath for what seemed like hours, humming a hilariously off-key hippo tune. And then, silence! The hiccups had vanished!

The high-society guests, initially horrified, now erupted in a fit of relieved laughter. Henry, red-faced but relieved, let out a hearty hippo chuckle. The soiree continued, the hiccup incident adding a hilarious twist to the evening. From that day on, Henry swore off habanero hummus and held his hors d'oeuvre portions to a healthy handful, forever haunted by the memory of his high-society hiccup extravaganza.

10. Hundreds of hungry hamsters, tired of their usual handful of hefty sunflower seeds, hatched a hair-brained heist. Their target? Hundreds of hoarded Halloween candies hidden haphazardly within hamster habitats by Herbert, the hapless head hamster handler.

Herbert, a hefty fellow with a heart of gold (and a head full of hay), had hidden the candy hoping to keep the hamsters healthy. But the hamsters, having honed their hunting skills through hours of hidden tunnels and hamster wheel dashes, were determined.

The heist began at the crack of hamster dawn (a time distinguished mostly by the happy hum of hamster wheels). Henry, the head hamster, hopped out of his habitat, his heart hammering with excitement. He hustled to Harold's habitat, a haven of hidden honeycombs and hoarded hazelnut shells. Harold, a hefty hamster with a healthy appetite, handed Henry a hairy helping hand.

Together, they hoisted open Herbert's hidden hatch, revealing a hoard of Halloween delights: heaps of Hershey's kisses, handfuls of gummy worms, and hidden stashes of chocolate bars. With happy hoots, the hamsters hauled the candy back to their habitats, hoping for a hoard-sized Halloween feast.

But alas, their happiness was short-lived! Herbert, awakened by the hooting and hollering, stumbled out of his hay-filled hut. He saw the hamsters, surrounded by sugary treats, their cheeks bulging like tiny hot air balloons.

Herbert, initially horrified, quickly hatched a humane plan. He hurried to the kitchen, humming a happy tune, and returned with a heap of healthy hamster treats – hulled sunflower seeds, juicy carrots, and hidden handfuls of hazelnuts.

The hamsters, initially hesitant, soon forgot their sugary dreams as they happily munched on their healthy feast. Herbert, relieved and a little wiser, decided to hide the Halloween candy in a much higher hollow next year. After all, a healthy hamster is a happy hamster, even if Halloween dreams are a little hard to handle.Helping hippos hop hurdles handicaps Hannah the horse horribly. Huffing and puffing, Hannah hopes her hippo helpers hurry up.

11. Hannah the horse, a hopeful hurdle hurdler, felt horribly handicapped by her hippo helpers. Henry and Henrietta, hefty hippos with hearts of gold, were enthusiastic but entirely unsuited for the task. Hannah huffed and puffed, her hooves tapping impatiently.

"Hurry, hippos!" she whinnied. "Helping me hop hurdles hinders my chances of winning!"

Henry, hoisting a heavy hurdle with a heroic heave, hollered back, "Hold on, Hannah! These hurdles are heavy! Hopping over them with hooves is hard for hefty hippos!"

Henrietta, holding another hurdle haphazardly, huffed, "Helping is how hippos show heart! Hannah, have a happy hop!"

Hannah, her patience wearing thin, highlighted the hazards. "Helping me with hurdles hinders my height advantage! Hopping over them myself is how horses hurdle!"

Just then, Harold, a helpful human happened by. Hearing the hippo hollering and the horse's huffing, he halted his hot dog hawking and hurried over.

"Hold on, everyone!" Harold hollered, his voice a welcome hush amidst the hippo havoc. "Hannah needs a human helper, not hippo helpers. Horses hurdle with hooves, not hefty hippos!"

With a sigh of relief, Hannah hopped off the starting platform. With Harold's help, the hurdles were hastily adjusted to a horse-friendly height. Hannah, finally free from hippo hindrance, took a deep breath and expertly hopped over each hurdle, her hooves leaving a happy hoofprint pattern in the dirt.

As she crossed the finish line, a triumphant whinny erupted from her throat. The hippo helpers, though a little humiliated, cheered for their horsey friend. Hannah, forever grateful for Harold's help, happily munched on a hefty helping of hay, her heart full and her hurdle-hopping handicap a hilarious memory

12. Harold the helicopter, hovering high above a herd of hungry hippos, hunted hotdogs hidden amongst hay bales. His high-powered heat sensors scanned strategically, searching for sizzling sausages. Hundreds of hungry hippos, hats held high, hoped Harold's hotdog hunt happened quickly.

Suddenly, Harold's heat sensors picked up a hidden heat signature! Horrified, he hollered, "Hungry hippos hiding heat-seeking missiles?" The hippos, holding hands and hiding hesitant smiles, hoped Harold wouldn't hover any closer.

Harold, hesitant to hover any lower, hovered high, hoping the hidden heat signature was just a hefty helping of hot sauce hidden amongst the hotdogs. The hippos, hungry and hopeful, held up handfuls of hamburgers for Harold to see.

Harold, happy hamburgers weren't hostile, hovered a little lower. He spotted the heat signature - a hidden hibachi grill, happily heating hefty hotdogs! Harold, his heart filled with relief, hovered down and happily handed out hotdogs to the hungry hippos.

News of Harold's hotdog hunt and the hippos' hidden hibachi grill hit the headlines. Hungry hippos from hundreds of habitats hailed Harold as a hero. Harold, happy to help, hatched a hopeful plan. He'd hover high above hungry hippos henceforth, hunting for hidden grills and hotdogs, forever ensuring no hungry hippo went home unhappy.

Harold's heroic hotdog hunts became legendary. From hippo habitats hidden amongst the Himalayan hills to herds holidaying by hidden Hawaiian beaches, Harold's heat sensors sniffed out sizzling sausages. Hungry hippos everywhere held up homemade signs of gratitude - "Harold the Hero!" "Hippos Love Hotdogs!" "Thanks for the Yum!"

Harold, his heart filled with the happy honks of grateful hippos, continued his hotdog hunts with renewed enthusiasm. He even upgraded his helicopter with handy hotdog holders, ensuring every sausage reached a hungry hippo safely. The hippos, in turn, used their newfound fame to promote hippo-human harmony. They hosted hotdog-eating contests, held hat-wearing hip hop concerts, and even started a line of hippo-themed hotdog stands.

Once a creature of solitude soaring through the skies, Harold became a symbol of hippo-human friendship. And it all started with a simple hotdog hunt, a hidden hibachi grill, and a helicopter pilot with a heart of hotdog-loving gold.

This act of kindness sparked a ripple effect that touched the lives of hippos and humans worldwide. Harold's hotdog hunts became international events, televised live and cheered on by millions. Children everywhere donned pilot costumes and dreamt of soaring through the skies in search of sausages. Hippo chefs became celebrities, their hibachi skills admired and emulated.

The hotdog stands, initially just a way for the hippos to express their gratitude, boomed in popularity. Their bright purple and yellow colours, emblazoned with cartoon hippos holding hotdogs, became a familiar sight on street corners around the world. The stands offered a delicious fusion of hippo and human cuisine, with hippopotamus jerky and hot sauces finding a place alongside the classic hot dog and bun.

The newfound appreciation for hippos extended beyond food. People began to see these once-feared creatures in a new light, marvelling at their intelligence, playful nature, and love of hotdogs. Hippo sanctuaries saw a surge in visitors, eager to learn more about these gentle giants.

Harold, though, remained humble throughout it all. He continued his hotdog hunts, his trusty helicopter a familiar sight in the skies. But for Harold, the true reward wasn't the fame or the fortune. It was the happy honks of the hippos, the smiles on the faces of children, and the knowledge that he had played a small part in bringing humans and hippos closer together, one hotdog at a time.

13. Her Majesty, the Queen, hesitantly held a hairy hermit crab perched precariously on her gloved hand. Hundreds of cheering well-wishers lined the streets, hoping for a glimpse of the royal visit. Suddenly, a horrified yelp escaped the Queen's lips! Clutching an oversized handkerchief to her face, Her Highness hoped her momentary lapse in composure had gone unnoticed.

A helpful royal guard named Harold, ever vigilant, hurried over. "Is everything alright, Your Majesty?" he inquired, his voice laced with concern. The Queen, flustered and flustered, could only manage a hurried nod, the handkerchief muffling any further explanation.

Harold, ever resourceful, scanned the situation. Spotting the culprit - the hairy hermit crab clinging desperately to the Queen's finger - a mischievous glint appeared in his eye. With a quick bow, he produced a beautiful, polished seashell from his pocket. "A happy hermit crab haven, Your Majesty," he announced, gently coaxing the crustacean into its new, more suitable accommodation.

The Queen, feeling a wave of relief wash over her, managed a weak smile beneath the handkerchief. Taking a deep breath, she composed herself and waved regally to the crowd, as if nothing out of the ordinary had transpired.

News of the Queen's hermit crab horror spread like wildfire. Royal commentators and reporters buzzed with speculation, while herpetologists from across the kingdom offered their expertise. The Queen, however, had other plans.

Emerging from Buckingham Palace the next day, a determined glint in her eye, Her Majesty announced a new and rather peculiar addition to the royal greeting protocol. Henceforth, all handshakes with the Queen would be conducted using a.specially designed seashell, ensuring the safety and comfort of any hapless hermit crabs that might find themselves in her presence.

The news sent shockwaves through the nation. Herpetologists, initially bewildered, were soon swept up in the excitement. They collaborated with the royal designers, creating a series of colourful, seashell-shaped handshakes, each a unique and whimsical addition to any audience with the Queen.

The public, ever fond of a bit of royal eccentricity, embraced the new protocol with gusto. Tourists flocked to the palace, eager to experience the seashell handshake for themselves. The Queen, once known for her stoic demeanour, became an unlikely internet sensation, her slightly bewildered expression as she held out the seashell becoming a meme.

More importantly, the Queen's actions sparked a

newfound appreciation for hermit crabs. People began to see these curious creatures in a new light, marveling at their unique shells and solitary lives. Charitable donations to marine conservation soared, and hermit crab-themed merchandise flew off the shelves.

The Queen, through her one small act of hesitant hospitality, had inadvertently fostered a wave of positive change. She had not only ensured the safety of a frightened hermit crab, but had also brought a smile to the faces of millions, and brought the wonders of the natural world a little bit closer to home.

14. Heaving Heidi, her heart hammering a hurried rhythm, hesitantly huddled behind a hundred-year-old haunted house. Hundreds of horrifying howls echoed from hidden hollowed-out halls, horrendous enough to haunt even the bravest hero.

Holding hands with Harold, her hesitant house-hunting companion, Heidi hoped her hiding place held strong. Harold, his head held high (or at least as high as his hammering heart allowed), hesitantly hollered, "Hello, house! Happy haunters here!"

Suddenly, a shadowy figure with glowing green eyes and a horrifying hooked head hungrily hooted from a hidden hole! Heidi, horrified beyond belief, held her breath, her heart hammering a frantic rhythm against her ribs. Harold, however, held his ground, his voice surprisingly steady.

"Hoping for hilarious house-hunters, not horrifying haunters!" he declared. The shadowy figure hesitated, its hooked head held high. "Honest house-hunters here!" Harold continued, his voice laced with hopeful hints.

The shadowy figure peered closer, its glowing green eyes

scrutinizing Harold and Heidi. Then, to their surprise, it hooted a high-pitched, happy hello! "Honest house-hunters, huh?" it boomed in a surprisingly friendly voice. "Hidden hallways hold harmless humorous happenings, happy to have you!"

Heidi, her heart hammering a happy rhythm now, hesitantly stepped out from behind the house. Harold, his fear replaced by hopeful curiosity, followed suit. The shadowy figure, who introduced himself as Humphrey the Headless Housekeeper, led them on a hilarious house-hunt through the hidden hallways.

They howled with laughter as hidden doors swung open to reveal harmless happenings - happy houseplants hiding behind headboards, hollowed-out hatstands holding humorous hats, and even a hidden haven for hungry house-hunting hedgehogs.

Heidi and Harold, their horrifying haunters turned into hilarious house-hunt helpers, happily decided to make the haunted house their home. News of Heidi and Harold's happy house-hunting adventure with Humphrey the Headless Housekeeper hit the headlines. Hundreds of hesitant house-hunters, hearts hammering with a newfound hope, hurried to the haunted house, eager for a hilarious house-hunt of their own. The once-horrifying haunted house became a haven for happy house-hunters, forever filled with harmless humorous happenings, thanks to Heidi, Harold, and their hilarious headless house-hunting helper, Humphrey.

15. Heaving Harold the hypnotist, head held high, held hundreds of hamsters huddled hypnotised. Holding hypnotising hands high, Harold hissed, "Hallucinate hot-air balloons shaped like hamburgers!" The hamsters, helpless against Harold's hypnotic hooey, hallucinated hefty hamburger-shaped hot-air balloons hovering happily high above.

Hundreds of hungry hamsters hopped haphazardly towards the hallucinatory hamburgers, hearts hammering with hope for a high-flying hamburger adventure. Harold, his hopeful plan hatching, hurriedly hung hidden wicker baskets beneath each hot-air hamburger.

Suddenly, the hamsters, hypnotized no more, stumbled and stopped, their hopeful expressions replaced by hungry confusion. Harold, hesitant to hinder their hamburger hankerings, hastily helped them hop into the hidden wicker baskets.

With a hearty heave, Harold hoisted the hot-air hamburger balloons high. The hamsters, hearts hammering with newfound excitement, held onto the wicker baskets tightly. Harold, happy his hypnotic hooey hadn't hindered their hamburger hot-air balloon hopes, happily handed them handfuls of hot dogs – a tasty treat to hold them over until their hamburger hot-air balloon adventure ended.

The hot-air hamburgers, propelled by hidden hot-air hand fans, hovered high above the happy, hot-dog-munching hamsters. News of Harold's hypnotic hot-air hamburger happening hit the headlines. Hundreds of hungry hamsters, holding hands and hoping for a high-flying hamburger adventure, hurried to Harold's haven.

Harold, happy to help, held hypnosis training sessions for other hypnotists. Soon, the sky was filled with hot-air hamburgers, each carrying a basketful of happy, hot-dog-munching hamsters on a high-flying adventure they'd never forget. The once-ordinary field became a haven for happy hot-air hamburger happenings, a place where hamster dreams of soaring through the skies and feasting on giant hamburgers became a delicious reality, all thanks to Harold's hypnotic talents and a whole lot of hot air (and hot dogs).

The craze didn't stop there. News of the hamsters' hot-air hamburger adventures reached intrepid explorers around the world. Inspired by Harold's ingenuity, they began crafting fantastical hot-air balloons in all shapes and sizes. There were hot-air pizzas for the cheese-loving adventurers, hot-air tacos for the spice aficionados, and even hot-air ice cream sundaes for those with a sweet tooth.

The skies became a vibrant canvas of culinary delights, each balloon carrying a happy load of hypnotised thrill-seekers on unforgettable journeys. Harold, once a simple hypnotist, became a legend. He was hailed as the "Father of Hypnotic Hot-Air Gastronomy" and lauded for his creativity and compassion. But for Harold, the true reward wasn't the fame or the fortune. It was the sight of those happy hamster faces, filled with wonder and delight as they soared through the sky in their very own hot-air hamburger. And that, he knew, was a sight that would stay with him forever.

CHAPTER 38: INSANE TONGUE TWISTERS FOR ALVEOLAR PLOSIVES: / T/ AND /D/

Alveolar plosives, /t/ and /d/, are foundational to English phonology. Produced through the occlusion of airflow by the tongue against the alveolar ridge, these consonants significantly impact speech clarity and intelligibility. This section provides targeted exercises to refine the articulation and accuracy of these sounds.

1. Ten determined dwarves darted diligently down dusty tunnels, their tiny pickaxes tapping a rhythmic tattoo against the dry earth. They were toiling on tiny Titan, a miniature world meticulously terraformed by their ancestors, and today's task was crucial. Disastrous downpours threatened to deluge the delicate desert landscape, so the dwarves were digging deep ditches to divert the destructive flow of water. Daylight dwindled, casting long, dramatic shadows across the miniature mountains, and a chill wind whispered through the canyons.

Dusk descended, painting the tiny Titan sky in hues of dusty orange and twilight purple. With a sigh of satisfaction, the dwarves dusted themselves off, their calloused hands a testament to their day's work. They gathered around a crackling campfire, fueled by dried twigs carefully scavenged from the desert scrub. Dinner, a delightful dish of dried dragonflies seasoned with a sprinkle of desert salt and served on flat, heated stones, was devoured with gusto.

Bellies full and spirits high, the dwarves huddled closer to the fire, their faces illuminated by the flickering flames. They discussed their daily duties, their voices low and serious. Their determined leader, a dwarf with a bushy beard the colour of sun-bleached sand, cleared his throat and declared, "Double duty diligently, dwarves! Don't dawdle, dismantle deadwood dams downstream. If those decaying logs remain, the diverted downpours will drown the delicate desert flowers and disrupt the delicate desert ecosystem we've sworn to protect!"

With a chorus of determined grunts, the dwarves rose from their fireside gathering. They donned their sturdy boots, adjusted their tool belts, and grasped their trusty pickaxes. Determinedly down dirty ditches, they dashed, their headlamps casting beams of light through the gathering darkness. They dug double-time, their pickaxes carving channels in the hardened earth, creating a network of bypasses to divert the impending deluge. Ducks, startled by the dwarves' rapid digging, quacked and flapped their wings, dodging the occasional shower of loose dirt as they frantically sought higher ground.

The dwarves worked tirelessly through the night, their only companions the rhythmic clanging of their pickaxes against rock, the mournful cry of a desert owl, and the distant rumble of approaching thunder. Finally, just as the first rays of dawn peeked over the horizon, they finished their task. Exhausted but exhilarated, they stood side-by-side, surveying their work. The diverted water flowed smoothly through the newly dug channels, bypassing the miniature villages and fragile flower beds below.

As the sun climbed higher in the sky, casting its warm light upon the tiny Titan, the dwarves watched with pride. Their hard work had ensured the safety of their miniature world, another day of successful defence against the harsh desert environment. Dusk might bring another threat, another downpour, but these determined dwarves would be ready. They would toil diligently, day and night, to protect their home, their legacy, and the delicate desert ecosystem that thrived under their watchful eyes.

2. Ten tiny tots, teeth tapping a frantic tattoo against translucent toy trumpets, tumbled towards a table overflowing with tempting treats. Towering over them, a thin tin toy train, its tracks twisting and turning like a miniature rollercoaster, toot-tooted teasingly. Tiny tongues tasting tantalizing treats – tangy tarts dusted with delicate sugar crystals, delightful doughnuts glazed with a shimmering sheen, and a terrific tower of tiny tricolour triangles tempting taste buds with a promise of citrus, chocolate, and vanilla.

Determined to delight the tots, their dad, a man with a twinkle in his eye and a talent for turning the ordinary into extraordinary, dusted off a dusty, dented toolbox. Dexterously, he dug deep, disentangling dozens of dazzling decorations – tiny twinkling twinkies strung on shimmering thread, delightful dangling dinosaurs crafted from colourful construction paper, and terrific toy trains in a rainbow of colours, each chugging along miniature tracks held in his calloused hands. Delicately, with the focused concentration of a master artist, he transformed the train from its once-ordinary state into a dazzling delight. The tracks became a glittering boulevard adorned with twinkling twinkies, the engine was adorned with a paper crown fit for a train king, and each carriage boasted a dangling dinosaur, its tiny claws playfully gripping the edges.

The toots of the train transformed into triumphant trumpets as it chugged along the tracks, its colourful cargo a captivating cavalcade for the tots. Tiny tongues tasting treats turned to tiny toes tapping in time with the train's rhythmic journey, their delight a delightful symphony of giggles and joyous shrieks. Dad, his task done, dusted off his dirty hands, a deep dimple in his delighted face, the reward of bringing joy to his children written in the creases around his eyes.

Dinnertime dawned, demanding a detour for delicious delights – a dish of delightful dumplings decorated with tiny twinkling twinkies, each bite a burst of savoury and sweet. The tots devoured their dinner, their tiny tummies full, their tired eyes drooping. Tucked into their tiny twin beds, each adorned with a miniature train mobile crafted from leftover decorations, they dreamt of dazzling trains chugging through fantastical landscapes, delightful decorations dancing in the moonlight, and a day filled with delicious delights and the memory of their dad-made decorations that brought a touch of magic to their ordinary afternoon.

3. Ten tiny tadpoles, translucent and trembling, tightly tied to a tangled clump of tangled teal-coloured twine, tussled together in their tank. Tiny tails thumped, a tap-dancing tattoo against the transparent tank walls. These tadpoles, timid at first, transformed with time. Tenacity took hold, teaching tiny tongues to target tasty treats, transforming their tails to powerful legs, perfect for propelling them through the tank's watery depths.

Days dwindled down to a dramatic dusk. Deep breaths filled tiny lungs, a thrilling transformation taking place. Tails shrunk, shrivelling into tiny stubs, replaced by ten terrific toes, twitching tentatively against the tank's transparent walls. Tadpoles, once timid tremblers, were now terrific toads, their tiny tongues tasting treats with triumphant trills.

Tuesday brought tank-tidying time. The teacher, a determined but tired soul, tapped a timetable to their temple, a testament to their tireless tasks. Tonight, the toads would be transferred to their new terrarium, a verdant wonderland teeming with thrilling things to tackle.

Tentative toes touched the terrycloth towel with a tiny tremor. Trepidation turned to triumphant leaps as the tiny toads tumbled into a world of delights – towering tiger lilies for sunbathing, tangled twigs for tunnelling, and a treasure trove of tasty treats tempting their newly acquired tongues. The terrarium, once quiet, now teemed with a chorus of triumphant trills, a testament to the teacher's tireless training and the tadpoles' thrilling transformation.

But the world outside the tank held dangers yet untamed. Towering tomato plants, once viewed from afar with wide-eyed wonder, now loomed as potential predators. Busy bumblebees, once a source of amusement through the tank's glass wall, buzzed by with a menacing hum. The tiny toads, their confidence momentarily shaken, huddled together under a broad lily pad, their triumphant trills replaced by a chorus of cautious chirps.

The teacher, ever watchful, observed their plight from a distance. With a gentle smile, they tossed a handful of juicy flies into the terrarium. The tiny toads, their primal instincts kicking in, abandoned their hiding place and launched themselves at the unsuspecting insects. A flurry of flicking tongues, a delighted dance of tiny legs, and the flies were devoured in a flash. Hunger sated, confidence restored, the triumphant trills returned, a chorus even louder and more exuberant than before.

The teacher, their heart brimming with pride, retreated from the terrarium. Their job was done. These tiny tadpoles, transformed into terrific toads, were now equipped with the skills and the spirit to conquer the challenges of their new world. The terrarium, once an empty vessel, now hummed with life, a testament to the enduring cycle of nature, the tireless dedication of a patient teacher, and the thrilling leap of faith taken by ten tiny tadpoles as they transformed into terrific toads.

4. Thick-thumbed Dr. Thaddeus, a determined dinosaur detective, donned his dusty diving suit, descending deep down into the dino-data depository. Dozens of dusty disks awaited, each a treasure trove of thrilling, thundering Triassic tracks, terrifying Tyrannosaurus teeth, and tantalising traces of Jurassic jawbones. Deciphering dinosaur DNA demanded diligence, declared Dr. Thaddeus, diving deeper into the dusty depths.

With a practised flick of his thick thumb, Dr. Thaddeus dusted off a disk labelled "Diplodocus Data." Downloading diligently, his digital decoder danced with dazzling displays as it deciphered the ancient DNA code. "Delightful discovery!" Dr. Thaddeus declared, his voice thick with delight. The decoded data detailed a previously unknown dipping mechanism in the Diplodocus's long neck, allowing it to drink from deeper depths than ever dreamed!

Disk after dusty disk Dr. Thaddeus devoured, decoding dinosaur datasets with dazzling dexterity. Triceratops tusks transformed from terrifying weapons into tools for tenderising tough treats. Stegosaurus plates, previously perceived as mere protective padding, were revealed to be intricate heat exchangers, regulating the prehistoric giants' internal temperatures.

Days dissolved into dedicated decoding. Dr. Thaddeus donned his dusty diving suit daily, descending ever deeper into the dino-data depository. The more he deciphered, the more thrilling the discoveries became. These weren't just monstrous movie monsters; they were magnificent marvels of machinery, meticulously designed by Mother Nature herself.

Finally, Dr. Thaddeus, drained but determined, dusted off the final disk. Labelled "Tyrannosaurus Rex," it promised to be the most thrilling decode yet. With a deep breath, Dr. Thaddeus initiated the download. The digital decoder whirred and clicked, deciphering the data with dazzling speed. Then, a triumphant "Eureka!" erupted from Dr. Thaddeus's lips. The decoded data revealed that the Tyrannosaurus Rex's fearsome roar wasn't just a threat, it was also a complex communication system, allowing these terrifying titans to talk tactics and trumpet territorial triumphs!

News of Dr. Thaddeus's discoveries detonated across the scientific community. Dinosaur documentaries were dusted off and rewritten, textbooks were tirelessly tweaked, and theme parks thundered with thrillingly accurate new dinosaur attractions. Dr. Thaddeus, the determined dino-data decoder, had single-handedly redefined the way we understood these magnificent, monstrous marvels of a bygone era.

5. Ten tired tasters, tongues tingling from a tempestuous tango with a tray of tremendously tart tangerine taffy, trudged towards a table overflowing with tins. Their task: to tirelessly track the texture, taste, and tooth-tearing tenacity of each tiny treat. Two timid tasters tackled the tangerine taffy first, their tongues tingling with the tangy citrus flavour. They declared it too tart, a terrible treat for tender teeth.

   Next, ten tough tasters tested the tropical taffy. This treat, thick and toothsome, threatened to topple their tiny teeth. Disgruntled and determined, the tasters dug deeper into the tin, their tired tongues tasting a trail of treats – tutti-frutti taffy too sweet, tutti-frutti taffy too sour, and a terrible, tasteless taffy tinted a terrifying shade of teal.

   Dejected but determined, the tired tasters continued their task. Tiny taste buds tingled, tongues tapped teeth in a frantic tattoo of frustration. Finally, a delightful discovery danced on their taste buds! This taffy, tinted a tempting shade of tangerine, tasted of tropical treats, tangy yet tolerable for tiny teeth. Triumphant at last, the tasters declared this the top toffee, a testament to their tireless taste-testing techniques.

   The tins of terrible taffy were tossed aside, destined to delight dentists with a terrible treat for toothaches. The top toffee, however, was carefully curated in a special tin, a trophy for their tireless tongues. News of their triumph traveled through the bustling candy company, delighting directors and designers. "Tireless tasters triumph over terrible taffy!" trumpeted the headlines, a testament to the tasters' meticulous methods.

Suddenly, a frantic factory worker burst into the room, his face a mask of worry. "Disaster!" he declared. "The temperature in the taffy-twisting tunnel has gone haywire! All the taffy is turning into terrifyingly tough, teeth-shattering torture!"

With a determined glint in their eyes, the ten tired tasters sprang into action. They weren't just meticulous taste testers; they were taffy troubleshooting titans! Racing to the factory floor, they tirelessly tweaked dials, tightened tubes, and tempestuously tinkered with the temperature controls. Finally, with a triumphant shout, they restored the taffy-twisting tunnel to its proper temperature.

The factory floor erupted in cheers. The directors, eternally grateful for their tireless efforts, declared the ten tired tasters honorary taffy technicians, forever safeguarding the company from terrible taffy and terrifyingly tough treats. And so, the day that began with a tempestuous tango with tangerine taffy ended with the ten tired tasters, their tongues triumphant, forever etched in taffy-testing lore.

6. Ten tiny toes tapped a frantic tattoo on the tattered tablecloth, telegraphing to tired Tom the torment of their tremendous tummies. Dinnertime dawdled, dishes dithered in the dishwasher, driving Tom to distraction. Dad dashed down the dusty driveway, declaring dinner delayed by a dozen dusty deliveries. Disgruntled but determined, Tom dug deep into a dusty drawer, disinterring a tattered deck of dinosaur dominoes. Delightedly, he dealt the dominoes, each depicting delightful dinosaurs devouring delectable dinners.

Tom's tiny toes tapped a slightly slower tempo, tamed

by the thrilling tale told by the tumbling tiles. Tyrannosaurus Rex tore through a tower of tasty triceratops, while the delicate Diplodocus diligently devoured dozens of delicious dandelions. Each domino depicted a delightful dinner devoured, a delicious distraction for Tom's demanding digestive system.

Just as Tom was about to declare defeat and demand a dry slice of toast, a delighted squeal erupted from the doorway. It was Daisy, Tom's younger sister, a tiny terror in a tutu, her arrival heralded by a trail of tinkling toys and triumphant shouts.

The sight of Daisy, all boundless energy and boundless hunger, momentarily distracted Tom from his own plight. He watched, a mischievous glint in his eye, as Daisy torpedoed towards the dominoes, a tiny tornado poised to topple the carefully constructed dinosaur dinner scene. With a lightning-fast reflex, Tom snatched the dominoes away just in time, Daisy's momentum carrying her into a surprised tumble onto the tattered tablecloth.

A moment of stunned silence followed, then both Tom and Daisy burst into giggles, the tension of the pre-dinner wait dissolving into delighted laughter. Dad's dusty delivery duty done, dinner finally arrived. Deliciously displayed on a delightful dish, a dozen delightful dumplings awaited Tom's determined digestion. Devouring them with delightful dispatch, Tom's tummy troubles transformed into triumphant contentment. Daisy, appeased by a plate of perfectly pink pasta shaped like playful pigs, settled into a satisfied silence, the clatter of her toys replaced by the contented slurping of noodles.

The tattered tablecloth lay forgotten, the dominoes neatly stacked, a testament to Tom's temporary torment, the thrilling triumph of a timely dinner, and the delightful distraction provided by a tutu-clad terror with a penchant for pasta pigs.

7. Ten tired teenagers, tummies rumbling with a tremendous hunger, tipped towards the table, tempted by trays overflowing with tempting treats. But disaster! A towering tide of dirty dishes deterred their delightful dinner. Disgruntled and determined, they decided to demonstrate their domestic duties. Donning dish gloves, they dove diligently into the dishwasher, deftly dodging dripping dishes and dodging dinnerware disasters. Dishes danced and clattered as determined dishwashers declared, "Dirty dishes don't delay delightful dinners!"

Determined dishwashing did the trick. Dishes didn't dare delay dinner any longer. Drained but delighted, the teenagers dried the dishes with dazzling dexterity, their teamwork a testament to their terrific table manners. Dinner, a delightful dish of delicately browned drumsticks and delightful diced potatoes, was devoured with gusto. Dishes deposited diligently in the dishwasher, the teenagers declared their domestic duties done. Delightful dinners, they decided, deserved dedicated dishwashers, and tomorrow, their turn at the table wouldn't be deterred by dirty dishes.

But wait! A bloodcurdling shriek pierced the post-dinner peace. The culprit? A forgotten, festering fruit fly infestation in a forgotten fruit bowl at the back of the counter. The teenagers, their delight dissolving into disgust, donned their dishwashing gloves once more. This time, armed with disinfectant spray and a renewed sense of purpose, they tackled the sticky mess, vanquishing the villainous vermin and leaving the kitchen sparkling clean.

Exhausted but triumphant, the teenagers collapsed onto the couch, their taste buds harbouring the sweet memory of dinner and their spirits buoyed by the satisfaction of a job well done. As they scrolled through their social media feeds, boasting about their culinary and cleaning conquests to their friends, a notification popped up – a reminder for tomorrow night's turn at dishwashing. A collective groan rippled through the room, but it was quickly replaced by a burst of laughter. They knew, deep down, that even though cleaning chores could be tedious, the reward of a delightful dinner and a sparkling clean kitchen was always worth the effort. After all, a little teamwork and a lot of determination could turn even the most daunting pile of dirty dishes into a distant memory.

8. Ten determined diners, tummies delighted after devouring delicious dinners of delicately browned drumsticks and delightful diced potatoes, discussed dirty dishes diligently. Dishes drying depended on dedicated dishwashers, they declared, their voices thick with the after-dinner contentment. But dawn, they knew from bitter experience, often delayed dish duty, duties inevitably delegated to diligent domestics. Dishes delayed delightful desserts, declared the determined diners, their eyes lingering on a plate piled high with tempting tiramisu.

Dropping dusty drapes didn't deter dish duty tonight. Determined diners donned dish gloves, their dexterity displayed as they dove into the dishwater with practised ease. Dishes danced and clattered, a delightful din that filled the kitchen like a rhythmic percussion performance during their dedicated dishwashing duty. Dishes drying demonstrated domestic devotion, declared the diners, their teamwork a testament to terrific table manners.

Plates piled high, gleaming and spotless, stood proudly in the drying rack, a silent salute to their collective effort.

But the battle wasn't over. A quick glance at the kitchen calendar revealed a terrifying truth - tomorrow was "Take a Turn Cleaning the Kitchen" Tuesday. A collective groan rippled through the room, the memory of overflowing bins and sticky stovetops sending shivers down their spines. Yet, even as groans turned into grumbles, a spark of determination flickered in their eyes. They knew, deep down, that even though cleaning chores could be tedious, the reward of a delightful dinner and a sparkling clean kitchen, shared with friends and family, was always worth the effort. After all, a little teamwork and a lot of determination could turn even the most daunting pile of dirty dishes into a distant memory, replaced by the warm glow of a shared meal and the satisfaction of a job well done.

9. Ten tattered textbooks toppled to the table, tumbling Ted towards a terrifying tower of tremendous tomes on tropical turtles. Tongue tied and terrified, Ted tried to twist his toes to topple the toppling terrors, but tripped again, tumbling further towards the teetering turtle towers. Determined to deter disaster, he darted desperately, dodging dusty dictionaries and delicate dinosaur dioramas like a frantic fly fleeing a fly swatter. Dishes danced and clattered, a delightful din as dinner plates dislodged by Ted's desperate dash toppled onto the dining room floor.

Disaster dawned - delightful dinner delayed! Dust devils danced across the disorderly dining room, a testament to Ted's terrible tumbling. Mrs. Tibbit, Ted's ever-patient housekeeper, surveyed the scene with a sigh. "Ted," she said, her voice laced with a hint of amusement, "it appears tropical turtles have taken temporary residence on your textbooks once more."

Ted, sheepishly untangling himself from a tablecloth adorned with a tangled tapestry of tropical fish, could only nod. "Terribly sorry, Mrs. Tibbit," he stammered. "My toes today seem to have a terrible tendency to trip over textbooks!"

A twinkle appeared in Mrs. Tibbit's eye. "Tell you what, Ted," she said, her smile widening. "Why don't we turn this turmoil into a terrific opportunity? While I tidy the toppled tomes and tend to the tumbled turtles, you can tackle those dusty dictionaries. Perhaps you'll even unearth some delightful definitions about diligent disaster prevention?"

With a grateful grin, Ted seized the opportunity. Together, they transformed the turbulent dining room. Ted, armed with a feather duster and a newfound determination, danced a delightful dust-banishing jig around the dictionaries, each swipe revealing a forgotten fact or a fascinating forgotten phrase. Mrs. Tibbit, with practised ease, righted the toppling tomes and relocated the displaced turtles to their rightful shelves.

Dishes dusted and dinner devoured, a delicious dish of delicately crusted cod and delightful dauphinoise potatoes, Ted declared, "Tomorrow, tidy textbooks and tempered toes, I promise!" Mrs. Tibbit chuckled, her eyes twinkling once more. "Tempered toes and triumphant tidying, Ted," she corrected gently. "That's the ticket!"

Exhausted but triumphant, Ted retreated to his room, a newfound respect for textbooks and tempered toes tingling in his tired but tidy body. As he drifted off to sleep, he dreamt of tropical turtles swimming serenely in a sea of sparkling dictionaries, a testament to the transformative power of a little teamwork, a dash of humour, and the importance of keeping textbooks firmly on tables and toes firmly on the ground.

10. Tiny termites, timid at first, transformed into tireless tunnelers, their tiny teeth tapping a frantic tattoo against the thick timber. Treasured trinkets tossed carelessly into the forest floor tempted their tiny tongues. Discarded dice became delightful dental tools, thimbles transformed into terrific toothpicks, and tattered tapestry threads turned into tempting termite treats.

Determined to delight their delightful queen, the termites dug deeper, dodging dusty detritus and delightful dandelions. Day and night they dug, their tiny bodies trembling with the thrill of the task. Dusk descended, draping the forest floor in a dusty twilight, but the determined diggers didn't dawdle. They discussed their duties in hushed, throaty whispers, their tiny torches twinkling like fireflies in the gathering gloom.

Disaster dawned! A dripping ditch, disregarded during their digging frenzy, diverted the delicate dewdrop drainage directly towards their newly built termite tower. Dismay danced in their tiny eyes, their triumphant thumps replaced by a chorus of terrified chirps.

Thinking swiftly, the termites took a daring detour. They dug diagonally, defying the downpour, directing the deluge towards a distant ditch filled with decaying debris. Determined digging delivered delightful deliverance! The diverted dewdrop disaster disappeared, and their delightful dwelling remained dry.

Triumphant trills filled the twilight air as the termites emerged from their daring detour. Ten tiny termites, timid no more, stood tall, their tiny chests puffed with pride. They had transformed once again – from tireless tunnelers to triumphant tide-turners, their teamwork a testament to their termite town's tenacity. The forest floor, glistening with the remnants of the downpour, now held a new kind of treasure – a tiny testament to the termites' terrific triumph against a terrible threat.

But the forest, a place of both beauty and danger, held more surprises in store. As the sun peeked over the horizon, casting its warm light upon the damp earth, a tremor shook the forest floor. A towering tree, its roots weakened by years of neglect and the termites' recent excavations, began to tilt precariously. The termites, sensing the impending danger, scurried back to their underground city, their tiny legs pumping in a frantic flurry.

Chaos erupted within the termite tower. Alarmed alarms echoed through the tunnels, termites tumbling over each other in a desperate dash for the nearest exit. The queen, her royal demeanour momentarily forgotten, squeaked out orders, her voice laced with panic.

Just as the termites braced themselves for the inevitable, the tilting tree met another obstacle – a massive boulder, immovable and eternally vigilant. With a shuddering groan, the tree halted its descent, its branches scraping harmlessly against the termite tower. Relief washed over the tiny termites, their trembling legs giving way as they slumped against the tunnel walls.

Exhausted but exhilarated, the termites emerged from their underground shelter. The forest floor, once again, seemed a peaceful place. But the termites knew better. The forest was a living, breathing entity, and danger could lurk around every bend. Yet, they also knew they were prepared. Their quick thinking, their tireless work, and their unwavering teamwork had seen them through two perilous situations in a single night.

As they surveyed the damage – a slightly tilted tree and a few toppled termite tunnels – a new sense of purpose bloomed within them. They would rebuild, stronger and more resilient than ever before. They would become living testaments to the enduring spirit of the termite colony, a tiny civilisation forever prepared to face whatever challenges the forest might throw their way.

CHAPTER 39: INSANE TONGUE TWISTERS FOR BILABIAL PLOSIVES: /P/ AND /B/ SOUNDS

The **bilabial plosives, /p/ and /b/**, form a foundational component of English phonology. Produced by a complete occlusion of the lips, these sounds are essential for clear and accurate speech. This section will focus on refining the articulation of these phonemes through targeted exercises and drills.

1. Peptic Peter, puffing past a pepper stand piled high with peculiar peppers, couldn't resist. "Perfect!" he proclaimed, puffing out his plump chest. "These peppers pack a punch! Precisely what pesky people deserve!" But Peter, perpetually unprepared, paid poorly for his purchase, leaving him penniless.

   Pondering his predicament, a plan popped into his perpetually plotting mind. "Pepper-painting!" he proclaimed, a mischievous glint in his eye. Packing his pockets with peppers, Peter positioned himself near a park playground, primed to pounce on playful pigeons.

Playful pigeons pecked at popcorn, completely oblivious to Peter's plot. With practised precision, Peter pelted the pigeons with perfectly painted peppers, transforming them into a rainbow-coloured spectacle. People passing by, previously preoccupied with their phones, paused in surprise. Pleasantly surprised by the peculiar, peppered pigeons, they paid Peter a pretty penny for pictures of these feathered friends.

Peter, pockets now plump with profits, puffed out his chest with pride. "Precise planning," he proclaimed, patting his pockets with a satisfied grin, "pays off perfectly, even when peppers are the only payment you possess!"

But Peter's pepper profits were short-lived. As the day wore on, the playful pigeons, tired of being painted projectiles, decided to peck back. With a flurry of feathers and feathery fury, they dive-bombed Peter, peppering him with payback pecks. Peter, propelled by pigeon power, tumbled through the park, his perfectly planned pepper scheme turning into a painful pepper pandemonium.

People, initially amused by the peppered pigeons, now doubled over with laughter at the sight of Peter's predicament. His pants, once pristine, were now a multicoloured mess, a living testament to his failed plan. The pigeons, victorious, perched on a nearby statue, cooing contentedly, their feathers ruffled but their revenge complete.

Peter, defeated and dusted with multicoloured pepper powder, slunk away, muttering under his breath about pesky pigeons and poorly planned pepper plots. As for the painted pigeons, they became local celebrities, their photos splashed across social media. Peter, however, became a cautionary tale, a reminder that sometimes, even the most perfectly planned plots can be peppered with problems.

2. Big, beaming Bob bobbed between bobbing bubbles, balancing precariously on a bright blue blimp. Below, beyond the bobbing bubbles, beautiful black holes beckoned. Bob, a bubbly but bumbling space explorer, bounced with glee. "Bubbles," he boasted, "best way to explore black holes!"

   Bubbles, propelled by Bob's breath, bounced between spaceships, their bright, beautiful colours a stark contrast to the black of space. But Bob, in his bobbing enthusiasm, bumped a button on his blimp. With a burst, the blimp began to deflate, bobbing lower and lower towards the black hole's pull.

   Panic seized Bob. Bubbles, beautiful moments ago, now seemed blunderous. But Bob, ever the quick thinker, grabbed a bucket of blueberries bobbing by his side. Blueberry by blueberry, he popped them into the deflating blimp, the blips of air puffing the craft back up just enough to bob safely away from the black hole's beam.

   Beaming with relief, Bob bobbed back up to the spaceships. "Bubbles," he sheepishly admitted, "brilliant for bouncing, but beware of black holes!" The spaceshippers, previously perplexed by Bob's bubbly black hole exploration, burst into laughter. Bob, the bumbling bubble-bouncing explorer, had become a legend, a testament to the fact that even the most beautiful of plans can burst unexpectedly.

   But space, as Bob was about to discover, held more surprises than black holes and bursting blimps. As he bobbed along, a bulletin blared from his spaceship's intercom. "Beware, Bob!" it beeped. "Asteroid alert! Brace for impact!"

Bob peered out the window. A gigantic asteroid, bigger than any blueberry he'd ever seen, hurtled towards his blimp. Panic surged through him again. But remembering his close call with the black hole, Bob sprang into action. He grabbed a paintbrush and a pot of bright blue paint, the last remnants of his bubble-blowing bonanza. With a flick of the wrist, he painted a giant bullseye on the front of his blimp.

"Brilliant!" he thought, channelling his inner blueberry. "Maybe the asteroid will mistake us for a giant blueberry and bounce off!"

The idea seemed preposterous, but Bob had no better options. He braced himself for impact and squeezed his eyes shut. A moment passed, then another. Bob hesitantly opened his eyes. The asteroid was gone! He looked down and saw the giant space rock bobbing harmlessly beside him, a giant, blue bullseye painted proudly on its side.

Bob, the bumbling bubble-bouncing explorer, had become Bob, the ingenious imposter of interstellar objects. News of his blueberry-inspired plan and asteroid-avoiding antics spread throughout the galaxy. Spaceshippers everywhere bobbed their heads in appreciation, their laughter echoing through the cosmos. Bob, forever changed by his bobbling mishaps and blueberry brilliance, continued his space exploration, a constant reminder that even the most unexpected blunders can become the stepping stones to interstellar stardom.

3. Professor Bob, a plump and portly fellow, proudly presented a peculiar project to his pupils. Perched precariously on a platform, stood a precarious pyramid of brightly colored beakers, each bubbling furiously.

"Behold!" boomed Bob, his voice booming through the brightly lit lab. "These bubbling beakers boast brilliantly coloured bubbles, brewed to bounce back better than boring black balloons!"

But Bob, bless his boisterous buttons, bobbled for a moment, his balance betrayed by a bouncing blue balloon wedged beneath his shoe. The pyramid wobbled, then with a bump! toppled to the table, sending a cascade of colourful concoctions coating the classroom in a sticky, sudsy mess.

Pupils shrieked with surprise as slippery suds splashed their spectacles. Bob, covered in bubbles of every hue, babbled apologies between sputters and spats. But amidst the bubbly bedlam, a bright-eyed student named Billy noticed something peculiar. The colourful bubbles, instead of bursting upon impact, bounced back with surprising resilience.

Intrigued, Billy grabbed a fallen beaker. Inside, a bright blue potion bubbled merrily. He dipped a finger in and blew a small bubble. It bobbed in the air, pulsating with an otherworldly blue light. To his astonishment, the bubble bounced back stronger than any he'd ever seen, defying gravity with a playful pop.

Excitement crackled through the classroom. Professor Bob, sheepishly wiping bubble goo from his brow, beamed with newfound pride. His botched experiment, born from bouncing balloons and bubbling beakers, had birthed a breakthrough in bouncy bubble technology!

News of Bob's blundering brilliance spread like wildfire. Scientists from prestigious universities begged for a peek at his "better-than-balloons" bubbles. Bob, once a bumbling professor, became a celebrated inventor, his bubbling beakers forever a testament to the fact that even the biggest blunders can bubble over with brilliant discoveries.

4. Busy Bobby Brown, a beekeeper brimming with beekeeping bravado, boasted about his beautiful beehives, built by his brilliant brood of buzzing bees. Between blooming blackberry bushes and plump purple pansies, Bobby's bees buzzed busily, bobbing from blossom to blossom, collecting pollen with playful precision. Their plump bodies, dusted with golden grains, were a testament to their tireless work ethic and Bobby's beekeeping expertise.

But Bobby, in his bobbing beekeeping bliss, blundered. He bumped a wobbly bucket brimming with blackberry brine, sending a sticky splatter spraying his pristine overalls. Bees, bewildered by the burst of brine, buzzed in a bewildered ballet around Bobby's bobbing head. He froze, visions of sluggish, brine-drenched bees dancing in his head.

Brushing himself off, Bobby began to babble apologies, his voice barely audible over the buzzing bee symphony. But then, a peculiar thing happened. The brine-splattered bees, instead of becoming sticky and sluggish, seemed to bob with renewed vigour. Their buzzing grew bolder, their pollen-collecting even more precise. They darted between the blossoms with an almost manic energy, their tiny legs laden with an impressive amount of pollen.

Bobby, perplexed but brimming with curiosity, dipped a spare paintbrush in the brine and dabbed a few bees with the purple liquid. The effect was phenomenal! The bees, adorned with tiny purple dots, buzzed with an unstoppable energy, collecting pollen at an unprecedented pace. The hum of their activity rose to a crescendo, a symphony of beekeeping brilliance.

News of Bobby's "buzzing brine" bee-boosting bonanza spread like wildfire. Beekeepers from neighbouring counties buzzed with excitement, their beehives echoing with the agitated chatter of eager bees. Bobby, once a bumbling beekeeper, became a beekeeping legend. Apiary associations across the land invited him to speak at conferences, his presentation slides buzzing with colourful charts and graphs depicting the exponential increase in honey production thanks to his accidental discovery.

Bobby, ever the humble beekeeper, chuckled at his newfound fame. He knew that even the busiest bees can benefit from a bit of an unexpected bob and a surprising splash. After all, sometimes the most brilliant discoveries are born from the stickiest of blunders. And so, Bobby Brown, the beekeeper who stumbled upon a secret by bumping a bucket of brine, became a permanent fixture in beekeeping lore, a reminder that a little bit of bumble can lead to a whole lot of buzz.

5. Big brown Barry, a baker with boundless brownie baking brilliance, balanced a big brown basket brimming with blueberries bigger than buttons. Breakfast for his bakery buddies, he boasted, would be blueberry bonanza! But Barry, bless his busy buttons, bobbed a bit too briskly, bumping a wobbly stool with his basket's bulky belly.

Blueberries bounced, bursting in a beautiful blue blizzard! Barry babbled in dismay, blueberries bobbing between his brown boots. But his bakery buddies, ever the brilliant bunch, didn't break into a panic. Brushing blueberries off their bibs, they began to babble their brilliant plan.

"Blueberry bramble bars!" they boomed, their voices

bubbling with excitement. "Best breakfast bonanza Barry's bakery ever baked!" Busy bakery buddies bustled about, grabbing bowls, whisks, and brown sugar by the bucketful. Soon, the bakery bustled with the beautiful aroma of baking bread, perfectly paired with the plump, bursting blueberries.

By breakfast time, the bakery was a beehive of hungry customers. Barry, his previous blunder forgotten, proudly presented his blueberry bramble bars. The first bite brought blissful babbles of approval. The bars were a brilliant blend of sweet and tart, the blueberries bursting with juicy goodness.

News of Barry's blueberry bonanza bars spread like wildfire. People lined up for blocks, begging for a bite of his bakery's best breakfast ever. Barry, the baker who began with a blueberry blunder, became a baking legend. His bakery bustled with business, a delicious testament to the fact that even the biggest bumbles can bake beautiful breakfasts.

6. Big, blue Bobby bibbled blueberry muffins, balancing precariously on a wobbly barstool. Belly full, Bobby bounced for the back door, but a loose button bounced free from his big, blue button-down shirt. The button bounced, bobbled, and landed right in Bobby's open backpack, burying itself beneath a bunch of bananas.

Bobby, bewildered by the bouncing button, babbled in confusion. "Button bandit?" he mumbled, searching his shirt in vain. But remembering his pressing appointment, he grabbed his backpack and bounced out the back door, the missing button forgotten for the moment.

However, Bobby's bouncing backpack became a bumpy banana bonanza! With every bounce, a banana bounced free, bobbing down the bustling sidewalk, creating a path of yellow peril. People yelped and yowled as bananas bounced off briefcases and bobbed between ankles. A bewildered beagle, chasing a bouncing banana, tripped a busy businessman, sending his briefcase clattering to the cobblestones.

The commotion grew louder, a bouncing banana symphony echoing through the streets. Bobby, blissfully unaware of the banana bedlam he'd unleashed, bounced along, whistling a cheery tune. But then, a particularly bumpy bounce sent his backpack flying. It landed with a thump, spewing forth not just bananas, but the missing button too!

The button, gleaming in the afternoon sun, rolled right to the feet of the bewildered businessman who'd been tripped by the beagle. The businessman, recognising it as Bobby's, scooped it up and raced after the bouncing boy, the beagle hot on his heels.

He finally caught up to Bobby just as he was about to bounce into a bakery. "Wait!" he wheezed, holding out the button. "Your bouncing button bandit!" Bobby, surprised and relieved, thanked the businessman profusely. He quickly sewed the button back on his shirt, a permanent reminder of his bouncing banana bonanza and the importance of a properly buttoned-up button-down.

News of Bobby's bouncing banana bedlam spread like wildfire. The bakery even created a new pastry in his honour – the "Bobby Bouncing Banana Bread," a delicious treat that came with a tiny, edible button decoration. And so, Bobby, the boy with the bouncing button, became a local legend, a reminder that even the smallest of things, like a missing button, can spark the biggest adventures, with a little bit of bounce and a whole lot of bananas.

7. Big, booming Bobby bounced between birthday balloons, begging Betty brightly, "Pick a perfect present, please!" Betty, beaming broadly, bought Bobby a beautiful, bulbous blue balloon, bigger than any Bobby had ever seen. Bobby bounced with glee, but his bobbing became too much for the balloon. With a loud "pop!" the balloon burst, bits of blue raining down on Bobby's bewildered face.

Betty, brow furrowed, battled back tears. But Bobby, ever the optimist, began to babble excitedly. "Best birthday bonanza ever!" he boomed, bobbing around in a blissful blue cloud of balloon bits. "Confetti cannon and birthday crown in one!" Betty, her birthday blues replaced by amused bewilderment, began to brush the blue bits from Bobby's hair.

Suddenly, Bobby noticed a glint of gold beneath the blue. It was the balloon's cap, a tiny crown in its own right! Bobby, grinning from ear to ear, plopped the cap on his head. "Perfect party prize!" he proclaimed, his voice punctuated by pops as he stomped on the remaining balloon bits, pretending they were celebratory fireworks.

Betty, her birthday blues transforming into birthday bubbles of laughter, ruffled Bobby's hair. "Well," she admitted, "that wasn't exactly the present I planned, but seeing your smile makes it the best birthday surprise ever!" Bobby, his heart brimming with birthday cheer, bounced around the room, a blue-dusted but beaming birthday boy with a lopsided crown, a testament to the fact that even a burst balloon can become the best birthday bash, with a little bit of imagination and a whole lot of bounce.

CHAPTER 40: INSANE TONGUE TWISTERS FOR LABIAL PLOSIVES: /P/ AND /B/ SOUNDS

This section focuses on refining the pronunciation of the labial plosives, /p/ and /b/. Formed by the complete closure of the lips, these sounds require precise articulation and release. Engage in these tongue-twisting exercises to improve your control over these essential building blocks of spoken language.

1. Plump Peter Piper, puffing past a pier piled high with peanuts, purchased a paper sack perfectly packed. "Perfect!" he proclaimed, puffing out his chest. "These peanuts will plump up those pesky purple puffins!"

   Peter, perpetually unprepared, paid poorly for his purchase, leaving him penniless. Pondering his predicament, a plan popped into his perpetually plotting mind. "Puffin-painting!" he proclaimed, a mischievous glint in his eye. Packing his paper sack with peanuts, Peter positioned himself near a park pond, primed to pounce on playful puffins.

   Playful puffins preened and preened, completely

oblivious to Peter's plot. With practised precision, Peter pelted the puffins with perfectly peeled peanuts, transforming them into plump, purple projectiles. People passing by, previously preoccupied with their phones, paused in surprise. Pleasantly surprised by the peculiar, peanut-covered puffins, they paid Peter a pretty penny for pictures of these feathered friends.

Peter, pockets now plump with profits, puffed out his chest with pride. "Precise planning," he proclaimed, patting his pockets with a satisfied grin, "pays off perfectly, even when peanuts are the only payment you possess!"

But Peter's peanut profits were short-lived. As the day wore on, the playful puffins, tired of being painted projectiles, decided to peck back. With a flurry of feathers and feathery fury, they dive-bombed Peter, peppering him with payback pecks. Peter, propelled by puffin power, tumbled through the park, his perfectly planned peanut scheme turning into a painful puffin pandemonium.

People, initially amused by the peanut-covered puffins, now doubled over with laughter at the sight of Peter's predicament. His pants, once pristine, were now a peanut-covered mess, a living testament to his failed plan. The puffins, victorious, perched on a nearby bench, preening their feathers and happily munching on the leftover peanuts.

Peter, defeated and dusted with peanut powder, slunk away, muttering under his breath about pesky puffins and poorly planned peanut plots. As for the painted puffins, they became local celebrities, their photos splashed across social media. Peter, however, became a cautionary tale, a reminder that sometimes, even the most perfectly planned plots can be peppered with problems.

2. Peter Piper, a portly puffin patroller, perched precariously on the pier piling. Plump purple puffins puffed out their chests, proudly pecking at Peter's plentiful peanut pile. Peter, puffing his pipe, politely pointed out, "Puffins, please! Play politely. Plenty more peanuts for everyone." The puffins, pausing politely, politely pecked their portions.

Peter, puffing peacefully, picked up a paintbrush. Patiently, Peter painted pictures of plump purple puffins politely pecking peanuts. Proudly presenting the pictures, Peter proclaimed, "Perfect portraits of polite puffins!" Pleased puffins politely preened, their purple plumage shimmering in the afternoon sun.

But Peter's peace was soon disrupted. A booming voice boomed, "Put those pesky puffins in their place, Peter!" Blushing, Peter bowed to Beatrice, the bossy but beloved beach bum. Beatrice believed puffins belonged bobbing on the buoys, not bothering beachgoers. Peter, ever polite, politely protested, "But Beatrice, puffins are part of the pier's charm!" Beatrice, barely budging, barked, "Poppycock, Peter! People pay for peace and quiet, not puttering puffins!"

Peter pondered. Picking up his paintbrush again, Peter painted a picture of Beatrice basking on a beach blanket, a blissful smile on her face, surrounded by happily playing puffins. Beatrice, bewildered, blinked. Peter presented the painting, "Behold, Beatrice! A vision of blissful beach harmony!" Beatrice, touched by Peter's portrayal, finally conceded, "Perhaps puffins aren't so pesky after all." From that day on, puffins pecked peacefully, pictures of Peter's perfect portrayal promoting peace on the pier.

3. Big brown Barry, a baker with boundless brownie baking brilliance, balanced a big brown basket brimming with blueberries bigger than buttons. Breakfast for his bakery buddies, he boasted, would be a blueberry bonanza! But Barry, bless his busy buttons, bobbed a bit too briskly, bumping a wobbly stool with his basket's bulky belly.

Blueberries bounced, bursting in a beautiful blue blizzard! Barry babbled in dismay, blueberries bobbing between his brown boots. But his bakery buddies, ever the brilliant bunch, didn't break into a panic. Brushing blueberries off their bibs, they began to babble their brilliant plan.

"Blueberry bramble bars!" they boomed, their voices bubbling with excitement. "Best breakfast bonanza Barry's bakery ever baked!" Busy bakery buddies bustled about, grabbing bowls, whisks, and brown sugar by the bucketful. Soon, the bakery bustled with the beautiful aroma of baking bread, perfectly paired with the plump, bursting blueberries.

By breakfast time, the bakery was a beehive of hungry customers. Barry, his previous blunder forgotten, proudly presented his blueberry bramble bars. The first bite brought blissful babbles of approval. The bars were a brilliant blend of sweet and tart, the blueberries bursting with juicy goodness.

News of Barry's blueberry bonanza bars spread like wildfire. People lined up for blocks, begging for a bite of his bakery's best breakfast ever. Barry, the baker who began with a blueberry blunder, became a baking legend. His bakery bustled with business, a delicious testament to the fact that even the biggest bumbles can bake beautiful breakfasts..

4. Pip, a picky poppy picker, perched precariously on a purple peak, peered between prickly pebbles. "Perfect!" he proclaimed, plucking a plump, purple poppy. But Pip, perpetually preoccupied with perfect poppies, paid poorly, pocketing pebbles as payment.

Plotting a poppy-painting plan, Pip positioned himself near a park pond, primed to pounce on playful pigeons. Playful pigeons preened and preened, oblivious to Pip's plot. With practised precision, Pip pelted the pigeons with perfectly picked poppies, transforming them into purple projectiles. Public park patrons, previously preoccupied with picnics, paused in surprise.

Pleasantly surprised by the peculiar, poppy-pecked pigeons, they paid Pip a pretty penny for pictures of these feathered friends. Pip, pockets now plump with profits, puffed out his chest with pride. "Precise planning," he proclaimed, patting his pockets with a satisfied grin, "pays off perfectly, even when pebbles are the only payment you possess!"

But Pip's poppy profits were short-lived. As the day wore on, the playful pigeons, tired of being painted projectiles, decided to peck back. With a flurry of feathers and feathery fury, they dive-bombed Pip, peppering him with payback pecks. Pip, propelled by pigeon power, tumbled through the park, his perfectly planned poppy plot turning into a painful pigeon pandemonium.

Public park patrons, initially amused by the poppy-pecked pigeons, now doubled over with laughter at the sight of Pip's predicament. His pants, once pristine, were now a purple mess, a living testament to his failed plan. The pigeons, victorious, perched on a nearby pumpkin, preening their feathers and happily nibbling on the leftover poppy petals.

Pip, defeated and dusted with purple pollen, slunk away, muttering under his breath about pesky pigeons and poorly planned poppy plots. As for the painted pigeons, they became local celebrities, their photos splashed across social media. Pip, however, became a cautionary tale, a reminder that sometimes, even the most perfectly planned plots can be peppered with problems..

5. Big Bill Baker, a blueberry blunderer turned babka baker extraordinaire, balanced a basket brimming with blueberries bigger than buttons. Breakfast for his bakery buddies, he boasted, would be a blueberry bonanza! But Bill, bless his busy buttons, bobbed a bit too briskly, bumping a wobbly stool with his basket's bulky belly. Blueberries bounced like bouncy blue marbles, bursting in a beautiful blue blizzard! Bill babbled in dismay, blueberries bobbing between his brown boots.

But his bakery buddies, ever the brilliant bunch, didn't break into a panic. Brushing blueberries off their bibs, they began to babble their brilliant plan. "Blueberry babka!" they boomed, their voices bubbling with excitement. "Best breakfast bonanza Bill's Bakery ever baked!" Busy bakery buddies bustled about, grabbing bowls, whisks, and brown sugar by the bucketful. Soon, the bakery bustled with the beautiful aroma of baking bread, perfectly paired with the plump, bursting blueberries.

By breakfast time, the bakery was a beehive of hungry customers. Bill, his previous blunder forgotten, proudly presented his blueberry babka. The first bite brought blissful babbles of approval. The babka was a brilliant blend of sweet and tart, the blueberries bursting with juicy goodness, their bursts of flavour a delightful contrast to the buttery, flaky dough.

News of Bill's blueberry babka bonanza spread like wildfire. People lined up for blocks, begging for a bite of Bill's Bakery's best breakfast ever. Bill, the baker who began with a blueberry blunder, became a baking legend. His bakery bustled with business, the delicious aroma of blueberry babka a constant reminder that even the biggest bumbles can bake beautiful breakfasts, with a little help from brilliant friends and a sprinkle of blueberry magic..

6. Plump plumber Pete, perched precariously on a pipe, pumped perfectly pink paint with practised precision. Painting pretty polka-dots on perfectly painted pipes, Pete puffed out his chest in pride. "Precise planning prevents poor piping!" he proclaimed, patting his pockets full of plump pennies.

But Pete, perpetually preoccupied with perfect pipes, paid poorly for his paint, pocketing pebbles as payment. Pondering his predicament, a plan popped into his perpetually plotting mind – "Public pipe portraits!" he proclaimed. Pete positioned himself near a park playground, primed to pounce on playful pigeons.

Playful pigeons pecked at popcorn, oblivious to Pete's plot. With practised precision, Pete painted the pigeons with perfectly pink polka-dots, transforming them into peculiar, pink projectiles. People passing by, previously preoccupied with their phones, paused in surprise. Pleasantly surprised by the peculiar, pink-painted pigeons, they paid Pete a pretty penny for pictures of these feathered friends.

Pete, pockets now plump with profits, puffed out his chest

with pride. "Precise planning," he proclaimed, patting his pockets with a satisfied grin, "pays off perfectly, even when pebbles are the only payment you possess!"

But Pete's pink-painted pigeon profits were short-lived. As the day wore on, the playful pigeons, tired of being painted projectiles, decided to peck back. With a flurry of feathers and feathery fury, they dive-bombed Pete, peppering him with payback pecks. Pete, propelled by pigeon power, tumbled through the park, his perfectly planned painting plot turning into a painful pigeon pandemonium.

People, initially amused by the pink-painted pigeons, now doubled over with laughter at the sight of Pete's predicament. His pants, once pristine, were now a pink-speckled mess, a living testament to his failed plan. The pigeons, victorious, perched on a nearby pumpkin, preening their feathers and happily pecking at leftover popcorn.

Pete, defeated and dusted with pink paint powder, slunk away, muttering under his breath about pesky pigeons and poorly planned painting plots. As for the pink-painted pigeons, they became local celebrities, their photos splashed across social media. Pete, however, became a cautionary tale, a reminder that sometimes, even the most perfectly planned plots can be peppered with problems..

7. Peter Proudfoot, plumber extraordinaire, puffed with pride at his perfectly painted pipes. Pipes snaked through the spotless sub-basement, a symphony of shiny, recently renovated steel. Peter, perpetually prepared, pulled on his pink painting pants, pockets plump with perfectly paired paintbrushes. Precisely positioned pumps pushed pink paint flawlessly, Peter's practised hand guiding the vibrant flow. Patterns pirouetted on the pipes - polka dots, playful stripes, and even a few playful puppies prancing in perfect pink.

Suddenly, Peter's peaceful painting was punctuated by a piercing pop! A pipe, neglected in a previous project, had burst, spewing a geyser of grimy, grey goo. Peter, peeved but undeterred, puffed out his chest. "Plumbing perils!" Peter proclaimed, promptly pulling on his protective pink plastic pants. With practised precision, Peter plugged the pipe, patiently patching the pesky leak.

Finally, peace returned. Peter, pink paint-splattered but pleased, surveyed his handiwork. The pipes, once perfectly painted pink, now boasted a unique blend of patterns and patches. A testament, Peter thought, to a plumber's perseverance in the face of plumbing problems. With a final pat on the patched pipe, Peter packed up his paints, prepared for the next plumbing predicament..

8.Busy Bobby Buoys, building brilliant blue buoys by the bay, balanced precariously on a bobbing boat. Below them, bobbing brightly, a bulbous blue bottle bobbed back and forth, bumping between bobbing boats. "Beware!" boomed Bobby, his voice booming through the bay. "Bobbing bottle! Big trouble!"

But Bobby's booming bellow bobbed unheard over the bobbing boats. Bump! The bottle bounced off Bobby's boat, spilling a bubbly blue goo that bobbed all around him. Bobby, bewildered by the bubbly blue mess, began to babble in dismay. "Brilliant blue blunder!" he blubbered, his boots bobbing in the blue goo.

But Bobby, ever the resourceful buoy builder, didn't break into a panic. Brushing blue goo off his bib, he began to babble a brilliant plan. "Bubbly buoy polish!" he boomed, his voice bubbling with excitement. "Best bobbing brilliance ever!" Busy Bobby grabbed a bucket and a brush, bobbing between the boats, collecting the blue goo.

Soon, Bobby's boat became a bobbing vat of blue goo. He dipped his brush and began to polish the buoys, transforming their dull blue into a brilliant, bubbly blue. Boat owners, initially bewildered by the blue goo, began to babble with delight. Their boats, once ordinary, now bobbed brilliantly in the bay.

News of Bobby's bubbly brilliance spread like wildfire. Boat owners from neighbouring bays bobbed their boats over, begging for a touch of his blue goo magic. Bobby, the bobbing buoy builder turned bubbly buoy polisher, became a legend of the bay. His boat, forever marked with a faint blue shimmer, became a reminder that even the biggest blunders can bob up into brilliant business opportunities, with a little bit of Bobby's buoyant .

9. Big, blustery Bill, a brave but bumbling botanist, balanced precariously on a bumpy brown mountaintop, bundled in a bright blue parka. Below, beautiful blooms boasted brilliant colours, but a blizzard brewed on the horizon. "Blast!" Bill bellowed, bracing himself against the blustery wind. "Blizzards burying blooms before I can begin breeding!"

Bill, ever the brilliant botanist, babbled a backup plan. Balancing a basket brimming with bulbs, he began bobbing between the blooming beauties, babbling a botanical bonanza. Busy Bill buried bulbs beneath bushes, hoping to outsmart the blizzard's blanket of white.

But Bill, bless his botanical buttons, bobbed a bit too briskly, bumping a boulder with his basket's bulky belly. Bulbs bounced like bouncy blue marbles, burying themselves beneath random rocks and reeds. Bill babbled in dismay, bulbs bobbing between his brown boots. "Botany blunder!" he blubbered, bewildered by the bulbous bedlam.

But Bill, ever the resourceful botanist, didn't break into a panic. Brushing dirt off his bib, he began to babble a brilliant plan. "Beautiful springtime surprise!" he boomed, his voice bubbling with botanical excitement. "Imagine the blooms popping up in unexpected places next spring!"

Bill, his previous blunder forgotten, proudly envisioned a mountainside bursting with blooms in unusual spots, a testament to his botanical brilliance. News of Bill's "blizzard-beaten-bulb-bonanza" spread like wildfire. Botanists from neighbouring mountains bobbed their heads in approval, their faces flushed with excitement. Bill, the bumbling botanist who began with a blizzard blunder, became a botanical legend. His mountaintop, forever marked with a mosaic of misplaced blooms, became a reminder that even the biggest blunders can blossom into beautiful surprises..

CHAPTER 41: INSANE TONGUE TWISTERS FOR VELAR PLOSIVES: /K/ AND /G/ SOUNDS

This section focuses on refining the production of the **velar plosives, /k/ and /g/**. These consonants are articulated through a complete closure of the soft palate by the posterior portion of the tongue. Exercises will target precise placement and release of these phonemes to enhance clarity and intelligibility.

1. Cracking knuckles, keen Kate kicked off her colourful canvas creation course, carefully constructing countless canvases kept perfectly coordinated. Keen-eyed students, captivated by Kate's colourful creations, kept asking countless questions. "Keep calm, crew!" Kate chuckled, kicking a kicked-over kickstand clattering across the concrete.

   Confused students kept asking, "Can kelly kettles keep kicking kettles?" Kate, keeping her cool, kicked the kicked-over kickstand countless times, causing countless clicking sounds. "Kickstands kick kettles, kettles keep kicking back!" Kate cackled, kicking the kickstand into a corner.

Suddenly, a gust of wind kicked open the classroom door, causing colourful canvases to crash and clatter. Kate, keeping her composure, calmly commanded, "Crew, keep calm! Carefully collect canvases!" Keen students kicked colourful canvases carefully into a colourful pile. Kate, kicking the kicked-over kickstand one last time, chuckled, "Colorful chaos creates character-building challenges!"

The students, giggling at Kate's kickstand kicking calamity, carefully collected canvases, their creative spirits kicking into high gear. News of Kate's colourful canvas chaos and creative kickstand kicking spread like wildfire. Soon, aspiring artists kicked down the door of Kate's course, eager to conquer colourful chaos and create countless colourful masterpieces.

2. Greg, a grinning green giant with gargantuan gardening gloves, grabbed his gigantic green goo gun. Grinning goofily, Greg gushed gloriously green goo, giggling as it gracefully glided onto gigantic gourds growing in his garden. Gigantic green goo gurgled gleefully, glistening in the golden glow of the afternoon sun.

Suddenly, a gust of wind kicked Greg's gigantic green goo gun, causing gooey green geysers to gush gloriously in all directions. Greg gasped, goggling as gigantic globs of green goo grappled his gardening gloves, glueing them together. Giggling geese, gossiping on the garden gate, goggled at the gooey green Greg.

Struggling and sputtering, Greg grabbed a gigantic green gourd and gingerly gouged a gap in its gleaming green gut. Grunting with glee, Greg grasped the gooey green gourd, giggling as it gurgled green goo gloriously, gracefully guiding the goo back onto the gigantic green canvases.

The geese, their gossiping forgotten, gaped in glee at Greg's green gooey glory. As the sun began to set, Greg, grinning goofily, gazed at his glistening green garden, a testament to his giggling green gooey gardening gaffe turned glorious green masterpiece.

3. Kick-crazy Kenny, a curious kid with ketchup-colored kicks, kicked a curious, kicking comet across the cosmos. Kenny cackled with glee, kicking the kicking comet countless kilometres, causing cosmic chaos. Confused constellations clustered closer, comets coughing in a coughing cloud.

   Confused creatures on countless colourful comets called out, "Kenny, kicking comets kicks cosmic calamity our way!" Kenny, keeping his cool, kicked countless coughing comets carefully into a colourful cluster. "Kicking comets keeps kicking comets calm!" Kenny cackled, kicking the kicked comet one last kick.

   Suddenly, a grumpy, glowing green guardian of the galaxy grabbed Kenny by his ketchup-colored kicks. "Kicking comets creates catastrophic consequences!" the guardian boomed. Kenny, keeping his composure, calmly commented, "Curious kicking keeps cosmic creatures curious!"

   The guardian, giggling at Kenny's curious kicking, gently guided him back to his own curious, ketchup-coloured planet. News of Kenny's cosmic kicking chaos spread like wildfire. Curious creatures across countless colourful comets kicked countless curious objects, keeping the cosmos curious and kicking.

4. Giggling Gary, a goofy green galactic guide, glided gracefully in his gigantic green gas-guzzling glider. Grinning goofily, Gary guided gigantic groups of giggling green guests across the glimmering galaxy. Glowing green gas trailed gracefully behind his gigantic green craft, giggling guests gasping at the glorious galactic sights. Spotting a colossal cluster of colossal comets casting curious, colourful contrails, Gary announced, "Gigantic green goody giveaway approaching!" The giggling guests shrieked with glee, their excitement echoing through the glowing green gas clouds.

   Suddenly, a grumpy, glowing green grouch guarding a gigantic gas giant glared at Gary's gigantic green gas guzzler. "Guzzling gas guzzlers gobble up galactic gas!" the grouch grumbled. Gary, grinning goofily, countered, "Giggling guests generate good galactic glee!"

   The grumpy grouch grumbled, "Giggling guests gobble up gigantic gobs of galactic goodies!" Gary, keeping his cool, countered, "Giggling guests generate generous galactic gratitudes!" The grouch, grudgingly giggling at Gary's goofy game of words, grasped a gigantic glowing green goody and granted Gary's giggling guests a gigantic goody bag each.

   Giggling guests gobbled up gigantic gobs of galactic goodies, their glee echoing across the galaxy. The grumpy grouch, no longer grumpy, began to giggle along. News of Gary's gigantic goody giveaway spread like wildfire. Giggling green guests from countless galaxies guffawed with glee, eager to join Gary's goofy galactic grub crawl. Soon, Gary's gigantic green gas-guzzling glider became a familiar sight across the cosmos, its glowing green gas trail a beacon for giggling green gourmands.

One particularly enthusiastic group of giggling guests hailed from a glistening green gas planet populated by polka-dotted gourmets. They guzzled gobs of Gary's galactic gummies with gusto, their polka-dotted bellies jiggling with joy. Another group, hailing from a grumpy grey asteroid belt, were initially guarded. However, after Gary gifted them gigantic bags of giggling green grapes, their grumpy grey frowns turned upside down.

News of Gary's galactic gastronomic generosity even reached the grumpy grouch guarding the gas giant. The grouch, now a giggling green gastronome himself, greeted Gary with a gigantic green grin and a gift basket overflowing with glistening green grapes, gooey green gummies, and giggling green ginger candies. Gary, his grin wider than ever, offered the grouch a goody bag overflowing with galactic goodies from across the giggling green galaxy.

From that day forward, Gary's gigantic green gas-guzzling glider became a symbol of galactic goodwill and gastronomic glee. Giggling green guests, polka-dotted gourmets, grumpy grey asteroid inhabitants, and even grumpy green gas giant guardians – all united by their love of Gary's goofy guiding and generous galactic grub crawls.

5. Keen Kate, kite kingpin extraordinaire, kept countless colourful cardboard containers crammed in her cluttered kingdom. Kids kicked around with chaotic energy, clamouring for kites like chattering kookaburras. Kate, kind and keen as ever, knelt kindly amidst the colourful cardboard chaos. With crackling concentration, Kate crafted colourful contraptions. Cardboard cut carefully with a keen karambit (curved knife), colourful kites took captivating concrete form. Keen Kate kicked kites kicking high, a kaleidoscope of colour kissing the clouds. Kids ki-yiied with kicking glee as their kites danced in the küchtig (cool) summer breeze.

One particularly curious kid, Kevin, kicked his kite a little too keenly. The kite, caught in a tricky thermal, kicked and coughed its way into the cosmos. Kate, never one to back down from a kite challenge, kicked off her shoes and with a mighty kingfisher-like leap, grabbed a hang-glider from the rafters. Kickstarting the engine, Kate rocketed into the sky, kicking after Kevin's kite.

The journey was gnarly. Gigantic gas giants loomed large, and glistening galaxies glittered all around. Kate, gripping the hang-glider with gusto, kicked and glided with grace, dodging giggling gremlins guarding galactic gates. Finally, after a gruelling trek through the cosmos, Kate caught up to Kevin's kite. With a gentle kick and a kind "kugelblitz, come kindly," Kate coaxed the kite back on course. Together, they rocketed back to Earth, kicking through the atmosphere with kite-flying glee. Landing with a soft thud, Kate and Kevin knew this was a kite adventure they'd never forget. From that day on, Kevin kicked his kites with a newfound respect, and Kate, the kite kingpin extraordinaire, continued to craft colourful contraptions that kicked joy into the cosmos.

6. Gleeful Greg, the gigantic green gargoyle guarding the gigantic green graveyard, gripped a gigantic green glass goblet gleefully. Grinning goofily, Greg gathered gigantic green glass goblets, gleaming gloriously in the golden glow of the graveyard gate. Gigantic green ghosts, giggling goofily, ghosted through the graveyard, gossiping about Greg's gigantic green glass collection.

Suddenly, a grumpy green ghoul guarding a gigantic green gateway glared at Greg's gigantic green glass goblets. "Glass goblets gobble up graveyard grass!" the grumpy ghoul grumbled. Greg, grinning goofily, countered, "Gigantic goblets gleam gloriously, good for graveyard ghosts!"

The grumpy ghoul grumbled, "Gigantic goblets gather gigantic green goo, gross for graveyard ghosts!" Greg, keeping his cool, countered, "Gigantic goblets gleam green, good for ghostly gatherings!" The ghoul, grudgingly giggling at Greg's goofy game of words, grasped a gigantic green garden rake and began raking gigantic green grass into gigantic green piles for Greg's gigantic green goblets.

Giggling ghosts gobbled up gigantic green goblets of graveyard goop, their glee echoing through the graveyard. The grumpy ghoul, no longer grumpy, began to giggle along. News of Greg's graveyard goblet giveaway spread like wildfire. Giggling green ghouls from countless graveyards guffawed with glee, eager to get their gigantic green goblets gleaming gloriously.

7. Curious kittens, kingdoms of claws unleashed, clambered cleverly across countless clean kitchen windows. Keen kitty eyes coveted plump, juicy goldfish gliding gracefully in glass globes. Giggles gurgled from gleeful Gloria, the giggling cook, grasping a gigantic green granny-smith apple for the greedy gang.

Suddenly, with a clumsy clatter, Kiki, the kingpin of the kitten crew, knocked a crystal cake stand cascading to the counter. Crystal clattered, cupcakes crumbled, and clouds of cocoa powder coated the curious kittens in a comical catastrophe. Gloria, gasping, grabbed a gigantic dishcloth and gently gathered the giggling, green-tinged gremlins.

While the kittens contentedly contended with clumps of clinging cocoa Katrina, the kitchen cat, casually strolled in. Keenly eyeing the cupcake carnage, Katrina casually snatched a scattered strawberry shortcake, strategically sauntering past Gloria with a nonchalant flick of her tail. Gloria, chuckling, decided a kitty council was clearly called for.

Gathering the curious crew around a cosy, cushioned basket, Gloria knelt carefully. "Keen kitties," she began kindly, "kitchen capers can cause countless catastrophes. Can we cultivate cooperation in the kitchen?" The kittens, captivated by Gloria's calming words and the promise of purrfectly delicious treats to come, all clambered curiously into the basket, a furry truce declared.

From that day forward, the kitchen witnessed a curious transformation. The kittens, no longer clumsy culinary critics, became Gloria's gleeful sous chefs. Clambering cleverly onto cute, custom-built cat platforms, they offered keen critiques on canapés, curiously contemplated cookie cutters, and gently guarded the goldfish from any greedy paws. Gloria's kitchen, once a site of comical catastrophes, became a haven of happy harmony, filled with the contented purrs of curious kittens and the delicious aroma of culinary creations.

8. Gregarious gardener Gus, gifted with gargantuan green thumbs, gleefully groomed gigantic green gardens. Glorious greenhouses glowed generously, glistening with glistening grapes, gigantic gourds, and grinning gourmets grinning goofily at Gus. Gigantic green glass windows granted glimpses of gorgeous greenery, a green galaxy gleaming gloriously. Gus, grabbing gigantic gardening gloves, grasped a glistening green garden hose, gently gushing gallons of glistening groundwater.

Suddenly, a giggling gaggle of geese, guardians of the gorgeous greenery, gandered grumpily at Gus, their goggling eyes gleaming with goosey disapproval. Gus, grinning goofily, grabbed a gigantic green watering can, generously gushing glistening groundwater elsewhere.

The geese, their grousing grumbles gradually replaced by gratified gobbles, gobbled gratefully at the glistening green goodness. Gus, gratified by the geese's grateful gobbles, continued his gardening gig, gleefully grooming the gigantic green gardens.

One particularly glorious day, Gus decided to cultivate a gargantuan pumpkin patch. Gigantic gourds, guarded by grinning gourmets, began to grow grotesquely, giggling gleefully at Gus's green-garbed gardening glory. The geese, gobbling gleefully on glistening grains scattered by Gus, occasionally goggled in disbelief at the grotesquely growing gourds.

Weeks later, Gus's gargantuan pumpkin patch was a glorious green and orange spectacle. Gigantic gourds, some as big as grinning gourmets themselves, gleamed golden in the glorious sunshine. Gus, grinning goofily with gargantuan glee, decided to throw a gigantic garden gathering.

Geese, gobbling gratefully on gigantic grains of golden corn, gossiped excitedly with grinning gourmets about Gus's gargantuan garden bounty. Gus, grabbing a gigantic carving knife, gleefully got to work on his gargantuan gourds, transforming them into grotesque grinning jack-o'-lanterns, glowing gloriously in the gathering gloom.

The garden, once guarded by grumpy geese, became a haven of gregarious gatherings. Gus, his gargantuan green garden thriving, continued to cultivate glorious greenery, gargantuan gourds, and goofy grins, forever grateful for the geese's grateful gobbles and the gourmets' goofy grins.

9. Cracking eggs with practised ease, keen kitchen crew Kevin and Kate cooked countless kilos of colourful kale. Kettles cackled, coffee cupped in calloused hands, keeping the kitchen crew keenly focused. Crisp, colourful kale crackled as Kate carefully coaxed it with a gigantic wooden spoon. Kevin, king of the kitchen counter, kneaded kilos of sticky, saffron-coloured cookie dough, humming a cheerful kitchen carol.

Suddenly, the kitchen door creaked open, revealing a gaggle of giggling girls, grandkids eager for after-school treats. Kate, kindness radiating from her kind eyes, grabbed a gigantic mixing bowl, generously gifting the girls gobs of glistening green goo – the leftover gooey goodness from the glorious green goop.

The girls, giggling uncontrollably, gleefully grabbed gorgeous green globs, giggling as they grappled with the gooey green mess. Kevin, chuckling at the girls' green-gooed glee, quickly whipped up a batch of gigantic ginger cookies, their golden goodness a welcome contrast to the green.

The kitchen, once calmly controlled by the keen kitchen crew, became a whirlwind of giggly girls, gobs of green goo, and the glorious aroma of golden ginger cookies. Kate, keeping her cool with kind commands, coached the girls on careful cookie construction, guiding giggly gloved hands in gentle circles.

Moments later, the girls, grinning from ear to ear, proudly displayed their gooey-green-trimmed, golden-gingerbread masterpieces. Kevin, his heart filled with grandfatherly glee, gathered the girls around a gigantic, gooey-green-splattered table, a haven for cookie decorating.

With glistening green frosting, glistening gumdrops, and gigantic handfuls of glittering sprinkles, the girls transformed their cookies into grotesque green ghouls, goofy grinning ghosts, and glorious green-trimmed gingerbread gardens. The kitchen, once keenly fragrant with colourful kale, became a haven of giggly girls, grotesque green cookies, and the glorious glee of grandparents and grandkids creating culinary chaos together.

10. Gleeful grape growers, Gus and Gertrude, guarded gigantic green grapes growing gloriously on gigantic green vines. Giggling goofballs, they gossiped about glistening grapes, guessing their gargantuan girth. Gus grabbed gigantic gardening gloves, gently guiding giggly grape clusters towards golden gratings. Gertrude, grinning goofily, grasped a gigantic green watering can, generously gushing glistening groundwater.

Suddenly, a gaggle of geese, guardians gone greedy, gobbled at the glistening grapes, their goggling eyes gleaming with grapey glee. Gus, groaning in grief, grabbed a gigantic green garden gnome, glaring grumpily at the geese. Gertrude, giggling uncontrollably, grabbed a gigantic garden hose, gushing glistening groundwater with grumpy goose-gobbling gusto.

The geese, grumbling about grumpy gnome glares, gobbled gratefully at the glistening groundwater geyser. Gus, grinning goofily once more, continued guarding the gigantic green grapes. Giggling goofballs once more, Gus and Gertrude gossiped about glistening grapes, grateful for the geese's grateful gobbles.

One particularly glorious day, Gus and Gertrude decided to create a gigantic grape guzzle. Gigantic goblets gleamed in the golden sunshine, glistening with glistening grape juice. Gertrude, giggling goofily, grabbed a gigantic grape grinder, gleefully grinding glistening grapes into glorious grape goo. Gus, grabbing a gigantic wooden spoon, stirred the grape goo with gusto, humming a grapey garden tune.

The geese, gobbling gleefully on glistening grains scattered by Gus, occasionally goggled in disbelief at the gargantuan grape guzzle preparations. Soon, the grape guzzle was ready, a glorious concoction of glistening grape juice, glistening grape goo, and gigabytes of Gertrude's giggles.

Gus and Gertrude, grinning goofily from ear to ear, invited the entire village to their gigantic grape guzzle gathering. Giggling guests gobbled gleefully on glistening grapes, guzzled gloriously from glistening goblets, and gossiped about Gertrude's gargantuan grape guzzle.

The garden, once guarded by grumpy geese, became a haven of grape-guzzling glee. Gus and Gertrude, their gigantic green grapevines thriving, continued to grow glorious grapes, giggle goofily, and guard their garden with gusto, forever grateful for the geese's grateful gobbles and the grape-guzzling glee of their gracious guests.

11. Gruff George the gorilla, gigantic and green-garbed, guarded a glorious garden of gigantic green gourds. Giggling gorilla girlfriends, Gertrude and Gladys, gracefully grasped gigantic green gourds, giggling about George's gruff guarding. George, grumbling gruffly, grabbed a gigantic gardening glove, gently guiding giggly gorilla girlfriends towards glistening green grapes.

Suddenly, a gaggle of goofy tourists, goggling at the gigantic gorillas, gasped in glee at the glorious garden of gourds. George, glaring grumpily at the gawking tourists, grabbed a gigantic green gourd, gruffly grunting a gorilla greeting. The tourists, giggling goofily, grasped their gigantic cameras, gleefully getting gigantic gorilla grins for their goofy holiday photos.

Gertrude, grinning goofily back at the tourists, grabbed a gigantic basket, generously gifting glistening green grapes to the grateful gaggle. The tourists, gobbling gratefully on the glistening grapes, continued their gorilla-gazing with giggly glee. George, his gruffness gradually replaced by gratified grunts, continued guarding the glorious gourds.

One gloriously sunny day, George decided to create a gigantic gourd-guitar. Gigantic green gourds, grasped by grinning gorilla girlfriends, were carefully carved with gigantic grins and glistening guitar strings. George, grunting with glee, grabbed a gigantic green gourd, gleefully strumming a gruff gorilla gig. Gertrude and Gladys, giggling goofily, grabbed gigantic gourds as drums, thumping out a glorious gorilla groove.

The tourists, gobbling on glistening grapes and grinning from ear to ear, gathered around the gorilla band, their goofy glee echoing through the garden. The once-guarded garden became a haven of gorilla gatherings. George, his gigantic green gourds still guarded (but now also gloriously musical), continued to grunt greetings to grateful tourists and groove with his giggling gorilla band, forever grateful for the grapes, the grins, and the glorious gorilla gig.

12. Crackling crowds, countless concertgoers captivated, crammed concrete concert halls, coughing occasionally. Keen conductors, Kurt and Kim, clutching crimson conductor's coats, conferred calmly, concocting captivating concert classics.

Kim, king of crescendos, cued kettledrums with a flick of his wrist, kicking off a captivating concerto. Kurt, king of calming codas, coaxed clarinets with careful cues, crafting crescendos that climbed and climbed. Concertgoers, captivated by the climbing crescendos, clapped contagiously, creating a captivating concert cacophony.

Suddenly, a gaggle of giggling girls, grandkids eager for giggly games, got up and began to gallop goofily around the gigantic grandstand. Kurt, keeping his cool with kind commands, called for a calming coda, gently guiding the giggling girls back to their giggling grandparents.

The concert hall, once calmly controlled by the keen conductors, became a whirlwind of giggly girls, galloping goofily, and the glorious gongs of a gradually calming concerto. Kim, keeping his composure with a kind smile, kept the captivating concert chugging along.

Moments later, the girls, grinning from ear to ear, settled back into their seats, captivated once more by the captivating concert. Kurt, his heart filled with conductorial glee, continued conducting captivating classics, keeping the countless captivated concertgoers captivated until the very last glorious gong.

13. Gleeful guitar gangsters, Gus and Gretchen, grinned goofily, glaring at gigantic green guitars gleaming gloriously beneath gigantic green stage lights. Gigantic green gloves gripped gargantuan guitar necks, gearing up for a gigantically glorious gig.

Gus, king of killer riffs, kicked things off with a knee-knocking, knuckle-busting Kombo, keeping the crowd kicking and clapping. Gretchen, queen of quick chords, countered with a cascade of cascading chords, creating a glorious guitar war that got the crowd going gaga.

Suddenly, a gaggle of giddy groupies, girls gone gaga for guitar gangsters, grappled for gigantic green guitar picks Gus and Gretchen occasionally flung into the crowd. Gus, grinning goofily, grabbed a gigantic green glittery guitar pick, gleefully gifting it to the giggliest girl in the front row.

The concert hall, once calmly controlled by the guitar gangsters, became a whirlwind of giddy groupies, grappling for guitar picks, and the glorious guitar groans of an electrifying guitar battle. Gretchen, keeping her cool with a kind wink, kept the gig going with gusto.

Moments later, the groupies, grinning from ear to ear, settled back, captivated by the glorious guitar gymnastics. Gus, his heart filled with guitarist glee, continued gigging with Gretchen, their gargantuan green guitars gleaming gloriously, forever granting glimpses of their glorious guitar gangster genius.

14. Keen kayakers, Kirk, Kelly, Kim, and Kris, kicked kicked kicked kicked kicked kicked kicked kicked kicked kicked through kelp-filled coves, conquering countless kayaking challenges. Kelp clung to kayaks, kicking up a cackle of kooky commotion. Killer krill krimped at kicking kayaks, causing kicking kayakers to cackle with glee. Kirk, king of kayak kicks, kicked his kayak king-kong fast, keeping kelp at bay. Kelly, kipping up after a kelp kerfuffle, kicked with kung-fu fury. Kim, kicking with krakengrip strength, conquered a colossal current. Kris, kayaking keenly, kicked through a kelp kingdom, kicking out a cunning course.

Suddenly, a gigantic green grouper emerged from the kelp, its gargantuan gaze gleaming with grouchy greed. The kayakers, momentarily forgetting their kelp-kicking camaraderie, kicked in a flurry of frantic paddling. Kirk, remembering his grandpa's gruff guidance about grouper greetings, grabbed a handful of glistening green glitter and tossed it towards the grouper. The grouper, momentarily stunned by the glittering glimmer, gave a grumpy gurgle and retreated back into the kelp kingdom.

Emboldened by their glitter gambit, the kayakers kicked on, their camaraderie kicking in stronger than ever. They kicked past playful pods of porpoises, their clicks and whistles keeping the kayakers kicking with renewed vigor. They kicked through caverns crawling with curious crabs, their claws clicking a castanet rhythm that matched the kayakers' kicking cadence. Finally, they emerged from the kelp clutches, kicking into a glorious, sun-dappled lagoon. Exhausted but exhilarated, the kayakers kicked back in their kayaks, kgiggling with triumphant glee. They had conquered countless kayaking challenges, proving that even when kelp, krill, and grumpy groupers ganged up on them, keen kayakers with a knack for kicking and a touch of glitter could always conquer the cove.

15. Graying Gary, glorious golfer, grasped a glistening green golf ball in his gigantic green glove. Gleaming galleries gathered, gossiping about Gary's gargantuan golfing game. Gary, grinning goofily, gripped the grip, his gigantic glutes wiggling with anticipation. Gleefully, he gave a gigantic golf ball a glorious whack, sending it soaring through the glowing green grassy expanse.

Suddenly, a gaggle of giddy geese, guardians of the green, gobbled gleefully at glistening grain scattered by groundskeepers. Gary, keeping his cool, grabbed a gigantic green golf club cover, gently guiding the geese towards a glistening grain getaway. The geese, grumbles replaced by grateful gobbles, gobbled gratefully, their goosey ganders giving way to giggly goose grins.

Moments later, Gary, grinning goofily once more, gripped the grip and gave another gigantic golf ball a glorious golf course getaway. The galleries gasped, their goggling eyes gleaming as the golf ball gracefully glided, seemingly defying gravity, before landing with a gentle plop in the glorious green cup.

Gary, king of golfing glory, grasped his gigantic green glove in a triumphant gesture, the galleries erupting in giggly glee. News of Gary's gigantic golf course getaway shot, gossiped about by grateful geese across the green, reached golfing greens everywhere.

Gigantic green gloves gripped gigantic green golf balls in gleeful anticipation, golfers across the globe mimicking Gary's glorious golfing getaway shot. Gary, grinning goofily, continued golfing gracefully, his gigantic green glove grasping gigantic green golf balls, forever granting glimpses of glorious golfing glory.

CHAPTER 42: INSANE TONGUE TWISTERS FOR NASAL SOUNDS: /M/, /N/, AND /Ŋ/

Nasal sounds are a distinctive feature of English pronunciation. Produced by allowing air to escape through the nose while blocking airflow in the mouth, these sounds require careful coordination of the oral and nasal cavities. This chapter focuses on refining your ability to produce the nasal consonants: /m/, /n/, and /ŋ/. Through a series of challenging tongue twisters, you'll develop greater control and clarity in your speech. Get ready to explore the nuances of nasal airflow and enhance your overall pronunciation.

1. Many marvellous manatees, munching merrily on mounds of mottled mussels, meandered amidst morning mist. Magnificent migrating mammals, mothers and minis alike, munched with mighty moos. Minnows darted in and out, mimicking the manatees' munching motions, making mesmerizing mini-manatee mayhem.

   Suddenly, a grumpy Gannett, guarding gigantic gobs of glistening guano, squawked squeamishly at the manatees' messy munching. Miffed manatees mumbled amongst themselves, munching more manically to mock the grumpy Gannett.

The Gannett, grumbling about guano-gobbling goofballs, gave up his grumpy guard and glided gracefully away. The manatees, munching merrily once more, meandered through the misty mangroves, making magnificent migrating mammal magic.

One morning, amidst the misty mangroves, mama manatee Matilda met a magnificent manatee named Marvin. Munching mussels merrily side-by-side, Matilda and Marvin made marvellous music with their mighty moos, a melody that mingled magically with the morning mist.

News of Matilda and Marvin's magnificent manatee meeting, amidst the misty mangroves munching mussels, mushroomed amongst the migrating mammals. Many more manatees meandered to the mangroves, munching mussels merrily and making marvellous manatee music together.

The mangroves, once guarded by a grumpy gannett, became a haven of harmonious humming, happy honking, and magnificent munching. Matilda and Marvin, munching mussels merrily with their magnificent manatee mates, continued migrating through misty mornings, forever making marvellous manatee music, a melody that would forever mingle with the memories of the mangroves.

2. Nine nimble night ninjas, noses nearly numb in the night's nip, navigated narrow, nagging night paths beneath a nearly new moon. Nimbly navigating, they napped not, noses twitching for nighttime noises:

nervous nighthawks napping, nocturnal newts nibbling, or neighbouring night owls nesting nearby.

Suddenly, a grumpy gander guarding glistening gooseberries gave a goosey groan, his grumpy gander gaze glaring at the ninjas. Nine nimble ninjas, none needing naps, never nervous, offered the grumpy gander nine glistening gooseberries, their night mission momentarily nixed.

The gander, gobbling gratefully, gave a gentle goosey grunt, his grumpy gaze replaced by a glimmering grin. The ninjas, nimbly navigating once more, navigated the narrow, nagging night paths beneath the nearly new moon, their nighttime mission nearly complete.

News of the ninjas' night manoeuvres and the grumpy gander's gooseberry gratitude nibbled its way through the nighttime network. Now, whenever nimble nocturnal nomads navigate narrow night paths, neighbouring creatures never neglect to offer nourishing nighttime nibbles. This ensures a night of neighbourly napping and nocturnal navigation without any nagging night noises.

In fact, the kindness of the ninjas became legendary. Nightingales, notorious for their nighttime serenades that sometimes turned into sleep-shattering screeching, now hummed soothing lullabies as the ninjas navigated nearby. Napping newts, often startled awake by the ninjas' nimble movements, now left calming, shimmering nightlights along the paths. And the grumpy gander, forever grateful for the ninjas' night-saving gooseberries, became their staunchest supporter, greeting them with a gentle goosey honk and a basket of glistening gooseberries whenever they passed through his territory.

The narrow, nagging night paths, once a source of

nighttime noise and neighbourly tension, transformed into a haven of harmonious humming, helpful newt-lights, and grateful gooseberry gifts. The nine nimble night ninjas, forever grateful for the nighttime network of kindness they'd inadvertently created, continued their missions beneath the moonlit sky, forever remembered as the ninjas who brought peace and quiet (and the occasional gooseberry) to the nighttime world.

3. Tenacious termites, tirelessly toiling in twilight, tunnel through towering terracotta towers. Their tiny translucent tools tirelessly tap, transforming treasured trinkets into toothpick-sized timber. Triumphant trumpets echo as the termites meticulously manoeuvre mounds of masonry. A grumpy gargoyle grumbles greedily at the glimmering gold, but a kitsune's cunning kick compels him to retreat.

The relentless clicking and clacking continues a symphony of industrious intent. The tan towers, once symbols of permanence, succumb to the relentless gnawing, transforming into a labyrinth of tiny toothpicks. Exhausted but exhilarated, the termites emerge triumphant, their minuscule mandibles leaving a legacy of industrious ingenuity etched upon the twilight landscape.

High above, a keen-eyed kestrel circles, casting a curious crimson gaze upon the toppled towers. The industrious insects, for a fleeting moment, become captivating characters in a grand, silent play. The kestrel lets out a shrill cry, alerting a colony of curious kobolds lurking in the crumbling cavities. The kobolds, wielding flickering torches, cautiously creep closer, their guttural gasps echoing through the twilight.

Unaware of the curious onlookers, the termites celebrate their victory. Their tiny antennae twitch in a silent toast, a testament to their unwavering work ethic. As the moon casts its silvery glow upon the scene, the toppled towers stand as a monument to the tenacious termites, a testament to the power of perseverance in the face of seemingly insurmountable challenges.

4. Many merry mole miners, munching merrily on mounds of monstrous mushrooms, meandered through moist, murky tunnels. Mustaches magnificent, muddy muck boots mucky, the miners mumbled merrily as they munched.

Suddenly, a grumpy gnome, guarding glistening goblets of glistening grog, grumbled about the miners' messy munching. Miffed miners mumbled amongst themselves, munching more manically to mock the grumpy gnome.

The gnome, grumbling about grog-guzzling goofballs, gave up his grumpy guard and gobbled down a glistening gobleted grog himself. The miners, munching merrily once more, meandered through the murky tunnels, making magnificent mole-mining magic.

One moist morning, amidst the murky tunnels, Marvin the mole miner met Matilda, a magnificent mole miner with a monstrous mane of mushroom-coloured hair. Munching mushrooms merrily side-by-side, Marvin and Matilda made marvellous music with their muffled mining melodies, a symphony that mingled magically with the moisture dripping from the tunnel walls.

News of Marvin and Matilda's magnificent mole-mining meeting, amidst the murky tunnels munching monstrous mushrooms, mushroomed amongst the mining community. Many more merry mole miners meandered to the tunnels, munching mushrooms merrily and making marvellous mining music together.

The murky tunnels, once guarded by a grumpy gnome, became a haven of harmonious humming, happy hollering, and magnificent munching. Marvin and Matilda, munching mushrooms merrily with their magnificent mining mates, continued mining through moist mornings, forever making marvellous mining music, a melody that would forever mingle with the memories of the murky tunnels.

5. Keen, courageous kobolds meticulously navigate kilometres of convoluted caverns, meticulously kicking, digging, and kicking again through countless kilograms of glistening, glimmering gemstones. Gleefully, they gather glistening gold, guarding gigantic glistening garnets, keeping coveted king-sized kunzites concealed from covetous creatures.

One particularly gruelling gig involved kicking through a gargantuan glistening gate guarded by a grumpy, grotesque gargoyle. Grunting and kicking with gusto, the kobolds finally gained access, greeted by a glistening grotto guarded by giggling gremlins.

Guffawing gremlins guarded gigantic glistening gears, giggling as they ground glistening gravel into glittering grit. Ignoring the gremlins' goading, the kobolds kept kicking, meticulously manoeuvring past grinning gremlins guarding glistening grates.

Finally, after kicking through kilometres of caverns, the kobolds reached their coveted king-sized kunzite. Kneeling with glee, they kicked countless kilograms of glistening gravel aside, carefully keeping the coveted gem concealed until their king could claim it.

Their next challenge: a gargantuan, glistening gryphon guarding a glistening grotto rumoured to be overflowing with glittering gems. Grunting with determination, the kobolds kicked a concoction of glistening gunk and glistening glue, creating a sticky, glistening gauntlet to get past the gryphon. The gryphon, grumpy and glistening with glue, shrieked in frustration, allowing the kobolds to kick their way past.

Inside, the grotto glistened with a kaleidoscope of glittering gems. Gigantic glistening geodes pulsed with vibrant hues, guarded by grinning, giggling gnomes. The kobolds, accustomed to kicking their way through challenges, opted for a different tactic this time.

Keeping their voices low, they kicked countless kilograms of glistening gravel into a glistening pile, catching the gnomes' attention. As the gnomes giggled and gawked at the glistening gravel growing by the kick, the kobolds swiftly kicked countless kilograms of glittering gems into their sacks.

Kicking their way back out, the kobolds emerged from the caverns, kings of countless kilograms of glistening, glittering gems. Their king, ecstatic with their success, kicked off a kingdom-wide celebration, with glistening goblets overflowing with glistening grog, and glistening grub kabobs sizzling on glistening grills.

6. Nine nimble oboeists, noses numb in the nippy November night, navigated narrow nooks near a nearly new moon, humming a new, nearly impossible nocturne. Never needing naps, noses twitching for nighttime noises (nervous night owls napping, nocturnal newts nibbling, or neighbouring nightingales nesting nearby), they meticulously memorised musical manuscripts.

Suddenly, a grumpy gander guarding glistening gooseberries gave a goosey groan, his grumpy gander gaze glaring at the musicians. Nine nimble oboeists, none needing naps, never nervous, offered the grumpy gander nine glistening gooseberries, their night mission momentarily nixed.

The gander, gobbling gratefully, gave a gentle goosey grunt, his grumpy gaze replaced by a glimmering grin. The oboeists, nimbly navigating once more, navigated the narrow nooks near the nearly new moon, their nighttime mission nearly complete.

News of the oboeists' night manoeuvres and the grumpy gander's gooseberry gratitude nibbled its way through the nighttime network. Now, whenever nimble nocturnal musicians navigate narrow nooks near the new moon, neighbouring creatures never neglect to offer nourishing nighttime nibbles. This ensures a night of neighbourly napping and nocturnal navigation without any nagging night noises.

In fact, the kindness of the oboeists became legendary. Nightingales, notorious for their nighttime serenades that sometimes turned into sleep-shattering screeching, now hummed soothing lullabies as the oboeists navigated nearby. Napping newts, often startled awake by the oboeists' nimble movements, now left calming, shimmering nightlights along the paths. And the grumpy gander, forever grateful for the oboeists' night-saving gooseberries, became their staunchest supporter, greeting them with a gentle goosey honk and a basket of glistening gooseberries whenever they passed through his territory.

The narrow nooks near the new moon, once a source

of nighttime noise and neighbourly tension, transformed into a haven of harmonious humming, helpful newt-lights, and grateful gooseberry gifts. The nine nimble oboeists, forever grateful for the nighttime network of kindness they'd inadvertently created, continued their missions beneath the moonlit sky, forever remembered as the musicians who brought peace and quiet (and the occasional gooseberry) to the nighttime world.

7. Nine nimble Norwegian knitters, needles never numb, nimbly knit knobby knee-high knit mittens for neighbouring Nordic nomads needing winter warmth. Nimbly navigating needles, never needing naps, noses numb in the nippy Nordic night, they natter non-stop about new knitting notions.

   Suddenly, a grumpy gnome guarding glistening gingerbread gnomes gave a grumpy groan, his grumpy gnome gaze glaring at the knitters. Nine nimble knitters, none needing naps, never nervous, offered the grumpy gnome nine glistening gingerbread gnomes, their nightly knitting mission momentarily nixed.

   The gnome, gobbling gratefully, gave a gentle gnomey grunt, his grumpy gaze replaced by a glimmering grin. The knitters, nimbly navigating needles once more, navigated the narrow, snowy Nordic night, their nightly knitting mission nearly complete.

   News of the knitters' night maneuvers and the grumpy gnome's gingerbread gratitude nibbled its way through the Nordic network. Now, whenever nimble Nordic knitters knit knobby knee-high knit mittens during the nippy Nordic nights, neighboring nomads never neglect to offer nourishing nighttime nibbles. This ensures nights of neighborly napping and nocturnal knitting without any nagging night noises.

In fact, the kindness of the knitters became legendary. Noisy night owls, notorious for their nighttime hoots that sometimes hindered sleep, now hummed soothing lullabies as the knitters navigated nearby. Neighborly newts, often startled awake by the knitters' nimble movements, now leave calming, shimmering nightlights along the paths. And the grumpy gnome, forever grateful for the knitters' night-saving gingerbread gnomes, became their staunchest supporter, greeting them with a gentle gnomey grunt and a basket of glistening gingerbread gnomes whenever they passed through his territory.

The narrow, snowy Nordic night, once a source of nighttime noise and neighborly tension, transformed into a haven of harmonious humming, helpful newt-lights, and grateful gingerbread gifts. The nine nimble Norwegian knitters, forever grateful for the Nordic network of kindness they'd inadvertently created, continued their missions beneath the moonlit sky, forever remembered as the knitters who brought warmth, peace, and quiet (and the occasional gingerbread gnome) to the Nordic night.

8. Many marvelous milliners, meticulously matching mohair shades, meticulously made magnificent mohair mittens for multiple magnificent mannequins. Mirrors magnified meticulous mitten marvels, making milliners murmur with immense millinery pride.

Suddenly, a grumpy gnat, guarding glistening goblets of glistening grape juice, grumbled grouchily about the mannequins' monotonous mitten modeling. Miffed milliners mumbled amongst themselves, maneuvering the mannequins more mischievously to mock the grumpy gnat.

The gnat, grumbling about grape juice-guzzling goofballs, gave up his grumpy guard and gobbled down a glistening gobleted grape juice himself. The milliners, manoeuvring mannequins merrily once more, meticulously modelled magnificent mohair mittens in the mirrored mannequins' magnificent midst.

News of the milliners' meticulous mitten modelling manoeuvres and the grumpy gnat's grape juice gratitude nibbled its way through the millinery network. Now, whenever marvellous milliners meticulously model magnificent mohair mittens, neighbouring gnats never neglect to offer nourishing nighttime nibbles. This ensures a night of neighbourly napping and nocturnal mitten modelling without any nagging night noises.

In fact, the kindness of the milliners became legendary. Noisy night owls, notorious for their nighttime hooting that sometimes hindered meticulous mitten modelling, now hummed soothing lullabies as the milliners modelled nearby. Neighbourly newts, often startled awake by the milliners' manoeuvring movements, now leave calming, shimmering nightlights along the paths. And the grumpy gnat, forever grateful for the milliners' mitten-modelling grape juice gift, became their staunchest supporter, greeting them with a gentle gnatty grunt and a glistening gobleted grape juice whenever they passed through his territory.

The mirrored mannequins' magnificent midst, once a source of nighttime noise and neighbourly tension, transformed into a haven of harmonious humming, helpful newt-lights, and grateful grape juice gifts. The many marvellous milliners, forever grateful for the millinery network of kindness they'd inadvertently created, continued their meticulous mitten modelling under the moonlit sky, forever remembered as the milliners who brought peace, quiet, and a newfound appreciation for grape juice (and the occasional gnat) to the world of nighttime mitten modelling.

9. Nine nervous newbies, noses nearly numb in the nippy November night, nervously navigated narrow aisles near a newly-opened bookstore, yearning for a newly-released novel. Never needing naps, noses twitching for new novelties (nervously nibbling on neon-coloured nibs, nervously navigating neon signs, or nervously noticing nearby napping bookstore cats), they nimbly navigated the numerous neatly-lined pages in a newly-released novel.

Suddenly, a grumpy gnome guarding glistening gnomes carved from neon nuts gave a grumpy groan, his grumpy gnome gaze glaring at the newbies. Nine nervous newbies, none needing naps, never nervous, offered the grumpy gnome nine glistening gnomes carved from neon nuts, their novel-night mission momentarily nixed.

The gnome, gobbling gratefully, gave a gentle gnomes grunt, his grumpy gaze replaced by a glimmering grin. The newbies, nimbly navigating the aisles once more, navigated the narrow bookstore near the newly-opened doors, their novel-night mission nearly complete.

News of the newbies' nervous navigation and the grumpy gnome's neon nut gratitude nibbled its way through the bookstore network. Now, whenever nervous newbies nervously navigate bookstores near newly-opened doors, neighbouring night owls never neglect to offer nourishing nighttime nibbles. This ensures nights of neighbourly napping and nocturnal novel-reading without any nagging night noises.

In fact, the kindness of the newbies became legendary. Noisy night owls, notorious for their nighttime hoots that sometimes hindered novel-reading, now hummed soothing lullabies as the newbies navigated nearby. Neighbourly newts, often startled awake by the newbies' nervous movements, now leave calming, shimmering nightlights along the bookstore aisles. And the grumpy gnome, forever grateful for the newbies' neon-nut novel-night gift, became their staunchest supporter, greeting them with a gentle gnomes grunt and a glistening gnome carved from a neon nut whenever they passed through his territory.

The narrow bookstore aisles, once a source of nighttime noise and neighbourly tension, transformed into a haven of harmonious humming, helpful newt-lights, and grateful neon-nut gifts. The nine nervous newbies, forever grateful for the bookstore network of kindness they'd inadvertently created, continued their novel-reading missions beneath the moonlit sky, forever remembered as the newbies who brought peace, quiet, and a newfound appreciation for neon nuts (and the occasional grumpy gnome) to the world of nighttime bookstores.

CHAPTER 43: INSANE TONGUE TWISTERS FOR FRICATIVES: /F, V, S, Z, Θ, Đ, Σ, 3, H/

Fricatives are the hissing, buzzing sounds that add complexity and nuance to spoken language. Produced by a partial obstruction of airflow, these consonants require precision and control. This chapter will challenge you to master the art of fricative articulation. Through a series of intricate tongue twisters, you'll refine your ability to produce these sounds clearly and accurately. Get ready to hone your hissing skills!

1. Feverish fibre-optic fanatics, faces flushed with future-forward fervour, frantically fashioned fantastic fibre-optic homes for five favourite fashion families. Fathers fussed over fibre-optic fireplaces, flicking switches with feverish fingers. Mothers meticulously measured magnificent multicoloured mood-lighting, marvelling at mesmerising mauve and mesmerising magenta hues. Children, captivated by the colourful chaos, chased chattering chipmunks crafted from colourful Christmas lights, their joyous shrieks echoing through the futuristic fibre-optic funhouses.

   Visiting friends fawned over the phenomenal feats of fibre-optic fancy. Fashionable females fingered flowing fabrics, oohing and aahing over outfits illuminated by strategically sewn-in strands of shimmering fibre optics. Fathers, fueled by futuristic fantasies, envisioned fibre-optic fishing rods that flashed and flickered, luring in legendary luminescent leviathans. Even family pets got in on the act, fluffy felines swatting playfully at shimmering butterflies crafted from coloured bulbs, their purrs providing a welcome counterpoint to the symphony of sighs and satisfied snorts emanating from the enthralled family members.

News of these phenomenal fibre-optic feats fizzed through the fashion world faster than a faulty filament. Fashion shows featuring frocks fashioned from fibre optics became all the rage, with models floating down runways like radiant, real-life rainbows. Furniture stores scrambled to stock shelves with fibre-optic floor lamps and fibre-optic fountains, desperate to keep up with the insatiable demand. The five feverish fibre-optic fanatics, forever famous for their fantastical creations, found themselves fielding frantic requests from fashion houses, furniture franchises, and even forward-thinking fish farms (who saw the potential for fibre-optic illuminated fish tanks to soothe stressed-out salmon).

Yet, amidst the fame and fortune, they never forgot the joy of creating those first five fantastic fibre-optic homes. It all began with a friendly Friday night gathering. Fueled by fizzy drinks and feverish brainstorming, the idea sparked – to craft custom living spaces that shimmered and pulsed with the magic of light. Friends became collaborators, sketching out dazzling designs on flickering fluorescent notepads. Fathers, with their fix-it expertise, tackled the technical aspects, weaving intricate webs of fibre-optic strands. Mothers, with their keen sense of style, curated colour palettes that danced and dazzled. The children, unburdened by adult inhibitions, provided a constant stream of whimsical suggestions – from fibre-optic fish that swam serenely through virtual aquariums to holographic houseplants that bloomed in response to whispered compliments. The result was a symphony of light, laughter, and limitless imagination, forever etching itself in the memories of the five families and solidifying the bond between the feverish fibre-optic fanatics.

2. Sprawling, subterranean suites, swathed in soothing silence, housed spacious sizzling saunas. Stressed souls seeking serenity shuffled silently towards the shimmering sanctuaries. Soft symphonic sounds surrounded them, seeping into their stressed spirits. Inside, scented steam swirled, swirling stress away with every swoosh of the whisks. Sweat soaked their skin, soothing sore muscles and sluggish systems. Silvery showers soothed further, sending shivers of satisfaction down their spines. Surrounded by smooth, sleek stone surfaces, worries fizzled and vanished like forgotten effervescent fizz. Finally, free from the frenzy of daily life, they found themselves floating in a blissful haze.

But the saunas offered more than just physical solace. Hunched over steaming mugs of herbal tea in plush, plush repose areas, guests found themselves fostering friendships with fellow serenity seekers. Soft-spoken conversations swirled, shared stories seasoned with sighs of satisfaction. Laughter, light and lufty, echoed softly through the caverns, a stark contrast to the harsh sounds of the world above. Here, time seemed to slow, measured only by the rhythmic hiss of the sauna stones and the soft sighs of contentment.

For those seeking an extra dose of invigoration, therapists wielding frosty flannels filled the air with the invigorating scent of eucalyptus. With practised precision, they'd flay away tension, kneading knots of stress into oblivion. Muscles loosened, minds meandered to mindful mantras. The entire experience, from the soft symphony of sounds to the subtle shift in soft lighting, was a carefully crafted symphony designed to soothe the soul.

Emerging from their subterranean sanctuary, guests re-entered the world transformed. Gone were the furrowed brows and hunched shoulders. In their place, a soft smile and a spring in their step. The spacious, sizzling saunas had served their purpose well, transforming stressed souls into serene spirits, ready to face the world with newfound zest.

3. Hefty helicopters hovered high, hunting for hidden headquarters. Headstrong heroes, hearts hammering, held their high-powered hoses high, hosing down rooftops relentlessly, revealing cleverly concealed hatches. Frustrated flyers fumed, forced to fly further afield, future follies firmly foiled by the fearless firefighters.

News of the firefighters' fantastic feat flashed across frequencies faster than a faulty filament. Fire stations across the nation fizzed with fervent activity. Firefighters, fueled by the heroes' bravery, furiously fastened fire-resistant jumpsuits, feverishly filling their fire engines with fresh foam. Fire chiefs, faces flushed with future-forward fervour, frantically formulated fire drills to counter increasingly fiendish fictional foes. Even firehouse pups got in on the act, fluffy fox terriers fetching fire hoses with ferocious focus, their playful barks providing a welcome counterpoint to the symphony of sighs and satisfied snorts emanating from the enthralled firefighters.

The cleverly concealed headquarters, once a haven for hush-hush hi-jinks, became a hotbed of hurried hide-and-seek sessions. Henchmen scurried about, hastily hauling heavy hi-tech weaponry from hidden compartments, their hurried hisses echoing through the high-ceilinged halls. The head villain, a heavy-set fellow with a penchant for houndstooth hats, hovered over holographic maps, his face flushed with frustration. Flustered flyers frantically fiddled with faulty flight controls, their once formidable flying machines sputtering and sputteringly backfiring.

Yet, amidst the foiled fiendish schemes and firefighter fanfare, a sense of fun remained. Firefighters, forever famous for flushing out fiendish foes, found themselves fielding friendly firetruck races from neighbouring stations, the flashing lights and blaring sirens transforming city streets into technicolour racetracks. The head villain, humbled by his hilarious helicopter mishap (his oversized hat becoming hopelessly entangled in the rotors), decided to put his high-tech talents to good use, designing a revolutionary flame-resistant firefighter suit. The once hidden headquarters, now a testament to friendly competition and creative collaboration, became a hub of heroic innovation, forever etching itself in the memories of firefighters and frustrated flyers alike.

4. Vexed vexillologists, vests very visibly violet, visited a vast, vaulted Victorian villa, visibly vibrating with vanished voices. Vigorously waving vibrant violet vexillums, vexillologists visualised vanishing vibrations, voices from vexing Victorian villains.

Frightful phantoms fluttered faintly, flickering forms

following furious flag-waving. Suddenly, a shadowy silhouette shifted, sending shivers shooting through the stoic scholars. Startled shouts sliced through the stuffy silence, swiftly followed by shrieks and sputtering coughs (a scholar, surely surprised, swallowed his sovereign's shilling). Spectral scoundrels, surprised by the sudden sensation, scurried swiftly through secret staircases, shadowy sighs swirling around startled scholars.

News of the vexillologists' valiant visit vanished virtually overnight, veiled in Victorian vagueness. However, whispers of violet vexillums vibrating villains vivified village taverns, forever fascinating fireside story spinners. Visiting vintners, voices laced with amusement, envisioned Victorian villains, vexed by violet vexillology, vowing vengeance (vaguely, of course). Even the village vicar, known for his fondness for fantastical fiction, found himself frequently fiddling with forgotten flags, half-heartedly humming forgotten Victorian fight songs.

The vast, vaulted Victorian villa, once a haven for vanished villains, became a venue for vigorous vexillological ventures. Vexillologists, forever fascinated by the faint vibrations of the past, continued their visits, valiantly wielding vibrant violet vexillums. But their quest wasn't just about vindicating the vilified Victorians. The scholars, fueled by a scholarly sense of adventure, hoped to unearth the villa's veiled secrets – hidden chambers, forgotten fortunes, or even fantastical flying machines sketched on dusty parchment.

One particularly vigorous vexillum-waving session sent a spectral scoundrel sprawling into a suit of shining silver armour. The startled scholar, a fellow with a fondness for forgotten fashion, momentarily forgot his scholarly pursuits and helped the dusty phantom don the dented breastplate. A hesitant friendship formed, a scholar and a scoundrel united by their fascination with the villa's veiled past. The phantom, with a surprising knowledge of secret passages, guided the scholar through hidden doorways, revealing forgotten libraries overflowing with leather-bound volumes and dusty telescopes pointed towards the inky night sky.

Together, they deciphered cryptic clues scribbled on the margins of faded maps, their scholarly pursuits punctuated by the phantom's ghostly giggles (a sound surprisingly similar to the wind whistling through broken windows). They unearthed forgotten fortunes in the form of shimmering sapphires and tarnished silver goblets, the scholar carefully cataloguing each treasure with a scholar's meticulousness. And in a dusty attic, beneath a pile of moth-eaten tapestries, they discovered a fantastical flying machine – a contraption of canvas and cogs that resembled a magnificent mechanical dragonfly.

News of the scholar and the phantom's fantastical discoveries fanned through the village like wildfire. The once-sceptical vintners, their amusement replaced by awe, flocked to the villa to witness the marvel. The vicar, his forgotten flag-fiddling replaced by a newfound fascination with aeronautics, spent his days tinkering with the flying machine, his humming replaced by excited shouts and the whirring of gears.

The vast, vaulted Victorian villa, once a haven for vanished villains, became a vibrant hub of historical exploration and fantastical invention. The vexillologists, forever grateful for the phantom's spectral assistance, continued their visits, their vibrant violet vexillums a permanent fixture against the villa's weathered facade. The scholar and the phantom, an unlikely duo bound by a shared sense of wonder, embarked on countless adventures in their rickety flying machine, soaring above the village rooftops and leaving behind a trail of laughter, scholarly pronouncements, and the faint, shimmering echoes of a Victorian villain's surprised shout.

5. Six sleek, silver spaceships, shields sizzling, soared swiftly through shimmering solar storms. Stealthy space sailors, scanning swirling sunspots, searched for safe, serene, and sun-dappled shore signs. Sudden static shrieks sliced through headsets, spaceships swerving sharply, shields sizzling furiously against solar flares.

   Startled space sailors scrambled, swiftly switching frequencies, searching for serene sectors shown on shimmering star charts. Spaceships shuddered, shields shimmering faintly, as ferocious firefights filled frequencies with frightening fizzes and bangs. Fortunately, futuristic force fields fended off fiery foes, forcing frightened fighter pilots to flee far from the fray.

   News of the spaceships' spectacular showmanship spread swiftly through spacefaring sectors, shared in hushed whispers over steaming space-brew. Space stations buzzed with feverish excitement, holographic news reports flashing stories of six sleek, silver spaceships and their swashbuckling space sailors. Fearsome fighter pilots, faces flushed with frustration, fumed in smoky space bars, vowing fierce revenge (vaguely, of course). Even fuzzy felines onboard, forever fascinated by flashing fighter controls, found themselves swatting playfully at shimmering space-mice simulations, their purrs a welcome counterpoint to the symphony of sighs and satisfied snorts emanating from the relieved space sailors.

The shimmering solar storms, once a source of fear for spacefarers, became a training ground for spectacular spacefaring skills. Space sailors, forever seeking serene shores, continued their soaring sojourns, shields sizzling with practised precision. But their quest wasn't just about seeking sandy beaches and sparkling seas. The spacefarers, fueled by a thirst for knowledge, hoped to discover forgotten alien artefacts, fantastical flora and fauna, or even hidden star charts leading to legendary lost civilizations.

One particularly sizzling solar storm sent a spaceship spiralling into a swirling vortex of shimmering space dust. The fearless space captain, a fellow with a fondness for forgotten frequencies, fought furiously against the ship's failing controls, his voice a steady stream of commands amidst the frightening fizzes and bangs. Suddenly, a faint signal flickered on the scanners – a melodic hum, unlike anything they'd ever heard before. The captain, with a hunch, steered the ship towards the signal's source, and emerged from the vortex to find a breathtaking sight – a hidden space city, constructed from shimmering crystals and pulsating with an otherworldly light.

News of the spacefarers' sensational discovery spread through the galaxy faster than a faulty fusion core. Fearsome fighter pilots, their thirst for vengeance replaced by awe, signed up for sightseeing tours of the spectacular space city. Fuzzy felines onboard, their fascination with space-mice simulations replaced by a newfound love for chasing holographic butterflies, frolicked joyfully in the city's crystalline parks. The shimmering solar storms, once a terrifying hurdle, became the key to unlocking a universe of hidden wonders. The space sailors, forever grateful for the fortuitous solar storm, continued their soaring sojourns, their sleek, silver spaceships forever a symbol of courage, curiosity, and the never-ending quest to explore the furthest reaches of the shimmering cosmos.

6. Five fierce female formula race fans, faces flushed with feverish fervour, frantically fastened futuristic flame-retardant fire suits, fingers flying over flickering fastenings. Fathers fussed over finely tuned Ferraris, fidgeting with futuristic fuel injectors, filling fiery fusion formulas into flaming fire tanks. Flags fluttered furiously, fans feverish with anticipation, focused on five flashy Ferraris poised for the phenomenal first lap.

Suddenly, a frustrated fire marshal frantically flagged furiously, a faulty fire alarm forcing a fiery fiasco. Frustrated female formula fans fumed, forced to forfeit front-row finishes, feverish frustration filling the fervent fans. Firefighters, fueled by frantic flags, furiously fought the faulty fire alarm, fixing faulty fuses with feverish focus. Finally, firefighters finished fixing the faulty fire alarm, flags flashing furiously once more, feverish fans filling the front rows with fervent cheers.

The five flashy Ferraris, finally freed from the fiery fiasco, flew furiously forward. Fearless female formula racers fought fiercely for first place, futuristic Ferraris flashing by in a flurry of furious fifths. Fans followed frantically, flags flailing fervently, feverish focus fixed on the phenomenal finish. Fathers, finally free from their fire-fixer duties, found themselves furiously flipping through futuristic financial reports, fantasising about fabulous fortunes from future Formula One finishes. Even fluffy felines, forgotten fans felines fast asleep on father's laps, found themselves twitching furiously in fantastical formula racing dreams, tiny paws chasing fuzzy flags in a flurry of ferocious feline frenzy.

News of the phenomenal female formula finish fizzed through the racing world faster than a faulty fuel injector. Female Formula racing fans, forever fascinated by the fierce female racers, flooded racing schools, their feverish fervour fueling a phenomenal influx of future female Formula One hopefuls. Fashion designers, fuelled by the frenzy, furiously sketched futuristic fashions for fearless female formula racers, featuring fire-resistant fabrics that flowed fantastically in the furious wind. Formula One factories, fueled by the financial frenzy, focused on futuristic features – self-fixing fire extinguishers, fabulous fog-eliminating visors, and even fluffy feline-shaped air fresheners to keep the cockpits smelling fresh.

The five flashy Ferraris, forever famous for their phenomenal finish, became rolling testaments to female fortitude and futuristic innovation. The female Formula racers, forever fierce and fabulous, continued their furious races, fueled by the fervent cheers of their fans. But their quest wasn't just about checkered flags and champagne showers. The racers, fuelled by a passion for speed and a thirst for knowledge, hoped to use their fame to fund fantastic new technologies – faster fusion formulas, fire-resistant fabrics that could withstand even the fiercest infernos, and maybe even a revolutionary new type of catnip that would keep even the most ferociously feline formula fan fast asleep during a race.

7. Six silly sightseers, faces flushed with feverish fascination, furiously fastened safety straps, fingers fumbling with flimsy fasteners. Fathers fumbled with fussy film cameras, fiddling with focus while fixing frightened faces. Flags flapped frantically, faces filled with fearful fervour, focused on six silly sightseers soaring skyward in stately steely zeppelins.

Suddenly, a strong, swirling southwesterly squall sent shivers shooting through the stoic sightseers. Startled shouts sliced through the stuffy silence, swiftly followed by shrieks and sputtering coughs (a silly sightseer, surely surprised, swallowed his souvenir seashell). Seagulls screeched shrilly, swooping swiftly around the swaying zeppelins, searching for salty snacks (stale sandwiches or soggy souvenir sausages).

News of the sightseers' sensational skyfaring spread swiftly through seaside resorts, shared in hushed whispers over steaming seafood stews. Souvenir shops buzzed with feverish excitement, holographic news reports flashing stories of six silly sightseers and their spectacular zeppelin voyage. Sceptical sailors scoffed, sipping sugary schnapps, scowling fiercely at the fanciful flying contraptions. Even feisty fleas found themselves fastened firmly to fluffy felines, frantically fleeing frightened friends, their furious scratching a welcome counterpoint to the symphony of sighs and satisfied snorts emanating from the soothed sightseers.

The azure expanse, once a source of fear for seaside strollers, became a stage for sensational skysailing sojourns. Sightseers, forever seeking sensational sights, continued their zeppelin sojourns, soaring swiftly through zestful zephyrs. But their quest wasn't just about sightseeing and souvenir shopping. The sightseers, fueled by a thirst for historical knowledge, hoped to discover forgotten shipwrecks, fantastical flying fish, or even hidden islands charted by swashbuckling sailors of yore.

One particularly sensational soiree saw a silly sightseer spot a shimmering shape sinking slowly through the swirling seas. The stoic ship's captain, a fellow with a fondness for forgotten folktales, steered the zeppelin swiftly towards the shimmering mass and emerged from the squall to find a breathtaking sight – a sunken shipwreck, its masts adorned with shimmering seaweed and its decks teeming with fantastical fish.

News of the sightseers' sensational shipwreck discovery spread through the seaside resorts faster than a faulty fog light. Sceptical sailors, their scoffs replaced by awe, signed up for sightseeing tours of the spectacular shipwreck. Feisty fleas, their frantic fleeing replaced by a newfound love for fish-flavoured treats, frolicked joyfully on the shipwreck's decks. The azure expanse, once a source of nervous seaside strolls, became the key to unlocking a universe of hidden underwater wonders. The sightseers, forever grateful for the sensational shipwreck serendipity, continued their zeppelin sojourns, their stately steely zeppelins forever a symbol of curiosity, courage, and the never-ending quest to explore the furthest reaches of the shimmering seas.

8. Six seasoned submariners, sporting sleek, streamlined suits, scurried silently onto a stealthy steel submarine. Strapping securely into swivelling seats smiles stretched across their serious, sun-kissed faces. Soon, the sensational steel submarine sliced silently beneath shimmering seas, searching for sunken ships shrouded in secrecy.

Suddenly, a startled starfish, startled by the submarine's silent shadow, sent shimmering seashells scattering across the sandy seabed. Startled submariners scrambled, swiftly searching for scattered seashells. Fortunately, swift sonar specialists, sporting stylish scarlet scarves, swooped swiftly, skillfully scooping up the scattered shells.

News of the submarine's sensational seashell skirmish spread swiftly through scientific societies, shared in hushed whispers over steaming mugs of soothing sea-kelp soup. Scuba-diving spots buzzed with feverish excitement, holographic news reports flashing stories of six seasoned submariners and their sensational seashell skirmish. Startled starfish, momentarily mortified by the misunderstanding, munched melancholically on microscopic mussels, missing their midday mischief. Even fuzzy fish onboard, fascinated by flashing sonar screens, found themselves frantically fiddling with fizzy fish-food feeders, their excited hisses a welcome counterpoint to the symphony of sighs and satisfied snorts emanating from the relieved submariners.

The shimmering seas, once a source of slight seasickness for some submariners, became a training ground for spectacular subaquatic skills. Submariners, forever seeking sunken ships shrouded in secrecy, continued their silent sojourns, skillfully scanning swirling schools of sand sharks and searching for signs of spectacular shipwrecks. But their quest wasn't just about snapping stunning sunken selfies. The submariners, fueled by a thirst for knowledge, hoped to discover forgotten fauna, fantastical fossil fuels, or even hidden shipwrecks holding secrets that could rewrite history.

One particularly sunny sojourn, a strong southerly swell sent the submarine swerving sharply, sending seasoned submariners swaying precariously in their swivelling seats. Shrieks and shouts filled the watery silence, submariners searching frantically for something solid to steady themselves. Suddenly, a sharp-eyed sonar specialist spotted a shimmering shape on the scanner – a majestic megafauna, its massive mouth agape in a silent yawn. The skilled submarine pilot, with a sigh of relief, skillfully steered the steel ship around the megafauna, their journey continuing with a newfound sense of awe.

News of the submariners' sensational megafauna sighting spread through the scientific societies faster than a faulty submersible signal. Startled starfish, their melancholy morphing into amazement, migrated in masses to witness the majestic megafauna. Fuzzy fish onboard, their fascination with fizzy fish-food feeders replaced by a newfound love for fluffy seaweed toys, frolicked joyfully in the submarine's pressurised cabin. The shimmering seas, once a source of slight seasickness, became the key to unlocking a universe of hidden wonders. The submariners, forever grateful for the strong southerly swell, continued their silent sojourns, their sleek, steel submarine forever a symbol of stealth, serenity, and the never-ending quest to explore the furthest reaches of the shimmering seas.

9. Five fearless firefighters, faces flushed from fighting fierce forest fires, furiously fastened fire-resistant gear, fingers flying over flickering fasteners. Fathers fretted over faulty fire hoses, fiddling with fickle fixtures, filling fiery fusion-powered firetrucks. Flags flapped frantically, faces filled with fearful focus, five firefighters focused on ferocious flames flickering fiercely across the forest floor.

Suddenly, a startled squirrel, scared silly by shrieking sirens, scurried nervously through sizzling undergrowth, sending showers of shimmering spruce needles scattering skyward. Startled firefighters stumbled, swiftly searching for scattered spruce needles. Fortunately, swift support specialists, sporting stylish safety squints, swooped swiftly, skillfully scooping up the scattered needles.

News of the firefighters' phenomenal forest firefight fizzed furiously through fire stations, firefighters fiercely fueled by the phenomenal feat. Fire drills focused on ferocious flames fanned by fierce winds, firefighters fiercely focusing on flawless form. Fire chiefs, faces flushed with feverish fervour, frantically formulated fire-fighting formations, featuring fabulous firetrucks fitted with futuristic flamethrowers (used defensively, of course, to fight fire with fire). Even frisky firehouse fox terriers, fascinated by flashing fire engine lights, found themselves furiously fetching fire extinguishers, their playful yaps a welcome counterpoint to the symphony of sighs and satisfied snorts emanating from the exhausted firefighters.

The once ferocious forest fire, a frightening force for firefighters, became a fiery furnace for forging phenomenal firefighting skills. Firefighters, forever fierce firefighters, fought furiously forward, fuelled by the fervent cheers of grateful families. But their fight wasn't just about felling fiery foes. The firefighters, fueled by a fiery sense of purpose, hoped to find forgotten fireflies, fantastical fire-resistant flora, or even hidden fire-breathing folklore etched onto ancient, fire-scorched rocks.

One particularly feverish firefight, a ferocious wind whipped the flames into a frenzy, forcing firefighters to fight fiercely from behind firebreaks. Fearful faces flickered in the flickering flames, firefighters furiously searching for a safe haven. Suddenly, a fearless firefighter spotted a shimmering shape through the smoke – a forgotten fire lookout tower, standing strong amidst the inferno. The firefighters, fueled by a surge of hope, fought furiously towards the tower, finding a safe haven and a breathtaking view of the fiery forest floor.

News of the firefighters' phenomenal fire lookout tower find fanned through the firefighting network faster than a faulty fire hose. Frisky firehouse fox terriers, their fascination with fire extinguishers replaced by a newfound love for fetching fire hoses, frolicked joyfully around the base of the tower. Families, forever grateful for the firefighters' fierce fight, flocked to the tower, leaving behind heartfelt messages of thanks scrawled on fire-resistant paper. The once ferocious forest fire, a symbol of fear, became a beacon of hope and a testament to the tireless efforts of firefighters. The fearless firefighters, forever fierce and forever grateful, continued their fiery fight, their firetrucks forever a symbol of courage, community, and the never-ending quest to extinguish ferocious flames.

10. Vexed veteran vintners ventured vigorously very early, venturing through verdant vineyards veiled in vaporous mist. Vivid violet vines vigorously vaulted vertically, vying for vital vernal sunlight. Vexed vintners, vexed voices barely audible, vigorously pruned vexing vines, envisioning voluminous vintages veiled in velvet.

Suddenly, a startled sparrow, startled by swiftly snipping shears, sent shimmering spiderwebs scattering through the silent space. Startled vintners stumbled, swiftly searching for scattered spiderwebs. Fortunately, swift seasonal specialists, sporting stylish straw sun hats, swooped swiftly, skillfully scooping up the scattered strands.

News of the vintners' vigorous vine-trimming venture vilified swiftly through villages, vintners vilified for vandalising valuable vines. Village vintners, voices laced with vehement vitriol, envisioned vanished vintages, veiled dreams of velvet-wrapped victories vanishing. Even frisky field mice, forever fascinated by fallen fruit, found themselves furiously fighting for fallen figs, their frantic squeaks a welcome counterpoint to the symphony of sighs and satisfied snorts emanating from the vindicated vintners.

The verdant vineyards once shrouded in suspicion, became a vibrant venue for vigorous viticulture ventures. Vintners, forever venerating the vine's vitality, continued their vigorous visits, violets valiantly vying for visibility amongst the verdant canopy. But their venture wasn't just about vintage victories. The vintners, fueled by a thirst for fruitful knowledge, hoped to discover forgotten fermentation formulas, fantastical flying fauna feasting on fat figs, or even hidden vine-coded messages whispered in the rustling leaves by the summer breeze.

One particularly vigorous venture, a valiant vintner unearthed a vast vat, veiled in verdant vegetation, its vinous vapours vaguely visible. The vintners, voices vibrating with vehement wonder, ventured cautiously closer, cautiously uncorking the ancient vessel. A heavenly aroma, heavy with hints of violets and vanilla, wafted from the vat, a fragrant testament to forgotten flavours. The vintners, forever fascinated by the vine's veiled past, vowed to continue their vigorous ventures, their verdant vineyards forever a testament to tradition, tenacity, and the never-ending quest to cultivate the most victorious vintages.

11. Silly schoolchildren, sporting stylish safari suits, skipped excitedly through a sun-dappled meadow. Smiling, they surrounded shimmering sunflowers, searching swiftly for sensational, six-spotted ladybugs. Suddenly, a startled spider, startled by swiftly skipping schoolchildren, scurried swiftly through a spiderweb strung sensationally between sunflowers. Startled schoolchildren shrieked, swiftly swatting at shimmering spiderwebs. Fortunately, swift summer supervisors, sporting stylish straw sunhats, swooped swiftly, skillfully scooping up scattered spiderwebs.

News of the schoolchildren's sensational spiderweb skirmish spread swiftly through summer schools, shared in hushed whispers over steaming mugs of soothing sunflower seed soup. Sun-dappled meadows buzzed with feverish excitement, holographic news reports flashing stories of six silly schoolchildren and their sensational spiderweb skirmish. Startled spiders, momentarily mortified by the misunderstanding, munched melancholically on microscopic midges, missing their midday mischief. Even fuzzy field mice, fascinated by fluttering butterflies, found themselves frantically fiddling with fizzy fruit-drink dispensers, their excited squeaks a welcome counterpoint to the symphony of sighs and satisfied snorts emanating from the relieved schoolchildren.

The sun-dappled meadows, once a source of slight sniffles from seasonal allergies for some schoolchildren, became a training ground for spectacular summer skills. Schoolchildren, forever fascinated by fantastic flora and fauna, continued their sunny sojourns, skillfully sketching shimmering sunflowers and searching for signs of secretive, six-spotted ladybugs. But their quest wasn't just about snapping stunning summer selfies. The schoolchildren, fueled by a thirst for knowledge, hoped to discover forgotten flower folklore, fantastical flying insects, or even hidden honeycombs overflowing with sticky, sweet sunshine.

One particularly sunny sojourn, a strong southerly breeze

sent shimmering sunflowers swaying sensationally. Schoolchildren shrieked and giggled, scrambling swiftly to steady themselves amongst the swaying stalks. Suddenly, a sharp-eyed student spotted a sensational sight – a busy bee buzzing between blossoming bushes, busily followed by a buzzing bumblebee. The excited schoolchildren, with sighs of relief, surrounded the sensational sight, forever fascinated by the frenetic dance of the busy bees.

News of the schoolchildren's sensational bee sighting spread through the summer schools faster than a faulty firefly. Startled spiders, their melancholy morphing into amazement, spun shimmering webs in the bushes around the blossoming flowers, hoping for a closer look at the busy bees. Fuzzy field mice, their fascination with fizzy fruit drinks replaced by a newfound love for sunflower seeds, frolicked joyfully in the meadow. The sun-dappled meadows, once a source of slight sniffles, became the key to unlocking a universe of hidden wonders. The schoolchildren, forever grateful for the strong southerly breeze, continued their sunny sojourns, their summer adventure forever a symbol of silliness, serenity, and the never-ending quest to explore the flourishing world around them.

12. Stylish steampunks, sporting shimmering steel suits, shuffled swiftly through a swirling snowfall, searching for sensational steam-powered snow sculptures. Suddenly, a startled squirrel, startled by the sputtering steam engine, scurried swiftly through a shimmering snowdrift, sending showers of fluffy snowflakes scattering skyward. Startled steampunks stumbled, swiftly searching for scattered snowflakes. Fortunately, swift snow specialists, sporting stylish scarlet scarves, swooped swiftly, skillfully scooping up the scattered flakes.

News of the steampunks' sensational snowflake skirmish spread swiftly through scientific societies, shared in hushed whispers over steaming mugs of soothing saffron soup. Snow-dusted slopes buzzed with feverish excitement, holographic news reports flashing stories of six stylish steampunks and their sensational snowflake skirmish. Startled squirrels, momentarily mortified by the misunderstanding, munched melancholically on microscopic mushrooms, missing their midday mischief. Even fuzzy ferrets onboard the steam-powered vehicle, fascinated by flashing steam gauges, found themselves frantically fiddling with fizzy fruit-drink dispensers, their excited hisses a welcome counterpoint to the symphony of sighs and satisfied snorts emanating from the relieved steampunks.

The swirling snowfalls, once a source of slight shivers for some steampunks, became a training ground for spectacular snow science skills. Steampunks, forever seeking sensational snow sculptures, continued their snowy sojourns, skillfully sculpting shimmering snow serpents and searching for signs of spectacular subterranean snow caves. But their quest wasn't just about snapping stunning snowy selfies. The steampunks, fueled by a thirst for knowledge, hoped to discover forgotten snow folklore, fantastical steam-powered snow vehicles, or even hidden snow crystals holding secrets to the universe's shimmering snowfall.

One particularly snowy sojourn, a strong southerly swell sent their steam-powered vehicle swerving sharply, sending stylish steampunks swaying precariously in their swivelling seats. Shrieks and shouts filled the snowy silence, steampunks searching frantically for something solid to steady themselves. Suddenly, a sharp-eyed snow specialist spotted a shimmering shape on the scanner – a majestic mountain range, its snow-capped peaks glistening in the sun. The skilled steampunk pilot, with a sigh of relief, skillfully steered the vehicle towards the mountains, their journey continues with a newfound sense of awe.

News of the steampunks' sensational mountain sighting spread through the scientific societies faster than a faulty snow shovel. Startled squirrels, their melancholy morphing into amazement, migrated in masses to witness the majestic mountains. Fuzzy ferrets onboard, their fascination with fizzy fruit drinks replaced by a newfound love for fluffy snowball fights, frolicked joyfully in the snow-covered fields. The swirling snowfalls, once a source of slight shivers, became the key to unlocking a universe of hidden wonders. The steampunks, forever grateful for the strong southerly swell, continued their snowy sojourns, their steam-powered vehicle forever a symbol of style, science, and the never-ending quest to explore the furthest reaches of the shimmering snowscape.

13. Vexed Vivian viciously vacuumed voluminous velvet Victorian valances, vowing vehement vengeance on vanished vermin. Visible frustration etched lines on her face. The vintage vacuum whined, a symphony of suction battling silence. Sunlight streamed through stained-glass windows, highlighting swirling dust devils dancing in the disturbed air. Vivian visualised villainous voles, vicious vandals of her valuable velvet. Each vicious vacuum stroke vanquished invisible invaders, vindicating Vivian's vigilance.

Vast improvements vindicated her efforts. The once-dusty valances shimmered, their rich hues revitalised. But vengeance wasn't enough. Vivian envisioned a future fortified against fiendish furballs. She fortified the foundation with fine steel mesh, effectively foiling future forays. Fragrant sachets of foxglove and viper's bugloss, strategically placed, served as a final, fragrant deterrent.

Victorious, Vivian ventured outside. Verdant vines, meticulously maintained, now veiled the Victorian villa. Vibrant violet blooms peeked from beneath, a testament to her triumph. A gentle breeze sighed through the swaying vines, whispering a soothing serenade. Leaning against the weathered brick wall, Vivian inhaled the fresh air, a sense of serenity settling over her. The vermin vanquished, the velvet vindicated, Vivian's Victorian villa was finally at peace.

14. Celebrity chefs, Chloe, Carlos, and Xavier, chopped with customary charisma. Countless colourful capsicums cascaded onto cutting boards, a symphony of sizzling sounds as knives sliced swiftly. Chloe, clad in a crisp white chef's coat, focused on crafting a vibrant vegetable vindaloo, her movements precise as if conducting an orchestra. Carlos concentrated on a sizzling seafood stew, his brow furrowed in concentration as he coaxed the perfect flavour from the shellfish. Xavier, with a flourish that sent a spray of saffron water into the air, flambéed scallops, a fiery flourish that fetched frantic flashes from food photographers.

Customers clustered around the open kitchen, captivated by the culinary choreography unfolding before them. Clinking cutlery chimed a counterpoint to the chefs' cheerful chatter, punctuated by the rhythmic sizzle of searing ingredients. The air buzzed with an intoxicating medley of aromas - the sharp tang of fresh herbs, the earthy musk of mushrooms, the sweet perfume of caramelised onions. It was a sensory feast even before the first bite.

Over on the grill station, Xavier seasoned skewered vegetables with a practised flick of his wrist, the spices sizzling as they hit the hot coals. Beside him, Chloe carefully arranged dollops of cooling raita on a bed of vibrant green mint chutney. Carlos, with a flourish worthy of a magician, unveiled a steaming pot of paella, the saffron-infused rice studded with plump mussels, succulent prawns, and tender chicken.

The waiters weaved between the tables, their movements a well-rehearsed dance. Plates heaped with culinary masterpieces were presented with a flourish, the aroma whetting the appetites of the eager diners. As forks dug into the vibrantly coloured creations, satisfied sighs rippled through the restaurant, a testament to the chefs' artistry. The clinking of glasses and murmurs of appreciation filled the air, the background music a mere whisper compared to the symphony of satisfied diners.

15. Fuming fifth-graders, frustrated by faulty fifth-generation phones, frantically fiddled with flimsy fibre-optic cables, frowning fiercely. Phones fizzled and flickered, flashing frantic error messages. Frustrated fifth-graders fumed, fervently flipping through flimsy user manuals. Suddenly, a flustered fifth-grade friend, flustered by frantic finger-fumbling, fumbled a phone, sending it flying through the flimsy fifth-floor window. Startled fifth-graders shrieked, swiftly scrambling to the window, searching frantically for the fallen phone. Fortunately, a fearless firefighter, featuring a fantastic flame-resistant fireman's hat, fetched the fallen phone from the fiery flowerpot five floors below.

News of the fifth-graders phenomenal phone fiasco flickered furiously through fifth-grade forums, friends furiously fascinated by the phenomenal feat. Fifth-grade classrooms fizzed with feverish excitement, holographic news reports flashing stories of six fuming fifth-graders and their phenomenal phone fiasco. Flustered fifth-grade friends, momentarily mortified by the misunderstanding, munched melancholically on mushy marshmallows, missing their midday Minecraft marathons. Even fuzzy ferrets fascinated by flashing phone screens found themselves frantically fiddling with fizzy fruit drink dispensers, their excited hisses a welcome counterpoint to the symphony of sighs and satisfied snorts emanating from the relieved fifth-graders.

The fifth-generation phones, once a source of frustration for some fifth-graders, became a training ground for fantastic fifth-grade technology troubleshooting skills. Fifth-graders, forever fascinated by futuristic features, continued their feverish FaceTime functions, filming fantastic feats of friendship and searching for signs of successful fifth-generation signal strength in secluded, shady spots. But their quest wasn't just about filming funny faces and flickering fireflies. The fifth-graders, fueled by a thirst for knowledge, hoped to discover forgotten features, fantastical fifth-generation filters, or even hidden fifth-grader forums filled with fascinating facts and fun facts.

One particularly frustrating Friday, a faulty fifth-generation feature froze all the phones' FaceTime functions. Fuming fifth-graders frantically fumbled with their phones, frustration filling the Friday afternoon air. Suddenly, a fearless fifth-grader spotted a shimmering signal on the screen – a forgotten fifth-generation forum filled with helpful hints and hilarious memes. The relieved fifth-graders, with sighs of relief, frantically followed the forum's instructions, successfully fixing their phones and continuing their FaceTime functions with renewed fervour.

News of the fifth-graders phenomenal forum fix spread through the fifth-grade forums faster than a faulty fifth-generation flashlight. Flustered fifth-grade friends, their melancholy morphing into amazement, flocked to the forum to find solutions to their own fifth-generation phone woes. Fuzzy ferrets, their fascination with fizzy fruit drinks replaced by a newfound love for fluffy finger puppets, frolicked joyfully in the classroom. The fifth-generation phones, once a source of frustration, became the key to unlocking a universe of hidden functionalities and fantastic friendships. The fifth-graders, forever grateful for the forgotten forum, continued their FaceTime functions, their phones forever a symbol of friendship, frustration, and the never-ending quest to explore the phenomenal features of the fifth generation.

16. Vicious VHS vultures, vexed by vanished video vixens, viciously ventured very early into a vast, vacant video vault. Vexed Vivian, wielding a vintage video viewer, vigorously vacuumed vanished videotapes, vowing vengeance on vanished vixens. Suddenly, a startled spider, startled by the vigorous vibrations, scuttled swiftly through a shimmering spiderweb strung strategically across a shadowed shelf. Startled video vultures shrieked, swiftly swiping at shimmering spiderwebs. Fortunately, swift security specialists, sporting stylish safety squints, swooped swiftly, skillfully scooping up scattered spiderwebs.

News of the video vultures' vicious VHS vault venture

vilified swiftly through villages, vultures vilified for vandalizing valuable video vaults. Village vicars, voices laced with vehement vitriol, envisioned video vixens vanished forever, veiled dreams of villains vanquishing victories vanishing. Even frisky field mice, forever fascinated by forgotten French fries, found themselves fiercely fighting for fallen fudge, their frantic squeaks a welcome counterpoint to the symphony of sighs and satisfied snorts emanating from the vindicated video vultures.

The vast, vacant video vault, once a haven for vanished video vixens, became a vibrant venue for vigorous video vixen vanquishing ventures. Video vultures, forever venerating vanished video vixens, continued their vigorous visits, vowing vengeance on vanished villainy. But their venture wasn't just about victorious video vixen vanquishing. The vultures, fueled by a thirst for forgotten knowledge, hoped to discover forgotten Victorian vaudeville videos, fantastical flying machines filmed on faded film reels, or even hidden video vaults veiled behind velvet Victorian valances.

One particularly vigorous venture, a valiant vulture unearthed a vast, veiled velvet vault, vibrations from the vacuum echoing strangely within. The vultures, voices vibrating with vehement wonder, ventured cautiously closer, cautiously cracking the combination lock. A heavenly aroma, heavy with hints of vanilla and forgotten film festivals, wafted from the vault, a fragrant testament to a bygone era. The vultures, forever fascinated by the vault's veiled past, vowed to continue their vigorous ventures, their vast, vacant video vault forever a testament to tradition, tenacity, and the never-ending quest to vanquish video villainy.

17. Stealthy secret service spies, sporting sleek, silver suits, scurried silently past shimmering security scanners, searching swiftly for stolen classified satellite secrets. Suddenly, a startled sparrow, startled by swiftly sliding spy shoes, sent shimmering security sensors skittering across the shiny steel floor. Startled spies stumbled, swiftly searching for scattered sensors. Fortunately, swift security specialists, sporting stylish safety squints, swooped swiftly, skillfully scooping up the scattered security systems.

News of the spies' sensational security system skirmish spread swiftly through secret societies, shared in hushed whispers over steaming mugs of soothing saffron soup. Spy schools buzzed with feverish excitement, holographic news reports flashing stories of six stealthy Secret Service spies and their sensational security system skirmish. Startled sparrows, momentarily mortified by the misunderstanding, munched melancholically on microscopic mosquito larvae, missing their midday mischief. Even fuzzy ferrets fascinated by flashing security screens, found themselves frantically fiddling with fizzy fruit drink dispensers, their excited hisses a welcome counterpoint to the symphony of sighs and satisfied snorts emanating from the relieved spies.

The shimmering security systems, once a source of slight stress for some spies, became a training ground for spectacular secret service skills. Spies, forever seeking stolen classified secrets shrouded in secrecy, continued their silent sojourns, skillfully scanning swirling streams of satellite signals and searching for signs of spectacular secret service satellites. But their quest wasn't just about snapping stunning secret selfies. The spies, fueled by a thirst for knowledge, hoped to discover forgotten spy tactics, fantastical flying submersibles, or even hidden secret societies shrouded in shadows, sharing secrets whispered on the summer breeze.

One particularly silent sojourn, a strong southerly signal surged through the satellite stream, sending the spies scrambling to decipher the scrambled message. Shrieks and shouts filled the silent surveillance room, spies searching frantically for the source of the signal. Suddenly, a sharp-eyed spy spotted a shimmering shape on the screen – a forgotten secret service satellite, reactivated and sending a faint, frantic message. The skilled spy chief, with a sigh of relief, skillfully sent a reassuring message back, their mission continuing with a newfound sense of purpose.

News of the spies' sensational secret satellite sighting spread through the secret societies faster than a faulty satellite signal. Startled sparrows, their melancholy morphing into amazement, migrated in masses to witness the majestic satellite soaring silently through the starry sky. Fuzzy ferrets, their fascination with fizzy fruit drinks replaced by a newfound love for fluffy souvenir space suits, frolicked joyfully in the spy school's training room. The shimmering security systems, once a source of slight stress, became the key to unlocking a universe of hidden secrets. The spies, forever grateful for the strong southerly signal, continued their silent sojourns, their sleek, silver suits forever a symbol of stealth, service, and the never-ending quest to safeguard the world's classified secrets.

CHAPTER 44: INSANE TONGUE TWISTERS FOR AFFRICATES: / TΣ/ AND /D3/

These **affricates** are unique speech sounds, combining the explosive force of a stop consonant with the continuous friction of a fricative, present a formidable challenge for speakers of all levels. From the sharp, incisive "ch" to the smoother, gliding "j," these sounds demand precision, coordination, and clarity. As you navigate through this chapter, you'll encounter a series of tongue twisters designed to test your ability to produce these sounds accurately and rapidly. Whether you're a seasoned speaker or a language learner, this affricate adventure is sure to enhance your articulation and overall speech fluency. So, fasten your linguistic seatbelt and prepare to conquer the complexities of these captivating sounds.

1. Six sharp stonemasons, sporting stylish suede suits, scurried swiftly through a sun-dappled sculpture garden, their footsteps leaving faint whispers on the soft, sandy pathway. Sunlight filtered through the leaves of ancient oaks, casting shimmering patterns on the weathered stone statues that lined the garden paths.

Suddenly, a startled squirrel, startled by the swiftly approaching stonemasons, scurried across a precariously balanced pile of polished pebbles, sending shimmering stones scattering like startled doves across the sun-dappled ground. The stonemasons shrieked in surprise, scrambling swiftly to prevent the precious stones from tumbling off the edges of the garden's raised flower beds. Fortunately, swift supervisors, sporting stylish straw sunhats, swooped swiftly from behind a towering topiary dragon, their movements resembling a silent ballet, skillfully scooping up the scattered stones with practiced ease.

News of the stonemasons' sensational stone skirmish spread swiftly through the stonemasonry societies, shared in hushed whispers over steaming mugs of soothing saffron soup. Stone sculpture seminars buzzed with feverish excitement, holographic news reports flashing stories of six sharp stonemasons and their sensational stone skirmish. Startled squirrels, momentarily mortified by the misunderstanding, munched melancholically on microscopic mites, missing their midday mischief of strategically pilfering forgotten French fries from unsuspecting picnickers. Even fuzzy field mice, forever fascinated by fallen figs, found themselves fiercely fighting for forgotten sunflower seeds, their frantic squeaks a welcome counterpoint to the symphony of sighs and satisfied snorts emanating from the relieved stonemasons.

The sun-dappled sculpture garden, once a place of peaceful contemplation for some stonemasons, became a training ground for spectacular stone sculpting skills. Stonemasons, forever fascinated by the stories whispered by the weathered stone, continued their sunny sojourns, skillfully sculpting shimmering sandstone serpents and searching for signs of spectacular, secluded stone structures shrouded in the mysteries of time. But their quest wasn't just about snapping stunning stone selfies under the dappled sunlight. The stonemasons, fueled by a thirst for knowledge, hoped to discover forgotten sculpting techniques, fantastical flying machines etched onto ancient stone tablets, or even hidden stone chambers filled with artifacts whispering tales of forgotten civilizations.

One particularly sunny sojourn, a young and eager stonemason, his heart pounding with excitement, spotted a figure hunched over a moss-covered rock nestled amongst the towering redwoods. As they approached cautiously, the figure came into sharper focus - a charming chieftain, his face etched with the wisdom of years, carefully crafting cherished chapters of his tribe's history onto a chipped chisel. The excited stonemasons, forever fascinated by the stories etched in stone, surrounded the chieftain, their hushed questions filling the air. The chieftain, a twinkle in his wise eyes, smiled warmly and beckoned them closer, eager to share the stories whispered by the stone and the skills passed down through generations of stonemasons. In that sun-dappled moment, surrounded by the silent sculptures and the chirping of unseen birds, a connection was forged between past and present, a testament to the enduring legacy of stone and the stonemasons who brought it to life.

2. Jaded judges, Jessica and Jenkins, jittered in their jewel-toned jackets. Jealous jewellers jostled for their attention, jangling jars of gems. Each jewel, a masterpiece, glittered for juicy-gem glory. Jessica scrutinised sapphires with a furrowed brow, her notes a cryptic code of cuts and clarity. Jenkins jotted down details about rubies, his gaze lingering on a fiery stone that pulsed like a tiny dragon's heart. The jewelers, a flamboyant bunch adorned in more jewelry than a pirate captain's treasure chest, fidgeted under the scrutiny.

Suddenly, a juggling mishap! A tray of emeralds, meant to showcase a dazzling cascade of green, went flying. Jewels jittered everywhere! Judges shrieked, jewelers jumped, the chaos jangling like a chorus of wind chimes caught in a hurricane. In the pandemonium, a crafty jeweler named Charles, known for his whimsical opal creations and even more whimsical waistcoats, chimed in, "Jumbled judging? Jellybean break, judges?"

Laughter erupted, a welcome break in the tense atmosphere. The tightly wound coil of competitive energy unraveled, replaced by smiles and a smattering of nervous giggles. Even Jessica and Jenkins, usually as stoic as statues, couldn't help but crack a smile. Maybe Charles was right. A break, a sugary burst of sweetness, might be just what they needed to refresh their palates and their perspectives.

"Jolly good idea, Charles!" boomed a voice from the back. A burly man with a handlebar mustache and a twinkle in his eye, sporting a tie clip fashioned from a giant amethyst, lumbered forward. "Jellybeans for everyone! Let's cleanse our palates and get back to judging these beauties with clear eyes and, perhaps, a touch more whimsy."

The room buzzed with approval. The jewellers, relieved by the reprieve, eagerly scooped up jellybeans from a crystal bowl that materialised in Charles's hand (perhaps a magician as well as a jeweller?). Jessica and Jenkins exchanged glances, a silent communication passing between them. The tension had eased, replaced by a newfound respect for the artistry and passion swirling around them. The judging would resume, a touch sweeter, a touch less judgmental, forever coloured by the memory of the jumbled jewels and the jellybean break that brought laughter and camaraderie to the most discerning court of gems.

3. Chubby chefs, sporting stylish checked chef hats, scurried swiftly through a shimmering seafood shack, searching swiftly for succulent, sizzling scallops sizzling on a stainless-steel stove. Suddenly, a startled seagull, startled by the sizzling sounds, swooped swiftly from the salty sea, sending shimmering seashells scattering skyward like startled silver stars. Startled chefs shrieked, swiftly swiping at shimmering seashells. Fortunately, swift sanitation specialists, sporting stylish safety squints, swooped swiftly, skillfully scooping up scattered seashells with practised ease.

News of the chefs' sensational seashell skirmish spread swiftly through seafood societies, shared in hushed whispers over steaming mugs of soothing saffron soup. Seafood shacks buzzed with feverish excitement, holographic news reports flashing stories of six chubby chefs and their sensational seashell skirmish. Startled seagulls, momentarily mortified by the misunderstanding, munched melancholically on microscopic mussels, missing their midday mischief of snatching sizzling shrimp straight from unsuspecting diners' plates. Even fuzzy ferrets, forever fascinated by forgotten French fries, found themselves fiercely fighting for fallen fish fingers, their frantic squeaks a welcome counterpoint to the symphony of sighs and satisfied snorts emanating from the relieved chefs.

The shimmering seafood shack, once a source of slight seasickness for some chefs, became a training ground for spectacular seafood culinary skills. Chefs, forever fascinated by the fantastic flavours of the sea, continued their sizzling sojourns, skillfully shucking succulent scallops and searching for signs of spectacular, secret seafood recipes shrouded in the mysteries of generations of seaside cooks. But their quest wasn't just about snapping stunning seafood selfies under the salty spray of the ocean. The chefs, fuelled by a thirst for knowledge, hoped to discover forgotten fish filleting techniques, fantastical flying fish recipes etched onto ancient, weather-beaten scrolls, or even hidden underwater caves filled with forgotten spices whispering tales of legendary seafood dishes.

One particularly sizzling sojourn, a sharp-eyed chef spotted a shimmering shape shimmering through the ocean waves – a sunken shipwreck, its masts reaching like skeletal fingers towards the sky. The excited chefs, fuelled by a sense of culinary adventure, donned their scuba gear and plunged into the shimmering sea. As they descended deeper, they discovered a treasure trove of forgotten flavours – spices nestled in weathered chests, ancient cookbooks etched onto seashells, and even a rusty old frying pan, still holding the faint aroma of a long-forgotten feast. With a sense of awe and excitement, the chefs carefully collected their treasures, their hearts filled with the thrill of discovery and the endless possibilities for creating new and exciting seafood dishes. The shimmering seas, once a source of slight seasickness, became the key to unlocking a universe of hidden flavours and culinary history. The chefs, forever grateful for the strong southerly swell that led them to the shipwreck, continued their sizzling sojourns, their stainless-steel stoves forever a symbol of skill, service, and the never-ending quest to explore the fantastic flavours of the sea.

4. Stylish sixth-graders, sporting shockingly short shorts, shuffled swiftly through a shadowy spruce forest, searching silently for singing songbirds. Sunlight sifted through the shimmering needles, casting shifting shadows across the silent forest floor. Suddenly, a startled squirrel, startled by the swiftly shuffling sixth-graders, scurried swiftly through a spiderweb strung sensationally between sunlit spruce boughs. Startled sixth-graders shrieked, swiftly swiping at shimmering spiderwebs. Fortunately, swift summer supervisors, sporting stylish straw sunhats, swooped swiftly, skillfully scooping up scattered spiderwebs with practised ease.

   News of the sixth-graders sensational spiderweb skirmish spread swiftly through summer schools, shared in hushed whispers over steaming mugs of soothing sassafras soup. Sun-dappled meadows buzzed with feverish excitement, holographic news reports flashing stories of six stylish sixth-graders and their sensational spiderweb skirmish. Startled squirrels, momentarily mortified by the misunderstanding, munched melancholically on microscopic mites, missing their midday mischief of strategically pilfering forgotten sunflower seeds from unsuspecting students. Even fuzzy field mice, forever fascinated by fallen figs, found themselves fiercely fighting for forgotten french fries, their frantic squeaks a welcome counterpoint to the symphony of sighs and satisfied snorts emanating from the relieved sixth-graders.

   The shadowy spruce forest, once a source of slight shivers for some students, became a training ground for spectacular summer survival skills. Sixth-graders, forever seeking signs of secretive songbirds, continued their silent sojourns, skillfully sketching shimmering spiderwebs and searching for signs of spectacular singing sparrows perched on sunlit spruce branches. But their quest wasn't just about snapping stunning summer selfies. The sixth-graders, fuelled by a thirst for knowledge, hoped to discover forgotten bird folklore, fantastical flying squirrels soaring silently through the forest canopy, or even hidden singing contests filled with chirping chickadees competing for the sweetest song.

One particularly silent sojourn, a sharp-eyed sixth-grader spotted a shimmering shape flitting through the sunlit leaves – a majestic blue jay, its vibrant feathers flashing like sapphires. The excited sixth-graders, with sighs of relief, surrounded the majestic bird, their hushed questions filling the silent air. The blue jay, perched proudly on a sunlit spruce branch, cocked its head inquisitively, its sharp eyes twinkling with amusement. In that silent forest moment, surrounded by the chirping of unseen birds and the rustling of leaves in the summer breeze, a connection was forged between nature and knowledge, a testament to the enduring wonder of the forest and the curious minds of the sixth-graders who explored it.

5. Jelliferous jigglers jostled jealously near jetties. Jewel-toned jellyfish, jiggling gently in the current, jeered at jet skiers zipping by. Each joyful jet skier left a trail of churning water, dislodging juicy jellyfish jewels – shimmering polyps prized by the jellies. With a surge of urgency, the jigglers surged, jostling for position. Jelly tentacles whipped through the water, a silent war for the jewel-like bounty. But the jet skiers were relentless, their joyful shouts echoing over the jealous jostle.

Finally, a particularly daring jellifer, translucent and tinged with envy, snatched a prized polyp just as a jet ski roared past. The jelly pulsed with triumph, a solitary victor in the jostling jelly joust. Yet, as the other jellies watched, their jellyfish jewels bobbing sadly in the current, a glint of determination flickered in their gelatinous forms. The joyful jet skiers might return, but the jigglers would be ready, their silent war for juicy jewels a constant undercurrent in the sun-dappled sea.

Unknown to the jet skiers skimming across the surface, a vital dance was playing out beneath the waves. The jellyfish, despite their lack of brains or brawn, possessed a complex and fascinating social structure. Communication rippled through the water as the jostled jellies pulsed messages to their brethren. Word of the jet skiers' disruption and the loss of precious jewels spread like wildfire. Soon, the entire jelliferous community was buzzing with a silent, stinging anger.

From the depths, colossal jellyfish, their bodies pulsing with an eerie luminescence, began to rise. These elders, rarely seen by human eyes, possessed the power to unleash stinging barbs that could send even the hardiest jet skier fleeing for the shore. As the playful shouts of the jet skiers grew closer, a wave of anticipation crackled through the jelliferous throng. The jellies, once translucent and benign, pulsed with an angry lavender, their delicate forms belying the potent sting they held. The playful chase for jellyfish jewels was about to take a shocking turn. The jet skiers were about to learn a valuable lesson about the power of a united, and rather jellied, front.

6. Cheerful chefs, clad in crisp white coats, juggled juicy jumbo jet-black jumbo shrimp with practiced ease. Their movements were a symphony of skill, each shrimp tossed and caught in a blur of white and black. But these weren't your average cooks – they were judges, tasked with the momentous decision of selecting the juiciest, most jiggly jumbo jet-black jumbo shrimp for a prestigious seafood competition.

Sunlight streamed through the spotless kitchen, illuminating the glistening bodies of the contenders. Each shrimp, a perfect specimen of jet-black brilliance, awaited its fate with a stillness that belied the impending culinary showdown. The chefs, their faces etched with concentration, meticulously examined each crustacean. They used a battery of tests – the weight in their hand, the translucency of the flesh, the satisfying snap when pinched – to assess the shrimp's juiciness and jiggliness. Every detail mattered, for only the most exceptional shrimp would be deemed worthy of the coveted title.

As the chefs worked, a delightful aroma of simmering butter and fresh herbs filled the air. Anticipation crackled in the kitchen, a delicious blend of competition and culinary artistry. Finally, after what seemed like an eternity, the chefs emerged from their huddles, a single, glistening shrimp held aloft by the head judge. This magnificent creature, its jet-black shell practically glowing under the spotlight, had conquered the competition. A cheer erupted from the assembled kitchen staff, a testament to the meticulous judging and the undeniable jiggliness of the champion shrimp.

But the journey wasn't over. This champion shrimp, soon to be transformed into a culinary masterpiece, would be the star of the show, a succulent reward for the discerning palate. Its journey from the depths of the ocean to the glistening plate was a story of skill, dedication, and the unwavering pursuit of jiggly perfection. And as the chefs prepped the winning shrimp, a silent promise hung in the air – a promise to honour its juiciness and jiggliness in a dish that would tantalize the taste buds and leave a lasting impression.

7. Jittery Johnny, juggling juicy jumbo jet-black jalapenos with jittery joy, jolted. One fiery pepper jettisoned like a rogue comet, jeopardising Jerry's jewel-like jumbo shrimp sizzling on the jet-hot grill. Jessica, judging the jiggling shrimp with judicious precision, jerked back with a yelp, a jolt of jalapeno juice splashing her jet-black chef's jacket like a miniature volcanic eruption.

   Jacques, the jolly giant of the kitchen, his booming laughter a constant undercurrent to the culinary chaos, jiggled a jelly jar with practised ease to distract Johnny. With a triumphant "Gotcha!" that echoed through the stainless steel symphony of the kitchen, Jacques caught the rogue jalapeno mid-air, chuckling as Johnny jutted his jaw in relief, beads of sweat clinging to his forehead. Jerry, jittery but unharmed, emerged from behind a towering wall of stainless steel pots and pans, brandishing a metal spatula like a knight's sword. He jeered at Johnny's jalapeno juggling fiasco, his voice laced with mock outrage.

   The near-disaster morphed into a moment of joyful camaraderie. Jessica, wiping the stinging jalapeno juice from her eye with a flourish, tossed a perfectly cooked shrimp onto a waiting plate. Jerry, appeased by the culinary feat, thumped Johnny on the back with the spatula, their playful argument dissolving into shared laughter. The kitchen buzzed with renewed energy, the near-jalapeno incident adding a dash of fiery excitement to the already vibrant atmosphere. The air, thick with the aroma of sizzling shrimp, sizzling peppers, and the sweet perfume of simmering sauces, vibrated with the rhythmic clanging of pots and pans, a symphony conducted by the ever-cheerful Chef Jacques.

8. Mischievous chefs, sporting stylish checked chef hats, scurried swiftly through a shimmering stainless-steel kitchen, searching frantically for forgotten flour sifters. Fuzzy feline friends, forever fascinated by fallen fish fingers, found themselves fiercely fighting for forgotten French fries, their frantic hisses causing a furry frenzy. Startled chefs shrieked, swiftly swiping at the feisty felines with shimmering spatulas. Fortunately, a swift security specialist, sporting a stylish safety squint, swooped swiftly, skillfully scooping up the scattered fries, sending the felines fleeing in a flurry of fur and frustration.

News of the chefs' sensational feline fiasco flickered furiously through food forums, fellow foodies fascinated by the phenomenal feat. Kitchens fizzled with feverish excitement, holographic news reports flashing stories of six mischievous chefs and their sensational feline fiasco. Fuzzy feline friends, momentarily mortified by the misunderstanding, munched melancholically on microscopic morsels of mozzarella, missing their midday mischief of strategically pilfering forgotten food from unsuspecting chefs. Even frisky ferrets, forever fascinated by fizzy fruit drinks, found themselves frantically fiddling with faulty fire extinguishers, their excited hisses a welcome counterpoint to the symphony of sighs and satisfied snorts emanating from the relieved chefs.

The shimmering stainless-steel kitchen, once a source of slight stress for some chefs, became a training ground for spectacular food finesse skills. Chefs, forever fascinated by fantastical flavour combinations, continued their frantic food flourishes, skillfully churning creamy cheese concoctions and searching for signs of sensational, secret spice blends shrouded in the mysteries of generations of master cooks. But their quest wasn't just about filming funny food fights for fizzing social media feeds. The chefs, fueled by a thirst for knowledge, hoped to discover forgotten fermentation formulas, fantastical flying fish recipes etched onto ancient, weather-beaten scrolls, or even hidden spice vaults filled with forgotten flavors whispering tales of legendary culinary creations.

One particularly frantic Friday, a fiery frenzy erupted as a faulty fryer flared, filling the kitchen with a thick cloud of smoke. Fearful foodies fumbled furiously with flickering fire alarms. Fortunately, the swift security specialist, ever the hero, skillfully seized a fire extinguisher and, with a sigh of relief, smothered the flames, saving the day and the chefs' fabulous Friday feast. News of the chefs' phenomenal fire-fighting feat fizzled faster than a faulty fryer through food forums, fellow foodies filled with fervent admiration. The shimmering stainless-steel kitchen, once a source of slight stress, became the key to unlocking a universe of hidden culinary knowledge and heroic skills. The chefs, forever grateful for the swift security specialist, continued their frantic food flourishes, their stainless-steel kitchen forever a symbol of flavour, finesse, and the never-ending quest to explore the phenomenal possibilities of food.

9. Six chubby chipmunks, cheeks stuffed with chocolate chip cookies, chattered cheerfully on a chilly, chestnut-coloured log. Suddenly, a startled squirrel, startled by the chattering chipmunks, scurried swiftly through a shimmering spiderweb strung strategically between sunlit spruce boughs. Startled chipmunks shrieked, swiftly swiping at shimmering spiderwebs, scattering chunks of chocolate chip cookies across the chilly forest floor. Fortunately, swift summer supervisors, sporting stylish straw sunhats, swooped swiftly, skillfully scooping up scattered cookie crumbs with practised ease.

News of the chipmunks' sensational spiderweb skirmish spread swiftly through summer schools, shared in hushed whispers over steaming mugs of soothing sassafras soup. Sun-dappled meadows buzzed with feverish excitement, holographic news reports flashing stories of six chubby chipmunks and their sensational spiderweb skirmish. Startled squirrels, momentarily mortified by the misunderstanding, munched melancholically on microscopic mites, missing their midday mischief of strategically pilfering forgotten sunflower seeds from unsuspecting students. Even frisky field mice, forever fascinated by fallen figs, found themselves fiercely fighting for forgotten french fries, their frantic squeaks a welcome counterpoint to the symphony of sighs and satisfied snorts emanating from the relieved chipmunks.

The chilly, chestnut-coloured log, once a source of slight shivers for some chipmunks, became a training ground for spectacular summertime survival skills. Chipmunks, forever seeking succulent snacks, continued their silent sojourns, skillfully shimmying up shimmering spruce trees and searching for signs of spectacular, secret stashes of sunflower seeds shrouded in the mysteries of the forest. But their quest wasn't just about snapping stunning summer selfies with cheeks full of chocolate. The chipmunks, fueled by a thirst for knowledge, hoped to discover forgotten forest folklore, fantastical flying squirrels soaring silently through the forest canopy, or even hidden honeycombs overflowing with sticky, sweet sunshine.

One particularly chilly sojourn, a sharp-eyed chipmunk spotted a shimmering shape nestled amongst the shimmering spruce needles – a forgotten backpack, its zipper slightly ajar. The excited chipmunks, with sighs of relief, scurried closer, their curious eyes peering inside. To their delight, the backpack overflowed with a treasure trove of treats – chewy chunks of cheese, juicy strawberries, and yes, even more chocolate chip cookies! The chipmunks, forever fascinated by the forest's hidden bounty, feasted joyfully on their newfound fortune, sharing their snacks with the relieved summer supervisors in a heartwarming gesture of chipmunk gratitude. In that chilly, sun-dappled moment, surrounded by the chirping of unseen birds and the rustling of leaves in the summer breeze, a connection was forged between nature and knowledge, a testament to the enduring wonder of the forest and the curious chipmunks who explored it.

CHAPTER 45: UNLOCKING THE VOWELS: A VOYAGE THROUGH VOWEL SOUNDS

Key Vowel Sounds:

- **Short Vowels (quick sounds):** /ɪ/ (pin), /ɛ/ (bed), /æ/ (cat), /ʌ/ (but), /ɒ/ (shop - British)
- **Long Vowels (sustained sounds):** /iː/ (sleep), /eɪ/ (name), /ɑː/ (father), /ɔː/ (boat), /uː/ (moon)
- **Bonus:** /ə/ (schwa - neutral vowel in unstressed syllables), diphthongs (combined vowel sounds)

Practice Techniques:

- **Mirror Work:** See how your tongue, lips, and jaw move for each vowel sound.
- **Minimal Pairs:** Distinguish vowels by practising words with only one vowel sound difference (ship vs. shop).
- **Shadowing:** Mimic the vowel sounds of native speakers as you listen.
- **Tongue Twisters:** Practice vowels in a fun way with tongue twisters like "She sells seashells by the seashore."
- **Record and Reflect:** Listen back to recordings to identify

areas for improvement.

CHAPTER 45A: INSANE TONGUE TWISTERS FOR LONG VOWELS (Ā, Ē, Ī, Ō, Ū):

Hone your vocal precision with these meticulously crafted tongue twisters designed to target **long vowels (ā, ē, ī, ō, ū)**. These exercises will challenge your ability to produce and extend these essential sounds, enhancing articulation and promoting clear, impactful speech.

1. A serpentine creature, scales gleaming an eerie lime, slithered with sinuous grace. Its forked tongue flickered, tasting the cool, damp air, searching for scents of unseen prey. Sunlight dappled the forest floor in fleeting patterns, illuminating the snake's silent, stealthy quest. With a flick of its powerful body, it propelled itself forward, a predator perfectly adapted to its verdant domain.

   The dense foliage whispered secrets in the breeze, a symphony of rustling leaves and chirping insects. But the snake was deaf to these sounds, its world dominated by vibrations travelling through the damp earth. Its keen senses, honed by millennia of evolution, detected the faintest tremor, a potential sign of a scurrying rodent or a plump frog hidden beneath the leaf litter.

The air grew thick with the scent of decaying vegetation, a familiar backdrop to the forest floor. But then, a new note pierced the familiar symphony – a musky aroma, foreign and intriguing. The snake's body coiled, its emerald eyes narrowing in focus. This was the scent it craved, the scent of its next meal.

With renewed purpose, the snake surged forward. The undergrowth parted silently before its sinuous form, its every movement imbued with predatory grace. It was a creature of patience, a master of the silent stalk. It could wait for hours, even days, until the opportune moment arrived. But today, fortune seemed to be on its side. The trail grew stronger, leading it deeper into the heart of the forest.

As the sun dipped below the horizon, casting long shadows across the woodland floor, the snake emerged into a small clearing. There, basking on a moss-covered rock, was a plump field mouse, oblivious to the danger lurking nearby. The snake froze, its body taut with anticipation. This was it. The moment it had been waiting for. In a blur of emerald scales and forked tongue, the snake launched its attack. The clearing erupted in a flurry of fur and frantic squeaks, but it was over in a heartbeat. The perfect predator had claimed its prize, a silent testament to the ruthless beauty of the natural world.

2. A lone wolf lopes along a lofty ridge, its lithe limbs leaving light tracks in the late-night loam. Lifting its long, lean snout towards the luminous moon, the lone wolf unleashes a mournful, melodious moan. The mournful moan meanders through the meadows, echoing eerily across the empty expanse. Every so often, the lone wolf pauses, its amber eyes gleaming in the pale moonlight, before continuing its mournful serenade. The sound seems to weave its way through the whispering pines and sighing spruces, a poignant plea for companionship in the vast, cool night.

Far off, another lone wolf, perched atop a towering peak silhouetted against the ethereal glow of the moon, hears the mournful cry. Its own long, lonely howl rises in response, a haunting counterpoint to the first. The two howls intertwine, creating a melancholic melody that hangs heavy in the cool night air. Perhaps they yearn for a pack, for the warmth of companionship on this desolate night. As the moon begins its descent, casting long, inky shadows across the land, the lone wolf's howls seem to take on a note of urgency. One last, long, lingering howl pierces the night, a final plea that seems to shake the very foundations of the ancient pines. The mournful song fades, leaving an emptiness in its wake, but the echo lingers, carried on the cool night breeze, a testament to the wolf's solitude.

The silence that follows is broken only by the occasional rustle of leaves or the hoot of an owl. The lone wolf, its amber eyes now reflecting a melancholic glint, retreats deeper into the shadows of the forest. Perhaps it seeks shelter amongst the towering trees or maybe it continues its solitary trek, hoping to find solace in the vast wilderness. The night stretches on, vast and uncaring, yet imbued with a strange beauty – the beauty of untamed nature, of raw emotion laid bare under the watchful gaze of the moon. The lone wolf's mournful cry may have faded, but its memory lingers, a reminder of the wild spirit that roams free in the heart of the forest.

3. The towering oak, its branches reaching for the smoky dome of the approaching evening, groaned with the weight of countless acorns. One by one, the ripe orbs broke free from their moorings, plummeting down through the cool, breezeless air. With a series of soft thumps and the occasional loud plop, the acorns landed upon the stone-strewn ground below. Some bounced with surprising vigour, their hulls rolling and clattering across the uneven terrain. Others nestled quietly amongst the pebbles and fallen leaves, their smooth, brown shells camouflaged against the stony backdrop.

A lone crow, perched atop a nearby branch, cawed with amusement as it observed the acornous avalanche. With a graceful dip of its wings, it swooped down, its keen eyes scanning the ground for the juiciest, most delectable morsel. It spotted a particularly plump acorn nestled between two smooth, grey stones and swooped in for the kill. Its sharp beak pried open the shell with ease, and the crow feasted upon the prize within, its long, black form silhouetted against the fiery hues of the approaching sunset.

As the last rays of the sun dipped below the horizon, casting long, inky shadows across the land, the shower of acorns subsided. The once-bustling scene beneath the oak tree became eerily still. The only sound that remained was the occasional rustle of leaves stirred by a gentle evening breeze. Yet, beneath the seemingly peaceful surface, a drama was unfolding. Deep within the cool earth, the fallen acorns, cradled in their stony resting places, began a slow and silent transformation. Fueled by the promise of spring, their dormant hearts stirred with the faintest pulse of life, a testament to the enduring cycle of nature – the old giving way to the new, the promise of a towering oak tree reborn from a single, solitary acorn.

4. The towering trees, their emerald leaves reaching for the smoky dome of the approaching evening, formed a cool, cohesive canopy overhead. Sunlight, filtered through the leafy expanse, dappled the forest floor in a mosaic of light and shadow. Beneath this verdant vault, a sense of cool, serene peace pervaded. The air, heavy with the sweet perfume of pine and damp earth, hung motionless.

A lone deer, its coat the colour of burnished copper, emerged from the dense undergrowth. Its long, elegant legs carried it silently across the forest floor, its keen eyes scanning the verdant surroundings for any sign of danger. The deer paused for a moment, its large, brown ears twitching at the faintest sound. Satisfied that all was clear, it bent its long neck to nibble on the tender shoots of a young fern.

Deep within the leafy labyrinth, a symphony of unseen creatures played out. A woodpecker tapped a rhythmic tattoo on a hollow tree trunk, its crimson crest flashing in the dappled sunlight. A colony of bees buzzed industriously around a hidden hive, their tireless work ensuring the delicate balance of the forest ecosystem. A lone owl, perched silently on a moss-covered branch, surveyed its domain with amber eyes that gleamed with predatory focus.

As the day wore on, the forest floor grew even cooler under the thickening canopy. The dappled light transformed into a soft, golden glow, painting the scene with an ethereal beauty. The air, now scented with the earthy fragrance of decaying leaves, hummed with a quiet energy. The towering trees, their leaves rustling gently in a nonexistent breeze, seemed to stand as silent guardians of this verdant sanctuary, a place where nature thrived under the cool, protective embrace of its leafy embrace.

5. The towering waves, their crests foaming like frothed cream, surged forward with unstoppable force. With a thunderous roar that echoed along the shore, they crashed upon the rugged coastline, sending plumes of salty spray skyward. The relentless rhythm of the ocean, a constant drone that seemed to permeate the very air, filled the ears with its primal symphony.

Seagulls, their white wings flashing against the azure expanse of the sky, soared and dipped above the churning water, their piercing cries adding to the cacophony. Below the surface, the ocean teemed with life. Schools of fish, their scales shimmering like scattered jewels, darted through the kelp forests, forever on guard against unseen predators. A lone whale, its immense form breaching the surface in a spectacular display of power, exhaled a plume of mist that hung suspended in the cool, salty air.

On the shore, a lone figure, her face weathered by the elements, stood transfixed by the spectacle before her. The wind, whipping her long hair into a frenzy, carried the salty spray against her cheeks. Yet, she remained rooted to the spot, her gaze fixed on the endless horizon where the ocean met the sky. The raw power of the sea, the constant ebb and flow of the tide, filled her with a sense of awe and a deep respect for the untamed beauty of nature.

As the sun began its descent, casting long, golden rays across the water, the waves seemed to soften their attack. The thunderous roar gentled into a rhythmic sigh, a lullaby sung by the mighty sea. The lone figure, her heart filled with the peace that only nature could provide, turned and began her trek back along the shore, the echoes of the ocean's song lingering in her ears.

6. The leaden clouds loomed low in the slate-grey sky, weeping long, lonely tears. Each teardrop, a glistening pearl, tumbled slowly from the heavens, its descent marked by a soft, sighing whoosh. Upon reaching the cool expanse of the window pane, the raindrops spread into tiny, shimmering pools. These miniature moats reflected the weeping sky above, their surfaces rippling ever so slightly with the gentle sighs of the wind.

A lone figure curled up on a window seat with a worn paperback clutched in their hands, watched the melancholic scene unfold. The rhythmic patter of the rain created a soothing lullaby, a gentle counterpoint to the hushed whispers turning the pages of the book. Every so often, a particularly large drop would race down the pane, leaving a glistening trail in its wake, momentarily obscuring the weeping world beyond.

As the afternoon wore on, the rain began to ease. The long, lonely tears morphed into scattered sprinkles, each one a tiny, fleeting diamond against the darkening sky. The miniature moats on the window pane dwindled, some merging into larger pools, others evaporating into wisps of steam that drifted skyward. A sliver of pale gold peeked through the parting clouds, painting the edges of the weeping sky with a hint of hope.

With a sigh, the figure on the window seat closed their book, the lingering scent of ink and aged paper a comforting presence. The rain had ceased entirely, leaving behind a world washed clean and glistening. A lone bird, its feathers gleaming in the watery sunlight, soared across the newly-washed sky, its joyful song a testament to the enduring beauty that followed even the weepiest of storms.

7. Screech! Sleepy owlet, perched on a weathered fence post, surveyed his supper scene with a hungry glint in his big brown eyes. "Where's the feast?" hooted the hungry hunter, his russet-feathered form a near-invisible silhouette against the pale moonlight. "A few more mice," he moaned, his voice morose and laced with a hint of desperation, "for this famished feathered fellow, indeed!" His stomach rumbled in agreement, a rumbly reminder of his recent rodent-less night. The owlet swivelled his head on a swivel joint, his keen eyes scanning the shadowy fields below like a feathered searchlight.

A rustle in the ryegrass! The owlet perked up, his posture rigid with predatory focus. Down he swooped a silent flurry of russet feathers, his wings slicing through the night air with barely a whisper. A plump meadow mouse, oblivious to the danger soaring silently overhead, munched contentedly on a juicy moth, its whiskers twitching with delight. But fate, that fickle friend of foragers, had a different dish in mind tonight. The owlet's talons struck with lightning speed, a blur of razor-sharp claws, snatching the squeaking squeakster mid-mognaw. The startled mouse let out a final, high-pitched squeak before disappearing into the owlet's grasp.

Back to his post, the owlet soared, a triumphant twit escaping his beak. Dinner, delicious and delightful, dangled from his grasp. With a satisfied hoot that echoed through the sleeping countryside, the owlet tore into his well-earned meal, the night resuming its peaceful symphony of hoots and chirps. But the hunt, never truly over for a predator, continued in the back of his mind. He would savour this victory, this plump morsel of protein, but as the moon crept higher in the sky, casting long shadows across the land, he knew the gnawing hunger would return. And when it did, the owlet, a silent sentinel of the night, would be ready, his keen eyes scanning the darkness for his next unsuspecting prey.

8. Skinny serpent, scales shimmering a dusty copper in the dappled sunlight, slithered silently through the summer grass. Its belly grumbled a low, rhythmic churn that echoed through the stillness. A sleek, sinuous shadow, the snake was on the hunt, seeking a scrumptious snack to quell its hunger pangs. With practised ease, it shifted its weight, its powerful muscles propelling it forward in a silent, sinuous dance.

Unaware of the silent drama unfolding beneath their beach towels, a group of sunbathers basked in the warmth of the afternoon sun. Laughter drifted on the gentle breeze, punctuated by the rhythmic clink of ice clinking in tall glasses. But beneath their carefree facade, a tiny tremor of fear flickered in a young girl's eyes. She had spotted a flash of movement in the tall grass, a fleeting glimpse of scales catching the sunlight. Her heart hammered against her ribs, a frantic drumbeat urging her to flee.

Suddenly, a plump frog, sunning itself on a lily pad, puffed up its throat in a comical display of bravado. But its bravado was short-lived. The snake, with the reflexes honed by years of hunting, lunged with lightning speed. The frog's bulging eyes widened in terror, its fat green legs kicking out in a desperate attempt to escape. But it was too late. The snake's coils wrapped around the struggling amphibian, a silent, constricting embrace. The frog's frantic struggles grew weaker, its once bright green skin turning a dull, sickly yellow. Then, with a sickening crunch, silence. The snake, its mission accomplished, slowly began to uncoil itself. Its forked tongue flickered out, savouring the scent of its victory.

With a satisfied hiss, the sated serpent slithered towards a nearby thicket, its scales catching the sunlight like scattered jewels. The sunbathers, blissfully unaware of the silent drama that had unfolded just inches from their beach towels, continued their carefree pursuits. The only clue to the events that had transpired lay on the lily pad – a single, crumpled frog leg, a stark reminder of the silent hunter that slithered unseen through the tall grass.

9. Busy bumble bees buzzed by, bright bodies flitting from flower to flower like fuzzy freighters ferrying floral fuel. Busy bees bobbed, their wings a whirring blur, searching sweet sips in summer's sugary bower. They bounced from blooms, bold and beautiful, big buzzing bodies brushing velvety bright bluebells. Higher they climbed, reaching for roses red, ruby rewards ripe for the taking instead. But clumsy bumble bees bumped and they bounced, their buzzy behinds brushing bright bougainvillea. Tumbling through tulips, tangled in thyme, those busy bumble bees buzzed one last time. Back to the hive, bellies full of bright blooms, a buzzing bonanza, a day filled with sweet perfumes!

But their work wasn't over. Inside the hive, a bustling beehive of activity awaited. Queen Beatrice, bigger than the rest with a regal glint in her compound eyes, surveyed her buzzing brood. Worker bees bustled about, unloading their pollen treasures and tending to the honeycomb, a masterpiece of waxy wonder. Drones, the male bees, lazed about in the fringes, waiting for their chance to mate with the queen. The hive hummed with a constant low drone, a symphony of industry composed of thousands of tiny wings.

Outside, the sun dipped lower, casting long shadows across the flower-filled field. The bees, their bellies full and their wings weary, began to return to the hive in a slow, buzzing ballet. One by one, they squeezed through the hive entrance, greeted by their buzzing brethren. Soon, the hive entrance was quiet, save for a lone bee, Henry, a particularly curious fellow. Henry hovered for a moment, gazing at the last rays of the setting sun painting the sky in fiery hues of orange and pink. He buzzed a farewell to the day, a tiny ode to the beauty that surrounded him, before finally following his kin back into the warm, buzzing heart of the hive. The night settled.

11. Six whistling woodwind players, perched precariously on a plush, velvety cushion, puffed furiously on their polished piccolos, their playful performance perfectly placed beneath a sheltering, leafy grove. Sunlight shimmered softly through the swaying leaves, casting shimmering shadows that danced silently across the peaceful picnic grounds. Suddenly, a startled squirrel, startled by the swiftly shifting shadows, scuttled swiftly through a shimmering spiderweb strung strategically between sunlit branches. Startled piccolos shrieked, swiftly swerving to avoid the shimmering strands, sending polished piccolos plummeting to the plush, velvety cushion with a soft, sighing thud. Fortunately, swift security specialists, sporting stylish safety squints, swooped swiftly, skillfully scooping up the scattered piccolos with practised ease.

News of the piccolos' sensational spiderweb skirmish spread swiftly through summer schools, shared in hushed whispers over steaming mugs of soothing sassafras soup. Sun-dappled meadows buzzed with feverish excitement, holographic news reports flashing stories of six whistling woodwind players and their sensational spiderweb skirmish. Startled squirrels, momentarily mortified by the misunderstanding, munched melancholically on microscopic mites, missing their midday mischief of strategically pilfering forgotten sunflower seeds from unsuspecting students. Even fuzzy field mice, forever fascinated by fallen figs, found themselves fiercely fighting for forgotten french fries, their frantic squeaks a welcome counterpoint to the symphony of sighs and satisfied snorts emanating from the relieved piccolos.

The peaceful picnic grounds, once a source of slight snoozes for some students, became a training ground for spectacular summer symphony skills. Woodwind players, forever seeking soothing sounds to soothe the soul, continued their silent serenades, skillfully shimmering through scales and searching for signs of sensational, secret sheet music shrouded in the mysteries of generations of travelling musicians. But their quest wasn't just about snapping stunning summer selfies beneath the whispering leaves. The players, fueled by a thirst for knowledge, hoped to discover forgotten fingering techniques, fantastical flying flutes soaring silently through the sky, or even hidden music boxes filled with forgotten melodies whispering tales of legendary composers.

One particularly silent sojourn, a sharp-eyed woodwind player spotted a shimmering shape nestled amongst the shimmering leaves – a forgotten sheet music stand, its brass base gleaming in the dappled sunlight. The excited players, with sighs of relief, surrounded the dusty stand, their curious eyes peering at the faded parchment sheets. To their delight, the music stand held a treasure trove of forgotten melodies – waltzes that whispered of bygone eras, jigs that jangled with joy, and even a lullaby so soft and soothing it could send even the weariest soul peacefully to sleep. With a sense of awe and excitement, the woodwind players embraced the music of the past, their hearts filled with the thrill of discovery and the endless possibilities for creating new and beautiful sounds to soothe and inspire the world. The whispering leaves, once a source of slight snoozes, became the key to unlocking a universe of hidden melodies and musical magic. The woodwind players, forever grateful for the forgotten sheet music, continued their silent serenades, their polished piccolos forever a symbol of skill, serenity, and the never-ending quest to fill the world with the soothing sounds of music.

12. Roaring rapids ripped and roared, rushing right down rugged rock faces. Frothing fury flung foam skyward, a frightening fight for fragile ferns clinging to the cliffside. The river roiled a relentless roar that echoed through the canyon, ripping rocks from the riverbed like pebbles. Rushing rapids raced on, a churning ribbon of rage, its colour a bruised red in the light of the rising dawn. But amidst the mayhem, a tiny trout, tight to the river bottom, held its ground. With powerful flicks of its tail, it battled the current, a speck of defiance against the raging torrent.

Above, a lone hawk, perched on a weather-beaten snag, watched with keen eyes. The hawk's screech, sharp and sudden, sliced through the roar of the river. Its gaze locked on the struggling trout, a silent promise of a coming struggle, another twist in the wild drama unfolding on the raging river.

Downstream, a weathered wooden bridge creaked and groaned as the water surged beneath it. A lone traveller, bundled in a thick oilskin coat, gripped the railing tightly, his face etched with concern. He had seen rivers rage before, but this one possessed a primal fury that sent shivers down his spine. The bridge swayed precariously, each crashing wave threatening to tear it from its moorings. Yet, the traveller held firm, his weathered face mirroring the resilience of the ancient bridge. He knew the river's fury would eventually subside, and the sun, peeking through the breaking clouds, promised calmer waters ahead.

Meanwhile, deep within a hidden cave nestled behind the cascading waterfall, a lone hermit stirred from his meditation. The tremors of the raging river had reached even his secluded sanctuary. With a sigh, he rose from his straw mat and shuffled towards the cave entrance. The roar of the water was a familiar lullaby, a constant reminder of the untamed power that coursed through the very heart of the mountain. He peered out at the churning torrent, a flicker of concern crossing his aged face. The river's fury seemed to intensify with each passing year, and he worried for the delicate balance of the ecosystem it sustained. With a muttered prayer, the hermit retreated back into the cave, his weathered hands clasped in silent contemplation.

The raging river continued its relentless course, oblivious to the drama it played out for the creatures who shared its domain. It was a force of nature, a symbol of both destruction and renewal, a constant reminder of the raw power that sculpted the very landscape.

13. I Seven mischievous moths, mesmerised by the moon's milky glow, fluttered frantically from fuzzy ferns, chasing shimmering fireflies flitting through the field. Suddenly, a startled skunk, startled by the swiftly fluttering moths, sprayed a shocking stench skyward, sending shimmering fireflies scattering like startled stars. Startled moths shrieked, swiftly swerving to avoid the shocking scent, sending fuzzy ferns flying in all directions. Fortunately, swift security specialists, sporting stylish safety squints, swooped swiftly, skillfully shooing away the startled skunk with practised ease.

News of the moths' sensational skunk skirmish spread swiftly through summer schools, shared in hushed whispers over steaming mugs of soothing sassafras soup. Starry meadows buzzed with feverish excitement, holographic news reports flashing stories of seven mischievous moths and their sensational skunk skirmish. Startled skunks, momentarily mortified by the misunderstanding, munched melancholically on microscopic mites, missing their midday mischief of strategically pilfering forgotten French fries from unsuspecting campers. Even frisky field mice, forever fascinated by fallen figs, found themselves fiercely fighting for forgotten french fries, their frantic squeaks a welcome counterpoint to the symphony of sighs and satisfied snorts emanating from the relieved moths.

The grassy field, once a source of slight shivers for some moths, became a training ground for spectacular summer survival skills. Moths, forever fascinated by the flickering firefly light, continued their frantic flits, skillfully searching for the sweetest-smelling flowers and shimmering signs of spectacular, secret summer solstice celebrations shrouded in the mysteries of the night. But their quest wasn't just about snapping stunning summer selfies beneath the milky moonlight. The moths, fueled by a thirst for knowledge, hoped to discover forgotten folklore of the night, fantastical flying fish flitting silently through the moonlight, or even hidden honeycombs overflowing with sticky, sweet nectar, whispering tales of legendary nocturnal creatures.

One particularly frantic flight, a sharp-eyed moth spotted a shimmering shape nestled amongst the shimmering wildflowers – a forgotten book, its leather cover weathered by time. The excited moths, with sighs of relief, surrounded the dusty book, their curious eyes peering at the faded pages. To their delight, the book held a treasure trove of forgotten night-time wisdom – secrets of navigating by the stars, the language of fireflies, and even a map to a hidden meadow overflowing with the sweetest-smelling flowers on Earth. With a sense of awe and excitement, the moths embraced the knowledge of the past, their hearts filled with the thrill of discovery and the endless possibilities for exploring the wonders of the night. The grassy field, once a source of slight shivers, became the key to unlocking a universe of hidden secrets and the magic of the moonlight. The moths, forever grateful for the forgotten book, continued their frantic flits, their iridescent wings forever a symbol of wonder, wisdom, and the never-ending quest to explore the beauty and mysteries of the night.

CHAPTER 45B: INSANE TONGUE TWISTERS FOR SHORT VOWELS (A, E, I, O, U):

Elevate your speech clarity and communication impact with this collection of tongue twisters designed to refine your **short vowel** (a, e, i, o, u) production. These meticulously crafted phrases will challenge your articulation, promoting precise and professional-sounding speech.

1. A timid tick-tock, a tiny tap, echoed from the turquoise tin perched precariously on the tap. Tim, the tea-loving tinker, his thirst a tiny tempest in his tummy, tiptoed towards the table. His worn boots squeaked softly against the wooden floorboards, the only sound daring to disturb the quiet of his workshop. Reaching out with a tentative tap, the tin revealed a tempting treasure trove - tiny, tempting teacups, nestled in a bed of soft, crimson velvet. Each cup, a masterpiece in miniature, boasted a delicate floral design, the colors as bright and vibrant as a summer meadow. Tim's heart skipped a beat. These weren't just any teacups; these were a collector's dream, a forgotten relic from a bygone era. A wide grin stretched across his face, crinkling the corners of his eyes. With a triumphant

chuckle, Tim carefully lifted the tin, the rhythmic tick-tock now a joyous symphony to his ears. Today, his usual cup of afternoon tea would be a truly extraordinary affair.

The workshop, usually a haven of whirring gears and clanging metal, was bathed in the golden glow of the afternoon sun streaming through the dusty windowpanes. Cobwebs, shimmering with the borrowed light, hung like ghostly tapestries in the corners, undisturbed by the gentle clinking of the teacups as Tim arranged them on his workbench. A well-worn teapot, its surface dented and scratched but polished to a warm gleam, sat patiently beside a chipped enamel mug filled with bubbling water from the rusty kettle perched on the ancient wood-burning stove. Tim, with the meticulous care of an artist, measured out a precise portion of loose-leaf tea, the fragrant aroma filling the air with a promise of warm spices and exotic flowers. As the tea steeped, its essence swirling in the amber liquid, Tim meticulously inspected his newfound treasures. Each cup, unique in its design, held a story waiting to be told. One, adorned with a delicate pattern of forget-me-nots, whispered of a lover's pledge. Another, decorated with bold sunflowers, evoked memories of a sun-drenched childhood. With a reverence that bordered on the sacred, Tim selected a cup – a simple design with a single, perfect rose – and poured the steaming tea. The warmth seeped into his chilled hands as he cradled the cup, his eyes closed, savoring the moment. This wasn't just tea; it was a journey through time, a connection to a world long forgotten. And as the first sip of the fragrant elixir touched his lips, Tim knew this was an afternoon he would never forget.

2. Busy bakers, Ben and Beth, bustled before the break of dawn, building blazing fires in brick ovens. Billowing billows of heat battled the bready breeze. Batter bowls brimmed, Beth beat batter briskly, bubbles bursting, batter thickening. Ben, with baker's finesse, braided beautiful brioche, baguettes begging to be baked. Bushels of bready bounty filled the oven, filling the bakery with a blissful, yeasty bouquet.

Bells boomed, bakers beamed, bread bursting from the oven, brown and beautiful. Baskets brimmed, breakfasts beckoned, bringing bustling business to the bakery. Bon appetit! Customers clambered in, captivated by the crusty creations. Croissants crackled, inviting fingers to reach. Doughnuts dripped with decadent delights, danishes danced with delight in the display case.

The scent of warm bread swirled a siren song for sleepy souls. Coffee cups clattered, conversations crackled, customers savouring their steaming sips and sunrise sustenance. Ben, balancing a tray of buttery biscuits, bantered with a businessman, both bemused by the spilt jam that resembled a jewelled masterpiece. Beth, busily bagging bagels, befriended a bashful ballerina, both bonding over their love for perfectly formed circles – one edible, one pirouetting with grace.

The bakery buzzed a beehive of happy activity. The rhythmic clatter of the cash register chimed in counterpoint to the contented sighs of satisfied customers. As the morning wore on, the bakers' bounty dwindled, replaced by the delightful disarray of crumbs and coffee grounds – a testament to a successful start to the day. But fear not, for Ben and Beth, with tireless dedication, would soon be back at it, their tireless hands shaping, kneading, and baking, ready to fill the bakery with the magic of bread once more.

3. Ten tiny tourists, ten tippy-tapping tots, toddled through towering temples, their eyes wide with wonder. Tropical birds twittered in the tangled treetops, their vibrant feathers flashing like jewels in the dappled sunlight. The tourists, led by Timmy, their tour guide with a tattered map and an infectious grin, tiptoed past towering statues of forgotten gods, their expressions etched in stone. Incense smoke, a wispy tendril, curled upwards, carrying with it the sweet, musky scent of sandalwood and exotic spices.

Timmy, his voice a hushed whisper, pointed out ancient murals depicting tales of bygone battles and mythical creatures. The tiny tourists, their imaginations ignited, gasped at the sight of ferocious tigers battling brave warriors and mischievous monkeys swinging through the jungle canopy. Stepping into a dimly lit chamber, their eyes adjusted to the flickering candlelight, revealing a treasure trove of trinkets – gleaming gold jewellery, intricately carved jade figurines, and silk scarves shimmering with every colour imaginable. Each trinket, a testament to the artisans' skill, whispered stories of a time-honoured tradition passed down through generations.

The tourists, their tiny fingers itching to touch, were gently reminded by Timmy to keep their hands firmly planted in their pockets. They giggled as a mischievous monkey, drawn by the commotion, swung down from a nearby rafter, snatching a tourist's hat in its nimble fingers. With a shriek and a flurry of activity, the hat was retrieved, a testament to the monkey's quick wit and the tourists' lightning-fast reflexes.

Emerging from the temple, blinking in the bright

sunlight, the tiny tourists buzzed with excitement, their tiny voices recounting the wonders they had witnessed. The timeless traditions, the breathtaking treasures, and the cheeky monkey encounter – all woven into a tapestry of memories they would cherish forever. The temple, a silent guardian of the past, stood tall, a testament to the enduring power of history and the boundless curiosity of ten tiny tourists.

4. Kit, a keen chronicler of kings, kept countless kingdoms' chronicles crammed in his cluttered attic. Musty manuscripts, meticulously marked, mingled with magnificent maps and miniature models of medieval moats. Each mammoth manuscript brimmed with monumental moments in monarchical madness, meticulously documented in Kit's spidery script.

There were tales of tyrannical tyrants who taxed turnips and terrified townsfolk, of valiant viziers who vanquished vicious villains, and of whimsical weddings where wigged walruses waltzed with winsome princesses. Kit, captivated by these chronicles, could spend hours hunched over a hefty history, his brow furrowed in concentration as he deciphered dog-eared documents detailing diplomatic disasters and daring duels.

One particularly perplexing parchment depicted a portly prince pilfering pastries from a palace pantry, pursued by a pack of particularly peeved pigeons. Kit chuckled, his keen eyes gleaming with delight. These chronicles weren't just dusty records; they were portals to a bygone era, brimming with bizarre behaviour and captivating characters.

As twilight tinged the attic with an inky hue, Kit

reluctantly shut the final manuscript. The chronicles, with their tales of triumph and treachery, would wait until tomorrow. But for now, Kit dreamt of daring deeds and delicious desserts, his mind swirling with the captivating chronicles of kings.

5. Five fearless firefighters, faces grim with gritty smudge, fought frantically to extinguish feverish flames. The forest, once a verdant haven, was a raging inferno. Fierce winds whipped the flames, twisting them into monstrous serpents that devoured trees whole. Flickering embers danced on the wind, a fiery ballet threatening to engulf everything in its path.

Sweat trickled down the firefighters' faces, stinging their eyes. Their hoses, thick black serpents themselves, sputtered and hissed, sending jets of water against the relentless inferno. But the flames, fueled by tinder-dry leaves and ferocious gusts, roared back with defiant fury.

The firefighters, a well-oiled firefighting unit, communicated with curt calls and determined glances. Fred, the fearless fire chief, directed them with a steely gaze. "Focus on the flank, fellas! Don't let it jump the ridge!" he bellowed, his voice hoarse from smoke inhalation.

Flick, the youngest firefighter, her nimble form a blur of frantic activity, hacked at burning undergrowth, creating a firebreak. Rick, the grizzled veteran, with muscles like knotted ropes, maneuvered the heavy fire truck, positioning it for a better attack.

The forest, once alive with chirping birds and rustling leaves, was now a symphony of crackling flames and hissing water. The air, thick with smoke and ash, tasted bitter on their tongues. But the firefighters, fueled by an unwavering determination, pressed on. They were the thin red line between the town nestled in the valley below and the fiery beast consuming the forest.

Hours bled into one another, the sun a hazy disk in the smoke-filled sky. But slowly, ever so slowly, the tide began to turn. The wind, sensing the firefighters' relentless assault, began to wane. The flames, starved of their oxygen supply, flickered and danced with a waning fury.

Exhausted but victorious, the firefighters watched the last embers of the forest fire sputter and die. The blackened landscape, a testament to the inferno's wrath, stretched before them. But amidst the devastation, shoots of green, signs of resilience, began to push through the scorched earth. The firefighters, weary but resolute, knew their work was far from over. But for now, they had won this battle, saving a town and preserving a vital ecosystem.

6. Doris, a dusty museum docent with a dull droning voice, mumbled muddled musings about mummies and mammoths of the Mesozoic Era. Drowsing dinosaurs dominated dusty dioramas, their dull, reptilian forms illuminated by flickering fluorescent lights. A bored bunch of students shuffled through the stuffy halls, their eyelids drooping like drowsy moths.

Doris, oblivious to their lack of luster, launched into a lecture laced with long, technical terms. "These magnificent mammoths," she droned, gesturing at a giant skeleton with missing tusks, "munched on massive mounds of misty mosses millions of miles in the past." A muffled snicker erupted from the back of the group, but Doris pressed on, her monotone a monotonous murmur.

Suddenly, a squawk shattered the soporific stupor. A

mischievous magpie, wings a blur of black and white, had snuck in through an open window. It landed with a cocky caw on the sarcophagus of a supposed pharaoh, its beady black eyes gleaming with amusement. The students, jolted awake, watched in fascination as the magpie hopped around, pecking at the pharaoh's painted nose.

Doris, flustered and flustering, shooed the bird away with a flimsy feather duster. But the magpie, a feathered trickster, wouldn't be deterred. It swooped down, snatching a mummy's dusty bandage in its beak and taking flight with a triumphant squawk. The students erupted in laughter, the sound a joyous melody that echoed through the stuffy halls.

Doris, defeated and deflated, sighed. The museum visit, meant to be a majestic march through time, had become a muddled mess. But as she watched the students, their faces alight with amusement, a tiny spark of amusement flickered in her own eyes. Perhaps, she thought, a little bit of muddle and a mischievous magpie were exactly what these students needed to remember the mammoths and mummies of the long-lost Mesozoic Era.

7. Stuart, a stubby, stuffy taxidermist with a sniffly snuffle, struggled to stuff stuffing into a fluffy stuffed puppy. Soft sobs escaped his lips, blurring his vision as he wrestled with the floppy fabric. The puppy, destined to be a delightful display in a child's room, lay limp on the worktable, its floppy ears drooping like deflated balloons.

Stuart, a man of meticulous methods, prided himself on his perfectly plump plushies. But this puppy, with its stubborn stuffing and uncooperative seams, was proving to be a prickly problem. He prodded and poked, his chubby fingers fumbling with the fluffy fabric. Each frustrated shove sent a puff of cotton fluff flying into the air, tickling his nose and making him sneeze.

"Just a bit more," he muttered, his voice thick with emotion. But the stuffing, as if possessed by a mischievous imp, stubbornly refused to cooperate. It clumped and bunched, leaving the puppy looking more like a lumpy sausage than a cuddly canine. Tears welled up in Stuart's eyes, blurring the already blurry seams. Was he cut out for this cuddly creature career?

Suddenly, a tiny voice piped up from behind him. "Mister, can I help?" Stuart sniffled and turned to see a little girl, her eyes wide with concern, clutching a tattered teddy bear.

With a shaky smile, Stuart nodded. Together, the unlikely pair wrestled with the wily wadding, the little girl's nimble fingers surprisingly adept at stuffing the stubborn seams. Slowly, the puppy began to take shape, its form rounding out with each gentle push.

Finally, with a triumphant sniff and a satisfied sigh, Stuart declared the puppy perfectly plump. The little girl beamed, her eyes sparkling with delight. As Stuart handed her the finished plushie, a warmth spread through his chest, chasing away the sniffles and replacing them with a contented chuckle.

Perhaps, he thought, creating cuddly creatures wasn't just about meticulous methods; it was about the magic that a little help and a lot of heart could bring to a fluffy stuffed friend.

8. Seven silly sailors, Skipper Finn, Pip, Gus, Chick, Cliff, Tim, and Will, set sail in a leaky little ship, the "Silly Shell

Seeker." Singing sea shanties with gusto, they skimmed shimmering sapphire seas, searching sun-dappled shores for shimmering seashells. Suddenly, a squall swept in, soaking salty sails and silly sailors! Sputtering, they scurried, scooping seawater with rusty sieves. "Quick, lads!" cried Skipper Finn, "Plug the pesky leaks with wads of kelp!"

With a splash and a sputter, the silly sailors plugged the leaky vessel, vowing to seek shelter in a secluded cove. Shivering slightly, they settled in for a sunset supper of salty salmon and soggy ship's biscuits. Though soaked to the socks, their spirits stayed sunny, for the silly sailors still sought shimmering seashells on shimmering sandy shores!

The next day, a crimson sunrise kissed the horizon, beckoning them onward. As the wind whispered secrets through the rigging, the "Silly Shell Seeker" bobbed merrily across the waves. Keen-eyed Pip, perched in the crow's nest, squinted and shouted, "Land ahoy, lads!" A thrill coursed through the crew. Soon, a lush, emerald island emerged from the misty blue. Palm trees swayed gently in the breeze, promising a haven of rest and, perhaps, a treasure trove of shimmering seashells.

With renewed vigour, the silly sailors steered towards the island. As they drew closer, the scent of exotic fruits wafted aboard, mingling with the salty tang of the sea. Crystal-clear lagoons beckoned, promising cool relief from the sweltering sun. But just as they neared the shore, a gruff voice boomed from the beach, "Avast, ye scurvy scalawags! This be forbidden territory!" A hulking pirate, Captain Cutlass, stood guard, brandishing a rusty cutlass. The silly sailors exchanged bewildered glances. This wasn't part of the plan!

9. A chubby cherub, Chuck, clung to his chubby, cuddly chum, Bun-Bun, chubby cheeks puffed with worry. Chuck's chubby chin quivered as a buzzing bumblebee bumbled by. The big, buzzing bee brushed by Bun-Bun's button buttonhole, making Chuck clutch him tighter.

"Waaaah!" wailed Chuck, chubby tears welling in his chubby eyes. "B-b-b-bee!" he stammered, pointing a chubby finger at the buzzing bug. Bun-Bun, though just a stuffed bunny, seemed to puff out his button nose in a comforting puff.

Chuck's sniffles subsided slightly as he snuggled Bun-Bun. Mommy bustled in, her brisk steps a comforting hush-hush. "What's the fuss, my little Chuck?" she cooed, scooping him up in her warm arms. Chuck, nestled in her comfy embrace, pointed again. "B-b-b-bee!" he mumbled, chubby face buried in her shirt.

Mommy chuckled, her eyes scanning the room. There, by the sunny window, she spotted the busy bee. With a calm hum, she grabbed a flimsy napkin and shooed the bee out the window. "There, there, Chuck," she soothed, "the busy bee is buzzing back to his bizzy business."

Chuck peeked out from his hiding place, his chubby cheeks still flushed. But a tiny smile tugged at his lips. The bee was gone, thanks to Mommy's quick cuff. Chuck snuggled Bun-Bun once more, feeling safe and sound.

Suddenly, a loud, buzzing sound filled the room again! Chuck squeezed his eyes shut, burying his face in Bun-Bun's soft fur. But to his surprise, the buzzing grew softer, then stopped altogether. Mommy giggled. "Look up, my little love," she said.

Chuck hesitantly opened his eyes. Perched on the

windowsill, buzzing contentedly, was a fuzzy little bumblebee. But this one wasn't big and scary. It was small and fluffy, with fuzzy black stripes and fuzzy yellow legs. It bobbed its fuzzy head at Chuck, then buzzed off towards a patch of bright yellow sunflowers blooming in the garden.

Chuck stared, wide-eyed. The bee wasn't scary after all! In fact, it was kind of cute. A giggle escaped his lips, turning into a full-blown belly laugh. Bun-Bun, the ever-faithful companion, seemed to chortle along with him. Mommy scooped Chuck up in a big hug, showering him with kisses. "See, sweetheart," she said, "there's nothing to be afraid of. Some bees just like to buzz around and collect pollen."

From that day on, Chuck wasn't afraid of bees anymore. He learned that there were many different kinds of bees, some big and some small, some scary and some not so scary. And whenever he saw a bee buzzing around the flowers, he'd smile and wave, remembering his adventure with the fuzzy little bumblebee.

CHAPTER 46: INSANE TONGUE TWISTERS FOR DIPHTHONGS

Prepare for a vocal workout like no other! This section is dedicated to the delightful but devilish **diphthongs** – those tricky two-vowel teams that can trip up even the most seasoned speaker. Whether you're wrestling with "oi," navigating the nuances of "ou," or conquering the challenges of "ow," these tongue twisters will put your pronunciation to the ultimate test. So, warm up those vocal cords, pucker those lips, and get ready to embark on a thrilling linguistic adventure. Can you conquer the chaos of these diphthong-filled phrases? Let's find out!

1. A playful clownfish, a splash of sunshine amidst the coral colonies, proudly displayed its showy, flowing fins. The vibrant orange stripes that bisected its body shimmered like painted flames, and its snow-white anemone home pulsed gently in the current.

   With a flick of its powerful tail (fin), the clownfish darted through a labyrinth of swaying sea fans, its beady eyes scanning for morsels to devour. Households of hermit crabs, their borrowed shells adorned with colourful anemones, scuttled across the sandy bottom, their claws clicking a rhythmic counterpoint to the clownfish's playful dance.

A school of shimmering sapphire fish, their scales catching the sunlight like scattered jewels, swooped past, their bodies forming a mesmerising underwater ballet. The clownfish, ever the showman, puffed out its chest (fin), its vibrant colours a stark contrast to the muted tones of the surrounding reef. It wiggled its feathery appendages (fins) playfully, a silent boast to the admiring audience of shrimp and starfish.

Suddenly, a sleek shadow darted past, sending shivers down the clownfish's spine. A lone barracuda, its body a steely grey, sliced through the water with predatory grace. The clownfish, its playful mood momentarily forgotten, sought refuge within the welcoming embrace of its anemone home, a silent prayer for safety whispered on the gentle current.

2. Five flabby flounders, with wide, surprised eyes, floundered foolishly in the flowing fountain. Their flat, brown bodies flipped and flopped clumsily, splashing fountain water high into the air. The cascading water, once a source of tranquillity, became a foamy frenzy, filled with scales and fishy flops. The fountain fixture, a bronze cherub with a perpetually surprised expression, sputtered and spluttered in outrage. Its once-gleaming surface was now fouled by a fishy film, and its carefully sculpted spout sputtered ineffectively, spewing out a gout of water mixed with indignant gurgles.

The commotion attracted the attention of a nearby park ranger, a stout woman with a no-nonsense demeanour. Her eyes narrowed as she surveyed the scene – the flustered fountain, the frustrated cherub, and the five flabby flounders still flopping about with reckless abandon. With a sigh and a shake of her head, she grabbed her trusty net. Stalking towards the fountain, she waded into the cool water, her boots leaving a trail of muddy footprints in their wake. The flounders, sensing danger, flopped with renewed vigour, their fins churning the water into a cloudy mess. But the park ranger was a woman of action. With a swift scoop of her net, she scooped up all five flounders in one smooth motion.

Dripping and gasping, the flounders were deposited back into the nearby stream, their natural habitat. With a final glare at the now-empty fountain, the park ranger turned and marched away, leaving the fountain to sputter and gurgle in an attempt to regain its composure. Slowly, the water began to clear, the fishy film dissipating with each passing moment. The bronze cherub, relieved of its watery torment, resumed its spout of gentle trickles. And the five flabby flounders, swimming free in the cool stream, undoubtedly learned a valuable lesson about the importance of finding the right floundering environment.

3. A loud shout echoed through the towering pines, rousing the rowdy scouts from their slumbering repose. With a startled shout, Scout Sarah scrambled out of her hammock, her paint-splattered smock flapping wildly. Grabbing her rusty canteen, she stumbled towards the source of the commotion. There, Scout Brian, his freckled face contorted in a shout, pointed towards the swiftly approaching cloud of dust.

"Cow stampede!" he bellowed, his voice hoarse from shouting. "Grab your buckets and cowbells, now!"

Pandemonium erupted. Scouts, a boisterous bunch at the best of times, descended into a flurry of frantic activity.

Stout Sarah, ever the reliable one, hauled out a dented metal bucket and a noisy brass cowbell. The other scouts followed suit, their movements a cacophony of shouts, clanging buckets, and the clanging, clanging of cowbells.

Moments later, a thundering herd of cows, their brown bodies a churning mass, rounded the bend in the dusty trail. The scouts, a determined line of mismatched footwear and wild determination, stood firm. With a synchronised shout and a cacophony of clanging cowbells, they charged towards the oncoming bovine brigade. The cows, startled by the sudden ruckus, bellowed in surprise and swerved, their hooves kicking up dust devils that danced in the afternoon sunlight.

The scouts, hearts pounding but faces alight with the thrill of the chase, expertly steered the cows away from the delicate ecosystem of the nearby meadow. After a few tense moments, the herd thundered off in a different direction, their disgruntled moos fading into the distance. The scouts, chests heaving and faces flushed, collapsed onto the dusty ground, a ragtag bunch of troupers who had saved the day with their rusty buckets and their loud, noisy cowbells. Laughter erupted, echoing through the trees, a testament to their teamwork and their unwavering spirit of scouting adventure.

4. Eight brightly painted pails, a rainbow collection in a row, awaited their juicy bounty. Inside, nestled in a bed of fragrant hay, lay eight perfectly ripe peaches, their fuzzy skins a canvas of sunshine yellow and blushing red. Each peach, a promise of summer sweetness, seemed to whisper tales of lazy afternoons spent picnicking in the park, chasing butterflies through wildflower meadows, and splashing in cool, refreshing streams.

The arrival of eight playful children shattered the afternoon's tranquillity, their laughter echoing through the air like wind chimes dancing in a summer breeze. Armed with tiny wicker baskets and infectious smiles, they descended upon the pails like a joyful swarm of bumblebees. Tiny hands reached in, carefully selecting the ripest peaches, their plump forms cradled with the utmost care as if they were precious jewels.

The children, a kaleidoscope of bright clothes and boundless energy, compared their treasures. Giggles erupted as a particularly juicy peach left a sticky stain on a freckled nose, and a playful water fight ensued, leaving them cool and refreshed under the summer sun. Soon, the air was filled with the sweet sounds of contented munching and the happy sighs of satisfied taste buds. Each bite of the peaches, bursting with sunshine flavour and dripping with sweet nectar, was a celebration of summer's bounty. The juice, staining chins and fingers a vibrant shade of red, became a badge of honour, a symbol of pure summer indulgence.

As the afternoon sun dipped below the horizon, painting the sky in hues of orange and pink, the eight empty pails stood as a testament to the delightful feast. The children, their faces sticky and their hearts full, chased fireflies that blinked on and off like celestial winks in the gathering twilight. Whispers of secrets and dreams for future summer adventures filled the air, punctuated by the contented chirping of crickets and the rustling of leaves in the gentle evening breeze. The day's simple pleasure, the joy of fresh peaches shared with friends, would be a cherished memory, a reminder of summer's sweetness long after the last peach had been devoured and the last firefly had faded into the night. Tucked away in their dreams, the taste of sunshine and the memory of laughter would linger, a promise of summers yet to come.

5. Proud, towering pines, their brown boughs reaching for the heavens like the gnarled fingers of ancient giants, whispered secrets in the howling clouds. The wind, a restless louse tormented by an insatiable itch, roused the house above, a churning cauldron of grey turmoil. Its voice, a mournful shout that seemed to emanate from the very depths of the storm itself, howled through the twisted branches of the trees, rattling their needles and sending showers of cones plummeting to the forest floor. Lightning, a fleeting white mouse arcing across the inky shroud, momentarily illuminated the scene – the stoic pines swaying in the gale, their rough bark etched with the stories of a thousand howling nights. Below, the once-peaceful town huddled together, a collection of fragile dolls' houses dwarfed by the immensity of the storm. Smoke, usually a gentle plume curling from chimneys, now whipped wildly from rooftops, a defiant wisp of grey against the encroaching darkness.

The storm raged on, a chaotic spouse locked in a tempestuous dance with the night. Its fury, a primal scream echoing through the ancient trees, rattled windows and shook the very foundations of the houses. Yet, the pines, their roots anchored deep in the earth, stood resolute. They had weathered countless storms before, their boughs bearing the scars of past battles with the elements. And within their woody brows, safe from the wind's icy touch and the lightning's blinding flash, the secrets they whispered – secrets of bygone seasons, of playful squirrels and soaring eagles – remained safe, a silent testament to the enduring strength of nature and the enduring stories whispered by the wind.

As dawn approached, painting the eastern horizon with

streaks of bruised purple and angry orange, the storm began to wane. The wind's mournful cries softened into a gentle sigh, and the rain, once a relentless torrent, became a pitter-patter on the windowpanes. The weary pines, their needles heavy with rainwater, seemed to exhale a collective sigh of relief. The house above, no longer a churning cauldron of fury, retreated into a bank of retreating clouds, its wrath spent. In the distance, a single tendril of smoke rose lazily from a chimney, a sign of life returning to the storm-battered town. The birds, their songs momentarily silenced by the storm's fury, began their morning chorus, a joyful melody that filled the air. And the secrets, safe within the boughs of the pines, awaited the next storyteller, the next gentle breeze that would carry them on its journey, weaving them into the fabric of the ever-changing forest.

6. A bright brown owl hooted in the towering oak's shadowy boughs. Moonlight, diffused by a veil of high-altitude clouds, painted the forest floor in an eerie, wavering glow. The owl, a silent sentinel perched on a gnarled branch thick with the memories of countless seasons, scanned the woods with eyes that gleamed like polished amber. A rustle in the undergrowth – a field mouse, its movements betraying a youthful naiveté. With a silent launch, as smooth as a shadow detaching itself from the darkness, the owl swooped. Talons, honed to razor-sharp points by a lifetime of hunting, snatched the prey in a blur of brown feathers and silent fury.

Back on its branch, the owl hooted – a victory cry that resonated through the stillness of the night. The sound echoed through the towering pines and ancient hemlocks, a chilling reminder to any other small creature foolish enough to venture out under the cloak of darkness. But the forest was a complex tapestry, woven not just with the threads of predator and prey. A family of foxes, their coats the colour of burnished copper, emerged from their den at the base of the oak. Kits, playful and rambunctious, tumbled over each other, their shrill barks a counterpoint to the owl's solemn call. The vixen, sleek and watchful, kept a wary eye on the owl, but knew its hunting grounds lay far above the forest floor.

Below, silence returned, broken only by the rhythmic chirping of crickets, an unseen orchestra serenading the forest floor. It was a reminder of the delicate balance that existed beneath the oak's watchful gaze, a predator-prey dance as old as time itself. The owl, its hunger momentarily sated, settled back onto its perch, its amber eyes scanning the darkness once more. The forest held its breath, waiting for the next act in this timeless drama to unfold. But the night was far from over. A lone wolf, its fur the colour of twilight, emerged from the dense undergrowth. Its silver eyes, filled with an ancient wisdom, met the owl's gaze for a fleeting moment. Then, with a soft whine, the wolf continued its solitary journey, a silent hunter on the prowl. The owl hooted again, its call tinged with a newfound respect. This vast ecosystem, bathed in the cool moonlight, was a shared kingdom, each creature playing its part in the grand symphony of the night.

7. A boisterous bunch, a gaggle of giggly clowns, tumbled out of a tiny house trailer, their painted faces beaming with merriment. In their wake followed a cacophony of clanging and clanging – a whole herd of happy helpers, proudly parading a collection of colourful cowbells. The townsfolk, roused from their usual routines by the joyful din, gathered around, faces creased with curiosity.

The lead clown, a portly fellow with a crimson nose and a shock of orange hair, bowed low. "Fear not, friends!" he boomed, his voice laced with playful theatricality. "We come in peace, and with noise!" He gestured towards his companions, each one outfitted with a brightly painted cowbell, their faces alight with anticipation.

With a flourish, the clowns launched into a chaotic symphony. Cowbells of all sizes and tones clanged in a merry jumble, the sound bouncing off the buildings and echoing down the quiet street. The townsfolk, initially startled, couldn't help but be swept up in the infectious energy. Soon, smiles were replacing frowns, and hesitant taps of the feet morphed into full-fledged dancing. Children, their faces alight with delight, chased after the clanging clowns, their laughter adding to the joyous cacophony.

For a brief, magical hour, the town square became a stage for unbridled merriment. The clowns, with their outlandish costumes and silly antics, brought out the inner child in everyone. The cowbells, once meant for cows, became instruments of joy, their clanging a joyful counterpoint to the usual humdrum of everyday life.

As the sun dipped below the horizon, painting the sky with streaks of orange and pink, the clowns announced their departure with a final, clanging flourish. The townsfolk, their hearts lighter and their spirits lifted, waved goodbye to their unexpected visitors. The clanging faded into the distance, a lingering reminder of the day a bunch of boisterous clowns, with their loud, noisy cowbells, brought a houseful of bouncing joy to their town.

CHAPTER 47: INSANE TONGUE TWISTERS FOR SILENT LETTERS

Here, we encounter a specific breed: words harbouring **silent letters**, those mischievous characters that lurk unseen, waiting to trip up the unwary speaker. Prepare to navigate a soundscape where pronunciation defies what the eye perceives. Sharpen your enunciation skills, for the challenge is delightful!

1. A ghastly ghast, more phantom than fish, gleams an eerie phosphorescent white beneath the emerald waves. Ghostly groans, mournful and low, rise from the depths, greeting unsuspecting sailors brave with a bone-chilling serenade. Billows churn, whipped into a frenzy by unseen currents, their crests foaming like phantoms' fingers reaching for the starlit sky.

   The rigging groans, taut as a haunted heartstring, sails shudder, and the once-proud ship heels sharply, its timbers creaking a mournful protest. Barnacles scrape the hull, sounding like skeletal fingers scraping a tomb. The crew faces etched with terror, clutch at anything solid, their eyes wide with dread. A spectral shroud of mist engulfs the vessel, isolating them in a world of whispering waves and ghostly moans.

   The weathered captain, a salty soul who had stared down

countless storms, fights to control the trembling helm. His weathered face, etched with a lifetime of battles against the sea, pales even further in the ghostly glow. But amidst the terror, a young cabin boy, barely out of his teens, steps forward. With a courage that belies his years, he grabs a lantern and shouts a defiant challenge into the swirling mist. The lantern's flame, a flickering ember against the encroaching darkness, casts long, grotesque shadows that dance on the deck.

For a moment, an unsettling silence descends. Then, from the depths, a colossal form begins to emerge. Its spectral outline, vaguely resembling a long-forgotten leviathan, chills the crew to the bone. The ghostly groans morph into a thunderous roar, a sound that seems to shake the very foundations of the sea. The young cabin boy, though visibly trembling, stands his ground, the lantern held high like a beacon against the encroaching darkness. In that moment, between the spectral monstrosity and the terrified crew, the cabin boy becomes a symbol of unwavering courage, a solitary spark of defiance against the overwhelming forces of the unknown.

2. Eight ebony eels, each enormous and equipped with eyes that gleamed like polished obsidian, writhed and entwined around eight enormous anchors, their slick, serpentine bodies forming a nautical nightmare. Kelp, caught in their writhing dance, whipped wildly, its fronds whipping and whistling an eerie song. The once-proud anchors, testaments to countless voyages, were now transformed into monstrous marionettes, their heavy iron forms yanked and twisted by the eels' relentless strength.

The ocean floor, usually a realm of hushed silence, erupted in a chaotic symphony of clicks, pops, and hisses. Schools of bioluminescent fish, startled by the commotion, scattered in shimmering bursts of turquoise and amethyst. Crustaceans scuttled for cover, their pincers clicking in a frantic rhythm. Crabs, their once-proud shells now askew, clung desperately to rocks, their beady eyes wide with terror.

The eels, oblivious to the havoc they wreaked, continued their eerie entanglement. Their bodies, slick with bioluminescent slime, pulsed with an otherworldly glow, casting grotesque shadows that danced across the seabed. The water itself, churned by their movements, became a murky, swirling vortex, a watery tomb for any unfortunate creature caught in its path.

The encounter, endless and eerie, stretched on. With each thrash of their powerful bodies, the eels tightened their grip on the anchors, their movements a macabre ballet of destruction. The once-peaceful ocean floor had become a battleground, a silent scream echoing through the depths.

3. Viscous volcanic viscera, a viscous vermilion ooze, spills outward, obscuring the opulent oasis overnight. Lush palm fronds, once swaying proudly in the desert breeze, now droop, choked by the creeping crimson tide. Crystal-clear pools, havens for hibiscus and herons, become cauldrons of churning, viscous venom, their once-vibrant reflections replaced by a malevolent glow. Marble statues, testaments to a forgotten time, stand like ghostly sentinels, half-swallowed by the volcanic ichor.

The once-bustling marketplace, a symphony of scents and spices, is reduced to a smouldering wasteland. Gingerbread houses, meticulously crafted from gingerbread and gumdrops, lie in smouldering ruins. Cobblestone streets, polished smooth by countless caravans, become slick obsidian pathways, reflecting the infernal glow of the encroaching doom.

Panic prickles the air, sharp as cactus needles. Scurrying sandpipers, their cinnamon-feathered wings frantic, abandon their nests, leaving behind speckled eggs that will never hatch. Fennec foxes, their oversized ears twitching in distress, dart between crumbling mudbrick houses, their mournful yelps echoing through the thickening smoke. The air itself seems to wheeze, heavy with the acrid stench of sulfur and singed earth.

In the distance, a lone date palm, its fronds reaching skyward in a final act of defiance, stands silhouetted against the blood-red horizon. A lone scarab beetle, its carapace gleaming like polished onyx, scuttles across the petrified dunes, a stark reminder of life persisting in the face of oblivion. The once-opulent oasis, a testament to human ingenuity and perseverance, is slowly consumed by the relentless tide of volcanic fury.

4. Hour after hour, the hungry hellmouth oozed. Molten rock, a viscous vermilion river, hissed as it snaked through the shattered streets with a slow, inexorable purpose. Homes, once havens of happiness, crumbled with heart-stopping coughs, their roofs and walls dissolving into molten slag. Furnishings flared briefly, casting grotesque shadows that danced on the advancing wall of fire. The terrified townsfolk huddled together on higher ground, the acrid stench of sulfur stinging their nostrils and bringing tears to their eyes. Hope, a flickering ember in the encroaching darkness, dwindled with each fiery huff of the volcano. The mountain rumbled with a deep, primal groan, its wrath a terrifying testament to the raw power of the earth, a power that dwarfed even the sturdiest human construction.

Elderly folks, their faces etched with the lines of a life lived in the shadow of the mountain, spoke of similar eruptions from years gone by. Back then, the volcano had been a sleeping giant, a source of awe and even reverence. But now, awakened from its slumber, it was a raging inferno, a destroyer of lives and dreams. Tears streamed down the faces of mothers clutching their children close, the acrid smoke a shroud that obscured the night sky and the indifferent glitter of the stars. Yet, amidst the terror, there were flickers of courage. Young men, adrenaline coursing through their veins, formed bucket brigades in a desperate attempt to save what they could. Women, their voices hoarse from shouting instructions, directed the evacuation of the elderly and infirm. The community, though fractured by fear, came together in a primal dance of survival, a testament to the enduring human spirit even in the face of unimaginable devastation.

As dawn approached, painting the horizon with streaks of bruised purple and angry orange, the eruption reached its peak. The earth itself seemed to convulse, and a towering plume of ash and smoke billowed into the sky, blotting out the weak morning light. The lava flow, momentarily impeded by a rise in the terrain, hesitated, then with a renewed surge of molten fury, carved a new path, deeper and more destructive than before. It was a scene of unimaginable chaos, a brutal tableau of nature's raw power on display.

But even the most violent storm eventually subsides. And so, too, did the volcano's rage. By midday, the tremors had lessened, the fiery spouts subsided to an occasional cough, and the lava flow began to cool, solidifying into a grotesque, blackened scar across the landscape. The townsfolk, emerging from their makeshift shelters, surveyed the devastation with a mixture of numb disbelief and a nascent determination to rebuild. Their homes were gone, their lives forever altered, but they still had each other. And in that shared experience of fear and survival, they found a newfound strength, a steely resolve to rise from the ashes, just as the mountain itself would one day return to a slumbering state, waiting for the inevitable cycle to begin anew.

5. Crumbling clodhopper Colin crushed crystalline castles with a clumsy catastrophe. Countless crystalline critters cavorted carelessly within, completely caught unaware by Colin's colossal klutziness. The collision caused cataclysmic chaos! Crystal candelabras combusted, chiming clocks clattered, and colourful candy cauldrons capsized, coating the cobblestone courtyard in a sticky, shimmering mess. Crystal creatures contorted in confusion as countless crowns clattered to the ground. Cobwebs, crafted with care by industrious crystal spiders, clung to Colin's oversized costume in shimmering strands.

   The once magnificent menagerie of mythical monsters was reduced to mountains of multicoloured shards, sparkling sadly in the sun. Colin, covered in crystal dust and utterly crestfallen, stood sheepishly amidst the shimmering wreckage, a monument to his own misfortune.

   A hush fell over the crowd. The joyous jester's performance, meant to be a centrepiece of the Crystal Jubilee, had devolved into a disaster of epic proportions. The King and Queen, their previously jovial faces etched with dismay, watched from the royal balcony. The assembled courtiers gasped, some even erupting in nervous snickers. The air crackled with a tension thicker than the spilt candy syrup.

Suddenly, a small, crystalline voice piped up. "Well, that wasn't very clownish, was it?" A tiny chipmunk fashioned entirely from rose quartz, its black bead eyes glinting with defiance, stood atop a precarious mountain of amethyst shards. Colin, mortified, could only stammer apologies. The chipmunk, unimpressed, flicked its tail dismissively.

"We crystal creatures are a resourceful bunch," it squeaked. "We can rebuild. But perhaps next time," it added, its voice laced with a surprising amount of sass, "hire a mime?" A ripple of surprised laughter broke through the tense atmosphere. The King, a hint of a smile playing on his lips, boomed, "Well said, Pip! Rebuilding efforts shall commence at once. As for you, Colin," he boomed, his voice softening slightly, "perhaps a career change is in order?" Colin, his face burning with shame, could only nod meekly. The chipmunk, Pip, hopped onto his shoulder. "Cheer up, clumsy one," it chirped. "Maybe you can help us gather the shards." And so, under the watchful eyes of the court, the unlikely duo began the long task of rebuilding the crystal castle, a testament to the resilience of both glass and clowns.

6. Wild wind, a banshee wailing its mournful song, whipped through the wiry willows that clawed at the inky sky. The weathered wooden house, a solitary sentinel guarding forgotten memories, creaked and groaned under the onslaught. Its warped windows, once welcoming portals to a world bathed in sunlight, now whined like weary souls surrendering to the storm's fury. Whispering drafts, cold fingers reaching from another realm, whistled through the cracked windowpanes, carrying ghostly greetings from the tempest outside. Inside, a flickering candle, the last bastion of defiance against the encroaching darkness, cast dancing shadows on the dusty walls. These phantoms, grotesque shapes morphing and twisting with each gust of wind that rattled the ancient windowpanes, seemed to writhe with unspoken stories.

The house, a testament to the relentless passage of time, whispered its own tales. Tales of bygone days, etched in the creaking floorboards and faded wallpaper, echoed in the mournful sighs that escaped the warped window frames. The wind, whistling its own mournful song, seemed to pick up these whispers, weaving them into its chaotic symphony. Together, they carried the secrets of the house – secrets of laughter and joy, of sorrow and loss – away into the night, on invisible currents that danced with the raindrops. These secrets, forever bound to the wild storm and the weathered house that stood defiant against its fury, would become part of the storm's legacy, carried on the wind's breath until the next time the tempest raged across the desolate landscape.

As dawn approached, painting the eastern horizon with streaks of rose and gold, the storm began to wane. The wind's mournful cries softened into a gentle sigh, and the rain, once a relentless torrent, became a pitter-patter on the windowpanes. The weary house, its battle scars etched deeper by the night's events, stood resolute. The silence that descended, broken only by the dripping of rainwater and the chirping of the first morning birds, was a stark contrast to the night's symphony of wind and wood. But within the silence, a sense of peace lingered. The storm had passed, and the house, battered but unbroken, remained, a silent guardian of its secrets, forever entwined with the whispers of the wind.

7. In a bygone era, shrouded in whispers of forgotten lore, Sir

Gareth, a knight renowned for his nobility and knightly bearing, ventured deep into the bowels of a forgotten castle. Cobwebs clung to the decaying stone walls, and the air hung heavy with the scent of damp earth and decay. The only sound was the rhythmic drip of water somewhere in the darkness, each drop echoing with an unsettling finality. Gareth, his heart hammering a steady rhythm against his ribs, pressed on, his courage fueled by a potent mix of duty and morbid curiosity.

Then, he saw it. Ethereal tendrils of mist coalesced in the gloom, solidifying into the spectral form of a knight. Its armour, once gleaming and polished, was now but a collection of spectral fragments, half-formed and flickering like a dying candle flame. A gaping wound marred its chest, a constant reminder of the violence that had claimed its life. Yet, within the hollow sockets of its helm, two ghostly eyes burned with an unnatural light, their gaze fixed upon Gareth with an intensity that pierced his very soul.

A wave of nausea washed over Gareth. The air around the apparition crackled with an unseen energy, a malevolent force that pressed down upon him like a physical weight. An icy dread gripped his heart, a primal fear that threatened to paralyse him. But Gareth was no ordinary knight. Years of combat and hardship had instilled in him an iron will. He steeled himself, forcing his trembling legs to hold him steady. With a deep breath, he drew his sword, its polished surface a defiant gleam in the oppressive darkness. Though fear gnawed at the edges of his resolve, Gareth knew he had to face whatever spectral entity loomed before him. The fate of the kingdom, perhaps even the world, might hang in the balance.

8. A shrill whistle shrieks, piercing the air. Eight fluffy crumpets, golden brown and begging to be devoured, sit perched upon a plate. The heat from their toasting lingers, a faint haze shimmering in the air. A rich, buttery aroma emanates from them, a siren song that tempts tiny tummies with promises of pure, wheaten delight. Each crumpet boasts a surface that begs to be explored, dimpled and dotted with the glorious remnants of their toasting. Imagination runs wild – are they miniature mountains, perfect for a dollop of jammy jam? Or perhaps they are spongy spaceships, ready for a voyage laden with butter and cream cheese? The possibilities are endless, and the only limit is the creativity of the tiny taste buds about to be indulged.

But the crumpets are more than just a canvas for culinary dreams. They are a promise of warmth and comfort, a familiar breakfast sensation that evokes cozy mornings and happy memories. The gentle give beneath a fingertip hints at the soft, pillowy interior waiting to be savored. A perfectly toasted crumpet offers a delightful textural contrast – a crisp exterior yielding to a yielding, spongy heart. Each bite is a symphony of tastes and textures, the wheaty flavour punctuated by the richness of butter and the sweetness of jam if that's the chosen path.

These are not mere crumpets; they are edible ambassadors of pure breakfast joy. They have the power to transform a grumpy morning into a delightful one, and their simple elegance is a testament to the enduring magic of breakfast time. So grab a plate, a knife, and a dollop of your favourite accompaniment. Let your imagination soar, and prepare to embark on a delightful journey with every bite of these perfectly toasted pillows of wheaty goodness.

9. With a shrill shriek, the shiny steel whistle pierced the sizzlin' symphony of the sausage stand. Chef Sergio, a swashbucklin' sausage sculptor with a smile as wide as a sunflower, swiftly snatched a succulent sausage from its sizzling perch on the grill.

The sausage, plump and juicy, glistened with a glistening glaze, the result of Sergio's secret blend of spices. It was a whistle-clean beauty, untouched by char or grime, a testament to Sergio's culinary craftsmanship.

Expertly, Sergio flipped the sausage, its plump form bouncing with a satisfying squish. As it sizzled and sputtered, a cloud of savoury smoke billowed upwards, tantalising the nostrils of the hungry customers who lined up expectantly.

One customer, a famished fellow with a rumbling stomach, tapped his foot impatiently. Sergio, with a wink and a flourish, announced, "Patience, my friend! A truly succulent sausage deserves a grand entrance!"

Finally, with a triumphant flourish, Sergio declared the sausage "done to a delightful degree!" He deftly slid it onto a warm hoagie roll, its soft innards yielding to the pressure with a satisfying squish.

Next came the sumptuous sweet potatoes. Sergio, usin' a silver spoon that gleamed in the afternoon sun, heaped a generous portion of mashed sweet potatoes onto the hoagie. The vibrant orange mash, flecked with golden brown bits of caramelised sugar, was a feast for the eyes as well as the stomach.

A dollop of creamy coleslaw, a sprinkle of crunchy chopped onions, and a drizzle of Sergio's signature sweet and tangy barbecue sauce completed the masterpiece. With a flourish, he presented the hoagie to the famished customer, its aroma a symphony of savoury and sweet.

The customer, his eyes wide with anticipation, took a huge bite. A blissful sigh escaped his lips as the symphony of flavours exploded on his taste buds. The succulent sausage, the creamy sweet potatoes, the tangy barbecue sauce – it was a culinary concerto conducted by the masterful Chef Sergio.

As the customer savoured each delicious mouthful, the whistle blew once more, a signal for Sergio to begin his culinary concerto all over again. The sizzlin' symphony of the sausage stand continued, a testament to Sergio's passion and the irresistible allure of a whistle-clean sausage served swiftly with sumptuous sweet potatoes.

CHAPTER 48: INSANE TONGUE TWISTERS FOR THE GLOTTAL STOP

The **glottal stop,** a silent pause in some British accents, is like a tiny hiccup in your throat. It replaces "t" sounds, especially at word ends ("wa'er" for "water"). More common in London and informal settings, it's becoming more widespread. Listen for pauses after vowels to spot it. Understanding it deepens your appreciation for British English pronunciation!

1. The verdant valleys echoed with the parrots' cacophony, a vibrant symphony for the visiting astronaut's curiosity. Captain Kaimana, her visor reflecting the emerald hues of the alien jungle, stood in awe. Here, on this uncharted planet, life exploded in a riot of colour and sound unlike anything she'd ever encountered.

   A kaleidoscope of parrots, their plumage shimmering with iridescent greens, reds, and blues, squawked and shrieked from the emerald canopy. Their calls, a cacophony to most ears, resonated with a strange beauty to Kaimana. It was a symphony, a complex language sung in clicks, whistles, and squawks, a vibrant tapestry woven by these feathered virtuosos.

Kaimana, an astronaut accustomed to the sterile silence of space, found herself captivated by the sheer oddity of it all. She trained her visor on a particularly flamboyant fellow perched on a branch, its emerald feathers catching the sunlight like a living jewel. The parrot cocked its head, its obsidian eye glinting with intelligence, and let out a sharp 'kack!'

Kaimana couldn't help but chuckle, a sound that echoed oddly in the verdant valley. Perhaps, she mused, there was a hidden order to this apparent chaos. Maybe with time, she could begin to decipher the parrots' symphony, to understand the language of this strange, vibrant world.

As the alien sun dipped below the horizon, casting long shadows across the valley floor, Kaimana knew this was just the beginning. This was a world teeming with life, a world that pulsed with an energy unlike anything she'd ever known. And she, Captain Kaimana, the lone astronaut amidst the parrots' cacophony, was determined to unravel its secrets, one click, whistle, and squawk at a time.

2. The stately canaries flitted through the leafy glades, their sweet melodies carrying for miles on the sultry summer airwaves. Sunlight dappled the verdant canopy, casting whimsical shadows that danced on the forest floor. Here, amidst the emerald embrace of the woods, the canaries reigned supreme, their songs a vibrant counterpoint to the rustling leaves and chirping crickets.

One canary, a fellow of feathery flamboyance with a crest of canary yellow, perched on a sun-drenched bough. He puffed out his chest, a tiny feathered maestro, and unleashed a cascade of crystal-clear notes. His song, a joyful ode to the summer's embrace, echoed through the glades, a sweet serenade for any creature lucky enough to hear it.

Another canary, a nearby neighbour, perched on a swaying branch, her voice a melodious echo. Her song, a gentle counterpoint to the first, intertwined with the original melody, creating a harmonious duet that filled the air. Soon, the entire glade was alive with song. Canaries, hidden amongst the emerald leaves, joined the chorus, their voices weaving together in a tapestry of sound.

The melody, a symphony of chirps and trills, carried for miles on the sultry summer airwaves. Hikers on distant trails paused, captivated by the ethereal music that drifted through the trees. Even the forest creatures, usually focused on their solitary pursuits, stopped to listen, their heads cocked in avian appreciation.

The canaries, oblivious to their audience, continued their joyous performance. They sang of sun-drenched meadows, crystal-clear streams, and the sheer delight of being alive on a glorious summer day. Their song, an echo of pure joy, resonated through the leafy glades, a testament to the beauty and wonder that nature held within its verdant embrace.

3. The distant comets, icy daggers slashin' the velvet night, streak across the inky expanse, their ghostly tails a hauntin' sight for the gazin' astronomer's delight. Dr. Stella Soong, bundled in a parka to ward off the desert chill, stood mesmerised beneath the glitterin' dome of the observatory. Her gloved hand tightened around the eyepiece of the telescope, her breath mistin' the cool glass.

There, in the velvet blackness, a celestial spectacle unfolded. A comet, a cosmic visitor from the farthest reaches of the solar system, streaked across the inky canvas. Its icy nucleus, a ghostly apparition, glittered with an otherworldly light. Behind it trailed a luminous tail, a diaphanous drape of dust and gas, shimmerin' in shades of emerald green and ghostly white.

Stella, an astronomer with a passion for the peculiar, couldn't help but grin. This wasn't just a comet; it was a cosmic question mark, a celestial cypher waitin' to be deciphered. Its icy composition, its unusual trajectory – these were all clues to the comet's origin story, a tale etched in ice and stardust.

For hours, Stella remained glued to the telescope, her keen eyes devourin' every detail of the ghostly visitor. She meticulously recorded her observations, jottin' down notes on the comet's speed, trajectory, and spectral composition. Each observation was a brushstroke on the canvas of scientific discovery, a piece of the puzzle that was this magnificent celestial oddity.

As dawn approached, paintin' the eastern horizon with streaks of rose and gold, the comet began to fade. Its ghostly form, a fleeting visitor in the grand cosmic ballet, dipped below the horizon, leavin' behind only a trail of celestial dust and a spark of inspiration in Stella's heart.

The observatory echoed with the soft click-clack of Stella's typin' as she transcribed her notes. The data, a treasure trove of information, held the potential to unlock the secrets of the comet's past and, perhaps, even shed light on the origins of our own solar system. The distant comet, a hauntin' sight in the velvet night, had become a beacon of scientific inquiry, a testament to the endless mysteries that glittered just beyond our reach in the vast expanse of space.

4. In the hushed heart of the night, crickets chirped their rhythmic tune, a chorus echoed by the occasional hoot of an owl perched high in a shadowy oak. The symphony of sounds, a lullaby for most, sent shivers down little Lily's spine. Clutching her teddy bear, Mr. Floofers, tighter, Lily peeked out from beneath her covers, her wide eyes scanning the darkness of her room.

   Every creak of the old house, every rustle of leaves outside her window, sounded magnified in the quiet night. Shadows danced on the walls, morphing into monstrous shapes in Lily's active imagination. The chirping crickets, usually a source of comfort, now sounded like the frantic chatter of unseen creatures. And the owl's hoots, once a soothing call, transformed into eerie pronouncements from some unknown entity.

   Lily, her heart thumping a frantic rhythm against her ribs, fought back the tears that welled up in her eyes. She wasn't scared, not really. Not with Mr. Floofers by her side, his button eyes staring bravely into the darkness. Mr. Floofers, her protector, her confidante, wouldn't let anything bad happen.

   Taking a deep breath, Lily forced a smile. She snuggled closer to Mr. Floofers, his soft fur a source of comfort in the vast unknown of her room. She shut her eyes tight, picturing Mr. Floofers standing guard, his fuzzy form a shield against the night's shadows.

   Slowly, the symphony of sounds outside began to work its magic. The crickets' chirping, once frantic, became a steady, lulling rhythm. The owl's hoots, once eerie, morphed back into the call of a solitary hunter. Lily's eyelids grew heavy, and the tension seeped out of her tiny body.

With a contented sigh, Lily drifted off to sleep. The night, no longer a place of fear, became a canvas for her dreams. In her dreams, Mr. Floofers soared through a starlit sky, a brave teddy bear knight on a quest to chase away the shadows and usher in the dawn. And as Lily slept, the crickets chirped and the owls hooted, their nighttime symphony a gentle serenade for the little girl and her trusty teddy bear protector.

5. Six dapper chaps, chins held high, strutted smartly down a slick, slick street. Their shiny shoes clicked a catchy clack, a rhythmic racket that rattled and smacked 'gainst the cobblestones slick with the city's sweat. Suddenly, a stray soccer ball, shot with reckless zest, rocketed right at the chaps, a shocking threat! The startled six scattered with shrieks, slick suits a-flutter, shoes clicking like castanets in a clatter. Swiftly, a street sweeper swooped, scooping the soccer ball with a practised flick of his wrist. Sighs of relief filled the air, the dapper chaps gathering their wits with a shared, sheepish grin.

News of the chaps' chaotic cobblestone clatter spread like wildfire through the city's streets. Shops shimmered with suppressed snickers, echoes of the click-clack echoing in every ear. The once-slick street, a source of silent swagger, became a training ground for swift reflexes. Chaps, forever focused on a flawless strut, honed their skills at spotting soccer balls, stray pigeons, and surprise sprinklers – all potential threats to their impeccable clicks. But their quest wasn't just about struttin' in style. Fuelled by a thirst for knowledge, they hoped to discover forgotten hat-tipping techniques, the secret society of sharp dressers, or even hidden tailor shops filled with forgotten fabrics whispering tales of legendary tailors.

One particularly crisp morning, a sharp-eyed chap spotted a shimmering storefront tucked away on a quiet side street. A forgotten sign, dusty and faded, proclaimed "Hattie's Haberdashery - Finest Threads & Forgotten Fashions." The excited chaps, hearts pounding with a mix of curiosity and sartorial delight, pushed open the creaky door, ready to unlock a universe of hidden threads and forgotten fashion secrets.

Inside, the air hung thick with the scent of aged wool and forgotten wax polish. Bolts of cloth in colours both familiar and fantastical lined the walls, whispering stories of bygone eras. A lone figure, a woman with a shock of white hair and eyes that sparkled with mischief, emerged from the back room. "Can I interest you gentlemen in a piece of history?" she boomed, her voice a delightful contrast to the hushed reverence of the shop.

The chaps, speechless at first, soon found themselves enveloped in a whirlwind of fabrics and forgotten fashion tips. Hattie, as they learned her name to be, regaled them with tales of double-breasted waistcoats and the art of the perfect pocket square fold. She showed them bolts of cloth woven according to techniques lost for centuries, their textures a revelation to the fingertips. As they ran their hands over the velvets and linens, the chaps felt a connection to a bygone era, a time when clothes were more than just fabric – they were a statement, a story waiting to be told.

Leaving Hattie's Haberdashery, the chaps carried more than just bolts of cloth; they carried a renewed appreciation for the art of tailoring and the stories clothes could tell. Their swagger, once reliant on the click-clack of their shoes, now held a depth and confidence that came from a deeper understanding of their sartorial heritage. The once-slick street became a runway for their newfound fashion knowledge, each click of their shoes a testament to their dedication to keeping the art of impeccable dressing alive. The dapper chaps, forever grateful to the stray soccer ball and the twist of fate that led them to Hattie's, continued their strolls, their impeccable attire a constant reminder of the day they rediscovered the forgotten language of clothes.

6. Dashing Desmond, decked out in a dapper double-breasted suit the colour of cobalt, strutted down cobblestone streets – with the confidence of a conquering king. His shiny shoes, polished to a mirror sheen, clicked a rhythmic counterpoint to the clip-clop of passing carriages.

Desmond, a fellow with a flair for the flashy, had just acquired this sartorial masterpiece from the city's most esteemed tailor, Mr. Higgins. The suit, with its sharp lapels and impeccably creased trousers, hugged Desmond's form like a second skin, accentuating his athletic physique. A crisp white shirt peeked out from the collar, adorned with a silk tie the colour of burnt umber. A jaunty pocket square, folded into a perfect geometric pattern, added the final flourish.

Heads turned as Desmond strolled down the street. Shopkeepers peeked out from behind awnings, their eyes following his path. Street urchins, usually a boisterous bunch, fell silent, momentarily awestruck by Desmond's dazzling display. Even the stray cats, usually lounging nonchalantly in sunbeams, seemed to take notice, their amber eyes gleaming with a hint of grudging respect.

Desmond, basking in the unexpected admiration, couldn't help but puff out his chest a little further. He tipped his fedora at a charming angle, the feather in its band bobbing jauntily. Today, the world was his oyster, and he, Desmond, was the dapper chap ready to shuck it open in style.

His walk took him past bustling markets, their stalls overflowing with colourful wares. He stopped to admire a glistening display of exotic fruits, their sweet fragrance mingling with the earthy scent of freshly baked bread. A vendor, a woman with a smile as bright as her crimson dress, offered him a taste of juicy mango, its tropical flavour exploding on his taste buds.

Desmond, ever the charmer, thanked her with a courtly bow and a wink. He continued on his way, the city's sights and sounds a symphony for his senses. The clatter of horse-drawn carriages, the rhythmic shouts of street vendors, the melodic calls of street musicians – all blended together to create a vibrant tapestry of urban life.

As the day wore on, Desmond's shiny shoes clicked their way through bustling markets, elegant promenades, and quiet alleyways. He savoured every moment, every appreciative glance, every whispered comment about his impeccable attire. For Desmond, this wasn't just a suit; it was a declaration, a statement of confidence and style that announced his arrival on the city's social scene.

By nightfall, as the city lights began to twinkle, Desmond found himself at a grand soirée, the talk of the town. He entered the ballroom, a vision in cobalt, and the chatter died down for a moment. All eyes were on him, the dapper chap who had conquered the cobblestone streets and captured the hearts (or at least the attention) of everyone he met.

Desmond, with a confident stride and a winning smile, walked across the polished dance floor. The evening stretched before him, filled with the promise of laughter, lively conversation, and perhaps even a captivating dance with a beautiful lady. The click of his shiny shoes continued a rhythmic beat to the melody of his triumphant night.

7. The cracklin' crowd roared with a thunderous intensity that shook the very foundation of the stadium. It was a primal sound, a guttural eruption of excitement that pulsed through the veins of every spectator. In the heart of this maelstrom of noise, eight athletes crouched low in their starting blocks, their muscles coiled like tightly wound springs. They were a kaleidoscope of humanity, each with their own story, their own dreams etched on their determined faces.

   The starter's pistol, a sharp crack that sliced through the roar, shattered the tense silence. With a synchronised burst of energy, the athletes exploded from their blocks, propelled forward by a cocktail of adrenaline and ambition. The track became a blur of straining bodies, legs pumpin' pistons driving them forward. Arms churned, elbows tucked tight, torsos bent low in a relentless pursuit of that elusive finish line.

   The stadium lights, like hungry suns, beat down on the track, illuminating the glistening sheen of sweat that beaded on the athletes' faces. Each laboured breath was a ragged rasp, a testament to the superhuman effort they were pouring into every stride. Yet, their expressions remained etched with an unwavering focus, their eyes fixed on the ever-nearing finish line, a shimmering mirage in the distance.

   As they rounded the final bend, the crowd's roar intensified, morphing into a cacophony of cheers and chants, each spectator willing their chosen champion onward. With a final, agonising surge of energy, the athletes lunged for the finish line. A photo finish couldn't have been tighter. One athlete, a blur of crimson and determination, dipped across the line a hair's breadth ahead of the pack. His arms shot up in a triumphant victory cry, a primal scream of joy that echoed through the stadium.

For the victor, the world seemed to slow down. The roar of the crowd faded into a distant hum, replaced by the exhilarating thrum of his own beating heart. This was the taste of victory, a bittersweet cocktail of relief and elation. He had pushed his body and mind to the absolute limit, and in that crucible of exertion, he had emerged triumphant.

But even amidst the euphoria of victory, there was a quiet respect for his fallen comrades. The athletes who had crossed the line after him, their faces etched with disappointment, were no less deserving of admiration. They had trained relentlessly, sacrificed countless hours, and poured their hearts into this singular moment. The sting of defeat might be sharp, a bitter pill to swallow, but their eyes held an unyielding fire. The roar of the crowd would echo in their ears, not as a taunt, but as a relentless mantra, a constant reminder of the challenges that awaited them. They would return, stronger, faster, more determined to conquer the track and silence the doubts that might whisper in the quiet moments.

The stadium lights dimmed, slowly plunging the arena into a warm twilight. The roar of the crowd subsided, replaced by the rhythmic thump of retreating footsteps. But the pursuit of excellence, a never-ending race, burned bright within each athlete. The echoes of this competition would reverberate long after the final runner had crossed the line, a testament to the unwavering human spirit and the relentless quest to be the best.

8. With a guttural groan and a shudder that shook the launchpad, the rusty rocket ship rocketed into the starry night. Its aged hull, a patchwork of peeling paint and faded glory, strained against the relentless pull of gravity. But its fiery exhaust, a defiant roar against the inky blackness, sparkled like a million scattered diamonds.

Captain Rex Rocket, a grizzled veteran with a beard as white as stardust, gripped the control panel, his knuckles turning white with the effort. His trusty robotic copilot, Bleep, whirred and clicked excitedly, its single green eye flashing with anticipation. Together, they were a mismatched pair – a relic of the space race and a cutting-edge piece of technology – but their bond was as strong as the metal hull that encased them.

The rocket, christened the "Rusty Rocket" with a wink and a sigh, was a far cry from the sleek, chrome spaceships that dominated the modern fleet. But Rex, a man who craved adventure more than comfort, wouldn't have it any other way. This ship, filled with the ghosts of past voyages and the echoes of forgotten dreams, was his chariot to the stars.

As the rocket punched through the atmosphere, the world below shrank into a swirling blue marble, a fragile oasis suspended in the vast emptiness of space. Rex, a seasoned traveller with a map etched into his memory, steered the Rusty Rocket towards a cluster of distant stars, their faint light a beacon in the cosmic ocean.

Their destination – a newly discovered planet, rumoured to be rich in untapped resources and shrouded in mystery. It was a place for pioneers, for those willing to brave the unknown and push the boundaries of human exploration. Rex, a restless spirit forever chasing the next horizon, felt a thrill course through him. This wasn't just a mission; it was a quest, a chance to carve his name into the annals of spacefaring history.

The journey was long and fraught with peril. Micrometeoroids pinged against the hull, a metallic rain that sent shivers down Bleep's circuits. Fuel reserves dwindled, forcing Rex to make difficult calculations, stretching the Rusty Rocket's capabilities to the limit. But through it all, the fiery exhaust continued to sparkle, a testament to their unwavering determination.

Finally, after weeks of hurtling through the void, a new world emerged on the viewport - a swirling blue and green orb, veiled in wispy clouds. Rex, his heart pounding with anticipation, steered the Rusty Rocket towards the planet's atmosphere. As they broke through the clouds, a breathtaking vista unfolded before them – verdant forests stretching to meet snow-capped mountains, crystal-clear lakes reflecting the distant stars. This was their prize, a world waiting to be explored, its secrets waiting to be unveiled.

The Rusty Rocket, with a final shudder, touched down on the planet's surface, its fiery exhaust now a wisp of fading smoke. Rex and Bleep, pioneers in a rusty ship, had reached their destination. The adventure had just begun. As they stepped out onto the alien ground, the stars above twinkled like diamonds, a celestial reward for their unwavering spirit and the rusty rocket's defiant roar into the starry night.

CHAPTER 49: INSANE TONGUE TWISTERS FOR CONSONANT CLUSTERS

Consonant clusters (consonants with no vowels in between) challenge non-native speakers. But listen and mimic native speakers! Practice pronouncing clusters slowly, then faster. Use minimal pairs (words differing by one sound) to isolate the sound. Tongue twisters can make practice fun! Remember, even native speakers stumble. Keep practicing, and you'll be a cluster pro!

1. Lady Beatrice "Butterscotch" Butterbur, Duchess of Dunvegan, never shied away from a challenge. Today, her challenge was a monstrous one – a slumbering, smoke-breathing dragon who guarded a vital trade route. Disguised in a flour-dusted smock and a kerchief tied haphazardly over her fiery red hair, Beatrice looked more like a baker's apprentice than royalty. But beneath the unassuming exterior burned the heart of a daring leader.

   With a basket overflowing with plump, glazed doughnuts, the fake "dough maker" Beatrice approached the dragon's cave. The air hung heavy with the dragon's snores, each exhales a tremor that shook the very stones beneath her feet. Beatrice, her heart pounding a frantic rhythm against her ribs, inched closer, the sweet scent of sugared dough wafting before her.

Finally, the cavern entrance loomed, its darkness swallowing the sunlight. Taking a deep breath, Beatrice called out in a voice as sweet as the doughnuts themselves, "Freshly baked doughnuts, delivered hot from the oven! Who wants a taste?"

Silence. Then, a colossal rumble echoed from within. A single, enormous eye, the colour of molten gold, cracked open and glared down at her. Beatrice, her smile unwavering, held up a glazed masterpiece. "See, your majesty? Still warm and fluffy!"

The dragon, sluggish with sleep, eyed the doughnut with suspicion. Then, with a deafening snort, it stretched out a massive claw, its tip the size of a carriage. Beatrice, nimble as a dancer, darted aside just as the claw snatched the doughnut. The dragon devoured it in a single bite, a shower of sugar raining down its snout.

Beatrice, her courage bubbling over, produced another doughnut and dangled it even closer. "Another, your highness? Perhaps with a hint of cinnamon?"

The dragon, seemingly intrigued by the sweet treat, lumbered closer, its massive form blocking the entrance to the cave. This was her chance. With a wink that wouldn't have been out of place on a battlefield, Beatrice slipped past the distracted dragon and into the cavern. The fate of the trade route, and perhaps Beatrice's secret identity, hung in the balance.

2. Duchess Diana, disguised in a dusty miller's dress, dangled delightful doughnuts with daring dexterity. Deep down in the dreadful dungeon, a drowsy dragon dreamt of dripping dumplings. Diana, determined to dispatch the dreadful dragon, devised a delicious distraction. Her plan? Dangle doughnuts dusted with dragonfire dust – a delicacy designed to disrupt the dragon's dreadful dreams.

Ducking down a damp, dripping dungeon passage, Diana reached the dragon's den. The air hung heavy with the dragon's dreadful drool and the stench of sulfurous sleep. The dragon, a dull, drab beast with dusty diamond scales, slumbered soundly amidst a scattered hoard of dusty doubloons.

Diana, her heart drumming a frantic rhythm against her ribs, dangled a doughnut dusted with dragonfire dust just above the dragon's dreadful drippy snout. The delectable scent, a delicious disruption to the dragon's dreamscape, caused the beast to twitch its whiskers and awaken with a dreadful yawn.

Blinking blearily, the dragon focused on the delightful doughnut dangling before its droopy eyes. "Doughnuts?" it rumbled in a voice that rattled the rusty dungeon bars. "Dragons don't devour doughnuts, delightful damsel!"

Diana, maintaining her disguise, dropped the doughnut with a delightful dink onto the dusty dungeon floor. "But Your Draconic Dreadfulness," she declared with delightful daring, "these are no ordinary doughnuts! These are doughnuts dusted with dragonfire dust, a delicacy designed to delight even the most dreadful dragon!"

The dragon, its dreadful drool dripping down its dusty diamond scales, eyed the doughnut with suspicion. But the delicious scent, a delightful disruption to its usual diet of damsels and dreadful dwarves, proved too tempting to resist. With a clumsy claw, the dragon snatched the doughnut and devoured it in a single, dreadful gulp.

A jolt of fiery surprise erupted in the dragon's belly. The dragonfire dust, a delightful deception concocted by the daring duchess, sent the beast into a frenzy. It snorted and stomped, its dreadful dream of dumplings replaced by a fiery nightmare of dancing doughnuts.

Diana, seizing her opportunity, whipped out a vial of dwarven dream draught – a delightful concoction guaranteed to induce a dreadful slumber. With a flick of her wrist, she doused the dragon's dreadful den in a mist of the dream draught. The dragon, overwhelmed by the delightful drowsiness, slumped back to sleep, its dreadful dreams replaced by visions of dancing doughnuts.

With a triumphant grin, Diana, the daring duchess disguised as a dough maker, secured the key to the dungeon hidden amongst the dragon's hoard. Her mission, a delightful deception fueled by delicious doughnuts and dwarven dream draught, was a delightful success. Now, all that remained was to free the damsels trapped deep within and escape the dreadful dungeon before the dragon awoke from its delightful, doughnut-induced slumber.

3. Sir Nigel Knotworth, renowned throughout the kingdom for his intricate and ingenious knots, found himself in a predicament as perplexing as any tangled fishing line. He knelt, his knees protesting against the unyielding earth, beside a gnarled, moss-covered oak. Nettles, those spiteful little barbs disguised as harmless greenery, lurked everywhere, their serrated edges itching to punish any careless touch. Sir Nigel, his normally immaculate armor now adorned with a haphazard collection of burrs and leaves, navigated the nettlesome obstacle course with the grace of a cow on roller skates.

His quest? Not a dragon, nor a damsel in distress, but a simple kite. A mischievous gust of wind, stronger than any foe he'd faced on the battlefield, had snatched the kite from his young niece, Lady Amelia's, grasp and deposited it precariously high in the gnarled branches of the oak. Now, the once-proud knight, whose reputation preceded him with whispers of intricate knots and cunning escapes, was reduced to a fumbling figure battling a tangled mess of string and a particularly belligerent patch of nettles.

Amelia, her face a mask of worry etched with the defiance of a young princess who wasn't afraid to get her hands dirty, watched from a safe distance. The kite, a fantastical beast crafted from crimson silk and adorned with a ferocious golden dragon, danced taunting just out of reach. It bobbed and dipped with the wind, a cruel reminder of her misfortune. Sir Nigel, ever the valiant uncle, wouldn't rest until Amelia's laughter filled the air once more.

He surveyed the scene with a furrowed brow. The trunk of the oak was too thick for him to climb, and any attempt to shake the branches loose risked sending the kite plummeting to its doom. But giving up was not in Sir Nigel's vocabulary. After all, he had outsmarted orcs, outs negotiated trolls, and even managed to untie the Gordian Knot that had baffled the kingdom's wisest minds for generations. Surely, a rogue kite tangled in a tree was no match for his legendary knot-tying skills.

With a determined glint in his eye, Sir Nigel rummaged through his pouch, a bottomless pit that seemed to hold every conceivable tool a knight might need. He emerged with a triumphant grin, brandishing a spool of sturdy twine and a selection of gleaming metal clasps. A plan, as cunning as any he'd devised to outwit an enemy, began to form in his mind.

4. Caspar the cook, coated in crimson cake crumbs, careened clumsily through the clanging castle corridors. Careless chaos clung to him like a cloud of flour. Kettles clanged, copper caldrons crashed, and countless cooking contraptions cascaded to the cold, cobbled floor in his wake.

His crimson-clad catastrophe began with a cake calamity. A colossal crimson confection, crafted to celebrate the conquering knight's coronation, had committed culinary suicide. Just as Caspar carried it, crowned with crystallized candies, through the crowded corridor, a rogue jester rounded a corner on a runaway rocking horse. The collision catapulted Caspar, cake, and cart into a whirlwind of crimson crumbs and clattering cookware.

Undeterred, if slightly dusted, Caspar scrambled to his feet. The knight's coronation cake was a catastrophe, but the castle still craved supper! He grabbed a gigantic griddle, its greasy surface reflecting his flustered face, and charged forth once more. This time, however, caution clung to him like a second skin. He crept cautiously through the corridors, casting a wary eye around every corner.

But fate, it seemed, had a fiendish fondness for food fiascos. As Caspar tiptoed past the tapestry-lined trophy room, a tremor shook the castle. A rogue catapult left carelessly loaded after the celebratory siege, had fired a stray boulder. It crashed through the trophy room window, sending a suit of gleaming silver armour tumbling headfirst into Caspar's path.

With a yelp that echoed through the echoing corridors, Caspar tripped over the fallen knight, sending the griddle flying. It landed with a resounding clang on top of the surprised knight's helmet, trapping him in a painful predicament. Caspar, covered once more in a crimson cascade, this time courtesy of a toppled vat of cranberry sauce, could only stare in bewildered dismay.

The castle clattered with laughter as the flustered cook and the hapless knight extricated themselves from their culinary calamity. The coronation cake might be a disaster, and supper slightly singed, but the castle echoed with a different kind of cheer – the joyous symphony of shared chaos and a clumsy cook's never-ending capacity for creating kitchen catastrophes.

News of Caspar's culinary calamities spread far and wide. Minstrels strummed lute strings and sang tales of the crimson-clad cook, his clanging cookware, and his uncanny ability to orchestrate edible emergencies. The king himself, a man with a hearty appetite and an even heartier appreciation for a good laugh, decreed that Caspar remain the castle cook. After all, a castle without a sprinkle of splatter and a dash of disaster was a dull castle indeed.

So, Caspar continued his reign in the kitchen, a whirlwind of flour and frenzy. He left a trail of overturned tarts and toppled tureens in his wake, but his mishaps were always delivered with a flourish and a sheepish grin. The castle echoed with the clatter of pots and the shouts of a harried cook, but more than that, it echoed with laughter – a testament to the fact that even in the heart of culinary chaos, a good dose of merriment could always be whipped up.

5. Blustery blizzards bullied the blustery bridge, bitter blasts buffeting beams with bone-chilling bravado. Billowing blankets of blinding white blotted out the bordering banks, blurring the boundaries between blustery bridge and belligerent blizzard. Bewildered birds, braving the biting breeze, battled for balance on bombasted branches, their bodies buffeted by belligerent gusts.

Beneath the bridge, the icy black broth of the brook boiled and bubbled, belligerent waves battling the encroaching ice. Blocks of brash, brittle ice, battered by the blizzard's belligerence, bobbed and bucked in the turbulent brew. A lone, bedraggled brown bear, blundering blindly through the blinding whiteness, stumbled upon the bridge, a beacon of brown amidst the belligerent bleakness.

He lumbered cautiously onto the bridge, its wooden planks slick and treacherous beneath his heavy paws. The blizzard, belligerent as ever, bullied the bewildered beast, buffeting him with bitter blasts that threatened to topple him from his precarious perch. But the bear, battling his bewilderment, pressed on, his powerful paws propelling him purposefully across the blustery bridge.

Reaching the other side, he shook the clinging snow from his thick fur and lumbered on, a solitary brown speck swallowed by the belligerent blizzard. The bridge, battered but unbroken, continued to bear the brunt of the blizzard's belligerence, a solitary sentinel against the blustery onslaught. And above it all, the bewildered birds, battling the biting breeze, continued their bravado-filled ballet - a testament to the enduring spirit of life in the face of the most belligerent of blizzards.

The storm raged on for hours, a relentless white maw gobbling up the world. But slowly, ever so slowly, the winds began to wane, their belligerent bluster replaced by a blustery sigh. The snowflakes, once falling in a thick, blinding frenzy, began to drift lazily from the leaden sky. A sliver of pale light peeked through the parting clouds, painting the bruised horizon with streaks of bruised violet and bruised orange.

The blizzard, defeated, began to retreat, its blustery belligerence replaced by a sullen sulk. The bridge, scarred but standing, emerged from the whiteout, its weathered timbers glistening with a sheen of meltwater. The birds, no longer bewildered, burst into joyous song, their sweet melodies a triumphant serenade to the retreating storm.

And in the distance, a lone brown bear emerged from the melting snowdrifts, his dark form a stark contrast to the pristine white landscape. He shook himself once more, sending a flurry of snowflakes scattering in the air, and continued on his journey, leaving behind a trail of paw prints in the freshly fallen snow - a testament to his resilience in the face of the blizzard's blustery wrath. The storm had passed, leaving behind a world cleansed and renewed, a testament to the enduring power of nature and the unwavering spirit of life.

6. Bernard the baker, bundled in billowing blankets that billowed in the blizzard's bluster, battled his way through the blustery blast. Balanced precariously on his broad biceps was a basket brimming with buttery brioche buns, their golden brown crusts beckoning warmth amidst the bone-chilling bite of the blizzard.

The wind, a belligerent beast with a blustery bark, buffeted Bernard from all sides, threatening to snatch his basket and send his precious pastries pirouetting through the air. Bernard, blinking back snowflakes that stung his bewildered eyes, battled back with a baker's brawn. He leaned into the wind, his bulky body a sturdy bulwark against the belligerent blast.

His breath puffed out in frosty clouds, a brief battle cry against the blizzard's bluster. Each step was a struggle, his boots sinking into the burgeoning blanket of white that stretched endlessly before him. The bakery beckoned in the distance, its windows glowing warmly, a beacon of buttery bliss amidst the belligerent blizzard.

But the closer Bernard got, the stronger the wind seemed to blow. The basket, precariously balanced, began to wobble precariously. Bernard grunted, his breath puffing out in a frosty flurry. He couldn't let the wind win. These buttery brioche buns, destined for a birthday breakfast, were his bakery's pride and joy.

With a burst of bakerly bravado, Bernard dug his heels into the snow-covered street. He gripped the basket handle tighter, his knuckles turning white with the effort. Inch by agonising inch, he battled his way forward, his bulky form a resolute brown bear against the blizzard's white onslaught.

Finally, with a triumphant sigh of relief, Bernard reached the bakery steps. He scrambled up the slick stone stairs, his heart hammering a frantic rhythm against his ribs. He flung open the bakery door and stumbled inside, a flurry of snowflakes swirling in his wake.

Safe and sound within his warm, yeasty haven, Bernard collapsed onto a nearby chair, his chest heaving. The basket of buttery brioche buns sat on the counter, not a single pastry lost to the blizzard's bluster. He had done it. He had braved the belligerent blizzard and emerged victorious, his precious pastries safe and sound.

As the wind howled outside, Bernard, a bewildered baker

who'd battled blizzards and emerged a brioche-balancing champion, allowed himself a weary smile. The warmth of the bakery seeped into his bones, chasing away the chill of the blizzard. He knew, with a baker's unwavering certainty, that no matter how belligerent the blizzard, his buttery brioche buns would always find their way home.

7. Groggy Griselda the gryphon, grumpy as ever, guarded a glittering grotto crammed with gleaming gold. Greed glinted in her golden eyes as she grumbled about grackles and goblins who might try to grab a glint of her glorious loot. Gigantic gems, glistening green and garnet-red, graced the grimy grotto walls, adding to the gryphon's glittering hoard.

Griselda grumbled under her grizzled beak, griping about greedy gnomes who might gnaw at her golden goblets or ghostly giants who might snatch shimmering statuettes. Glittering gargoyles, grotesquely grinning guardians, perched on the grotto's grimy pillars, their vacant eyes offering Griselda scant comfort.

Suddenly, a gravelly groan echoed through the gloomy grotto. Griselda, her grip tightening on a golden goblet, spun around, her golden eyes gleaming with suspicion. A gaunt, ghostly giant, his grey form barely visible in the gloom, materialised before her.

"Greetings, grumpy gryphon," the giant rumbled in a voice that grated like gravel. "I've come to claim a curio from your collection – a glistening gryphon egg, rumoured to be hidden within this gloomy grotto."

Griselda scoffed a guttural sound that echoed through the cavern. "Gryphon eggs? Grubby giant, you must be dreaming! My grotto glitters with gold, not grotesque gryphon young!"

The giant chuckled, a sound like boulders tumbling down a scree. "Gryphon or no gryphon, grumpy one, I shall search your grotto from grinning gargoyle to grimy ground."

With a groan that shook the very stones of the grotto, the giant began his search. Griselda, her grip tightening on the golden goblet, watched him with narrowed eyes. She wouldn't let this ghostly giant plunder her precious possessions!

As the giant lumbered towards a glistening golden chest, Griselda made her move. With a powerful flap of her griffin wings, she sent a gust of wind whistling through the grotto, scattering glittering goblets and gremlins carved from green gemstones. The startled giant stumbled back, momentarily disoriented.

Seizing her opportunity, Griselda swooped down, snatching the giant's ghostly grey staff from his grasp. The staff, the source of his ghostly glow, clattered to the grimy ground with a dull thud. The giant, his form fading rapidly without the staff's power, let out a final, frustrated groan before vanishing completely.

Griselda, perched triumphantly on a grinning gargoyle, surveyed her grotto. Glittering gold and glistening gems lay scattered on the ground, but her most prized possession - the gryphon egg, if it ever existed - remained hidden. With a grumpy grumble, Griselda began the tedious task of restoring order to her glittering grotto. The ghostly giant might be gone, but Griselda knew other greedy creatures lurked in the shadows. She, the grumpy gryphon guardian, would be ever vigilant, forever protecting her glittering hoard.

8. Wilbur the worm, a wriggling wonder with a woeful whine, writhed through a watery wormhole, wishing wildly for warmer weather. Winter's wrath had whipped the world white, wrapping Wilbur's world in a wet, woollen shroud. The once-vibrant wildflowers had withered, their vibrant hues replaced by the dull drab of dormant dreams.

Wilbur yearned for the warmth of the summer sun, for the whispering wind that waltzed through the wildflowers, and for the juicy, wiggling worms that wiggled alongside him in the wormy world. But winter's icy grip held him hostage, and the watery wormhole, a swirling vortex of woes, beckoned him onward.

With a wiggle and a woeful wobble, Wilbur plunged forward. The swirling vortex whipped him around, a watery washing machine of woes. Whispering voices, wispy and weak, echoed in his wake - the voices of fellow worms yearning for warmth.

Suddenly, the swirling vortex softened. Wilbur emerged on the other side, not into a winter wonderland, but a world washed in warm, watery hues. Coral castles cast curious crooked shadows, and schools of shimmering fish swirled around him in a silent, swirling symphony.

A wave of wonder washed over Wilbur. He was no longer a wriggling worm in a woeful world, but a wiggling wonder in a watery wonderland! Here, the water was warm, the sun was a shimmering orb, and wiggling worms were not just welcome, but celebrated! Wilbur, his woes forgotten, began to wiggle with renewed vigour. He wiggled through warm waters, wiggled past waving coral, and wiggled alongside other happy, wiggling worms.

Winter's wrath might still grip the world above, but for Wilbur, the watery wormhole had become a doorway to a warm, wonderful world. He wiggled with glee, a woeful worm transformed into a wiggling wonder, living proof that even the wildest wish can sometimes wiggle its way true.

Life in this underwater utopia was a constant wiggle of delight. Wilbur befriended Wanda, a wise old worm with a fondness for weaving tales of legendary worms who could wiggle at the speed of light. Wilbur, inspired by Wanda's stories, practised his wiggling with newfound fervour. He wiggled through shipwrecks teeming with bioluminescent creatures, wiggled past playful dolphins with permanent toothy grins, and even wiggled alongside a grumpy old octopus who grumbled about the incessant wiggling but secretly admired Wilbur's enthusiasm.

Days turned into weeks, and Wilbur, the once-woeful worm, became a wiggling sensation. Other worms, tired of winter's woes, began to arrive through the watery wormhole, their wiggles transforming the underwater world into a vibrant tapestry of colour and movement. They wiggled in unison, creating mesmerising underwater ballets, and wiggled in friendly competition, racing through coral reefs and around swaying kelp forests.

News of the wiggling utopia eventually reached the surface world. Birds, tired of the winter chill, began to migrate downwards, drawn by the tales of warmth and constant wiggling. They perched on coral castles, singing songs of summer, and some even joined the underwater wiggling routines, their feathers shimmering like jewels in the sunlit water.

The once-isolated underwater world became a beacon

of joy, a testament to the transformative power of a single wiggle and a wild wish. Wilbur, the unlikely hero, continued to wiggle with infectious enthusiasm, a constant reminder that even the smallest creature, with a little bit of wiggle, can make a big difference in the world.

9. Fern, a fawn with fur the colour of autumn leaves, trembled in the twilight. The day's warmth had surrendered to a cool embrace, and shadows stretched long and menacing from the towering pines. It was the witching hour, the time fireflies emerged, their tiny lanterns a frightening sight for a young fawn.

One firefly, then another, blinked into existence like malevolent stars descended from the darkening sky. Fern's heart hammered a frantic rhythm against her ribs. These weren't the friendly fireflies she played with during the day, their gentle glow a source of amusement. Tonight, their flickering light seemed to mock her, daring her to chase them into the unknown depths of the forest.

With a panicked snort, Fern took off, her small hooves pounding a desperate rhythm against the soft earth. The fireflies, seemingly amused by her fear, flitted closer, their tiny lights taunting her every turn. She weaved through the undergrowth, branches whipping at her fur, the forest a maze of looming shadows and flickering menace.

Suddenly, a comforting scent reached her – the warm, familiar musk of her mother. Relief washed over Fern, dispelling the terror. She stumbled out of the undergrowth and into the soft embrace of her mother's flank. The doe snorted softly, nuzzling Fern with a gentle reassurance. The fireflies, sensing the shift in power, drifted away, their playful taunts forgotten.

Fern nestled against her mother, the forest sounds

no longer frightening but familiar. The fireflies, once a source of terror, now seemed like distant, harmless embers. As the moon cast its silvery light upon the clearing, Fern drifted off to sleep, the memory of her fright a fading echo in the tranquil embrace of the forest night.

CHAPTER 50: INSANE TONGUE TWISTERS FOR HOMOGRAPHS

Homographs (same spelling, different meanings/pronunciations) can be tricky! Like twins, they share a look but have different personalities (meanings & sounds).

1. A furrow deepened between the teacher's brows. "Write with your right hand," they instructed, gesturing towards the blank page. "But is it right to right what's already been read?" they added, a hint of philosophical curiosity peeking through their stern demeanour.

   A student, a mischievous glint sparkling in their eyes, piped up, their voice barely a whisper. "But isn't writing about righting wrongs always right, even if it's a right already written? Think about it," they continued, their voice gaining volume. "A ship's captain rights a ship, don't they? Setting it on a course that's right, even if the water's already been sailed countless times before."

   The teacher, momentarily stunned by the student's well-reasoned retort, paused, their expression thoughtful. Perhaps, they mused, there was more to the act of writing than simply copying characters onto a page. Maybe it was about wielding words as tools to right wrongs, to illuminate truths hidden beneath layers of what had already been written. A flicker of amusement danced in their eyes. "Well-reasoned," they conceded, a smile tugging at the corner of their lips. "Perhaps there's always a new way to use the right words to make things right, even if the story itself has already been told."

The classroom, once filled with the monotonous scratching of pencils, fell silent as the weight of the student's words settled in. A new understanding dawned on the other students, a spark igniting in their eyes. Writing wasn't just about replicating, it was about rectification, about using the power of language to rewrite narratives, to challenge the status quo, and to shine a light on injustices, even if they were already well-documented. From that day forward, the classroom became a vibrant arena, not just for copying information, but for crafting compelling arguments, for righting wrongs with the written word, and ensuring that the rights of all were not only read about, but actively fought for.

2. The tawny tiger, travel-worn and weary, took a well-deserved doze at the witching hour of three. But slumber wouldn't fully subdue this striped seeker of thrills. Deep within his tigerish mind, a playful plot preened and purred – a quiet spree to satisfy his sweet tooth.

With a stealthy stretch, the tiger slunk from his shady slumber spot. Silently slipping through swaying swamp reeds, he stalked towards the settlement at the swamp's edge. There, nestled amongst flickering fireflies, stood a quaint little bakery, its window a beacon of buttery bliss. Tonight, the tiger wouldn't be troubling troublesome tourists or tussling with territorial turtles. Tonight, his target was altogether tastier – a tempting tower of tea cakes, their sugary scent swirling on the still swamp air.

Reaching the bakery, the tiger's brow furrowed in feline frustration. The tempting treats resided tantalisingly behind a transparent, treat-taming barrier. But a tiger with a taste for tea cakes wouldn't be deterred by a trifling trifle. With a well-placed paw, he nudged open a nearby window, its hinges groaning in protest. Slipping through the slim opening with the grace of a greased, glittery eel, the tiger found himself face-to-face with a flustered baker, flour dusting his face like a bewildered blizzard.

"Well, well, well," the baker stammered, his voice a wobbly warble. "Looks like we have a rather unusual customer this evening." The tiger, unfazed, let out a low, rumbling purr, a sound both playful and persuasive. Understanding dawned on the baker's flour-dusted face. With a chuckle, he reached for a towering tray of tea cakes. "Seems you have a sweet tooth, my striped friend," he said, offering the tray with a wink.

The tiger, his mission accomplished, retreated back through the window, leaving behind a bewildered baker and a trail of paw prints leading back to the swamp. Once safely nestled amidst the reeds, the tiger savoured his stolen treats, the sweetness a delightful reward for a well-timed, thrillingly quiet spree. Back in his slumber spot, a contented purr rumbled through the swamp, a lullaby to his daring afternoon adventure.

3. We spied a solitary sailor upon a slumbering sea, his sloop slicing silently through the swells. Solitude stretched endlessly around him, the sky a seamless steel dome mirroring the metallic sheen of the ocean. His weathered face, etched with lines that spoke of countless voyages, was locked in a look of resolute resolve. Was he seeking a fabled isle, its shores lined with luminous loot? Or perhaps a mythical monster, its lair lurking beneath the languid waves?

No, a different desire drove this determined mariner. He clutched a weathered, worn chart, its parchment whispering tales of a secret cove, a secluded sanctuary said to hold a key. A key not of gold or gleaming gemstones, but a key whispered to hold the power to unlock a long-lost legacy, a lineage shrouded in swirling sea-mist and forgotten folklore. The sailor, the sole scion of this sunken saga, sailed relentlessly, his weathered vessel a vessel of veiled yearning.

Days bled into weeks, the sun a relentless ruler in the sky. The sailor, fueled by flickering hope and fuelled by frugal fare, steered his course with unwavering resolve. Then, one twilight, as the sun dipped below the horizon, painting the sky in streaks of fiery scarlet and bruised violet, a sliver of land pierced the watery veil. His heart hammered a wild rhythm against his ribs. Could this be it? The sailor, his weathered hands gripping the wheel with renewed vigour, urged his vessel onward.

As dawn painted the sky in hues of pearlescent pink, the sailor drew closer to the island. Jagged cliffs, cloaked in a verdant cloak of vegetation, rose from the sea. Following the cryptic clues on his chart, he navigated a treacherous channel, the churning water threatening to swallow his sloop whole. Emerging on the other side, he found himself cradled in a secluded lagoon, its emerald waters shimmering serenely.

There, nestled amidst the tangled roots of an ancient banyan tree, the sailor found it – a weathered stone chest, adorned with cryptic symbols that echoed those on his chart. His breath caught in his throat. With trembling fingers, he pried open the heavy lid. Inside, nestled in a bed of velvety black velvet, lay a key. A simple, unadorned key, yet it pulsed with an otherworldly luminescence. The sailor, his eyes glistening with a mixture of relief and wonder, grasped the key. He had found it, the key to unlocking his legacy, the key to unravelling the mysteries of his shrouded past.

4. Fair skies unveiled a veil of vibrant hues, a playful palette splashed across the world. The air once filled with a chill, now held a welcome warmth, whispering promises of blissful summer days. Laughter lilted on the gentle breeze, a melody weaving through the streets and parks. Everywhere, flowers flaunted their flamboyant finery. Lavish lilies lolled languidly in lazy sunlight, their luminous lavender petals a feast for the eyes. Butterflies, their wings like stained glass, flitting from flower to flower, a kaleidoscope of colour flitting through the flourishing flora. Children, filled with unbridled glee, wove whimsical wreaths from wildflowers, their playful laughter echoing through the fragrant air.

   The once-dormant gardens hummed with renewed life. Sun-dappled lawns became vibrant stages for buzzing bumblebees and industrious ladybugs. Honeysuckle, its heady fragrance a sweet perfume, draped itself languorously over fences, its golden blooms beckoning hummingbirds with iridescent throats. Sunflowers, their faces turned towards the life-giving sun, swayed gently in the breeze, their cheerful visages radiating warmth. Even the most ordinary window boxes burst forth with colour, a testament to the tenacious spirit of life.

   Park benches, once deserted, became coveted perches for sunbathers and picnickers. Ice cream vendors, their carts adorned with colourful umbrellas, hawked their wares, their cheerful chimes a welcome addition to the symphony of summer sounds. The world, bathed in the golden glow of sunshine, seemed to sigh in contentment. It was a time for throwing open windows, for casting off heavy clothes, and for embracing the simple joys of the season. The fair weather, a farewell to winter's woes, had brought with it a wave of flair, a flourishing festival for the senses, a vibrant invitation to celebrate the glorious return of life.

5. A wizened old owl hooted hollowly at the luminous moon, his amber eyes alight with a playful glint. "Can you," he hooted, his voice a mellow, melodious hoot, "wear a new, shimmering suit of silver, or would one that's in tune with the twilight gloom suit you better, moon?"

The moon, a luminous orb lulled by the lullaby of the loon, shimmered and swirled, its silvery sheen shifting with amusement. "Wise owl," it cooed in a voice that echoed through the cool, calm night, "a new suit would be lovely, but wouldn't a cloak of cool, celestial blue be more in tune with the mood of the moonlit milieu?"

The owl hooted thoughtfully, his feathers fluffing with amusement. "A celestial cloak, you say? A most splendid notion, moon! It would surely suit your silvery splendour and soothe the slumbering world below." The moon chuckled, its light rippling across the tranquil trees. "Then let it be, wise owl," it cooed. "A cloak of cool celestial blue it shall be."

But the conversation wasn't over. The owl, ever the philosophical creature, hooted again. "Tell me, moon," he mused, "do these adornments – the suits of silver, the cloaks of celestial blue – do they truly define you? Or are you, like the world below, a constant interplay of light and shadow, ever-changing with the moods and moments of the night?"

The moon paused, its luminescence flickering thoughtfully. "A wise question, my friend," it replied, its voice tinged with a touch of awe. "Perhaps you are right. Perhaps the truest essence of the moon lies not in the garments we wear, but in the ever-shifting tapestry of light and shadow we weave across the night sky, a silent symphony for all who care to look up and wonder."

The owl hooted softly, a sound of agreement. He looked down at the world bathed in the moon's ethereal glow. Below, fireflies twinkled like celestial confetti, and crickets chirped their gentle lullabies. A hush had fallen, a hush filled with the quiet magic of the moonlit night. The owl knew, in that moment, that the moon's true beauty wasn't just in its attire, but in its ability to cast a spell of wonder and serenity over the world, a spell that soothed weary creatures and ignited the imaginations of stargazers young and old. And so, the owl and the moon continued their celestial dialogue, their words weaving through the night, a testament to the enduring power of curiosity and the ever-shifting poetry of the moonlit sky.

6. The writer, well-versed in the moral code, wrestled with a welling tide of worry. The perfect prose, penned with painstaking precision, the perfect package prepped with pride, now lay tainted by a single, soul-crushing blunder. A bewildering betrayal of brain and brawn! The right envelope, crisp and ready, held the wrong, wretched address scrawled upon its surface.

Would the rightful recipient receive their reward, a reward meticulously crafted with righteous words? Or would the carefully constructed sentences, meant to illuminate and inspire, end up in the realm reserved for the wrong reader, a bewildered soul who might misinterpret their meaning entirely?

The writer, wracked with remorse, ruminated on remedies. Repacking, rewriting – a race against relentless rhyme and reason. Should they chase down the errant envelope, a desperate knight on a quest to rectify their wrong? Or should they start anew, fingers flying across the keyboard to recreate the lost masterpiece?

The question gnawed at them. Would the recipient, upon receiving the misplaced missive, recognise the rightness within the wrongly addressed words? Or would the well-intended work wander forever, lost in the labyrinthine lanes of the postal service, a silent testament to the writer's woe?

Sleep offered no solace. The image of the misplaced package loomed large, a constant reminder of the writer's fallibility. Dawn finally broke, painting the sky in hues of hopeful orange and pink. With a deep breath, the writer decided. They wouldn't succumb to despair. They would rewrite, recreate, and rectify their error. The rightful recipient would receive their due, even if it arrived a tad belated.

And perhaps, just perhaps, the writer would learn a valuable lesson – a lesson about the importance of double-checking, the fickleness of fate, and the unwavering power of perseverance in the face of well-meaning blunders.

7. Lost in the labyrinth's looping lanes, his brow furrowed in frustration. Everywhere loomed looming limestone walls, each identical, each an impassable barrier. He clutched a worn leather pouch, its contents meagre – a crust of bread, a well-worn map, and a single, silvery key. This key, whispered legends, held the power to unlock the labyrinth's labyrinthine lair, leading him to liberty.

The map, however, was maddeningly cryptic. Symbols swirled, swirling lines leading to nowhere and everywhere. But one detail stood out – a depiction of the key, its twin gleaming beside an illustration of the exit. "The left key unlocks the leftward path," the inscription beside it declared in a language long lost. Hope flickered, a fragile flame in the oppressive gloom.

Clutching the key, he embarked on a relentless quest. Left turns he took, leftward passages he explored, his heart hammering a frantic rhythm against his ribs. Dead ends mocked him, identical to the paths he'd already traversed. Desperation gnawed at him, a relentless wolf at his heels. Was the map a malevolent mockery? Was there no escape from this endless loop?

Suddenly, a glint caught his eye. Nestled amidst the gnarled roots of a lone, lichen-laden lantern stand, lay another key. It was identical to the one he held, save for a single, subtle difference – a minuscule inscription on its handle, barely visible in the dim light – "Right."

A wave of revelation washed over him. The map wasn't mocking, it was mirroring! The key in his hand wasn't the left key, it was the right key in disguise! Elated, he swapped the keys, his heart pounding with renewed hope. He retraced his steps, this time turning right at every junction. And there, bathed in the warm glow of a hidden torch, stood a doorway, its hinges whispering promises of freedom.

With trembling fingers, he inserted the key. It clicked, a sound as sweet as salvation, and the doorway swung open, revealing a sun-dappled path leading out of the maze. He emerged, blinking in the sudden sunlight, a wave of relief washing over him. The labyrinth had tested him, twisted him, but in the end, a little faith, a little lateral thinking, and the right key in disguise had led him to liberty.

8. The benevolent baker, with a practised flourish, wielded a well-worn serrated slicer. Sunlight streamed through the bakery window, glinting off the gleaming metal as it descended upon the magnificent creation. This wasn't your average cake; it was a masterpiece, a symphony of flavours built layer upon layer. Vanilla sponge, light and airy as a cloud, alternated with tangy lemon curd and bursts of sweet, seasonal strawberries. A delicate blanket of whipped cream, flecked with vanilla bean, adorned the top, punctuated by a cascade of glistening raspberries.

With a reverence reserved for the most precious works of art, the baker meticulously separated the sumptuous sponge cake. Each slice emerged a testament to their skill, sizable and similar, a perfect rectangle showcasing the vibrant layers within. Satisfied smiles stretched across the faces surrounding the scrumptious spread. They weren't just grins of anticipation for the sugary treat; they were expressions of appreciation for the baker's artistry, their talent for transforming simple ingredients into a visual and edible delight.

But this wasn't just about the cake itself. It was about the ritual of sharing, of savouring a sweet morsel in the company of loved ones. As the baker placed a slice on each plate, a sense of community bloomed in the bakery. A young child, eyes wide with wonder, received their first taste of strawberry sunshine, the sweetness exploding on their tongue. A weary worker, their brow furrowed with the day's troubles, found solace in the tangy lemon curd, a burst of brightness amidst the afternoon slump. An elderly couple, their hands clasped across the table, shared a knowing smile as they savoured the familiar vanilla, a reminder of countless birthday celebrations and shared moments of joy.

The clinking of forks against plates mingled with murmurs of appreciation, a symphony of delight. The bakery, once filled with the rhythmic whoosh of the mixer and the measured tapping of dough, now hummed with a different kind of energy – the warmth of connection, the simple pleasure of sharing a delicious treat. In that moment, the baker realised that their creation wasn't just a cake; it was a catalyst for connection, a shared experience that transcended the sum of its ingredients. It was a reminder that even the most ordinary act of dividing something sweet could weave a thread of joy through the fabric of the day, leaving a taste of sunshine on everyone's tongue and a smile in their hearts.

9. The museum unveiled a unique exhibition, a thought-provoking interplay of past and present. Glass cases shimmered, filled with an eclectic collection of "presents," a delightful juxtaposition of historical and heartfelt.

On one side, a velvet-lined display showcased a gilded snuffbox, a symbol of aristocratic indulgence from a bygone era. Beside it, a well-worn teddy bear, its fur faded with love, whispered tales of childhood comfort. A jewelled music box, its melody a delicate echo from the past, shared a shelf with a child's brightly coloured hand-drawn card, its wobbly letters proclaiming unbridled love for a grandparent.

The juxtaposition sparked curiosity. What was a "present"

then, and what is it now? Did the value lie in the craftsmanship and cost, or in the wellspring of emotion that flowed from giver to receiver?

A gleaming silver locket, its inscription proclaiming eternal love, lay near a simple friendship bracelet, woven with colourful beads and imbued with the giggles of two schoolyard chums. A dusty travel journal, filled with tales of faraway lands, found a companion in a well-worn backpack, its pockets bulging with travel brochures and dreams of future adventures.

The exhibit wasn't just about objects; it was a portal into the human heart. It explored the timeless act of giving, the desire to connect, to express love, and to leave a lasting impression on another soul. Whether through a carefully chosen, precious object or a simple, heartfelt creation, a present, the exhibit whispered, held the power to bridge time, to weave a thread of connection, and to remind us that the most valuable gifts are often the ones that come from the heart.

Beyond the glass cases, visitors pondered, their expressions a mix of amusement and introspection. Were the "presents" of the past more valuable simply because of their age? Or did the well-loved, well-worn objects of the present hold a deeper meaning, a testament to the enduring power of human connection? The museum's exhibit offered no definitive answers, but it sparked a delightful dialogue, a conversation that whispered through the halls, a testament to the timeless power of a well-chosen, well-placed present.

CHAPTER 51: INSANE TONGUE TWISTER FOR THE DARK "L"

The following tongue twisters are meticulously crafted to hone your proficiency in producing the **dark "l"**. Each bite-sized challenge is designed to loosen up your tongue and refine your pronunciation. Remember, practice makes perfect! So, clear your throat, focus your tongue, and prepare to embark on a thrilling journey into the heart of the dark "l"!

1. Beneath the stooped shoulders of ancient oaks, a carpet of sapphire bloomed. Delicate bluebells, swaying in a gentle ballet choreographed by the blissful breeze, painted the forest floor in a breathtaking display of colour. Sunlight, filtered through a canopy of emerald leaves, cast dappled patterns on their upturned faces, each a tiny chalice brimming with the promise of spring. The air hummed with the soft drone of unseen bees, pilgrims drawn to the sweet nectar hidden within the bluebells' fragile forms. A sense of serenity, thick as the moss clinging to the ancient bark, hung heavy in the air, broken only by the occasional chirp of a curious robin or the rustle of a field mouse weaving through the vibrant tapestry of blue.

   Here, in the cool embrace of the timeless trees, the bluebells thrived, a testament to the delicate beauty that can flourish even in the shadow of giants. Their presence, a whisper against the stoic silence of the oaks, spoke of renewal and resilience. Theirs was a fleeting dance, a performance that unfolded over a handful of precious weeks before the forest floor surrendered once more to the dominion of fallen leaves and whispering shadows. But for this brief, enchanted time, the bluebells reigned supreme, transforming the once-sombre earth into a breathtaking canvas of sapphire, a fleeting masterpiece painted by the very breath of spring.

2. Bartholomew Brickfist, a man whose hands resembled cured slabs of beef, surveyed his latest creation with a callous pride. It was a building. Not just any building, mind you, but a bulbous behemoth that defied all architectural conventions. Its walls curved outwards like a pregnant pufferfish, windows were randomly scattered like misplaced freckles, and the roof resembled a giant, misshapen mushroom cap. Bartholomew, impervious to the bewildered stares of passersby, puffed out his chest. "Behold," he bellowed, his voice as rough as sandpaper, "the pinnacle of bulbous beauty!"

Whispers rippled through the crowd like tumbleweeds. "Bulbous? More like bewildering," one muttered. "Looks like a giant stepped on a playdough factory," another snickered. Bartholomew, blissfully unaware of the mockery, continued his self-congratulatory monologue, pointing out the "ingenious" angles and the "daring" disregard for symmetry.

The wind, as if to punctuate the public's opinion, howled around the building, tugging at its bulbous protrusions. A particularly strong gust rattled a loose windowpane, sending it crashing to the sidewalk with a resounding SMASH. Bartholomew, finally jolted from his self-absorption, stared at the shattered glass with a frown. Perhaps, just perhaps, bulbous beauty wasn't as practical as he'd initially thought. As a chagrined Bartholomew scurried to clean up the mess, the crowd dispersed, leaving behind a trail of stifled laughter and the lingering memory of the most peculiar, and least beautiful, bulbous building the town had ever witnessed.

3. A willow, its weeping limbs laden with luminous leaves, loomed lonely by the well's worn wheel. Wildly wailing, it whipped the willow wisps that clung clinging to its weeping wood. Wistful whispers welled within the willow's weeping form, words of woe wishing for a world where willows weren't weeping. The wind, a gentle swell sighing through the swaying scene, swirled the willow's whispers, swirling them skyward, swirling them far and wide.

Will the willow's wishes ever wander where willing ears will welcome them, wonders the world, watching the willow weep wildly by the winding well. Perhaps a wayward woodlark, its lullaby lost on the wind, will catch a wisp of the willow's woe. The woodlark, a weaver of twilight melodies, might carry the willow's wistful words to a distant, welcoming willow, a willow with wise, ancient boughs that whisper tales of resilience on the breeze. Or maybe a wandering well-mender, his weathered tools well-worn from countless well-work, will hear the willow's wails. Touched by the tale of a weeping willow, he might mend the well's wheel, coaxing cool, clear water to well up once more. With renewed life pulsing through its roots, the willow's wild weeping might waver, replaced by a gentle sigh, a sigh of hope whispered on the wind's gentle swell.

But what if the whispers travel further? What if they reach a wandering well-wisher, a woman with eyes as deep as the well and a heart as wide as the weeping willow's branches? Drawn by the willow's woes, she might approach, her weathered wellingtons whispering on the worn Wellstone path. With a wellspring of empathy welling within her, she might weave a wish of her own into the wind's gentle swell. A wish for the willow to find solace, a wish for the well to flow freely once more, a wish for the world to hold a little less weeping and a little more well-being. And perhaps, in the whispering interplay of wind, willow, and well-wisher, a flicker of hope might bloom, a promise of a world where even lonely willows can find solace by the winding well.

4. Herman the Hippo, a hulking hulk of muscle and misplaced manners, lumbered through the savanna, his back groaning under a mountainous pile of dented helmets. Beside him, a ragtag group of heroes – a clumsy cheetah in ill-fitting armour, a nervous meerkat clutching a chipped sword, and a bumbling bat draped in a bedsheet – hurried with all the grace of newborn foals.

"Hurry!" squeaked Bartholomew the bat, his voice high-pitched with panic. "The hyenas are gaining on us!"

Herman grunted, his beady eyes scanning the tall grass for any sign of striped pursuers. A chorus of cackling howls confirmed Bartholomew's fear. The hapless heroes stumbled and swore, their valiant efforts hampered by their oversized equipment and lack of coordination.

With a mighty heave, Herman reached a cluster of enormous termite mounds, their hardened earth offering a temporary haven. He lumbered towards them, creating a path with his massive bulk as the heroes scurried after him, helmets clanging in a symphony of disarray.

Just as they reached the termite mounds, a pack of hyenas emerged from the tall grass, their eyes gleaming with hungry anticipation. The heroes yelped in unison, scrambling to climb the smooth mounds.

But their attempts were comical at best. The cheetah, despite his impressive speed, was too clumsy to get a foothold. The meerkat, valiant but small, could barely reach the first level.

Herman, ever the unlikely hero, let out a bellow that shook the ground. He lowered his head and scooped up the struggling heroes, stacking them precariously on his broad back like a living helmet pyramid. Then, with a surprising burst of speed for such a large creature, he charged towards a nearby watering hole, kicking up dust and sending the hyenas scattering in confusion.

Reaching the water's edge, Herman plunged in, creating a temporary moat between them and the frustrated hyenas. The water washed away the fear and the mud, revealing a group of rather bedraggled but undeniably grateful heroes.

5. Percival the pelican, a feathered fiend with a penchant for plums, perched precariously on a prickly plum tree. Sunlight glinted off his enormous bill, a comically oversized utensil for the task at hand. The branches, laden with plump purple orbs, were a formidable defence, a thorny gauntlet guarding the juicy treasure within.

   But Percival was undeterred. With a playful glint in his beady black eyes, he shimmied along the branch, his webbed feet surprisingly adept at navigating the spiky terrain. He zeroed in on a particularly perfect plum, its skin taut and its colour a deep, mesmerising purple. Inching closer, he stretched his neck to comical lengths, his enormous pouch rippling with anticipation.

With a deft flick of his head and a lightning-fast jab of his bill, Percival snagged the plum. The branch, momentarily relieved of its burden, twanged back with surprising force, sending Percival wobbling precariously. But the master pilferer, a veteran of countless plum-plundering expeditions, remained unfazed. With a triumphant squawk, he tossed the plum into his cavernous pouch and launched himself into the air, a plump purple prize dangling from his bill like a pirate's stolen treasure. His laughter, a series of loud honks that echoed through the orchard, was a victory cry for the playful pelican who had once again outsmarted the prickly plum trees.

6. Seraphina, a sculptor whose whispered legend echoed through the industrial district, stood bathed in the steely blue glow of her workshop. The air hung heavy with the tang of molten metal and the rhythmic hiss of escaping steam. Sparks danced like a swarm of fireflies around her as she wielded her torch, its brilliant white tip the sun in her own personal galaxy. With a practised ease that belied years of honed skill, she sculpted a block of silvery steel. Her hands, strong and calloused yet surprisingly nimble, flowed with an almost musical grace. Each twist and turn of her wrist seemed to follow an unheard melody, transforming the raw material into a sleek, sinuous shape.

The rhythmic clang of her hammer against the metal wasn't just noise, it was a percussive counterpoint to the hiss and crackle of the forge. Every weld was a precise note, each measured blows a rhythmic beat composing a symphony unlike any other. The industrial symphony swelled and contracted with the intensity of her work, a testament to the raw power and delicate artistry that coexisted within her.

From under her focused gaze, a magnificent creature slowly emerged. Its form, though abstract, spoke volumes. It conveyed a powerful sense of movement and strength, its metallic curves hinting at a predator poised for the pounce. The finished sculpture, a dazzling chimaera of light and shadow, reflected the workshop lights in a thousand shimmering facets. It stood, not just a testament to Seraphina's mastery over the unforgiving material, but a silent poem forged in steel. It was a creature of the industrial age, a mechanical phoenix rising from the flames of the forge, a breathtaking fusion of raw power and breathtaking beauty. It was a masterpiece, whispering tales of the woman who coaxed magic from the most unyielding elements.

7. Chester the cheetah, notorious for his cheerful chirp and charmingly chaotic chase tactics, was on the prowl. The chaparral shimmered with the heat of the midday sun, casting dancing shadows on the dusty ground. Chester, his sleek spots glistening in the light, crouched low, his yellow eyes gleaming with playful anticipation.

Suddenly, a twitch in the tall grass caught his attention. A chubby chipmunk, cheeks bulging with juicy berries, emerged from its hiding place. It froze for a moment, its beady black eyes wide with surprise. Before it could even chirp a warning, Chester was off!

He sprang forward in a burst of speed, his powerful legs churning the earth. The chipmunk, with a shriek of startled surprise, dashed for cover. A hilarious chase ensued, a chaotic choreography of cheetah and chipmunk. Chester, ever the cheerful chaser, let out a series of playful chirps, urging the chubby chipmunk on. The chase wound through the chaparral, weaving between prickly pear cacti and dodging scraggly shrubs.

The chipmunk, surprisingly nimble for its size, darted and jinked, leaving Chester momentarily confounded by its erratic movements. But Chester, a champion chaser, was relentless. He matched the chipmunk's agility turn for turn, his laughter echoing through the dry air.

This wasn't a serious hunt, of course. Chester, despite his cheetah instincts, preferred playful pursuits to actual predation. He simply enjoyed the exhilarating dance of the chase, the shared laughter echoing through the chaparral.

Finally, after a good long chase, the chipmunk reached its burrow, a tiny hole nestled at the base of a weathered rock. With a final defiant chirp, it disappeared into the cool darkness. Chester, panting slightly but brimming with cheerful satisfaction, slowed to a stop. He watched for a moment, his chest heaving with the remnants of laughter.

Then, with a satisfied shake of his head, he turned and sauntered away. The chaparral, once again, fell silent, save for the chirping of unseen insects and the gentle rustling of leaves in the warm breeze. But the memory of the chase, a joyous symphony of cheetah and chipmunk, lingered on, a testament to the playful spirit that lived within the heart of this most cheerful cheetah.

8. Jubilant Jasper, the jolliest jester in the jungle, embarked on a journey unlike any other. His mission: is to deliver a collection of jewel-toned juggling balls to the joyful jays residing in the tallest trees. Jasper, a fellow with a penchant for flamboyant flair, wouldn't settle for a simple stroll. Oh no, his journey would be a spectacle, a performance fit for the jungle's finest feathered friends.

He set off at sunrise, his crimson cloak billowing behind him like a joyful flag. Atop his head, a jaunty jester's hat perched precariously, adorned with jingling bells that chimed a merry tune with every bounce and jostle. In his hands, a cascade of colourful juggling balls – amethysts, jade, sapphires – shimmered like captured rainbows. Each jewel, meticulously chosen, held a specific meaning for the jay who would receive it.

Jasper's path was far from smooth. Jagged vines snagged at his cloak, jolting him sideways. Gnarled roots tripped his boots, sending him into a series of joyful stumbles. Yet, through it all, the juggling never faltered. With practised ease, Jasper kept the vibrant cascade in a mesmerising dance. Laughter echoed through the jungly passage as monkeys peeked down from the trees, marvelling at his jovial perseverance.

Finally, after a journey filled with jolts and jangles, Jasper reached the towering trees inhabited by the jays. There, perched on a branch, awaited a delegation of the most joyful jays imaginable. Their vibrant blue feathers gleamed with the same intensity as the jewels Jasper carried, and their excited chirps filled the air.

With a flourish, Jasper launched into his grand finale. The jewel-toned balls soared through the air, a kaleidoscope of color against the verdant backdrop. The jays, captivated by the display, swooped and dived, their joyful calls blending with the jingling of Jasper's bells. One by one, he deftly caught the balls and tossed them to their rightful avian recipients.

As the final jewel found its home, a chorus of grateful chirps erupted from the jays. Jasper, his face beaming with joy, bowed deeply. His mission complete, he knew that the laughter and merriment he brought were the truest treasures of all. With a final wave and a jaunty jig, Jasper set off on his journey back, his laughter echoing through the jungle, a joyful melody long after he disappeared from sight.

Made in United States
Orlando, FL
26 January 2025

57832341R00254